The New Black Middle Class
in South Africa

The New Black Middle Class
in South Africa

Roger Southall

First published in southern Africa by Jacana Media (Pty) Ltd in 2016
10 Orange Street, Auckland Park 2092, Johannesburg, South Africa

First published in rest of world by James Currey,
an imprint of Boydell & Brewer Ltd
PO Box 9, Woodbridge, Suffolk IP12 3DF (GB)
www.jamescurrey.co.uk

and of Boydell & Brewer Inc.
668 Mount Hope Ave, Rochester, NY 14620-2731 (US)
www.boydellandbrewer.com

ISBN 978-1-84701-143-5 (James Currey cloth)
ISBN 978-1-4314-2316-3 (Jacana paperback)

A CIP catalogue record for this book is available
from the British Library

The publisher has no responsibility for the continued existence or accuracy
of URLs for external or third-party internet websites referred to in this book,
and does not guarantee that any content on such websites is, or will remain,
accurate or appropriate.

Jacket design by David Rodgers
Front cover image: 'Nomthandazo and Kgomotso Letsebe, Meadowlands,
Zone 5, 2009' (© Jodi Bieber from the book *Soweto* published by
Jacana Media with support from the Goethe-Institut, www.jodibieber.com)
Set in Sabon 10.2/13.87 pt

See a complete list of James Currey titles at www.jamescurrey.com

Contents

Preface

This book was originally inspired by a rereading of Leo Kuper's *An African Bourgeoisie: Race, Class and Politics in South Africa*, which was first published in 1965, and was based on research carried out in the late 1950s and early 1960s. It portrayed the black middle class of that time with intimacy and deep understanding, sympathetically depicting what he termed 'the pathos in their position, in the contrast between the narrow restraints and low status of systematic racial discrimination in a society dominated by white settlers, and the almost boundless opportunities for power and fulfilment in the independent African states'. My original intention had been to attempt something of a repeat of Kuper's work, but it soon became evident that times had changed so much – for all the continuities with the past, post-apartheid society is really *very* different – that I would have to adopt a very different plan of analysis. Nonetheless, I have found myself constantly referring back to Kuper, and trust that readers and reviewers will identify at least some respectable degree of continuity with his marvellous work.

Inevitably, I have accumulated numerous debts to both individuals and institutions. Above all, I am indebted to all those people who lent of their time by participating in focus groups or by being interviewed. As they are too many to list, I thank them collectively and hope that they will not judge the final product too harshly. Henning Melber of the Dag Hammarskjøld Foundation generously shared his own thoughts and writings on the African middle class. Leslie Bank, Linda Chisholm and Francine de Clercq provided valuable comments on individual chapters. Amuzweni Ngoma's own work on black professionals provided a basis for constant discussion, alongside much fun and laughter. Other scholars kindly provided access to their unpublished work. And I am hugely indebted to Colin Bundy, Deborah James and Dieter Neubert, who served as (originally anonymous) referees for the publishers, and offered extraordinarily constructive suggestions for improving the original text.

Much of the early work on this book was undertaken when I held the Van Zyl Slabbert Visiting Professorship in the departments of Political Studies and Sociology at the University of Cape Town in 2013. This was to prove a hugely influential period, not least because of the assistance provided by the African Studies library at UCT. My thanks are also due to the Open Society of South Africa, which funded the chair. Similarly, I am deeply indebted to the Konrad Adenauer office in South Africa which, under the direction of Dr Holger Dix, provided financial and logistical support for the conduct of black middle-class focus groups in Johannesburg, Cape Town and East London. As ever, Nancy Msibi of the Foundation was extraordinarily helpful, and even found herself participating in the Johannesburg focus group with very interesting things to say.

An earlier version of ch. 3 was published as 'The African Middle Class in South Africa, 1910–1994' in *Economic History of Developing Regions*, 29, 2, 2014, pp. 287–310, and ch. 8 as 'The Black Middle Class and Democracy in South Africa', *Journal of Modern African Studies*, 52, 4, 2014, pp. 647–670. I am grateful to the editors of both journals for permission to reproduce much of the text of those articles in the present volume.

Russell Martin of Jacana has proved a superb editor, imposing firm discipline upon someone who always wants to ovewrite, and has rendered the text far more intelligible and readable than if it had been left to my own devices. Jaqueline Mitchell of James Currey has been hugely encouraging throughout. Margaret Ramsay demonstrated once again her consummate skill in devising the index.

Finally, I give thanks as ever to my wife, Hilary, for her tolerance of my being too long stuck in front of the infernal machine which occupies my desk.

I conclude on a personal note. In writing about the struggles for upward mobility and respectability of the black middle class in post-apartheid society, I recognised much from my own family background in 1950s and 1960s England, in particular the determination and sacrifices made by my own parents to provide myself, my brother and sister with a good education. It is in grateful recognition of this that I dedicate the book to the memory of my mother and father.

Roger Southall
Cape Town, November 2015

Abbreviations

ADB	African Development Bank
ANC	African National Congress
BBBEE	Broad-Based Black Economic Empowerment
BEE	Black Economic Empowerment
BEEC	Black Economic Empowerment Conference
BMF	Black Management Forum
CA	chartered accountant
CBD	central business district
CCP	Communist Party of China
CDE	Centre for Development Enterprise
CEE	Commission for Employment Equity
COPE	Congress of the People
COSATU	Congress of South African Trade Unions
CPSA	Communist Party of South Africa
DA	Democratic Alliance
DENOSA	Democratic Nursing Organisation of South Africa
ECSA	Engineering Council of South Africa
EFF	Economic Freedom Fighters
GEAR	Growth, Employment and Redistribution strategy
HBU	historically black university
HDSA	historically disadvantaged South African
HSRC	Human Sciences Research Council

IDC	Industrial Development Corporation
IMF	International Monetary Fund
JSE	Johannesburg Stock Exchange
LEAP	Leadership Exchange and Advancement Programme
LRA	Labour Relations Act
LSM	Living Standards Measure
LSSA	Law Society of South Africa
NADECO	National Deployment Committee
NAFCOC	National African Federated Chamber of Commerce
NAIL	New Africa Investments Ltd
NAPTOSA	National Professional Teachers' Organisation of South Africa
NDR	national democratic revolution
NEC	National Executive Committee
NEHAWU	National Education, Health and Allied Workers' Union
NGO	non-governmental organisation
NPC	National Planning Commission
NUMSA	National Union of Metalworkers of South Africa
PAC	Pan Africanist Congress
RAIL	Real Africa Investments Ltd
RDP	Redistribution and Development Programme
SAARF	South African Audience Research Foundation
SABC	South African Broadcasting Corporation
SACP	South African Communist Party
SACTU	South African Congress of Trade Unions
SADTU	South African Democratic Teachers' Union
SAICA	South African Institute of Chartered Accountants
SAIRR	South African Institute of Race Relations
SAMWU	South African Municipal Workers' Union
SANNC	South African Native National Congress
SAOU	Suid-Afrikaanse Onderwysersunie
SGB	school governing board
SMME	small, medium and micro enterprise
SOE	state-owned enterprise
UCT	University of Cape Town
UDF	United Democratic Front
UDM	United Democratic Movement
UNDP	United Nations Development Programme
UNISA	University of South Africa

Introduction:
Why study the black middle class?

I come to this problem as a writer who belongs to the middle classes, i.e. is neither a capitalist, or person existing mainly by dividend drawing, nor a member of the working class. As a man I am keenly interested in the future of my own kind. As a writer ... – and by writer I understand a constructively critical depictor of human society – I am obliged to be keenly interested not only in the future of my own kind, but in the future of the whole.

– Alec Brown, *The Fate of the Middle Classes*, 1936

Writing during the global depression of the 1930s, when the future seemed to herald a titanic struggle between Fascism and Communism, Alec Brown offered an analysis in which he urged the middle class to throw off its servitude to capital and the bourgeoisie and go over to 'the great social class, the proletariat'[1] in the interests of a brave and better world for the whole of humanity. My book has no such Promethean mission; its modest aim is to make some contribution to the greater understanding of contemporary South African society. Nonetheless, the opening lines of Brown's book, which was one of the few considered attempts to depict the character of the English middle class of the time, continue to resonate for me. I am, after all, (some would say, 'incorrigibly') 'middle class', as indeed are the overwhelming majority of academics, and as a sociologist I am interested in what it means to be 'middle class'. Unsurprisingly, I also have an interest in its character, fate and future. But as well as being 'middle class', I am also white. Unlike my class position, which through opportunity or choice I might at times have been able to change, I was born into my whiteness, and am stuck with it, however much I might choose to decry the salience of race in shaping social inequality. So I come to the task of writing about the 'black middle class' as both an insider and outsider, with all the strengths and weaknesses that this implies. But these considerations apart, there are sound reasons why an exploration of the composition and character of the black middle class is a pressing project.

First of all, although the 'rise of the black middle class' is one of the most visible aspects of post-apartheid society, it has been of far more interest to the advertising industry and journalists than it has been to social scientists. One consequence has been the image presented to society, through the media, of the black middle class as 'black diamonds' – as consumers of the products of advanced industrial society, notably cars, electrical goods, computers, tablets and the ubiquitous cell phones. This perspective implies that the black middle class is essentially shallow, if not actually parasitic, and lacks the industrious and productive character which has traditionally been associated with its historical counterparts in, especially, Western capitalist society. Indeed, the notion of the black middle class as somehow lacking the essential prerequisites of 'a proper bourgeoisie' has been further propelled by the focus of the media on corruption in post-1994 South Africa, notably on the phenomenon of 'tenderpreneurs', social actors who use their political connections with individuals within the state to obtain contracts which, in a properly competitive situation, they would be denied. Undoubtedly, both these images present an aspect of reality; yet caution, if nothing else, suggests that it is likely to be dispiritingly one-dimensional. Sadly, social scientists have done little to complicate and correct this picture. There have been efforts – assessed in the chapters that follow – to estimate the size of the black middle class, and to ascertain its political roles and attitudes, but there has been remarkably little attention paid to developing a more comprehensive and better-rounded picture of a grouping in society which, everybody seems to agree, is of major importance.

In part, this lack of focus upon the black middle class has its roots in the past. It has been nearly half a century since Leo Kuper penned his magisterial *An African Bourgeoisie,*[2] the most famous of a small number of similar studies in the 1960s which examined the small African middle class (often referred to as 'an African elite') in detail. Subsequently, Alan Cobley provided an overview of the development of the 'black petty bourgeoisie' up to the 1950s;[3] and there have been occasional thematic studies of particular occupational groups and of middle-class development in particular urban areas.[4] Furthermore, there have been numerous works which have dealt with the intersection, across diverse sectors of South African society, of 'race, class and nationalism', in which the middle class receives some (usually subsidiary) attention; and, above all, historians have paid major attention to the role taken by the early, largely mission-educated African elite in the formation and development of the African National Congress (ANC).[5] Nonetheless, on the whole it is fair to say that the black middle class has been, if not actually ignored, then largely pushed in analysis to the margins of South African society,[6] even while there has been enormous attention paid to the formation of the black working class.

To some extent, this marginalisation of the black middle class reflects social realities, and how these were reflected in ANC and wider Marxist theorising about the impact of segregation and apartheid upon African class structures. In crude summary, such work has argued (quite reasonably) that the massive restrictions placed upon black professional and entrepreneurial activity stunted the development of black capitalism in particular and the black middle class in general. Meanwhile, the requirement of a minerals-driven capitalist economy led, over time, to the growth of a very substantial black working class which became the class vanguard of the struggle against apartheid and for the political liberation of South Africa. Within this heroic context, the black middle class has been presented as playing either a subsidiary or an actively antagonist role. On the one hand, squeezed by apartheid restrictions, the more politically progressive elements of the black middle class were thrust into alliance with the working class under the umbrella of the ANC and such popular organisations as the United Democratic Front (UDF); on the other, minority segments of the black middle class were drawn into collaboration with the apartheid regime as petty capitalists, homeland leaders or urban Bantu councillors, thereby becoming objective enemies of the liberation movement.

There is no need to dwell here upon the lack of complication of this picture (which, admittedly, at times was not entirely without nuance), save to note that its overall impact was always to locate the black middle class as playing a very junior role in the unfolding of the drama of South African history.[7] Sadly, it has been an invitation to social scientists (historians are probably less guilty) to continue largely ignoring it, even though post-apartheid developments suggest that there is an accompanying need for viewing this category of people through a new lens.

This leads to a second reason why the black middle class is in need of further study: simply that the contemporary world is changing fast, and South Africa with it. The black middle class is being shaped by the impact of globalisation and democratisation, while simultaneously it is becoming a major actor in the reshaping of South African society. For one thing, the opening up of the economy after apartheid has introduced a host of new factors. These range from access to new forms of communications technology to foreign investments by multinational corporations, such as Walmart, which market cheaper goods to consumers while posing potentially disastrous competition to local businesses. For another, the greater freedoms of post-apartheid society offer greater work and living opportunities to the black middle class, enabling individuals to become upwardly mobile, gain access to higher incomes and social status, and move into old-established and newly built suburbs in formerly segregated 'white' areas. All such changes mean that the black middle class is acted upon, in terms of its being channelled into various forms of behaviour, as well as becoming an active respondent to new opportunities and an active participant in the restructuring of the world around it. There is no clean divide here between 'structure' and 'agency'; rather, there is a complex interaction which is reshaping both the black middle class itself and the environment in which it is located.

An important element of change is that brought by the post-apartheid order to relationships not merely between classes, but between 'races' historically divided into dominant whites and subordinated blacks (Africans, Coloureds and Indians). In terms of the ideals of the constitution of 1996, democracy was intended to bring about a 'non-racial' society. Certainly, looking back over two decades, it is evident that significant changes have occurred in what – using a rather old-fashioned phrase – may be labelled as 'race relations'. Whether one takes an optimistic or pessimistic view of the extent to which the desired transition to 'non-racialism' has come about (and the controversies on this subject are huge), very few would deny that the relationship of the races has been restructured in significant ways. Hegemonic white political power under apartheid has given place to majority rule and, hence, largely 'black' government; black economic empowerment (BEE) has provided access for a small elite of blacks to significant economic opportunities for ownership and control of industry; while affirmative action strategies in recruitment to positions in government and public institutions have massively increased opportunities for blacks and, to a significant if lesser extent, the professions and private sector. In turn, these changes have brought about the reappearance, if to a limited extent, of white poverty, the abolition of which was a principal mission of white governments from the 1920s.

The point is not simply to lament the failure to achieve a truly deracialised society, but to argue that an expanding black middle class has arguably been the major beneficiary of the post-apartheid dispensation. From this perspective, one might liken the contemporary South African social structure to a pyramid, with blacks able to mix far more freely and equally with whites at the apex, even while the patterns of the past ensure that most blacks remain firmly rooted, and largely segregated, at the much broader base. Any attempt to understand the character and quality of democracy in contemporary South Africa seems to require the unravelling of the dynamics of both race and class in the construction and lived experience of the 'black middle class'. This is not a straightforward task. Cultural divisions between Africans, Coloureds and Indians, exacerbated by past and even present political practice, render perilous any collapsing of the previously subordinated races into one homogeneous grouping labelled 'black'. This is well recognised, not least by ANC theorising, which has long argued that differential levels of oppression of Africans, Coloureds and Indians require different levels of 'racial redress'. Liberation was fought for all blacks, but especially for Africans, who constitute the overwhelming majority (just under 80 per cent) of the population.

In what follows, I am going to negotiate this problem by concentrating my focus upon the specifically 'black African' middle class, while recognising that together with Coloureds and Indians they will at times constitute, or be categorised as constituting, a broader collective class entity. This focus has been chosen because the Coloured and Indian communities have been forged through significantly different historical experiences. Generally, therefore, when I speak of the 'black middle class', I will be referring to the 'black African middle class'. While some object quite strenuously, this is the now generally accepted practice in political debate and the media, although, confusingly, much of the historical literature refers simply to the

'African' middle class. Readers will hopefully forgive me for adopting both usages, according to the particular context. When I use the term 'black middle class' in a more inclusive manner (including Coloureds and Indians), I will be explicit in doing so. I acknowledge immediately that this is not wholly satisfactory, and I stress that by concentrating on 'black Africans' I am not suggesting that what has happened among the Coloured and Indian components of the population is not important. But I plead that because of the complexity of South Africa, there is only so much that can be satisfactorily done within the limits of a modestly sized book.[8]

A further justification for a concerted analytical focus upon the black middle class is that today it is widely depicted as a key actor in the processes of modernisation and development. As implied above, the role of the black middle class in the making of South African democracy has been seriously understated, in part for ideological reasons derived from the dominance in ANC theorising of the influence of the South African Communist Party (SACP). To this day the party continues to adhere to a peculiarly rigid form of Marxism-Leninism which emphasises the leading role of the proletariat. Within this context, the ANC is presented as pursuing a 'national democratic revolution' (NDR) whose unfolding will see a deracialisation of capitalism and the emergence of a 'patriotic' bourgeoisie and black middle class, which will remain guided by the revolutionary party. Today, SACP theorising is becoming increasingly anachronistic, while the effects of globalisation have begun to pose important questions about how the status and role of the middle classes are understood.

The shift to financial and service industries in much of global capitalism has seen the decline of the traditional working classes in many countries of the world, and a corresponding increase in the size and significance of 'new' middle classes. Political independence expanded the size and power of indigenous middle classes in former colonial territories, with outcomes generally more favourable in developmental terms in Asia than Africa. Today, the shift of global economic power to the East and South is having major repercussions, one of which is the stimulation of Chinese, Indian and other Southern investment in the African continent. This has resulted in the rapid growth of the still relatively small African middle classes, which are commonly seen as both the drivers and recipients of a new prosperity in what, not so many years ago, *The Economist* notoriously labelled the 'hopeless continent'.[9] In contrast, African middle classes are today regularly presented as the agents of modernity and hope, their style and standard of life the envy and aspiration of those below them in the social pecking order.[10] Who wants to work in a grubby factory, when the alternative is an air-conditioned office? Who wants to live in a shack or slum, when the alternative is a private flat or a house with garden? Who, whether trade union official or ordinary worker, wants to decline the material seductions of 'embourgeoisement', and the chance for his or her children to live a better life, even if it means a loss of proletarian class consciousness? The answer, the contemporary world tells us, is 'very few'.

Meanwhile, and perhaps above all, the middle class is often seen as the harbinger of democracy; in the view of some, the principal actor demanding freedoms and challenging tyranny, from Tiananmen Square to the Arab Spring. All these changes insist upon the need to take the black middle class in South Africa seriously. As we shall see, the questions posed will allow for no easy answers, and often the answers will themselves be simultaneously inspiring, hopeful, disappointing and unpalatable – in a word, contradictory. Yet nothing will be gained by continuing to ignore the issue; and the opening chapter explores precisely what is meant by that manifestly conglomerate term, 'middle class'.

1

The 'middle class':
Problems and controversies

Few terms are so widely used and misused as that of 'middle class'. There is general agreement that 'middle class' refers to a category of people who are in the middle range of hierarchies of income, wealth, property ownership, occupation or whatever. Equally, the term invites massive confusion, with a cacophony of voices using it in different ways. Nonetheless, the sheer persistent use of the term suggests that it points to a social phenomenon of lasting significance that will not easily go away. In other words, however hard we may find it to pin its meaning down, we are unlikely to be able to do without the term 'middle class'.

Why this is so is simple to relate. In short, some notion of social class or social stratification is at the heart of explanations of the development of the modern world. Whether we are trying to understand the dynamics of advanced capitalist states, those states which like the former Soviet Union or Communist China pursued a path of 'socialist industrialisation', or those today (the large majority) which are in the throes of, or aspire to, rapid industrialisation, we seem to come back to class. Accordingly, if we want to explore the meaning of 'middle class', we have to locate that term in a wider body of theory.

Theories of class or stratification seek to account for patterns of systematised social inequality which are characteristic of all industrialised or industrialising societies, whether capitalist or (formally) socialist. When we address the issue of inequality, we are asking about the causes of the differential allocation of rewards or goods in society to various categories of people. In turn, we have to ask about the underlying causes of such inequality, and its implications for social coherence, economic efficiency and political stability or change – all this apart from normative questions about social justice, from which the prior issues cannot be separated.

Two grand traditions of class analysis

Two major traditions of analysing class follow from the work of Karl Marx and Max Weber. These traditions are simultaneously complementary to, and in constant debate with, each other. This is another way of saying that while many Marxists or neo-Marxists violently disagree with the Weberians or neo-Weberians, there are equally many who agree with each other across a whole set of issues, even while they may use different terminology. In what follows, I focus upon how these two traditions understand in particular the middle class.

Marx and the middle class

As with other nineteenth-century thinkers, Marx was concerned to explore the origins of capitalism, choosing England as his model, as it was the most advanced industrial country of his time. To his mind, England showed to other countries advancing along the same path 'the image of their own future'. Even so, Marx did not set out any systematic exposition of class, and the well-known observations scattered throughout his writings – notably the assertion in the *Communist Manifesto* (1848) that advanced capitalist society would split up into two hostile classes, the bourgeoisie and the proletariat – are heavily qualified. Thus in later work, notably in the third volume of *Capital*, Marx observed that even in England, where capitalism was most advanced, 'middle and intermediate strata' blurred the boundaries between capitalists, land owners and wage labourers.[1] Likewise, elsewhere he argued that it was a trend of bourgeois society that 'the middle class will grow in size and the working class will form a continually diminishing proportion of the total population'.[2] Hence, while it is often asserted that Marx insisted that the middle class was merely a transitional class, condemned to disappear in the culminating crises of capitalism, his legacy was actually more ambiguous.[3]

This ambiguity in Marx left plenty of scope for debate. Thus Eduard Bernstein, the German social democrat who attempted at the turn of the nineteenth century to revise Marx, argued that in capitalist Germany the classes were not polarising, and instead of the social structure becoming more simplified, it was in fact becoming more complex and differentiated. The concentration of capital in large enterprises was being matched by the growth of new small and medium-sized businesses; property ownership was more widespread; living standards were rising; and, instead of becoming smaller, the middle class was increasing in size.[4]

Subsequently, Marxist thinking about the middle class was to proceed in two directions. First, there were those who argued that the development of capitalism would bring about the proletarianisation of the middle class. This tradition came to the fore in the 1930s, during the course of the Great Depression, when writers such as Francis Klingender (in his work on the class location of clerical workers in Britain)[5] anticipated the later work of Karl Renner, especially his analysis of the development of a 'service class' (basically, administrative workers in the public and private spheres) as a new type of middle class. Members of this class were neither capitalists nor workers, they did not own capital, and they did not create value by their work, but they did control values created by others. Furthermore, they were distinguished from the working class by virtue of their possession of a salary, and the relative security and prospects of advancement this offered. Nonetheless, because the working class itself had become more organised, more secure in employment and a more constituent element of society, the workers and the service class were moving more closely together.[6]

Strong echoes of this approach were to be found in the work of sociologists in the post-1945 period. For instance, David Lockwood, while drawing primarily upon the work of Max Weber, argued that clerical workers in Britain in the 1950s were beginning to identify with manual workers by viewing their work situation as having much in common with the proletariat.[7] Considerably later, and from a very different perspective, Harry Braverman investigated what he called the 'deskilling' of 'white-collar' labour, implying its incipient proletarianisation. Deskilling involved the elimination of skilled labour by the introduction of technology operated by semi-skilled or unskilled workers, thus reducing costs to employers and weakening the bargaining power of labour.[8] Such approaches concentrated mostly on economic changes, however, and failed to address the difficult question of whether these were likely to be accompanied by new social and political attitudes among the middle class.

Hence there followed a second line of analysis among Marxist thinkers who rejected the proletarianisation thesis, and who gave as much weight to ideological and political factors as economic relationships in the constitution of social class. Most notably, Nicos Poulantzas proposed that the middle class (or petty bourgeoisie), which included both the 'old' middle class (lawyers, doctors, shopkeepers and the like) and the 'new' middle class (those filling managerial, semi-managerial and lower administrative positions), had become a distinctive class, sharply separated from the working class. The political implications he drew from this were not entirely clear.[9] More satisfactory, in this respect, was the work of Erik Olin Wright, who, while similarly recognising the distinctiveness of middle-class groups in various ways, argued that there were intermediate strata between the capitalist class and the working class whose members occupied 'contradictory class locations'.[10]

Such studies led on to the question of the relations between the capitalist class and the upper sections of the middle class in particular, and the extent to which they were forging a joint interest. In contrast with early industrial capitalism, when the capitalist owned and directed the means of production, modern capitalism has seen a significant divergence between ownership and control. Although there remain important exceptions, large corporations are today rarely owned by a single person or a few individuals, and are mostly run by managers on behalf of shareholders. This shift was referred to by James Burnham as 'the managerial revolution',[11] although his argument that managers were replacing capitalists as a ruling class was to be strongly disputed. Nonetheless, the problem remains of whether to conceive of managers as 'capitalists' or as falling into an intermediate category, somewhere between capitalists and workers, and the issue is rendered yet more complicated by the fact that today a number of managers are also shareholders. For many, in both the Marxist and Weberian traditions, a distinctive class characteristic of managers is the authority they wield over subordinate employees. For instance, Nicholas Abercrombie and John Urry were to return to the idea of a 'service class', which was 'taking on, and concentrating within itself, the functions of capital, namely, conceptualization, control and reproduction'. Meanwhile, the 'class position of the capitalist class [was] being transformed', and its functions were becoming more and more indistinguishable from those of the service class.[12]

In contrast, on the basis of studies that demonstrated the continuing importance of family wealth in establishing control over the large corporations that dominate modern capitalist society, Tom Bottomore argued that the service class does not displace the capitalist class, nor even merge with it to any considerable extent. Certainly, the massive growth which has taken place in public-sector employment in capitalist societies since Marx's time ensures that the service class plays an important role in the management and regulation of public agencies as well as private corporations, yet for Bottomore it does so in a largely subaltern (or junior) role as the executor of decisions made elsewhere. Nonetheless, the growth of the middle class is hugely important in two other ways. Firstly, it increases the diversity of civil society, and gives rise to new forms of political activity; this tends to reduce the salience of class-based political activity, mainly at the expense of the working class (and of trade unions). Secondly, by virtue of its economic and social location, a large part of the middle class generally lends its support to the capitalist order.[13]

The fundamental problem posed by the Marxist tradition is how a conception of class, based upon the ownership or non-ownership of property, translates into collective class behaviour and political action. As Frank Parkin has noted, this problem draws attention to the institutional and political arrangements which underlie the distribution of advantages in society, and the ways in which, within a two-class model, the dominant class seeks to preserve its rewards and privileges vis-à-vis the subordinate class.[14] To answer this, many have turned to the work of Max Weber.

Weber and the middle class

Throughout his writings, Marx showed an acute consciousness of the variations in historical development which had produced enormous differences in the social and political patterns of the European countries of his day. Nonetheless, he based his writings on the assertion that, 'in analytic terms, economic power is everywhere the foundation of political domination'.[15] In contrast, Max Weber, much of whose work was undertaken in direct refutation of Marx or in dialogue with him, was concerned with an appreciation of the significance of political as distinct from economic power. In particular, he sought to understand the role played by the state under Bismarck, and especially the bureaucracy, in promoting the internal consolidation and economic development of Germany. Ultimately, he concluded that Germany lacked the parliamentary autonomy needed to take control of the bureaucratic machine which Bismarck had bequeathed to the country. At the same time he dismissed radical revolution as the only means for the political emancipation and economic advancement of workers. Rather, Weber held that the improvement of the material circumstances of the working class as well as the growth in its political power was wholly possible within capitalism, and both were in the true interests of the bourgeoisie.

The major political problem facing Germany was, therefore, how to escape bureaucratic domination rather than how to avoid revolution.[16]

Weber's greatest contribution to the study of stratification was to expand Marx's notion of class by defining it in terms not simply of property but of market situation. While he acknowledged that property and lack of property were the 'basic categories of all class situations', no less important were factors such as income, security of employment, promotion opportunities, long-term income prospects and the general array of social and material advantages that Weber referred to as a person's market situation or 'life chances'.

Related to this was the distinction Weber drew between class and status, or social honour. Weber maintained that, alongside class, status was also an unevenly allocated resource. Very often, the distribution of social honour would correspond to the distribution of material reward, yet the two were distinct and could display considerable inconsistency. Thus in nineteenth-century Europe the upwardly mobile bourgeoisie enjoyed major wealth, but did not rank so highly in terms of social honour as the landed aristocracy, many of whose members were materially less well-off. Nonetheless, class and status were closely related, and the predominance of the one or other in society as a whole was influenced by general economic conditions. Whereas in times of economic stability status tends to predominate, in times of economic stress it is class that tends to come to the fore. At the same time, although class and status could form the basis for political parties (or behaviour), political power as an independent phenomenon could be based, variously, upon the bureaucracy, the use of violence or the vote.

Weber contended that inequality is founded upon a multiplicity of structural determinants including, in addition to property, marketable skills, prestige and political power. Arguably, the central concept is the market, where property and skills are exchanged, for the market determines the class situation of individuals according to their marketable value. In other words, from a Weberian perspective, those at the top of the social hierarchy in a capitalist society typically owe their class position to large-scale ownership of property (capital or land); while those at the bottom are non-owners who are required to sell their labour to survive. In-between the two we find the middle classes, who derive their income and status from their small-scale ownership of land, from their occupation (which is strongly linked to their education), or from both.

In sum, Weber's conception of the system of social stratification differed from Marx's in two significant ways. Firstly, he interposed a range of status groups to bridge the gap between the two major classes in capitalist society. Secondly, by suggesting a different idea of social hierarchy, as a continuum of more or less clearly defined status positions determined by a variety of factors and not merely by property, he questioned whether a fundamental conflict really exists between classes.

Key problems surrounding the middle class

Even from this cursory overview of the two grand traditions, it is possible to point to key problems concerning the middle class. In what follows, I am going to focus upon issues which have particular salience for the subject of this book – the black middle class in South Africa.

Class analysis and terminology are never value-neutral

Thomas Piketty has reminded us that the terminology of class is rarely innocent. 'The way the population is divided up usually reflects an implicit or explicit position concerning the justice and legitimacy of the amount of income or wealth claimed by a particular group.'[17] In regard to the 'middle class' in particular, he observes how broad definitions of the term, suggesting that its members earn incomes and own resources that are average for the society concerned, imply that such individuals are not privileged and deserve the indulgence of government, especially when it comes to taxes. On the other hand, if the middle class is viewed as closely aligned in interest and income to a society's elite, quite the opposite conclusion could be drawn. In other words, how the term 'middle class' is used is not just a linguistic issue, but is distinctly political. In the United States, for example, politicians refer to the 'middle class' in such a broadly encompassing way that it seems to apply to all Americans, and thus discounts any suggestion of a major conflict of interest between an elite and a working class. Indeed, American workers are explicitly urged to define themselves as 'middle class'. This is merely one illustration of the fact that analyses of the middle class are virtually always imbued with political meaning.

The differentiation of the middle class

A fundamental starting point, about which most agree, is that 'the middle class' is increasing in size and proportion in virtually all societies in the contemporary world, whatever pattern of development they are pursuing. Contrary to Marx's expectations, as capitalism developed, the class structures

7

associated with it became more highly differentiated, along the lines elaborated by Weber. Furthermore, given the apparent tendency for the social structures of capitalist and socialist societies to 'converge' to a significant degree (for the production process in both needs to be managed and administered), such convergence involved the growth of highly similar administrative and white-collar positions. Consequently, it would seem that inherent in the process of industrialisation is an increasing complication of class structures. This does not mean that Marx was 'wrong', for there are substantial indications in his writings that he recognised that intermediary class elements would not easily disappear, and indeed might multiply as capitalism moved forward. Nonetheless, it is difficult to deny that the multidimensional approach to class espoused by Weber (in a critique of Marx) seems to offer more purchase in analysing the patterns of stratification that have accompanied capitalism and industrialisation. In effect, this has been acknowledged by later Marxist theorising, which, with different emphases and outcomes, has sought to grapple with the growing differentiation of the social structures of modern societies. This, however, is only the start of our problems.

If we accept that there is more to stratification than ownership or non-ownership of property, and that we need to take into account such factors as income, occupation and status, then we have to confront the situation of how to weight them. Putting aside the (very considerable) matter of possession or otherwise of capital (or wealth),[18] occupation provides the foundation for the class structure in capitalist societies: even other sources of material and symbolic advantage (such as prestige) have their roots in the occupational structure. Indeed, even the hierarchy of political power seems to derive from occupation, for today political authority is largely exercised as a full-time occupation.

Nonetheless, problems arise in thinking through this idea, for while we may argue that there is a broad congruence of occupation and income, with managers earning considerably more than manual workers, the textbooks are full of instances where, for instance, better-off manual workers, such as plumbers, earn more than modestly paid semi-professionals, such as teachers, whose occupation generally ranks more highly in terms of status. Consequently, if we rely upon income as the major proxy of class (as occurs, for instance, in many surveys), the outcome may be very misleading, especially at middling levels, where – apart from matters of status – other factors should really be taken into account, such as long-term employment prospects and accompanying benefits.

Furthermore, the issue of why occupation is so important poses the additional problem of why some occupations should be better paid than others. Generally, the Weberian response would be that this derives from market situation; that is, the higher-paid occupations, such as those of banker, doctor or dentist, demand more skill and training than those required by manual or white-collar work. One response to this is that differential incomes often derive from some exercise of power – whether it be that those high up in large corporations or financial services possess considerable autonomy to decide their own income or that professional associations operate to restrict entry into their professions in order to maintain the market scarcity of those with the requisite qualifications. All this confirms that the manner in which the social analyst chooses to define and measure classes (and subgroups within them) will do much to determine how their attitudes and behaviours are assessed – yet at the same time, this is not likely to be entirely arbitrary, for, very often, there are strong historical, social and cultural reasons why certain factors are more important than others in structuring a class system.

The middle class and political identity
A related problem is that of linking class and status to political attitudes and behaviour. In Marxist terms, a worker who chooses to vote for a capitalist rather than a socialist party is very probably the victim of 'false consciousness', for his or her true interests lie in identifying with political movements which have workers' interests at heart. The reality, of course, is much more complicated.[19] Leaving aside the fact that people's political orientations can be shaped by a whole host of other factors, such as nationality, ethnicity, religion or lifestyle, it is by no means clear in practice whether the self-employed tradesman is better off voting for parties representing the interests of property or those of the workers. Thus to a much-asked question in Britain in the 1950s and 1960s about what motivated a substantial minority of working-class people to vote Conservative (the party of property), one significant answer was that they did so either out of 'deference' to their perceived 'betters' or that they were seeking to elevate their status, either in their own eyes or those of others, by voting 'upwards' with the Conservative Party rather than 'downwards' with the Labour Party.[20]

Long before this, the European sociologist Werner Sombart had asked why there was no socialism in the United States, and found the answer in factors which explained 'American exceptionalism' (later expressed as the 'American dream'), including the purported ability of every person to

9

climb a relatively open class system by dint of hard work.[21] In a related manner, C. Wright Mills portrayed the US middle class of the early 1950s as so threatened by the prospect of being thrust back into the ranks of the working class by impersonal forces such as deskilling and bureaucratisation, that, without an independent class agenda of their own, they sought safety by aligning themselves with the 'ascendant' class, the 'power elite', in whose hands economic, political and military power was concentrated.[22] What we can conclude from this is that while class (understood as occupation) will more often than not be strongly associated with political orientations, there is no straight line between class and politics, and, in any case, status may intervene to produce an apparently contradictory result.

It is in this context that Erik Olin Wright's notion of 'contradictory class locations' can be useful in understanding the political orientations of different segments of the middle class. Going beyond matters of status (which may prove particularly salient for certain occupations, such as established professions like the law), Wright focused on the particular role an occupation plays in shaping relations between classes. Fundamentally, he identified three central processes underlying the basic capital–labour relationship in advanced capitalism: control over the physical means of production (plant and machinery); control over labour power; and control over investments and resource allocation.

> The fundamental class antagonism between workers and capitalists can be viewed as a polarization on each of these three underlying processes or dimensions: capitalists control the accumulation process, decide how the physical means of production are to be used, and control the authority structure within the labour process. Workers, in contrast, are excluded from the control over authority relations, the physical means of production, and the investment process. These two combinations of the three processes of class relations constitute the two basic antagonistic class locations within the capitalist mode of production.[23]

When the capitalist system is analysed in the abstract, the only class positions defined by the relations of production are those of capitalists and workers. However, when we move to the analysis of 'real capitalist societies', the neat coincidence of the three dimensions of class relations separating capitalists from workers disappears – and 'contradictory class locations' appear.[24]

The contradictory location closest to the working class is that of foremen and line supervisors. They have little real control over the physical means of production, but exercise control over labour power – although increasingly this control has become institutionalised and bureaucratised (so that a 'rule of law' replaces a 'rule of personal command'). At the other end of the spectrum, because their ownership of capital is generally limited, senior managers occupy a contradictory location at the boundary of the capitalist class (which enjoys control over all three productive resources), although 'at the very top of the managerial hierarchy, corporate executives essentially merge with the capitalist class itself'. The most contradictory location between the bourgeoisie and proletariat is that of the middle managers and technocrats. While enjoying a limited degree of autonomy over their own work and a limited control over subordinates, the middle managers are not in control over the productive apparatus. In contrast, they control various aspects of the labour process and immediate subordinates. Consequently, unlike line supervisors and foremen on the one hand, and top managers on the other, middle managers and technocrats do not have a clear class pole to which they are attached. As a result, 'it is much more difficult to assess the general stance they will take within the class struggle'.[25]

The notion of 'contradictory class location' implies that the relationship between class position and political orientation can be difficult to pin down. Wright's contribution is particularly useful on two counts. Firstly, it suggests that particular class locations – while possibly pulled in different directions by the three dimensions that compose the capital–labour relationship – are likely to gravitate over the long term towards one class pole or the other (that is, towards the bourgeoisie or the proletariat). Secondly, it suggests that the key issue involved in defining political position may be the function that individuals perform in the process of capitalist production. But this does not particularly help us if and when class position, middle class or otherwise, seems to stem rather more directly from the relation of individuals to the state.

The middle class and the state

For Marx in the *Communist Manifesto*, the state was the committee of the ruling class. In essence, he argued that the capitalist state expressed the coercive power of the bourgeoisie, and facilitated the conditions for continued capitalist accumulation. Yet the state also had an ambiguous character, in that it provided the social foundation for the form of society that would ultimately transcend capitalism. Thus the objective of the workers' movement was to convert the state 'from an organ superimposed upon society into one completely subordinate to it'; that is, in a future Communist society, the state would lose its political (its coercive) character and perform only non-coercive administrative functions. However, the transitional phase of the 'dictatorship of the proletariat' would represent a concentration of the political power that already existed in a more diffuse form in bourgeois society: this would make possible the centralisation of production and distribution, and an increase in the total of productive forces as soon as possible. For this reason, the eventual abolition of the state would not involve a sudden reversal in the social organisation of society, but would form an aspect of a more extensive transformation of society.

While we might draw from this the idea that state officials in capitalist society perform their administrative tasks on behalf of the interests of capital (or in the interests of particular 'fractions' of capital), this does not satisfactorily explain the class location of the state officials themselves. The difficulty can be highlighted by referring to contemporary analysis of the development of the Soviet state.[26] Soviet theorists were inclined to argue that those who ran the Soviet state – 'the intelligentsia', which was a broad term inclusive of government ministers, party officials, managers of industrial enterprises, intellectuals proper, administrative workers and technicians – constituted an intermediate 'stratum' which was in a 'non-antagonistic relation' to the two basic classes of Soviet society, the working classes and the peasantry. The problem with such interpretations was not only that they were unconvincing (not least because the Soviet state under Stalin had engaged in campaigns of mass terror against the peasantry), but that they ignored the issues of power and bureaucracy. Unsurprisingly, they were to be challenged even from within the Soviet bloc.

One of the most foundational critics was Milovan Djilas, a Yugoslav thinker who, while applying a broadly Marxist approach to the study of Communist society, argued that those elements (state and party bureaucrats) whom Soviet theorists so confusingly lumped together as 'the intelligentsia' had transformed themselves into a new ruling class with its own special characteristics. Basically, it was the bureaucracy, controlled by the party elite and state managers, which had come to assume control over nationalised property, and which monopolised control of the distribution and control of national income and production. In so doing, they had secured for themselves positions of material and symbolic privilege. 'Ownership is nothing other than the right of profit and control. If one defines class benefits by this right, the Communist states have seen, in the final analysis, the origin of a new form of ownership or of a new ruling and exploiting class.'[27] Furthermore, being the deliberate creation of the party elite, the rule of this 'new class' was more brutal than that of any other class in history. As with previous ruling classes, its dominance was based upon ownership; but the 'collective ownership' which the new class formally exercised on behalf of society was merely a façade behind which it enjoyed 'totalitarian authority'.

While finding Djilas useful in showing how some form of Marxism could be used for analysing Communist societies, Ralf Dahrendorf argued that he had been ambiguous about the determinants of social class. As a Marxist, he had sought to locate the characteristic of the new class in property and ownership – in this case, collective ownership. On the other hand, he had also argued that the party elite had used its political and bureaucratic power to maintain its domination. In other words, 'there is at least a hint here that it is ultimately not the ownership of the means of production that determines a class, but that this very ownership is only a special case of a more general social force, power. While Marx ... subordinates relations of authority to those of property, Djilas seems inclined to subordinate ownership to power.'[28]

From this perspective, the theories of Djilas and other Marxist critics who argued for the important role of the state in creating a new social hierarchy had strong affinities with those of Weber and various elite theorists (such as Gaetano Mosca and Vilfredo Pareto) who followed after him. Weber offered the much-cited view that a transition to socialism would more likely lead to the 'dictatorship of the bureaucrat' than the 'dictatorship of the proletariat', while elite theorists tended to argue that the division of society into dominant and subordinate groups or classes was inevitable. Robert Michels, for instance, formulated his famous 'iron law of oligarchy' according to which leaders of parties (including socialist ones) and classes came to constitute a dominant elite.

It is not a far cry from this to arguing, with Dahrendorf, that though industrial society might have grown out of capitalist society, it has superseded it, and as a result capitalist society is merely one form of industrial society. In contrast, 'post-capitalist' societies, while continuing to be driven by the desire to maximise gains, have experienced a second industrial revolution whose logic is based on the imperative of organising production more rationally (by means of such notions as 'scientific management' and 'social engineering'). The successful functioning of such post-capitalist societies is founded upon merit and achievement, and this requires a reasonably high level of social mobility. However, though based upon formal legal equality, these societies embed levels of social and economic inequality, which flow in considerable part from occupation. Furthermore, as with capitalist society, post-capitalist societies involve relations of power and authority; at the same time they also embody a rationalised tendency towards the regulation of conflict. Within the state, conflict with and between citizens is regulated by the rule of law. In industry, conflict between capital and labour is regulated by institutionalised bargaining. Thus, while 'the institutionalization of class conflict implies its continued existence', this is far removed from 'the ruthless and absolute class struggle envisaged by Marx'.[29]

Such an industrial society also requires an expanded middle class. 'Rationality and bureaucracy are never very far apart; in one sense the rapidly growing demand for clerks and office employees, accountants and supervisors, statisticians and submanagers is but a concomitant of the "rational" organization of enterprises.'[30] This notion of industrial society remains powerful today, though many theorists doubt whether today's industrialised societies can be accurately described as 'post-capitalist'.

The middle class as 'precariat'

With the collapse of the Berlin Wall in 1989, Communist societies tumbled back into forms of capitalism. Whether this was through 'shock' treatment that dissolved Communist political monopolies and privatised economic structures (as in the former Soviet Union), or through a Communist Party-controlled shift to a form of state capitalism (China), the result was a move towards the neo-liberalising market model, which was sweeping all before it throughout the West and elsewhere. But rather than advanced capitalism and Communism 'converging' in the form of an 'industrial society', many capitalist societies were in fact undergoing a process of 'deindustrialisation'.

From the 1970s on, the capitalist world has been driven by the ideology of neo-liberalism. According to this ideology, economic growth depends on market competitiveness, efficiency demands a maximisation of competition, and market principles should permeate all aspects of life. Central to neo-liberalism has been an emphasis upon 'labour flexibility'. Because revolutions in communication and technology have rendered the world an increasingly interconnected market in which investment flows to countries offering the most welcoming conditions, workers must abandon previously hard-won protections to render themselves competitive. In turn, the entry to the capitalist market of hundreds of millions of workers in the former Communist states, notably China, has swelled a global surplus of labour and had a massively depressing effect upon wages internationally. The outcome has been that multinational corporations have globalised by minimising costs, shifting operations to countries which offer lower taxes and cheaper labour than their competitors. The more corporations have globalised, the more they have further cut costs by reducing their core workforces and 'outsourcing' segments of their production processes to smaller employers who feed upon the 'informalisation' and greater 'flexibility' of labour. Consequently, Western countries which after the Second World War erected welfare states have now adapted to the new conditions by dismantling the costs of social protection, and reduced labour costs by weakening trade unions and adopting labour-saving technologies in a bid to stem the migration of investment capital to sites elsewhere. In turn, notwithstanding the growth of 'service' sectors, notably in finance and internet technology, the 'deindustrialisation' of the North has involved increasing unemployment, slowing growth and increasing poverty alongside a dramatic reversal of the trend to greater social equality, which was a significant feature of the post-1945 world.[31]

It is within this context that we see an increase in 'precarious labour' and the massive growth of the 'precariat'. Guy Standing, the principal proponent of this term, defines the precariat as a 'class-in-the-making'. Arguing that globalisation has resulted in a fragmentation of national class structures as inequalities have grown and the world has moved towards a more flexible labour market, he proposes that class has not disappeared but has taken a more fragmented, global form. Leaving aside agrarian societies, he identifies a global class structure composed of the following tiers:

- The elite, consisting of a tiny number of 'absurdly rich' global citizens.
- The 'salariat', still in stable employment, some hoping to move into the elite, but the majority just enjoying their pensions, paid holidays and enterprise benefits, often subsidised by the state. This grouping is concentrated in large corporations, government agencies and public service.
- The 'proficians', a grouping which combines the traditional characteristics of 'professionals' with those of 'technicians', adding to these bundles of skills they can market so as to earn incomes on contract, as consultants or independent 'own account' workers.
- A shrinking working class (the traditional proletariat), a category

15

which is now being shrivelled by the reduction of protections and which is losing its sense of social solidarity.

• Finally, under these four groups, a growing 'precariat', characterised by 'precarious' employment, which is flanked by an army of the unemployed and a detached group of 'social misfits' living off the dregs of society (what Marx referred to as the lumpenproletariat).[32]

Standing argues that traditional understandings of class, notably the division into wage labour and salaried employee, break down when considering the precariat. On the one hand, the precariat

> has *class* characteristics. It consists of people who have a minimal trust relationship with capital and the state, making it quite unlike the salariat. And it has none of the social contract relationships of the proletariat, whereby labour securities were provided in exchange for subordination and contingent loyalty, the unwritten deal underpinning welfare states. Without a bargain of trust or security in exchange for subordination, the precariat is distinctive in class terms. It also has a peculiar *status* position, in not mapping neatly onto high-status professional or middle-class status craft occupations ... Its structure of 'social income' does not map neatly onto old notions of class or occupation.[33]

Basically, the precariat consists of people who once enjoyed the labour-related security that social democratic parties and trade unions pursued after the Second World War. They are now workers beset by multiple forms of insecurity, subject to temporary, short-term, often part-time, employment contracts; to the erosion of their benefits if in employment; and vulnerability to loss of income, rendered more acute by the reduction of state benefits. Critically, all this (and more) leads to a lack of work-based identity. When employed, they have a sense that they are in careerless jobs with no prospect of improvement; and they do not feel part of a solidaristic labour community. This intensifies their sense of alienation; a sense that they have no meaningful or worthwhile future; and they also lack a sense of occupation, even if they have vocational qualifications and even if many have fancy titles. Precariousness defines their existence, as work is reduced to a means for survival. Indeed, Standing refers to them as a 'new dangerous class': internally divided, and highly susceptible to siren calls of political extremism.

The notion of the precariat has major implications for our traditional understandings of the term 'middle class'. Standing admits that the precariat lacks homogeneity and that it is made up of significantly different elements: from the mother wanting to feed her family and worrying where the next week's income is coming from, through migrants who live on their wits, to youths and consultants who have no immediate wish for permanent employment, and older people who, already on pension, choose to supplement their income by taking temporary or part-time work out of choice. Yet amid all this, we can identify two broad groupings within his schema that are elsewhere depicted as 'middle class'. These are the 'salariat', who are closest to, and in a sheltered relationship with, the elite; and the 'proficians', who constitute a middling tier of the middle class as it is conventionally understood. Beyond them, it would also seem that categories of salaried workers that have traditionally been described as 'clerical', administrative or 'white collar' now constitute a significant element of the 'precariat'.

There is little to be gained by quibbling with particular aspects of Standing's depiction of the emergent class structure of the globalised world. It is far more important to grasp the fundamental reality he is presenting of a labour market that for the majority of people, even those traditionally included within the middle class, is becoming more 'precarious'.

A valuable illustration of this is provided by Leela Fernandes in her analysis of India's 'new middle class'. She explores how the condition of a rapidly expanding middle class, mostly in 'new' occupations such as salaried professional jobs, and managerial and white-collar occupations (rather than in 'old' occupations such as the law and civil service), is related to the neo-liberalisation of the economy and how it influences the country's political dynamics. In particular, she seeks to challenge existing treatments of this new middle class which have portrayed it as overwhelmingly a beneficiary of market liberalisation through the expansion of job opportunities and increased opportunities for consumption. In contrast, she argues that these approaches ignore important internal differences within the middle class. Certainly, she concurs that the new middle class has given rise to an emerging political elite that is shaping responses to economic reform, and has gained access to high-paying, secure jobs which can provide for a remarkably high standard of living. On the other hand, she identifies major segments of the middle class, employed in both the private and public sector, that have been subject to a restructuring of their class location as a result of economic liberalisation. From the 1990s:

The labour market was marked by a decrease in job security mani-
fested by an increasing movement from permanent to temporary or
contract-based work on the one hand and retrenchment in both the
public and private sectors on the other. The shift from a state-managed
to a liberalized economy has begun (albeit gradually and in hidden,
informal ways) to downsize the traditional middle class basis of state
enterprises. For example, in the context of middle class, white collar,
public-sector employment, the banking and insurance industries
have represented sites of political contestation. The banking sector in
particular has been identified as a critical arena for retrenchment in
order to cut costs and make public banks competitive in the context
of new financial standards of liberalization.[34]

Meanwhile, within the private sector, corporations have implemented processes of restructuring that have ranged from lower-level white-collar employees to the upper echelons of the managerial staff, with the downsizing of
white-collar jobs leading to 'jobs relocated, work outsourced. People given
golden handshakes, pushed down with a golden parachute, or plain axed.'[35]
Though she does not use the term, her new middle class is clearly joining
the precariat.

What are the implications for their political attitudes and behaviour?

The middle class and democratisation

'No bourgeoisie, no democracy,' stated Barrington Moore in one of the
most important modern discussions of historical development and political
forms.[36] Yet, in contrast with a widely held Western belief that capitalism
and democracy automatically go hand in hand, and indeed in disagreement
with the quite similar view of Lenin that 'bourgeois democracy' was the
political form that most perfectly suits the capitalist economic order (for,
while proclaiming the rule of the many, it in practice protects the interests of
the owners of capital), Moore identified three paths to political modernity:
the path to parliamentary democracy, the path to Fascist dictatorship, and
the path to Communist dictatorship. These routes, he argued, were not
alternatives for countries to pick and choose to follow as they liked, but
were tied to specific conditions characteristic of world history.

Notwithstanding criticisms of Moore (notably, that he largely excludes a
role for the working class in struggles for democracy), what we should draw
from his work is the fundamental point that the link between the bourgeoisie

and democracy cannot be assumed, and that it is contingent on an array of historical and structural factors. In other words, the bourgeoisie may be necessary for democracy, but it is not necessarily democratic.

This aphorism is broadly supported by Dietrich Rueschemeyer, Evelyne Stephens and John Stephens, whose wide-ranging survey of *Capitalist Development and Democracy* concludes that the bourgeoisie have rarely been the primary agents of democracy. Generally, the posture of the bourgeoisie towards democratic reforms has varied from case to case, and from period to period, depending upon the class alliance options available to them as well as upon the ideological legacies of the past. Certainly, in many countries, the bourgeoisie supported the introduction of parliamentary government, which in turn allowed for the inclusion of the middle class and, later, the working class. Ultimately, rather than being the historical project of the bourgeoisie, democracy is the outcome of the contradictory nature of capitalist development, which, in creating the working class, created a class that exhibited a remarkable capacity for self-organisation. Although the working class has not proved to be the grave-digger of capitalism, it has frequently been capable of successfully demanding its own political incorporation and the accommodation of at least some of its interests. Indeed, 'no other subordinate class in history has been able to do so on anywhere near the same scale'. Democratic capitalism, Rueschemeyer and his associates argue, rests upon a class compromise in which the interests of both sides, the bourgeoisie and proletariat, are to varying extents accommodated.[37]

All the same, the idea that the middle class is intrinsic to democracy remains hugely influential. As far back as Aristotle, the middle class has been widely viewed as vital for a stable democracy (serving as a balance between rich and poor). This tradition was embodied in seminal post-Second World War texts, notably Seymour Martin Lipset's foundational study, which correlated high levels of education, income, industrialisation and urbanisation with liberal democracy. In turn, a large middle class in modern society plays a mitigating role in moderating conflict since it is able to reward moderate and democratic parties and penalise extremist groups.[38] Scholars such as Gabriel Almond and Sidney Verba subsequently endorsed Lipset's approach by linking the existence of a 'civic' political culture, which seemed to rest upon suspiciously middle-class attributes (in particular, higher levels of education), to democracy.[39]

Numerous other social scientists were to associate the rise in living standards of the working class, and their merging into an enlarged middle class, as a key characteristic of the post-1945 democracies in the West. In more recent years, what Samuel Huntington has called the 'third wave of democracy', which began in southern Europe in the 1970s and culminated in the collapse of Communism in Eastern Europe, and hugely increased the number of electoral democracies, has been seen as having promoted and been promoted by the growth of middle classes, which are relatively better off and more demanding of their governments.[40] Higher levels and changing patterns of economic growth are also widely feted as having encouraged the rapid emergence of new middle classes in the countries of the South, where demands for jobs and political participation have provided the basis for such sustained challenges to dictatorship as the Arab Spring. Yet even Francis Fukuyama, who pronounced liberal democracy as the 'end of history', recognises that middle-class people do not support democracy in principle: rather, they are self-interested actors who want to protect their property and position, and may feel threatened by the demands of the poor, and hence may line up behind authoritarian governments that safeguard their interests.[41]

Indeed, there are today worrying indications that the post-2008 global capitalist crisis has led to a significant reversal of democracy. The Economist Intelligence Unit, for instance, argued that democracy had deteriorated in 48 out of 167 countries surveyed in 2011. Even in the long-established democracies of Europe, there has been increased support for populist and far-right parties with little commitment to democratic norms, and governments have shown greater willingness to clamp down on information flows and political dissent. According to John Kurlantzick, the middle class may have exploded globally (the World Bank estimated that it tripled in size in developing countries in Asia and Africa between 1990 and 2005), but it seems to be opting for political stability over democracy. The economic crisis may be laying the basis for the rise of the 'new authoritarians'.[42] Similarly, Guy Standing views 'the commodification of politics', which has accompanied the rise of neo-liberalism, as having encouraged a 'thinning of democracy'. The precariat, in particular, seems torn between political apathy and a turn to parties of the right, which appeal in the most ugly ways to the fears of those whom changes have rendered increasingly insecure.[43]

The debate about the middle class and democracy remains inconclusive, precisely because it is so problematic. Nonetheless, even if we can no longer (if ever we could) neatly identify the 'bourgeoisie', as owners of capital, with the wider middle class, it would seem credible enough to assert that the emergence of a significant middle class is necessary for the triumph and sustainability of democracy. The rise of a 'civic culture' implies a 'thickness' of civil society, which is today unimaginable without the considerable presence of educated, urbanised and globally connected middle-class citizens. Nonetheless, what the critical tradition of scholarship from Barrington Moore onwards insists upon is that, while the existence of a significant middle class may be a necessary condition, it is not sufficient in itself to make or guarantee a stable democracy. In any given situation, we need to examine how the middle class relates to wider progressive and democratic forces.

Conceptualising the middle class

This all-too-brief chapter has sought to provide a preliminary guide to the varied ways in which the middle class has been understood, in terms of its origins, dynamics, motivations and relations with other classes and strata in society. Hopefully, at least three generalisations stand out. Firstly, the middle class has become increasingly differentiated over time, as capitalist industrialisation has advanced, and it has changed. Indeed, it is a point often made that we should not refer to the 'middle class', but rather to the 'middle classes'. Secondly, while at times we may be able to identify a broad direction in which the 'middle class' or 'middle classes' are moving, their contradictory class locations may pull different segments of the middle class in different directions. Such heterogeneity is likely to be related to their different relations to capital and the state.

Thirdly, their work, life, occupation, income and status are becoming inherently precarious for large segments of the middle class. This poses worrying questions about the widely assumed commitment of the middle class to democracy. In our case, there is the further problem of just how far class theory, which has largely been developed in relation to countries in the global North, can be applied to the global South, where social conditions are very different. Structural unemployment may be more rife in the industrialised North today, but in very few such countries does it compare with the extent of unemployment and underemployment in numerous countries in the South.

Finally, it is apposite to conclude by reminding ourselves of the view of E.P. Thompson that 'class' is neither a structure nor a category but a historical phenomenon, something in human relations that 'happens'. While class experience is largely determined by the productive relations into which people are born or into which they enter, we cannot mechanically read off class consciousness from occupation or class situation, because consciousness of class arises in different ways, at different times, and is mediated by culture, ideas and institutions. 'If we stop history at a given point, then there are no classes but simply a multitude of individuals with a multitude of experiences.' Class is 'defined by men as they live their own history', and we can only grasp its nature if 'we watch these men over an adequate period of social change', and observe patterns in their relationships.[44]

It is with these thoughts in mind that we now turn to the experiences and perceptions of the black middle class in South Africa.

2

The black middle class in South Africa, 1910–1994

The history of the black middle class in South Africa has for long received comparatively little attention. Even though the emergent black middle class attracted some interest from liberal scholars in the mid-twentieth century, it is fair to say that it was dealt with spasmodically, and then very often largely as an appendage of the black proletariat. It is only now that the black middle class, notably as it participated in and shaped the African National Congress (ANC), is really beginning to receive its due. In part, this is because the lot of the middle class is often deemed in 'struggle history' to have been unheroic: indeed, in some tellings, the only way for the bourgeoisie to contribute to liberation was by subjecting itself to the leadership of the working class. Yet even while there is a growing interest today in the multifaceted nature of the struggle against apartheid, there has been a failure to trace the holistic evolution of the black middle class. This chapter thus provides an overview of the development of the specifically 'black African' segment of the black middle class in the pre-democratic era.

African classes under segregation and apartheid
The formation of the Union of South Africa in 1910 granted effective sovereignty to a white settler minority at the expense of the political rights of the indigenous black majority. Thereafter, white power and privilege were secured by means of an industrialising economy which was based upon the exploitation of cheap black labour. Discriminatory laws legitimised the

appropriation of the vast portion of previously black-occupied land, severely impeded black capacity to acquire capital, restricted black urbanisation, blocked access to upward social mobility of all but a tiny minority of blacks, and first eroded and later eliminated completely the rights of blacks to participate in the country's central political structures. It was only as a culmination of long-term historical developments, not least of which was an increasing tempo of black resistance reflective of rising levels of black urbanisation and proletarianisation, that white political monopoly gave way to a democratic settlement. This ushered into power the African National Congress, a political organisation formed in 1912, which had survived numerous travails, notably when it was banned by the government in 1960 and forced into exile, to assert its status as the predominant vehicle of black nationalism.

The class structure fashioned by settler capitalism left little room for a black middle class. Indeed, during the long course of history it was designed to inhibit this class's growth, save in so far as the white minority regime required a class of subaltern black allies and, from the 1970s, began to address growing shortages of skilled white labour by increasing the provision of black education and housing. The overwhelming characteristic of the black middle class, therefore, was its small size, together with its limited opportunities for upward mobility. This accounts for the theorisation of the black middle class by the Communist Party of South Africa (CPSA)[1] as a historically progressive class whose interests lay in allying with the black working class in pursuit of nationalist struggle and political freedom. From 1927, when the CPSA adopted the thesis of the 'Native Republic', it forged an alliance with the ANC, which, for all its limitations, it regarded as the principal vehicle of an anti-colonial, nationalist bourgeoisie.[2] Whatever the limitations of such analysis, it was undoubtedly correct in identifying the black middle class as frustrated by the racialised polity.

The emergence of the African middle class in colonial society

From the later nineteenth century a process of class stratification within African societies becomes … discernible. One begins to observe the emergence of something like an African petty bourgeoisie, a group who can be differentiated according to their economic position and lifestyle, their self-identification as an elite superior to the rank and file, and their values, one of which laid great stress on individual accumulation.[3]

Following this observation, its author, Paul Maylam, remarked that the concept of an African petty bourgeoisie was 'problematic'. If anything, this was an understatement, and in the decades to come there were to be complex debates about the character of the black African middle class.[4] Suffice it to say here that the black middle class came to occupy an intermediate position between white capital and the black working class, and between the state and the black population it ruled. During early decades of Union, this class was defined by its employment in professional, 'service' and clerical spheres and, subsequently, under apartheid, increasingly in political and managerial positions. Its status was dictated not only by its standard of living, but by its education, literacy, lifestyle, political authority and its orientation towards material improvement and individual betterment.

The origins of the black middle class, variously depicted as an emergent African elite or petty bourgeoisie, lie in the scattered educational efforts of the Christian missionaries of a variety of nationalities and denominations which became increasingly active from the early nineteenth century.[5] 'The missionary endeavor was crucial to the future character of the black petty bourgeoisie.'[6] The saving of souls demanded the promotion of literacy and the teaching of the English language so that earthly sinners could read the word of God, and with that came the missionaries' commitment to spreading 'civilisation'. 'The basic elements were a westernized lifestyle – ranging from style of dress and eating habits to housing based on the nuclear family, a mode of employment suited to the early industrial age (whether cash-cropping farmer, artisan or wage-labourer), aspirations which were westernized and capitalistic though tempered by personal humility, and above all, rigid conformity to Western norms in all questions of morality and deportment.'[7]

To ensure that this Westernising project endured, missions formed their own Christianised communities – known in Natal as the *amakholwa* or 'believers' – often settled on mission-owned land and isolated geographically from non-Christian neighbours. The relations between Christian and non-Christian were often strained and discouraged by the missionaries, who believed that indigenous African customs were backward if not actually sinful.

Many missionary societies granted individual title to parcels of land to their most loyal converts, or assisted their adherents to acquire land, believing that this would help entrench solid Christian values. Here was the origin of various African landed enclaves scattered around the country (which were later to complicate the apartheid government's efforts to bring about a tidy allocation of land between the different races).Yet, by far the most important advantage available to the *kholwa* was access to education, for this was a 'vital asset' for those wishing to prosper. The ability to read, write, add up, subtract and communicate with the colonists in their own language involved skills that were required by the colonial economy. Nonetheless, educational opportunities were severely limited. Mission schools were relatively few; they were usually poorly equipped; and not many were able to offer more than the most elementary teaching. This 'fell far short of a comprehensive and effective schools network even for the Christianized African population', with the result that only a small minority of children had access to formal education, and most of those were confined to lower grades. According to the country's first census, in 1911, only 6.8 per cent of the black African population was able to read or write.[8]

Beyond elementary level, *kholwa* communities enjoyed a 'virtual monopoly on opportunities in education'. A prime purpose of the missionaries' efforts was the training of ministers and teachers, to which end, from the middle of the nineteenth century, the different missionary societies established a number of 'Native training institutions'. The earliest and most prominent of these was Lovedale College in the Eastern Cape, established by the United Free Church Mission in 1841. This was followed by other institutions such as St Matthew's, established by the Anglicans near Grahamstown in 1855, Healdtown by the Methodists at Fort Beaufort in 1857, the Amanzimtoti Institute (later renamed Adams College) by the American Board of Commissioners for Foreign Mission near Durban in 1853, and St Francis's by a Catholic Trappist order at Mariannhill in Natal in 1909. Overwhelmingly, the objective of such institutions was to create 'educated men', for African women were largely excluded from the benefits of formal education. Nonetheless, there were pioneering institutions for women, the most famous being the Inanda Seminary just north of Durban, founded by the American Board in 1853, and the Lovedale School for Girls.[9] Elsewhere, opportunities were provided for a few women to train as nurses, initially at Victoria Hospital (Lovedale Mission Hospital) in Alice, which started a three-year general nursing course in 1902. Here, Cecilia Makiwane was one of the first two African women to pass her examinations and graduate in 1908.

The educational fare provided by the mission schools was basic, the large majority of such institutions preparing pupils to teach at the lower levels of the primary school system.[10] The South African Native College, or Fort

Hare, founded in 1916 at a site close to Lovedale, became the first and, for a long time, the only institution available for the training of African secondary school teachers.[11] These institutions did provide a rudimentary framework of further education for Africans, although the costs involved ensured that only those students who obtained scholarships or had relatively wealthy parents could hope to progress beyond the lowest levels. In turn, the scarcity of opportunity was to impart to higher education an aura of exclusiveness.

During the entire period from 1901 to 1934, despite the fact that mission schools received modest financial support from the state (though this came along with increased regulation), there were only 253 Africans who successfully passed their matriculation, while by 1935 only 49 students had graduated from Fort Hare with BA degrees and just two with BSc degrees, although the college also successfully trained some 370 students at sub-degree level to become teachers, ministers of religion, clerks, agricultural demonstrators and the like.[12] At school level, as late as 1958, there were just 723 African boys and 215 African girls in Standard 10 throughout the country.[13] Limited opportunity at home necessitated training abroad for a fortunate few. For instance, aspiring black doctors had to seek education abroad until the outbreak of war in 1939 prompted the admission of blacks to medical schools at the universities of the Witwatersrand in 1941, Cape Town in 1943, and Natal in 1951.[14] Even then, graduation amounted to no more than a miserable 6.2 black doctors per annum throughout the period from 1946 to 1956.[15]

Mission education sought primarily to civilise 'the Natives', who for their part prioritised the acquisition of useable and marketable capacities. Thus, there was a basic tension at the heart of 'Native education'. For the overwhelming majority of whites, educated blacks were subjects of deep suspicion, as likely to have acquired ideas above their station. Educated Africans were left in no doubt about their subordinate status in the colonial social hierarchy. However, within their own communities, their education brought both significant material rewards and social respect. Certificated teachers could earn double the amount paid to uncertificated teachers in primary schools, while those who emerged from Fort Hare with degrees could earn up to five times as much.

Those few Africans who obtained an education came to regard themselves, and became regarded by both uneducated Africans and colonists, as an 'African elite'. An elite they were, for they numbered little more than a few thousand, amounting to no more than 11,067 'professionals and salaried personnel' in 1936 and increasing to 18,165 in 1946[16] (the bulk of these being teachers and clergymen), together with some 6,400 'managers-proprietors', clerks, shop assistants and hawkers in 1936.[17] Yet even among this elite, there was an upper stratum composed of successful farmers along with the most highly educated teachers, ministers, professionals and clerks, who together with their spouses established themselves as leaders of their communities. Their relative privilege was to become entrenched by laws of inheritance, by intermarriage among leading families, and by the advantages that their social background gave them for acquiring access to higher education.[18] In illustration, Nkululeko Mabandla demonstrates how African access from the early 1900s to an area of freehold land in the otherwise exclusively white municipality of Mthatha (Umtata) provided the means to acquire middle-class status, which extended over successive generations.[19] In turn, his study poses the intriguing question of the extent to which the more successful of Colin Bundy's commercially oriented peasantry managed to parlay their agricultural resources into urban social advantage, despite the increasingly brutal limitations imposed upon African independent agricultural production by white appropriation of land.

The best opportunities for employment were in the rapidly industrialising cities, although even in the smaller towns a growing demand for teachers, nurses, clerks, interpreters and ministers of religion complemented the increasing scope for black Africans in trade and business to service the needs of growing township communities. (Given restrictions and lack of capital, trading generally remained a highly precarious occupation, and only relatively few entrepreneurs were able to sustain a position among local elites.) Thus, while their counterparts in *kholwa* communities continued to enjoy relative privilege among the rural African population, a recognisable black elite took shape in urban areas, its position reinforced by individuals' ability to acquire certificates or letters of exemption from the provisions of 'Native laws'. This was crucial for their legal ability to conduct business and acquire land outside locations, and could free them from demeaning restrictions on movement, from curfew regulations and from the requirement to live in a location.

The grant of exemptions varied across the provinces. Formally, at least until 1936, they were not required in the Cape, where a legally defined status of civilisation was notionally admitted by the inclusion of qualifying black individuals on the common voters' roll. Across the other three provinces, the extent to which exemptions were granted reflected local circumstances, yet during the first decade following Union the number of exemptions amounted to no more than about 1,550 in total. Although the number was to increase after it was made easier for municipalities to grant exemptions within their boundaries, those who benefited always remained a tiny minority. Nonetheless, by the 1920s 'even the smaller dorps [villages] in South Africa had a nucleus of successful black citizens ... who were the authoritative heart of their communities'.[20]

'The shared origins of rural and urban black elites' were constantly reinforced with 'bonds of friendship and marriage', often across ethnic lines, which bolstered their homogeneity as a privileged social group across the urban–rural divide.[21] Furthermore, social activities such as 'white weddings', funerals and dances, along with cultural bodies such as debating societies, choirs and literary groups, strengthened a sense of elite identity. Likewise, the formation of professional associations, especially for teachers, nurses and ministers of religion, served to promote elite coherence and a sense of mutual interest. Teachers' associations, in particular, became vehicles of representation on matters such as salaries and conditions, although it was only a Native Mine Clerks' Association on the Witwatersrand that was to achieve a modicum of success in the form of recognition by the Chamber of Mines as a negotiating body. At a lower level in the social hierarchy, black traders and businessmen were also to form their organisations, but it was only with the foundation of the African Chamber of Commerce in the early 1950s that they acquired an association of any lasting consequence and importance.[22]

Even though liberal education implied the potential of 'Native peoples' to achieve Western standards of civilisation, the black elite was subject to legalised racial barriers that blocked their upward mobility. The gap between the promise and reality was readily apparent to the black elite, especially when the politer paternalisms of white churchmen, senior administrators and professionals were crudely challenged by the rougher and ruder treatments of poorer and less privileged whites to whom educated blacks represented a grave threat in both market and status terms. Unsurprisingly, reactions varied. One response, reflective of the frustrations of black ministers with discriminatory pay levels and limits on opportunities for promotion within the missionary societies and established religious denominations, led to the formation of African independent churches. These sought to combine the Christian message with aspects of indigenous beliefs, culture and expression.[23] Another response, of which the formation of the Inkatha movement in the 1920s by the emergent Zulu petty bourgeoisie and aristocracy was the most prominent, was a reassertion of the value of African culture in defiance of its negative evaluation by white society.[24] Yet another was the leading role taken by members of the African elite in the formation and activities of political associations, of which the South African Native National Congress (SANNC), later to become the African National Congress, was key.

The African elite and the ANC: from Union to apartheid

The formation of the SANNC on 8 January 1912 came in response to African military defeat and land loss during the nineteenth century, and the entrenchment of white privilege, power and political domination under Union in 1910. Embodying an appreciation that all black African classes, social strata and ethnic groupings were subordinate to white rule, and drawing upon prior African experiences of organisation in the colonial societies that preceded Union,[25] the inaugural meeting of the SANNC was hailed as 'nothing less than a Native parliament'. Thereafter, 'Congress began to develop nation-wide contacts and attract support from diverse African social strata'.[26] Emblematic of this was the provision in its 1919 constitution for a House of Chiefs, the intention being that chiefs would represent 'their districts and places under their rule or control' – this implied the indirect affiliation to Congress of African people under their jurisdiction. The early meetings of the SANNC were attended by 'clerks, messengers, and servants, members of the new African urban proletariat',[27] and soon rural working people became involved in SANNC protests against the Natives Land Act of 1913. Nonetheless, the founders of the SANNC were overwhelmingly drawn from the emergent black petty bourgeoisie: 'ministers, teachers, clerks, interpreters, a few successful farmers, builders, small-scale traders, compound managers, estate and labour agents',[28] some of whom on that momentous day in January 1912 were formally dressed, 'in frock-coats with top hats, carrying furled umbrellas'.[29]

Such proto-middle class elements were chiefly drawn from among that 'sprinkling of educated men and representatives of political associations',[30] whose hopes for inclusion as citizens of a common, non-racial society had been disappointed. Although their stance was informed by Christian and liberal conceptions of justice and humanity, they were 'proud of their African identity'.[31] Accordingly, while the SANNC's nationalism was 'tempered by the demand of its members for incorporation into South African political life, Congress presented an anti-colonial variety of nationalism', which 'required African middle strata to return repeatedly to the need for cross-class unity in order to survive'.[32] The SANNC, renamed the ANC in 1923, consistently reiterated its status as the embodiment of the black nation and stressed the need for national unity, even in the face of inescapable organisational weaknesses and divisions among black Africans along lines of class, ethnicity, ideology, religion and region.

Although most historians have chosen to portray the ANC during its early decades as largely dominated by a middle-class elite, Peter Limb in a recent study has set out to challenge this 'simple axiom'.[33] While accepting that the ANC switched back and forth during the period from the 1920s to 1940s between centrist, constitutionalist and more strident approaches, and that such moderation was 'largely the product of the class composition of its leaders', he argues that Congress was nonetheless perpetually pushed towards a latent supra-class unity with workers because of 'the basic contradiction between white rule and black national oppression'. If the thesis is scarcely new, his detailed exploration of what he deems to be virtually inescapable linkages between middle-class leaders of the ANC and labour throughout the four provinces offers an antidote to the predominance hitherto of 'top-down' history. It argues his case that 'the gradual development of a distinct African political culture with a constituency including workers and propertied strata was crucial in embedding Congress in the gaze and memory of African society'. For all its much documented failings, the ANC outlasted and outperformed its various rivals as a necessary preparation for the qualitative changes that occurred during the 1950s.[34]

The black middle class under high apartheid

The triumph of the National Party (NP) in the election of 1948 ushered in the era of apartheid – a political project intended to reverse tendencies to racial integration inherent in urbanisation and industrialisation, and to promote the 'separate development' of races. This in turn was to intensify a process of radicalisation which the ANC had begun to undergo during and after the Second World War. The key features here were the influence of an increasingly assertive black trade-union movement, rising rank-and-file militancy, and the defeat inflicted by the ANC Youth League on the organisation's conservative leadership at its conference in 1949. In following this direction, the ANC forged strong linkages across racial groups by means of the Congress Alliance (formed in 1953).[35] The mass mobilisations of the 1950s – from the Defiance Campaign in 1952 through successive bus boycotts, stayaways, campaigns around the Freedom Charter and mass protest meetings – saw the emergence of a Congress movement that was distinctively less elitist and more manifestly rooted among both the urban and rural masses throughout the country. Even so, argues Limb, the ANC continued to be viewed as dominated by middle-class elements (notably intellectuals, lawyers and other professionals), even while it found itself at the head of an increasingly working-class base. Whether or not this involvement of the ANC middle-class leadership was positively reluctant,[36] and whether or not the Congress Alliance and its prioritisation of national over class struggle served to inhibit the radicalising impact of the black trade-union movement,[37] historians agree that workers and their organisations became increasingly influential throughout the 1950s. It was during this period, in short, that the ANC was transformed into a radical movement of national liberation, with middle-class individuals among the party's elite preparing the ground for the turn to armed struggle.

That the black middle class was becoming more radically disposed is unsurprising. Notwithstanding official determination to limit black aspirations, signified most notoriously by the introduction of Bantu Education in 1953, the demands of an increasingly industrialised economy brought about both quantitative and qualitative shifts. The number of African children in school increased from 588,000 in 1945 to over 2,741,000 in 1970;[38] the launch of the university colleges of the North (1959) and of Zululand (1960) brought about a modest increase in enrolment for Africans at tertiary level (this would have dramatic, unanticipated political consequences in so far as they were to foster Black Consciousness);[39] and, by the mid-1970s, the number of African 'salaried employees and businessmen' had grown to just over 94,000 – this included the dramatic increase in the employment of women as teachers and nurses (aided by their significantly lower salaries compared with those paid to men).[40] Even so, the structural position of the black middle class remained fundamentally unchanged.

The most comprehensive effort to portray the composition and contradictions of the African middle class during this period was provided by Leo Kuper's study of *An African Bourgeoisie* in Durban in the 1950s and early 1960s.[41] He justified the use of the word 'bourgeoisie' by virtue of the fact that the class to which it referred formed 'the "upper" occupational strata of African society', even though he admitted that it was misleading to suggest there was 'a well-defined class structure in the African communities'. Of course, he allowed that the bourgeoisie in Marxist theory referred to the class that owns the means of production, and wields political power by its control of the state and the propagation of ideologies promoting its domination. As such, the term usually referred to large land owners, industrialists, merchants, bankers and financiers. In contrast, he was applying it to African 'professionals, traders and senior government and municipal clerks'.[42]

Kuper's bourgeoisie, as depicted by his study of intellectuals, teachers, nurses, clergy and other professionals, consisted of rising groups which had struggled against the traditional privileges of African aristocracies, and which in other African territories were providing presidents, government ministers and 'new men of wealth'. In contrast, the black bourgeoisie in South Africa was largely denied the opportunity to acquire significant property and was poorly remunerated. Nonetheless, collectively, they were considerably better off than the mass of blacks, distinguished from the latter by their more educated backgrounds, higher incomes, better life chances and superior styles of life. Generally, too, they sought to put their relatively elevated positions to advantage, not least by dominating the leading positions in the various voluntary associations, municipal advisory boards, and sporting and social bodies open to blacks. But, because their lack of property and opportunity was dictated by their racial subordination, this bourgeoisie shared much in common with the black masses.[43]

The black bourgeoisie's ambiguous situation provided them with three political options. Firstly, in line with the government's evolving bantustan strategy, they could opt for the 'separate development' of tribal states in rural areas. Secondly, they could seek fulfilment through evolutionary change. In this context, they were perpetually frustrated by the contradiction that, while they enjoyed high regard within the black community, their achievements were systematically denigrated by white society, especially by lower strata of petty officials and policemen who were most threatened by their higher social status. The resulting tension engendered a more pronounced sense of grievance among the black bourgeoisie than among black proletarians and peasants, and resulted in their being more demanding of social change. Consequently, and thirdly:

> thrown back on the African masses by the denial of entry into the dominant society, [the bourgeoisie] may interact with them to forge a nationalist movement with the goal of African domination, in which case the development would be from political power to bourgeois property, and not from property to power. Or the bourgeoisie may be divided, and sections may seek fulfillment in a revolutionary

struggle aimed at the creation of a socialist state and the destruction of bourgeois property.[44]

For all that Kuper used Marxist terminology, there was nothing particularly Marxist about his analysis, for he was as much concerned with status and 'life chances' as any Weberian. Status was similarly a marked theme of *Langa* by Monica Wilson and Archie Mafeje. Despite its diversity – 'decent people' were 'mixed up' with town toughs (*tsotsis*) – the township of Langa was presented as 'the most "middle class" of the black communities in the Cape'.[45] The 'decent people', only some of whom formed an 'educated middle class', were known as the *Ooscuse me*, while the others constituted a 'respectable lower class'.[46] The former were composed of the familiar categories of teachers, nurses, lawyers, doctors and clergymen, who, while not necessarily emerging as leaders in bodies such as churches and sports clubs, tended to be favoured when it came to dealing with whites. Yet this carried costs, for 'Africans who are in any position of authority have conflicting obligations, to the blacks they control and to the whites who are in authority over them. They are in an inter-calary position,' and if they were seen to be timid rather than expressing opposition to white authority, they were likely to be dismissed as 'Uncle Toms'.[47]

Similar patterns were explored by Mia Brandel-Syrier's *Reeftown Elite*, an anthropological study conducted at around the same time in a township to the south-west of Johannesburg. Rich in detail, it is notable for its recording of change in the composition of the elite. As white township officials increasingly withdrew into a more impersonalised municipal bureaucracy, they were replaced by a 'new elite of public servants' as the administration of housing, welfare and community centres was handed over to black control. Evident, too, was 'the beginning of a managerial elite', as white retailers opened up branches in townships, staffed by black personnel who were knowledgeable about changing black consumer trends. Brandel-Syrier also identified 'the rise of an entrepreneurial elite', who were held up by local society as the token by which 'the so-called African middle class could become a "true" middle class'. These developments were accompanied by 'the decline of the first urban aristocracy', those whose status had been founded upon their occupation of stands when the township was first set up; and, significantly, by the replacement on the Reeftown Advisory Board of earlier 'notables' (stand-owners, businessmen, tribal aristocrats and an occasional professional) with professional politicians. Although the elite was contemptuous of the local political leadership that 'played to the gallery', they were happy enough for it to do their 'dirty work' for them, as 'township politics had changed from co-operation to resistance'.[48]

A similar study was undertaken by Thomas Nyquist in the mid-1960s (although it was only published in 1983). Rather than identifying members of the black elite by occupation and profession, he asked the inhabitants of the townships adjacent to Grahamstown in the Eastern Cape whether they believed that their community had an 'African upper stratum' which constituted a 'distinct group bound together by common characteristics and a high degree of interaction'.[49] His respondents identified three major strata,[50] of which the 'upper stratum' consisted of the *abaphakamileyo* or 'high ones', composed not merely of lawyers, teachers, social workers, nurses and ministers of religion but also shopkeepers, carpenters and taxi drivers (a finding which indicated that black perception of middle-classness was both extensive and flexible). In familiar fashion, he characterised the upper stratum as located in 'an acute position of sociological marginality' in that, while its members were success-oriented, their success was restricted by racial barriers and limited opportunities. This led to high levels of psychological frustration, and to their engagement in 'debilitating competition with one another and Africans of other strata' in struggles for the most desirable leadership positions within the community. Yet few were attracted by the government's bantustan ideal, even while Nyquist, who had returned to his field site in 1975, could see little immediate future for them beyond more frustration.[51]

These studies, the principal ones of their era, were distinguished by their empirical research, which linked contemporary black middle-class perceptions of their location in society to their social behaviour and attitudes. There were to be few significant equivalent efforts during the later apartheid period.[52] Thereafter, for whatever reason, writing on the black bourgeoisie was largely carried on from a social or political distance, in the sense that it rarely involved actual engagement with black middle-class people themselves and was largely presented in terms of their political relationship to the liberation struggle.

The black middle class under late apartheid
The banning of the liberation movements in 1960 was followed by a decade of political quiescence during which the regime oversaw a booming economy. This changed rapidly from the early 1970s. The Durban strike wave of 1973 was followed by the Soweto uprising of 1976, itself a prelude to more

intensive political resistance throughout the 1980s. Meanwhile, the economy entered a long decline, featuring much-reduced rates of growth, falling investment, skilled labour shortages resulting from white upward mobility, and an increasing mechanisation of industry. External pressures – military, political and diplomatic – also rose dramatically. The apartheid government was faced by the contradictory challenges of implementing political and economic reforms while placating the more insecure segments of its own constituency. Yet the project of reforming apartheid was an 'impossible art'.[53] The more the government sought to modernise apartheid, the more it alienated major segments of its own followers while simultaneously raising and disappointing hopes among the black population.

The changing racial division of labour involved a significantly faster pace of black upward advance into occupational spheres previously dominated by whites, themselves upwardly mobile.[54] More and more, industry declared the lack of trained personnel a massive brake upon the economy. This in turn required a major increase in the provision of education to black children, 'who now rose to levels their parents could only dream about'.[55] The number of black African children in school leapt from 2.7 million in 1970 to over 7 million in 1988; and the opening up of new universities in black areas and increased black access to 'white' universities saw the enrolment of blacks grow to over 98,600 (33 per cent of all students, while another 11,000 blacks enrolled in technikons).[56] Although still concentrated in the law, medicine, teaching and nursing, the black middle class increasingly began to penetrate the corporate sector as managers.[57]

Initially, the government had sought to confine black African political aspirations to the homelands. As studies of the Transkei revealed, while the bantustan project was rejected by the majority of Xhosa upon whom it had been imposed, there was an emergent petty bourgeoisie – chiefs, politicians, civil servants, teachers and traders – on whom it conferred substantial material benefits. There was a steady increase in salaries paid to state functionaries, the size of the public service grew, and the black businessmen derived opportunities from the extrusion of white traders from Transkei and the generous loan facilities provided by such bodies as the Transkei Development Corporation. The closer such petty bourgeois elements were to the bantustan state, the stronger their political adherence to it (so that while the chieftaincy and the politicians were the most loyal, the teachers were more ambivalent and the most likely to exhibit political dissidence).[58] But, as the apartheid regime's crisis intensified, the extent to which the bantustans could satisfy the class interests of even the core members of the homeland petty bourgeoisie was brought into question.[59] Resulting doubts were to be confirmed in the early 1990s when, faced by the political pressures of the transition, the various bantustan regimes 'imploded'. As a study of the Transkei and Ciskei has shown, different elements of the homeland petty bourgeoisie either clung haplessly to independence or lined up behind popular forces (for most, the ANC).[60]

Similar forms of petty bourgeois collaboration occurred in the urban areas, which became sites of government reform in the late 1970s and 1980s. Here, attempts to address the voracious needs for a better-educated workforce merged with desperate efforts post-Soweto by the regime to create a supportive black middle class. What to do about urban blacks became 'a major preoccupation of the Botha government'. This led to important changes to the overall conception of grand apartheid, whose central strategy was to divide blacks into urban 'insiders' and rural 'outsiders'. Close to the government's heart was the cultivation of an urban black middle class as a bulwark against revolution. 'New housing, education and employment policies now offered limited but real social mobility to this diffuse stratum', including the lifting of various restrictions upon black business.[61] By 1988, spaza shops in the townships accounted for a turnover of more than R3,150 million.[62]

Despite an easing of restrictions on blacks in urban areas, both the 'old' and 'new' black middle class were still prevented from entering the economic mainstream by multiple obstacles.[63] Yet things were changing. Indeed, the origins of Black Economic Empowerment, a major thrust of the ANC after it moved into government in 1994, and the makings of a more assertive black business class lie very much in the changing conditions of the 1980s. For all the assertion by liberation theorists that 'the immediate fate of the black middle sections [was] linked much more with that of the black workers and peasants than with their equivalents across the colour line',[64] the liberation that dawned was far from radical – and the black middle class was to prove a primary beneficiary of the 'elite transition'.

The black middle class and the politics of liberation

The late 1980s was to see the final unravelling of the apartheid enterprise. The various political reforms enacted by the government – the tricameral constitution of 1983 (which granted separate representation to Indians and Coloureds in the central polity but continued to exclude blacks), the granting of full municipal status to elected Black Local Authorities, and the significant extension of urban privileges and services – all failed miserably. Although P.W. Botha's 'Total Strategy' was intended to secure support from the black middle class against the threat of 'Marxist tyranny', it instead drove the bulk of them into the welcoming arms of the ANC. Nor did the government's reformist efforts convince large-scale business, which now came to view apartheid as an obstacle to profitability. Alarmed by the urban-based mass revolt of the mid-1980s (triggered by mass rejection of the tricameral constitution), white business geared up to embrace 'democracy', so long as it could be tailored to its interests. When the fall of the Berlin Wall signalled the withdrawal of active Soviet support for the ANC, large corporations proved a major force backing the efforts of the National Party under F.W. de Klerk to fashion a political solution that would render the transition to democracy safe for capitalism. Although the National Party was to be thoroughly outplayed by the ANC during the course of negotiations, the ANC's more radical ambitions were to be reined in by the power of business, backed by international financial institutions and the West, as well as by its own character as a multiclass alliance.

Radical theorists aligned with the liberation movements had been scrambling to discern the class implications of the changes taking place under late apartheid from the early 1980s. Essentially, they sought to ascertain the political affiliations of the black middle class, which they felt had for too long been dismissed by the ANC as insignificant. Yet the vigorous efforts of the regime to woo the black petty bourgeoisie had increasingly called this assumption into question, raising the issue of how the ANC should respond. In particular, if it was the case that the black middle class was being drawn into collaboration with the regime, should the ANC respond by moderating its programme? The answer given by Pallo Jordan was a resounding no. In a paper that analysed the vacillating political stance of the National African Federated Chamber of Commerce (NAFCOC), he argued that the organisation had only begun to adopt a more assertive stance towards the regime in the wake of mass struggles. Consequently, 'It is not by pandering to petty bourgeois sensibilities that the movement will retain its allegiance. It is only when the mass movement, under the leadership of the Black working class, gives a bold lead that it will be able to draw the petty bourgeoisie into its train.'[65]

In contrast, a more cautious note was sounded in 1986 by Bonginkosi (Blade) Nzimande when he assessed the political and ideological position of the 'new' black middle class, by which he meant in particular the small, but growing, number of Africans employed as managers by the large corporations. This was a trend that had been increasing since the early 1970s, as the corporations responded to a mix of labour market shortages and international pressures (such as the codes of conduct introduced by Western investor countries to appease their anti-apartheid critics). Nzimande warned that the ideological influence of this group, which he saw as articulated by their various professional associations, notably the Black Management Forum (BMF), founded in 1976, should not be taken lightly. Despite its small size, it performed two clearly identifiable functions in favour of the ruling class: 'It legitimates an ideology of professionalism and careerism; and reinforces the belief within the working class that their only salvation out of shop-floor exploitation and repression is by becoming professionals.'[66]

The deracialisation of industrial relations, undertaken as part of the government's reform strategy, had enabled white capital to argue a distinction between apartheid and the free-enterprise system. In turn, black managers had largely responded by internalising capitalist ideology. Certainly, the mass struggles of the mid-1980s saw the BMF backing popular political demands, not least because black managers continued to be confronted by racial obstacles in the workplace. However, their political interventions should be understood as attempts to enter the terrain of class struggle on their own terms. 'This is an embryonic form of class consciousness development which realizes that the class interests of the new African middle class, and its survival, are inextricably linked with the continued survival of capitalism in its deracialised form.'[67] They were 'reluctant partners' of white capital, but only because racial domination was interfering with the advancement of their class position within capitalist structures. The liberation movement should therefore be alive to the danger of worker interests being subsumed under a 'people's alliance' led by the middle class.[68]

Looking back upon that era, many critics have argued that the class character of the political transition provided for little more than a deracialisation of capitalism. Philip Eidelberg, in echo of Nzimande, has suggested that this can be explained by the capture of the ANC by the black middle class during the 1980s. In arguing against the view that the ANC's close relationship with the burgeoning black trade-union movement indicated it was becoming 'more working class than nation-oriented', he proposed that the liberation movement's turn to urban guerrilla warfare had rendered it more community-oriented and gave it a social base quite different from that of the industrial unions. 'It was ultimately township support, including elements of the African middle classes, most notably the civics, which would provide the ANC with the main source of its strength.'[69] Rather than urban reform being viewed as merely an attempt by the regime to co-opt the middle class, it should be read as 'a growing loss of political control over the very class upon whose suppression apartheid had been posited'.[70]

After Soweto, most radical Black Consciousness adherents lined up behind the ANC, just as conservative organisations such as NAFCOC were later to do. The adoption of a 'People's War' gave the ANC credibility with emerging radical middle-class civic associations, which were soon to form the United Democratic Front (UDF), itself aligned with the exiled liberation movement. The UDF was dominated by an urbanised petty bourgeoisie, and was to reinterpret the radical content of the Freedom Charter in a reformist manner. This paved the way towards the far more limited political objective of securing the ANC's 'seizure of power at township, and ultimately at national level'.[71] In the long run, it would lead to the transformation of the ANC into a predominantly middle-class, rather than multiclass, organisation and the scaling down of its institutional ties with organised labour. Eventually, the union federation COSATU was to recognise the ANC's leadership in the liberation struggle and, in effect, reinforce the political hegemony of the middle class.

Although we may take issue with aspects of Eidelberg's argument (black workers, as distinct from the 'urban poor', are largely omitted from his analysis), the thrust of his thesis is powerful. The interests of 'big capital' and the ANC's middle-class township constituency would not always coincide – but that was a problem for the future. In the shorter term, 'the end of white rule would permit the accelerated expansion of the new African middle class'.[72] In short, after 1994 the ANC was set to become 'the party vanguard of the black middle class'.[73]

3

The black middle class in post-apartheid South Africa: Size, shape and structure

Present interest in the middle class in South Africa revolves overwhelmingly around the extent and consequences of black upward social mobility, yet this only highlights the lack of attention to the wider middle class generally.[1] While there is a very significant literature on the white working class, for example, there is little that is specific to the 'white middle class' as such. And, although there is a substantial body of work on the history of the black middle class, integral as it was to the rise of the ANC and black resistance to apartheid, the literature on the Indian and Coloured middle classes is almost as meagre as that available for the white middle class.[2]

Despite this lack of a coherent history of the middle class, one thing that can be stated for sure is that its development has been racially skewed. Nonetheless, a growing theme of present-day analysis is that while levels of social inequality in South Africa remain extraordinarily high, interracial disparities in the upper reaches of society are diminishing. It is against this background that we need to profile the black middle class in post-apartheid South Africa, although that is no easy task given the wide variety of approaches adopted in examining the problem.

The problem of size

One of the few certainties about the black middle class in post-1994 South Africa is that, while it remains relatively small in both absolute terms and as a proportion of the total population (reckoned at 51.5 million in 2013), it has experienced significant growth as a result of the democratic transition. ANC rule has driven the removal of all apartheid-era formal racial barriers which operated to bar black upward social mobility. Notably, educational options for blacks have been greatly improved, and official strategies of affirmative action and BEE have massively increased job opportunities for blacks at middle and managerial levels within the public and private sectors alike (see chapter 4). However, apart from broad consensus that the black middle class is 'growing fast', there is little agreement about its size, shape and structure. For instance, the Human Sciences Research Council (HSRC) calculated that in 2004 the black middle class comprised around 2.5 million people,[3] while other estimates have varied widely. One, by Carlos Garcia Rivero and his colleagues, calculated its size at 3.6 million in 2003.[4] Attracting most publicity has been the work of the Unilever Institute for Strategic Marketing at the University of Cape Town (UCT), which asserted that the black middle class had grown from 1.7 million in 2004 to 4.2 million in 2013.[5] However, even this figure is dwarfed by that proposed by Eric Udjo, a highly respected researcher at Statistics South Africa, who had previously estimated the size of the black middle class as 9.3 million in 2008.[6]

That there should be disagreement about such a matter as size should not surprise us. As we saw in chapter 1, definitions of 'middle class' vary widely, reflecting different theoretical traditions and purposes, not only whether the approach is broadly Marxist or Weberian, but whether research is being conducted for reasons of social analysis, policy or marketing. Indeed, any attempt to undertake research into the black middle class requires treading one's way across an ideological, conceptual and methodological minefield in full knowledge that one is unlikely to emerge sound in body and limb on the other side. Furthermore, whatever approach researchers adopt, they are then confronted by a host of problems about where the middle class begins and ends; and whether it comprises only those who are 'economically active' or should include their dependants, such as unemployed partners, children and the old. Clearly, choices have to be made, even if on somewhat arbitrary grounds. To state the obvious, the size of the black middle class depends not only on how one chooses to define it, but the methodology one chooses to count it.

In what follows, I make an initial distinction between two broad approaches into which existing work about the size, shape and structure of the black middle class has fallen. Broadly, these cluster around whether the black middle class has been defined according to criteria of consumption or of production. Garcia Rivero and his associates, from whom this useful distinction is drawn, suggest that this depends on whether the primary unit of analysis is the household (as the unit of consumption) or the individual (as the unit of production), and, in turn, on whether definitions are constructed around income or occupation respectively. In what follows, my study leans strongly towards the second approach, principally because it is based upon the notion of work, which I believe is fundamental to understanding the type and mode of functioning of society. Nonetheless, the argument here is that although there are obvious difficulties in seeking to combine the two approaches, they can be utilised (with all due caution) to complement each other, to enrich one another's findings and understandings. It is in this spirit that I turn now to an elaboration of the consumptionist approach.[7]

Consumptionist approaches to the black middle class

Consumptionist approaches to the black middle class have been at one with a much wider focus on the growth of the middle class throughout the African continent. The thrust of such analysis, undertaken by bodies like the African Development Bank (ADB) and by consulting firms, is concerned with what is seen as a dramatic increase of the African 'middle classes' in one country after another, the resultant expansion of markets for consumer goods and services, and the spillover effect in areas such as construction, infrastructure development and agriculture. One survey pictured the continental African middle class as having risen from 111 million (or 26 per cent of the population) in 1980 to 313 million (or 34.3 per cent) in 2010, and projected it as reaching 1.1 billion (or 42 per cent) by 2060. As in South Africa, this middle class is presented as predominantly youngish, overwhelmingly urban, higher-educated, salaried or self-employed, highly aspirational in terms of their standards of living and hopes for their children, technologically aware, culturally self-confident and, not least, politically assertive.[8] Notwithstanding the extremely modest definition used to distinguish this 'middle class' (according to the African Development Bank, those spending between just US$2 and $20 a day),[9] the socio-demographic changes involved have been widely used to give substance to the notion of 'Africa rising' and of a continent on the verge of a historic surge in economic growth.[10]

When we come to look at South Africa, it is useful initially to draw a broad distinction between the approaches of the marketing industry and of academic economists and policy-makers (although of course they do overlap).

The approach of the marketing industry

By far the most widely cited studies of the changing black middle class in South Africa are those presented since the mid-2000s by UCT's Unilever Institute. These caught the public imagination by introducing the term 'black diamonds' to refer to the increasing numbers of blacks who since 1994 have become upwardly mobile and have breached the racial barriers of apartheid society.

The 'black diamond' profile has been located in a wider sociological context by Hilde Ibsen. She notes the extent to which this phenomenon was predated by key developments within the economy in the late-apartheid era, in particular the greater attention paid by white companies to blacks as potential consumers. Already in the 1980s black-owned shopping malls opened in some townships (such as Lesedi City in Soweto), and blacks began to move into larger and better homes, some in white suburbs, and to register changing consumption patterns.[11] This was accompanied by growing media attention, symbolised by the coining of the term 'Buppies' (for Black Upwardly Mobile Professionals) by *Time* magazine in 1988,[12] though it never gained currency in South Africa. Although it is the 'black diamond' surveys which have earned most attention, earlier surveys, notably by the Bureau for Market Research of the University of South Africa (UNISA), broke the ground which the UCT researchers were later to plough.[13]

Such marketing surveys, while making a cursory nod in the direction of the diversities of sociological tradition, adopt empirical definitions of what it means to be middle class, usually based on either income bands or (increasingly) Living Standards Measures (LSMs) as created and refined over the years by the South African Audience Research Foundation (SAARF). Given that the 'black diamond' surveys are themselves largely based upon LSMs, these measures need a brief explanation. Developed from the 1970s on behalf of Unilever, the LSM index

> is designed to profile the market into relatively homogeneous groups. It is based on a set of marketing differentiators which group people according to their living standards, using criteria such as degree of urbanization and ownership of cars and major appliances (assets). Naturally, the LSM bands are not airtight pockets. LSMs bring together groupings of people out of the total population continuum into contiguous and sometimes slightly overlapping groups. Essentially, *the LSM is a wealth measure* based on standard of living rather than on

44

income – in fact, *income does not appear anywhere within the LSMs at all*
… Variables such as income, education and occupation were tested as
part of the first LSM but did not add anything to the strength of the
measure. (Original emphases)[14]

By 2004, for LSM purposes, the population was divided into ten groups,
from 1 at the bottom end, to 10 at the top, using some 29 descriptors,[15]
which could be omitted, varied or added to over time according to changing
living trends. Generally, it is only people falling into LSMs 5–10 who are
regarded as middle class, with one researcher describing those in LSMs 5–7
as the 'emerging' middle class and those above that level as the 'realised'
middle class.[16] Proponents have argued that LSMs offer far higher reliability
for marketing strategies than income bands, and are definitely not a proxy
for race, even though in apartheid South Africa they had tended to reflect it.
Since 1994, it has been noted, the impact of race as a differentiating variable
has been declining.[17]

LSMs were taken as the major basis for the first UCT Unilever
survey, conducted in 2004. However, the survey (carried out among 750
appropriately identified individuals, with a 50/50 gender split) made clear
that LSMs were not wholly adequate for identifying the black middle class,
because their product ownership went ahead of their income and because
it is important to enquire about such issues as where black middle-class
individuals live and what their 'state of mind' is. Nonetheless, selecting its
respondents from LSM 4 and above, or from those with a personal income
of R7,000 per month, or with a tertiary education, or from those young
enough and qualified enough to gain a better education, the Unilever survey
identified black diamonds as 'People who are wealthy or salaried in "suitable"
occupations; well educated people; younger individuals who live in middle
class circumstances; own certain goods such as homes, cars, household goods;
have aspirations, confidence about the future; credit worthy.'

Using these criteria, the survey estimated that the size of the black middle
class was 1.7 million out of a total black population of 21.9 million; it had
an average monthly household income of R5,900 (as against R5,800 for
whites); and it had a consumer buying power worth an annual amount of
R300 billion.[18] By 2013, the latest follow-up survey reported that the size of
the black middle class had risen to 4.2 million in 2012, and that its buying
power had increased to over R400 billion.[19] This contrasted with R3.8
billion spent by white middle-class adults.[20]

According to the results of the 2004 survey, 94 per cent of black diamonds lived in a formal home (58 per cent in the townships, 23 per cent in the suburbs, the remainder in flats or 'cluster homes'), and displayed high levels of middle-class consumer ownership (with 100 per cent owning such goods as televisions, 94 per cent owning or having access to cell phones, and 71 per cent having at least access to a car). Even so, while they were clearly drawing nearer to whites in terms of lifestyles and behaviour, the majority remained strongly rooted in 'traditional' African custom and beliefs, with 86 per cent believing in lobola (bridewealth), 75 per cent in slaughtering animals to thank the ancestors, 47 per cent in traditional healers and, interestingly, 71 per cent feeling guilty about owning so much when many members of their family were continuing to live in poverty.

Nonetheless, the 2004 survey sought to challenge any idea that the black middle class was homogeneous. It divided the class into four segments, each of which was further divided according to whether members favoured the 'status quo' or had a 'future focus'. The first segment, composed of those aged between 35 and 49, constituted 'The Established', accounting for some 39 per cent of all black diamonds and 58 per cent of black diamond consumer power. The status quo group was largely settled in the townships, in contrast to those with a future focus, a third of whom had moved to traditionally white suburbs and who exhibited a different consumer pattern, with for instance a higher rate of car ownership. The second segment, some 22 per cent of the sample with 20 per cent of black diamond consumer power, was made up of 'Young Families' with children under six and very often young women who were either single or lived with their parents. Within this category, the status quo group was largely content to remain in the townships, while those with a future focus were eager to move to the white suburbs, were better educated, took more financial risks, and were highly ambitious for themselves and their children. The third segment, the 'Start-me-ups', who constituted 21 per cent of the total, with 19 per cent of the consumer power, were aged between 18 and 29. They were largely male and childless, and were generally oriented to enjoying the high life; those who belonged to the status quo subgroup were less educated and more township-rooted than their future-focused peers, who were more prepared to take financial risks. Finally, the 'Mzansi Youth', 18 per cent of black diamonds with just 3 per cent of the buying power, were identified as the first genuinely post-1994 'born-free' generation, still living at home, but looking to enjoy opportunities denied their parents, and highly optimistic and aspirational.

Such marketing studies, though often reported breathlessly in the media,[21] lack sociological depth (their purpose, after all, is to assist companies to sell their goods to a growing sector of the market), but they are nevertheless informative in that they highlight broad social trends and orientations among a class which, apart from growing apace, is 'catching up' with whites and generally enjoying the benefits of liberation. According to the Unilever Institute's John Simpson, 'the aspiration to have a better and financially secure life' is the principal driving force behind the growth of the black middle class.[22] To that extent, this class has been strongly welcomed by the ANC government as proof of the beneficial impact of its policies. 'Black South Africans', remarked Joel Netshitenzhe, whom the *Financial Mail* once described as the Mbeki government's most strategic thinker, had 'shattered the glass ceiling created by apartheid', and had contributed to growth in demand in the economy and to social cohesion.[23]

Despite its descriptive value, the black diamond approach tends to feed a popular notion of the black middle class as essentially shallow, showy and materialistic, when – notwithstanding some highly publicised cases of individual excess – it might be fairer to say that they are merely aspiring to, and beginning to enjoy, the sort of opportunities and benefits enjoyed by other 'ordinary' middle-class people around the world. In this regard, Ibsen points out how the black diamond profile fits into celebrations of neo-liberalism, along with Western cultural attributes of individualism, happiness and freedom, while at the same time being associated with ideas of African renaissance and development. Black diamonds, she says, are popularly presented as 'enchanted consumers', and their growing freedom and wealth are often loosely linked to their involvement in a participatory and democratic culture. Yet in reality, for the present at least, the prospects of the black middle class may be strongly linked to just one party, the ANC. Ibsen's fundamental point is that black diamonds are not so much the spontaneous creation of post-1994 capitalist democracy, as a direct product of the ANC's struggle for liberation.[24]

Different methods, different results: the approach of economists
Less tendentious (if less fun) than marketing surveys relying largely on LMS data[25] are careful studies by economists that rely upon more comprehensive data sets and are theoretically and methodologically more rigorous. Here I will draw upon key studies by Justin Visagie and Dorrit Posel which, in seeking to assess the size and state of the middle class as a whole, allow us to

locate the black middle class within that wider framework.[26]

Visagie and Posel distinguish between two definitions of the middle class regularly employed by economists.[27] On the one hand, a middle class is often defined by its middle share of the national income distribution; on the other hand, it is equally often defined by an absolute level of affluence and lifestyle. As they demonstrate, both the size and composition of the middle class vary according to these two approaches. They also show that, given the very high levels of poverty and inequality in South Africa, there is limited overlap between these two definitions of the middle class.

Basing their analysis upon the first wave of the National Income Dynamics Survey of 2008, a nationally representative survey which captures a wide array of individual and household sources of income,[28] they observe that the first approach, identifying middle income strata, presents a middle class that varies in size according to the methodologies employed to identify it.[29] They proceed to employ a 50–150 per cent median definition of the middle class as the most appropriate, noting that this selects households which are generally close to, and even below, the poverty line. They accordingly identified the middle class in 2008 as having had an upper boundary for monthly household income of R1,058 per capita and a lower boundary of R353 per capita.[30]

In contrast, the affluence and lifestyle approach bases itself upon absolute standards of what would normally be considered a 'middle-class' standard of living. Typically, 'middle-class affluence' is identified by using a threshold of household income, adjusted for household size. However, this involves the problem that the choice of income threshold is inherently subjective, particularly in developing countries where household incomes vary widely, with the result that studies range from those which set the lower threshold well above the poverty line, to others, like those of the African Development Bank, barely above it.

Visagie and Posel note that studies of the South African middle class using this approach have adopted a wide range of thresholds: for instance, while a much-cited study by Lawrence Schlemmer published in 2005 used a household income of R12,000 per month (in 2003 prices),[31] Eric Udjo employed a household income that went as low as R2,436 per month (in 2000 prices), neither adjusting adequately for household size. A further problem is that the affluence approach fails to distinguish between middle and 'upper' classes.

Visagie and Posel seek to deal with these problems by, firstly, considering

▌ Table 3.1: Earnings (in rands) and occupational status, 2008

Occupation	Mean monthly earnings (individuals)	Mean per capita income (using occupational category of highest earner in household)
Upper middle class		
Legislators, senior officials and managers	R12,878	R8,228
Professionals	R9,214	R5,266
Lower middle class		
Technicians and associate professionals	R6,517	R3,729
Clerks	R4,221	R2,749
Working class		
Service, shop and market sales workers	R3,047	R2,093
Skilled agricultural and fishery workers	R1,436	R829
Craft and related trades workers	R3,835	R2,399
Plant and machinery operators and assemblers	R3,150	R1,985
Elementary occupations	R1,261	R948

Source: Visagie and Posel, 'Reconsideration', Table 3 (simplified).

the earnings of individuals working in occupations typically associated with the middle class (managers, senior officials, legislators, professionals, semi-professionals, technicians and clerks), using these to distinguish between upper- and lower-middle-class occupations according to international criteria; and by, secondly, reporting mean per capita income for households, using the occupational status of the highest income earner in the household to represent the occupational status of the household. This accordingly provides a set of income rankings by class groupings, as Table 3.1 shows.

In turn, Visagie and Posel present their findings on the size of the middle (and other) classes, according to their instrumentalisation of the two approaches, as Table 3.2 indicates. They also proceed to demonstrate certain trends. Firstly, the middle class identified by affluence relies primarily upon labour market income (85.3 per cent), followed by income from investments (8.8 per cent), whereas the middle class defined by the middle strata, while also relying heavily upon the labour market (58 per cent), is

▌Table 3.2: Size of classes, 2008

	Income strata			Affluence			
	Lower class	Middle class	Upper class	Lower class	Middle class	Upper class	Population
Number (millions)	19.9	15.4	13.4	37.7	9.9	1.0	48.7
% of population	40.8	31.6	27.6	77.4	20.4	2.1	100.0
% of total household income	5.2	13.2	81.6	22.6	49.6	27.7	100.0

Source: Visagie and Posel, 'Reconsideration', Table 4 (simplified).

also heavily subsidised by income from government grants (30.9 per cent) and remittances (8.3 per cent). Secondly, the average number of years of education for individuals aged 15 to 62 (the working-age population) within the middle class identified by affluence is 11.3, compared with 8.6 years for the middle class defined by the middle strata. The upper 'affluent' class is particularly well educated, with 59.6 per cent of individuals possessing a tertiary-level education. 'Hence part of the difference in earnings and employment outcomes across the two conceptions of the middle class is likely to be explained by considerable differences in education.'[32]

It is against this broad background that Visagie and Posel present data on the racial composition of the middle class in South Africa, according to their two approaches (see Table 3.3). Unsurprisingly, the size of the middle class (across all racial groups) varies significantly across the two approaches. When defined by the income strata approach, it comprises 15.4 million individuals (31.6 per cent of the population); and when defined by the affluence approach, only 9.9 million individuals (20.4 per cent of the population). From these figures, we may infer that by 2008 the size of the black African middle class according to the income strata definition had climbed to approximately 12.8 million people (in excess of even Eric Udjo's estimate), while, when calculated by affluence, its number shrinks to some 4.9 million (approximating the Unilever Institute estimate). Furthermore, the affluence approach shows that the middle class as a whole has become significantly more multiracial, recording a growing presence of black Africans (4.947 million in 2008, compared with 2.217 million in 1993) as against a declining presence of whites (down to 3.093 million in 2008 from 4.175 million in 1993) and an increasing presence of Coloureds (up from 767,000 in 1993 to 1.159 million in 2008) and Indians (increasing from 516,000 to 662,000).[33]

❚ Table 3.3: The racial composition of the middle class, 2008 (expressed as percentages)

	Income strata			Affluence			
	Lower class	Middle class	Upper class	Lower class	Middle Class	Upper class	Population
Black	94.3	83.4	51.3	88.3	49.8	20.3	79.0
Coloured	4.6	11.1	12.6	8.2	11.7	4.2	8.9
Indian	0.6	1.8	6.3	1.2	6.7	10.5	2.5
White	0.4	2.8	29.2	1.8	31.1	65.0	9.1
Missing	0.1	0.8	0.6	0.4	0.8	0.0	0.5
Total	100	100	100	100	100	100	100

Source: Visagie and Posel, 'Reconsideration', Table 5.

Clearly, the two approaches indicate fundamentally different conceptions of the class structure: for instance, the upper class defined by the middle strata approach forms 27.6 per cent of the population, while under the affluence approach it forms only 2.1 per cent. Indeed, Visagie and Posel highlight how under the former definition the middle-class stratum receives only 13.2 per cent of household income, whereas under the affluence definition it receives some 49.6 per cent.[34]

Visagie and Posel conclude on a note of 'horses for courses', suggesting that the definitions are likely to serve different purposes. The income strata approach draws attention to the status of the 'average' South African. 'Growing the proportional size of the middle class would imply supporting economic policies that favour those in the middle of the income distribution, thereby decreasing income inequality.'[35] On the other hand, the middle class defined by affluence highlights living standards generally conceived of as middle class. 'Given South Africa's history of racial exclusion and discrimination, this definition ... typically is used to assess racial transformation in opportunities and access to resources.'[36] The adoption of economic policies that would increase the size of this class would therefore tend to increase income inequality.

Overall, consumptionist approaches can provide enormously valuable data about living standards, income, spending power and lifestyles of different class segments of a given population. Importantly, too, they can differentiate by race, and in so doing map how – with due regard to enduring cultural beliefs and attitudes – the racial profile of the South African class structure is changing, with the 'middle class' becoming more racially diverse. However, while they are perhaps of particular utility to economists and policy-makers, sociologists are likely to argue that consumptionist approaches are largely descriptive, and that to understand the dynamics of class and class behaviour we must turn to more dynamic interpretations, which revolve around work, occupation, wealth and education, and how these reflect (or result from) the wielding of power in society.

Productionist approaches to the black middle class

Whereas the competing consumptionist orientations to class in South Africa can lead to widely differing definitions of middle-classness, shared concerns about power and societal function lead to considerably greater agreement between what, in a very broad sense, we can term neo-Weberian and neo-Marxist approaches. In what follows, I shall proceed from the former to the latter, outlining convergences and differences.

As with the work of Visagie and Posel, the post-apartheid black middle class is often located in the neo-Weberian perspective within a wider understanding of the middle class as a whole. One of the first holistic treatments of this class was provided by Carlos Garcia Rivero, Pierre du Toit and Hennie Kotze, who described their own approach as specifically Weberian. Whereas Marxism was 'embedded in political promotion' and the analysis of class conflict, their approach treated the middle class as just one social group among others, without any predefined relationship of cooperation or conflict between them. Within their approach, they made an occupational distinction between a 'new middle class' composed of professionals, managers and white-collar workers, and an 'old middle class' composed of the self-employed who fell into the same income groups as the former.

Basing their analysis upon income data drawn from opinion surveys conducted in 1994 and 2000 by the HSRC, they divided the population into five quintiles. The three middle quintiles (overwhelmingly white under apartheid) were identified as the middle class, which they then further differentiated by occupation into its old and new components. The resulting profile of the middle class, racially differentiated, is represented in Table 3.4.

From this data, their principal empirical findings were twofold. While its black membership had marginally increased, the 'old middle class' had decreased in its relative size – this was consistent with what had generally occurred in 'advanced societies'. In contrast, the 'new middle class' had increased quite dramatically, the advance of the black population (proportionately the largest) being the main factor for the enlargement of the

▌ Table 3.4: Percentages of population groups falling within the South African middle class

Population group	Old middle class 1994	Old middle class 2003	New middle class 1994	New middle class 2003	Total middle class 1994	Total middle class 2003
Black	0.3	0.5	3.0	7.3	3.3	7.8
White	5.1	2.0	23.0	31.0	28.1	33.0
Coloured	1.9	0	9.1	15.6	11.0	15.6
Indian	4.6	0	18.5	20.7	23.1	20.7

Source: Garcia Rivero, Du Toit and Kotze, 'Tracking the Development of the Middle Class', Tables 3, 4 and 5.

middle class as a whole. Further, when dissecting the HSRC survey responses into four occupational components (professional, managerial, clerical and 'old middle class'), they found that the proportion of blacks within the professional category had advanced from 1.7 per cent in 1994 to 4.9 per cent in 2000, whereas the proportionate increases in the managerial categories had been much lower (a 0.4 per cent increase for clerks and 0.7 per cent for managers over the period). 'Thus the real enlargement of the black middle class has only occurred at the top level.'[37] Overall, whereas 29 per cent of the middle class was black (defined extensively) in 1994, the corresponding figure for 2000 bordered on 50 per cent. Whites had been overtaken by blacks as the largest population group within the middle class.

Garcia Rivero and his associates concluded that the liberation process since 1990 had resulted in Africans, Coloureds and Indians moving into middle-class occupational spheres previously largely reserved for whites. At the same time, the democratic government had failed to stem the growth in unemployment for the majority of its constituency, and Garcia Rivero and his associates therefore proposed that 'the years of struggle for democracy may have produced benefits for a qualified minority only'.[38] This raised the further issue of whether class rather than race would become the major cleavage bisecting South African society.

Certainly, their basic empirical findings were suggestive. Beyond that, however, they sought neither to explain the significance of their distinction between the new and old middle classes, nor to provide any explanations for the differential rates of black movement into the various components of the new middle class, nor to reconcile their starting assumption that the growth of the middle class would help consolidate democracy with their speculation about a possible increase in class conflict. In short, even while adopting an approach based upon the nature of work undertaken by different classes within society, they failed to move meaningfully beyond what was, in essence, merely a skeletal description of black upward mobility.

In sharp contrast, Jeremy Seekings and Nicoli Nattrass have provided a far more sophisticated analysis of the class structure in the post-apartheid period. Initially, they offer a discussion of the way in which the two grand traditions of class analysis have been transposed to South African conditions. They argue that while the neo-Marxist, 'revisionist' tradition concentrated on 'the big picture', notably on the presumed functionality between capitalism and the apartheid state, it largely 'focused on the political behaviour of different classes rather than class *and* structure per se'.[39] In particular, neo-Marxists largely ignored, if they did not actively disdain, quantitative analysis. As a result they more or less left the field to neo-Weberian scholars, who, from the late 1970s, began to explore issues such as class and inequality and the changing racial composition of different occupations, using a wide array of sources (official and otherwise) as the basis for a more comprehensive picture of the changing social structure before and after apartheid. Consequently, while lamenting the flaws but celebrating the strengths of both approaches, Seekings and Nattrass sought to build, locally, on Owen Crankshaw's work on the changing occupational division of labour under apartheid (which, while espousing a broadly Marxist perspective, had used operational categories of class that had much in common with Weberian understandings);[40] and internationally, on Erik Olin Wright (who had sought to demonstrate 'the usefulness of class analysis to non-Marxists *and* the usefulness of quantitative analysis to Marxists') as well as on the work of some pre-eminent Weberians, notably John H. Goldthorpe.

It is important to stress, first of all, that their particular interest stretches far beyond the black middle class, which for them has no particular significance apart from the fact that it is located within their broader context. Secondly, they insist that class is only important if it is 'consequential', by which they mean if it is linked to what Weber termed 'life chances', so that, for instance, the better-off in society are more likely to access better education, jobs, standard of living and so on. Following on from that, classes are likely to have certain interests; and class location is likely to be related to attitudes, which can shape individuals' motivation. Thirdly, Seekings and Nattrass stress that while they are guided particularly by the neo-Weberian approach of Goldthorpe (centred around occupations), they also appropriate aspects of the neo-Marxist approach of Wright, notably the idea of mediated class relationships (whereby, notably, individuals' class locations can be 'contradictory'). Fourthly, they recognise that analyses of class based on surveys can only provide 'snapshots' of class configurations at a particular time, whereas class locations and systems change over time. For instance, individuals can change class by moving to other occupations (or losing their jobs), while the shape and interrelationship of classes can also be changed by intergenerational mobility. While not citing E.P. Thompson, it would seem that they would approve of his notion that class is a historical phenomenon and can ultimately be studied only over time. Finally, while acknowledging that theorisations of class have been overwhelmingly developed to help us understand industrialised (or 'Northern') countries, they argue that these cannot be applied mechanically to semi-industrialised or underdeveloped countries in the South. In South Africa, for instance, many 'proletarians' retain strong links to the countryside.[41]

Basing their classification upon a comprehensive survey conducted under the auspices of the Project for Statistics on Living Standards and Development,[42] supplemented by other sources, Seekings and Nattrass mapped South Africa's classes by way of three steps. First, they classified the occupations of individual respondents. This resulted in a five-category class schema, which in turn was differentiated by the nature of the employment relationship (see Table 3.5). Importantly, they note that this has particularly 'Southern' characteristics, especially in respect of the erosion of formal protections for workers, increasing casualisation of work, and general precariousness.

Secondly, having given individuals an occupational classification, they categorised the households of which these were members. Households with one person in employment were classed according to that person's occupation. Households with two persons in employment in the same occupational category were classified accordingly. Finally, households with two or more persons in employment were classed according to the highest individual occupation classification of their members (so households with, for instance, a manager and also a secretary were assigned to the 'upper-class' category of the former). Although they noted various complications, overall they found 'very few surprising combinations'.

However, the second stage left something like 33 per cent of households uncategorised – and unclassifiable according to the denominated categories. Such households ranged from those composed of unemployed people dependent upon government grants through to a relatively small number of people enjoying a prosperous retirement funded by pensions and investments.

▌Table 3.5: Class structure, occupation and employment relationship

Class category	Typical occupations	Typical employment relationship
Upper class (UC)	Managers and professionals	Based on 'service' within a structured career path; degree-level qualifications; employment security; authority in workplace; high autonomy
Semi-professional class (SPC)	Teachers and nurses	Limited upward career prospects; diploma-level entry; no authority in workplace
Intermediate class (IC)	Routine white-collar, skilled and supervisory workers	Employment based on both 'career service' and labour contract.
Core working class (CWC)	Semi-skilled and unskilled (except farm and domestic workers)	Labour under formal contract, highly supervised, within a closely regulated payment system; increasing tendency towards casualisation
Marginal working class (MWC)	Farm and domestic workers	Labour often without formal contract, highly supervised, within a closely regulated payment system; regularly casualised labour

Source: Seekings and Nattrass, *Class, Race and Inequality*, pp. 241 and 260–270.

Accordingly, in the third stage, Seekings and Nattrass catered for this 'residual' and very heterogeneous group by categorising households according to whether their incomes were 'unearned' (from financial investments, rents or profits) or primarily from earnings from entrepreneurial or informal employment. Ultimately, they divided such households into three categories, labelled 'wealth and entrepreneurship' (from WE1 to WE2 and WE3 downwards). This in turn allowed for households classed by occupation to be moved to one of these WE categories, if 'wealth and entrepreneurship' proved to be the major source of their income.

From these three stages, Seekings and Nattrass derived eight main class categorisations (to which they subsequently added an 'underclass' at the bottom) and proceeded to rank them by income, relating this to household size (the details of which we do not need to discuss here). Ultimately they arrived at a schema of the South African class structure, which is represented in Figure 3.1. This they constructed by ranking average household incomes according to how they compared with the overall mean (average) and median incomes of all households. Thus, in 1993 the mean household income, according to the PSLSD data, was about R11,960 per month, and the median income little more than R900 per month. Accordingly, the average income of households in the upper, semi-professional, intermediate, WE1 and WE2 classes was above both the mean and the median incomes for

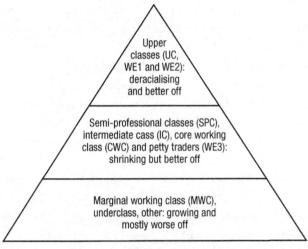

**Figure 3.1: Stratification after apartheid

Source: Seekings and Nattrass, *Class, Race and Inequality*, p. 337.

society as a whole. The average income for households in the core working class and WE3 classes was below the mean but above the median. Only in the marginal working and residual classes were the average household incomes below the median as well as the mean. Hence, households in the core working class were not privileged in that they had average incomes below the mean for society as a whole, but were privileged in that their incomes were above the median.[43]

Unsurprisingly, in 1993, at the end of apartheid, the upper-class categories were predominantly white (between 55 and 70 per cent of households); the semi-professional, intermediate and petty trader (WE3) classes were predominantly, but not exclusively, black African (between 62 and 71 per cent of households); while the core, marginal and residual classes were overwhelmingly black African. Geographically, the upper-class households were overwhelmingly located in metropolitan and urban areas, particularly Gauteng and Western Cape; the semi-professional class was distributed more evenly across the provinces (many teachers were located in rural areas), although the intermediate classes were more concentrated in provinces with large metropolitan areas (43 per cent in Gauteng and Western Cape); the core working class was concentrated in KwaZulu-Natal, the Western Cape, Gauteng and North West Province (63 per cent); while the largest concentrations of the marginal working class were to be found in KwaZulu-

Natal and Mpumalanga; and the residual class was heavily concentrated in the Eastern Cape, Limpopo and, to a lesser but nonetheless significant extent, in KwaZulu-Natal.[44]

Finally (for our purposes), Seekings and Nattrass arrived at a discussion of 'the new African elite and "middle" classes' in the post-apartheid period.[45] According to their previous categorisation, 'these were members of the upper class, the clumsily labelled WE1 and WE2 classes, and "perhaps" also the semiprofessional class comprising households headed by teachers or nurses' (although it is not clear why they excluded their intermediate category from this grouping). Such classes were, in household income terms, either privileged or relatively privileged, and 'were in no way in the middle of the class structure' according to the data for mean and median household income. Indeed, from this point of view, it was the core working class that was really the class in the middle. Nonetheless, it was to the black people in salaried jobs (such as managers and teachers, and professionals), as well as entrepreneurs and capitalists, that the term 'middle class' was generally applied. As the authors of the study noted, the 'accelerating growth' of these classes had proved 'the most dramatic shift in the social landscape' after 1994.

The work of Seekings and Nattrass provides a solid basis for further exploration of any notion of the 'black middle class' in South African society today, some two decades after the defeat of apartheid. But how does it square with a previous (2005) characterisation of the black middle class by the present author in which that class was differentiated into four 'fractions' (state managers, a corporate bourgeoisie, a civil petty bourgeoisie and the black trading bourgeoisie) on the basis of broad occupational categories? My understanding of the black middle class was most immediately based upon the prior work of Blade Nzimande,[46] which had been firmly planted within the theorising of the national liberation movement. In his study Nzimande had discussed how the consolidation of what he termed 'monopoly capitalism' and apartheid had changed the composition of the African petty bourgeoisie.[47] Having made suitable adjustments to reflect the changes of the post-apartheid period, I endorsed Nzimande's decomposition of this petty bourgeoisie into four categories, using census and other official data to demonstrate their changing patterns and growth since 1994. 'State managers' referred largely to those who had assumed high position in the ranks of the public service, parastatals and the ANC; the 'civil petty bourgeoisie' (a far more heterogeneous fraction), to those located in white-collar and service occupations (including independent professionals and semi-professionals);

the 'corporate bourgeoisie', to blacks who had begun entering managerial ranks of the large corporations from the early 1980s and who, boosted by affirmative action and Black Economic Empowerment, had assumed a growing presence not only as managers, but as shareholders and directors after 1994; and, lastly, the African trading petty bourgeoisie – small-scale business persons who in the latter years of apartheid had largely aligned themselves with the ANC, but had remained too weak to constitute a capitalist class as such.

The thrust of the analysis was that in the post-apartheid period these four fractions were all heavily aligned with, or dependent upon, the state for growth, opportunity and influence (although the development by the corporate bourgeoisie of greater autonomy through the accumulation of independent wealth implied a growing ambivalence to the ANC's proclaimed project of promoting greater social equity). Indeed, in general terms, rapid upward mobility and the consolidation of the black middle class suggested 'that the egalitarian aspirations of the NDR [national democratic revolution] are now at risk, and that differences of interest between the middle class and the poorer mass of the population are increasingly likely to arise'.[48]

In retrospect, if my approach had any merit, it was that it placed much greater emphasis upon the nature of the post-apartheid state than Seekings and Nattrass did, while indicating the manner in which the ANC's political project was increasingly assuming a class form. On the other hand, it was neither so well-grounded methodologically as the grander work of Seekings and Nattrass, nor indeed did it adequately locate the black middle class within the class structure as a whole. It is against the background of these diverse treatments of class and class structure that I now attempt to sketch a plausible approach to the black middle class during the post-apartheid period.

Reconceptualising the black middle class

It is worth re-emphasising that there is no single 'correct' way of thinking about class. The marketing industry will continue to identify blacks as consumers; economists will still differentiate between large categories of people for policy purposes; the different sociological traditions will continue to do battle without end; and many will try to draw inspiration from all simultaneously, and seek ways to combine their different insights. Furthermore, different approaches to 'measuring' class lead to different outcomes, whose utility varies according to purpose. It is against this background that priority is given here to 'productionist' approaches to class, grounded in both Weber and Marx; consumptionist approaches, by contrast, are far less concerned with causality, consequence and social explanation.

Fundamentally, class location is founded on occupation and possession or non-possession of wealth, upon which the income and lifestyles with which the consumptionist school is preoccupied are fundamentally based. However, it is here that I part company with Seekings and Nattrass, for if we base our conception of class upon occupation or possession or non-possession of wealth, then we need to link these to differential levels, types and sources of power and authority. In other words, if we are to more fully grasp the significance and meaning of class in South Africa, we need to build upon the scheme of the contemporary social structure offered by Seekings and Nattrass, by attempting to link it to 'the big picture', which, for all its flaws, the Marxist school has generally attempted to present.

The problem can best be illustrated by the blandness of Seekings and Nattrass's categorisation of those at the top of the social structure as simply 'the upper class'. While clearly locating a small category of people at the top of the social pile in terms of their income and wealth (although admittedly relating this to the authority which managers and professionals typically wield in the workplace), this approach avoids dealing with the sources of its wealth, power and authority in post-1994 South Africa, and the sort of society that the country has become. Quite simply, my argument here is that we cannot talk sensibly about 'class' without simultaneously linking it to the possession or otherwise of 'power' within the post-apartheid political economy.

The major debate that took place from the 1970s between liberal historians and their Marxist or revisionist opponents revolved around whether there was a functional relationship between apartheid and the interests of capital. On the one hand, liberal historians argued that there was considerable contestation between political and economic power-holders; on the other, the revisionists proposed that the relationships between them were mutually rewarding. The debate was inconclusive, but in later years there was growing convergence around the idea that, from the mid-1970s, the mounting costs of adherence to apartheid in the face of renewed black resistance became increasingly burdensome to capital. As a result, from the early 1980s large-scale capital came to exert growing pressure on the government to enter negotiations with the ANC. In due course, this was to lead to white minority rule giving way to a non-racial democracy in 1994. However, the nature of the negotiated settlement was such that, while the ANC was enabled to gain control of the state after winning the first democratic election, the overwhelming weight of economic power was retained in white hands or, more correctly, in the hands of the white elite that owned and controlled the large corporations. The problem for the ANC then became how to promote a 'national democratic revolution' that would allow for a deracialisation of capitalism. Subsequently, the broad strategy of the ANC's liberation project was to 'capture state power' and build upon this to extend its control over the economy.

Basing itself upon its political hegemony, the ANC has sought to bring public institutions deemed politically independent in terms of the constitution under the control of a hybrid 'party-state'. Winning state power has made the ANC the major fount of opportunity, for both employment and access to resources, for a black majority which previously had been blocked from competing freely in the market. As a result, the party-state has become the fulcrum around which upward social mobility, and chances for 'private accumulation', revolve for historically disadvantaged segments of the population.[49] All the same, while the ANC has assumed political power, and wields considerable derivative economic power from its control of state revenue, expenditure and the parastatals, the economy remains overwhelmingly dominated by large, internationally or domestically owned corporations and financial institutions. State power therefore coexists, cooperates and contests with corporate power, while power is simultaneously contested and shared by a 'power elite', which remains largely fractured along lines of race.[50]

Any attempt to understand the social weight and significance of the 'black middle class' has to be located in this broader context. Thus, while we may broadly accept the social rankings (and associated employment relationships) proposed by Seekings and Nattrass, they need to take more account of the reshaping of South African society under the ANC 'party-state' alongside our depiction of the different sources of class power. Table 3.6 is therefore offered as a supplement to understanding.

It must be acknowledged right away that it is enormously difficult to put this schema into practice. While it is conceptually possible to link types and sources of power to particular occupational categories (so that, for instance, corporate managers wield corporate power and state managers wield state power), it is far more difficult to assess 'how much' power particular classes possess, and even how they use it (until they take actions

▌Table 3.6: Class structure and power in post-apartheid South Africa

Class category	Typical occupation	Power location or limitation
Power elite or bourgeoisie	Senior state managers	High position in party or state
	Corporate owners and managers	Private assets and corporate authority
	Residual upper class	Assets and investment
Upper middle class	Middle-level state managers	Location within party or state bureaucracy
	Middle and lower corporate managers	Location within corporate hierarchy
	Independent professionals	Dependent upon access to state and market
Lower middle class	Lower-level state managers	Low position in party or state bureaucracy
	Semi-professionals	Location in public or private bureaucratic hierarchy; membership of trade unions
	White-collar employees and supervisors	Subjection to routinised bureaucratic or corporate authority; membership of trade unions
	Small-scale business owners and operators	Access to market opportunity
Core working class (CWC)	Formally employed skilled or semi-skilled workers	Membership of trade unions; industrial action; political protest; collective action
Marginal working class (MWC) and underclass	Farm and domestic workers; informally employed or unemployed	No membership of trade unions; political protest; collective action

which give us clues). Not only are power relationships highly fluid and variable, but the class power of the corporate power elite (or bourgeoisie, according to the terminology preferred) is often exercised indirectly, for control of corporations is normally separated from ownership, and mediated through share ownership of corporations or financial institutions (which are very often largely or partially owned by other such institutions). Likewise, although Seekings and Nattrass were able to allocate some individuals to classes upon the basis of income derived from wealth (assets), this sort of information is rarely available to researchers. Indeed, while we now know much about *income* distribution and social inequalities, it is more difficult to obtain reliable information about the distribution of *wealth*, even though we are uncomfortably aware that this remains heavily skewed in favour of whites.[51]

Nonetheless, despite such problematic issues, if we want to understand the nature and salience of class in contemporary South Africa, we need to move beyond more easily measurable 'hard' data to pose awkward questions about the relations of class to power, whether power be publicly sourced from the state or privately sourced from corporate and financial institutions. In line with the Marxist tradition, the approach here will assume that classes (and perhaps fractions within them) have different interests and that these will often lead them into conflict with other classes or segments of classes. However, it will also be argued that patterns of conflict or cooperation cannot be simply read off from class location. In other words, while we can probably assume that in many or most instances the interests of the power elite will clash with those of the working class, its relations with the different layers of that class (core or marginal) may prove to be very different.

It is against this background that this book will seek to explore the growth and social character of the upper echelons of black society in South Africa today. Both in the past and now, they have been variously referred to as a black bourgeoisie, a black petty bourgeoisie and a black middle class. Perhaps the first term simply gained its currency from its snappy alliteration, despite the acknowledgement by authors such as Leo Kuper that blacks were systematically disadvantaged in South African society and, lacking access to wealth, income and property, could never become a 'proper bourgeoisie'. At least the other two terms more accurately depict social strata that are somehow lodged between higher and lower classes, with their interests and social leanings consequently conflicted. However, in the more fluid social conditions of post-apartheid society, there are now greater (if still heavily circumscribed) opportunities for blacks to move upwards into the bourgeoisie proper, as well as into the upper-middle and the considerably more numerous lower-middle class.

Because this significantly increased rate of upward social mobility has been associated with ANC rule, it makes sense to begin my empirical analysis by tracing how the party's policies and practices have widened the doors of entry to the upper layers of society and to the middle class for its black constituents.

4

Black class formation under the ANC

The expansion of the black elite and middle class has been very deliberately engineered by the ANC. In line with its theory of the 'national democratic revolution', the ANC after 1994 set out to transform South Africa's 'racial capitalism'. This it sought to achieve by 'seizing control of the command posts' of society, deracialising patterns of privilege and power, and promoting a black capitalist class. As the ANC saw it, this class would be enabled to compete on increasingly equal terms with white business but, under the ANC's guidance, it would remain true, as a 'patriotic bourgeoisie', to the vision of 'a better society for all'. Although not widely acknowledged, these very deliberate efforts to promote a black middle class would build upon the changing strategies pursued by the apartheid government and large-scale capital since the 1970s.[1]

Black upward mobility under late apartheid

Passing reference was made in chapter 2 to changes during the late-apartheid period that promoted limited yet nonetheless significant opportunities for black upward mobility. By the mid-1970s South Africa was entering a period of economic decline. Factors as diverse as the oil shocks of 1973, growing shortages of skilled labour, quickening black urbanisation, an increasingly assertive black labour force and associated political challenges induced what Sampie Terreblanche has termed crises of accumulation and legitimacy.[2]

The outcome was the ending of a period of estrangement between the government and the corporate sector and the forging of a new partnership between the two that was designed to restore growth and corporate profitability. This was to revolve around a 'free-market' restructuring of traditional apartheid strategies, notably with regard to black urbanisation and black labour. Plans for reform were elaborated by the Riekert and Wiehahn commissions, both of which issued their reports in 1979. The former recommended that blacks with residential rights in urban areas should be granted unrestricted freedom to work in any 'white' urban area and improvements made to their quality of life by the grant of property rights, better housing and higher wages (although it also prescribed a sharp distinction between 'urban insiders' and 'migrant outsiders', who were condemned to political and economic marginalisation in the bantustans). At the same time, the Wiehahn Commission recommended that blacks should be accorded the right to join registered trade unions.

These measures failed to stem the crisis of accumulation. Nor did the government's attempt to contain political insurrection by the introduction in 1984 of a tricameral parliament (designed to incorporate Indians and Coloureds into the central legislature while continuing to exclude the black majority) succeed in resolving the 'legitimacy' crisis. Indeed, they backfired by inspiring the formation of the United Democratic Front. As a result, the government succumbed to pressure from business by also abolishing influx control (long-standing measures to restrict black entry into urban areas). In so doing, it hoped that a larger influx of blacks into the cities would decrease pressure from rapidly unionising black workers for higher wages. Rather than using legal measures to differentiate between urban insiders and migrant outsiders, it proposed that class differentiation among blacks should now be left to market forces. 'Those who could afford to live in the new middle class suburbs should be allowed to do so, while those who could not (mainly the unemployed) should be accommodated in squatter settlements on the peripheries of the cities.'[3]

By now, the government of P.W. Botha was increasingly reliant upon brute military force to repress opposition. In response, the corporates swung their support behind an accommodation with the ANC, combining this with deliberate efforts to co-opt prominent blacks. Major discord with the government of Botha was followed by corporate support for his successor as president, F.W. de Klerk, who in February 1990 announced the unbanning of the ANC and the start of formal negotiations for a political settlement.

It was in this dramatic context of the late-apartheid era that the racial division of labour underwent restructuring. This involved a significant level of black upward advancement into broadly middle-class jobs. After carefully mapping this process, the sociologist Owen Crankshaw arrived at three major conclusions.[4]

The changing racial division of labour during late apartheid
Crankshaw's first finding was that there had been marked black African advancement into the professions, albeit mainly into what he termed 'semi-professional' jobs. Specifically, these were the occupations of 'schoolteacher, nurse, technician and priest'. Whereas blacks accounted for only 3 and 11 per cent of managerial and professional occupations respectively in 1990, the black proportion of semi-professional employment grew from 24 per cent in 1965 to 41 per cent in 1990. Most of these jobs were in the public sector, mainly within the segregated health and education services for blacks.[5]

The second finding was that there had been substantial black advancement into routine white-collar jobs, most of them in the private sector. The black proportion of routine white-collar employment doubled between 1965 and 1990, rising from 15 per cent to 31 per cent, while the number of black wage-earners in these occupations increased from 89,000 in 1965 to nearly 301,000 in 1990. A shortage of whites meant that employers increasingly turned to black employees to staff white-collar jobs in the services, retail and transport sectors. This pattern contrasted sharply with black advancement into skilled trades, where white craft unions blocked black entry until the Wiehahn reforms widened the doors during the 1980s. The expansion of black employment in the mining, manufacturing and construction sectors was therefore achieved largely through the entry of blacks into semi-skilled machine operative jobs and not through skilled employment.[6]

Finally, Crankshaw demonstrated that although black upward occupational mobility was 'fairly extensive' in the late-apartheid period, it still followed the pattern of an upward 'floating colour bar': black advancement took place only as whites moved upwards into more skilled and better-paid jobs.[7] Nonetheless, throughout the 1980s, the large corporations and government became increasingly eager to promote support for capitalism by the encouragement of black entry into business.

Decreasing the odds: black participation in business[8]
Despite the destruction of black peasants and small-scale commercial farmers in the early years of the twentieth century, there remained a small capital-

accumulating class in the reserves and urban areas of the country. It survived because of the contradictions of racial separation. 'Native stores' were allowed to operate, albeit under severe restrictions, in the African reserves. Similarly, because racial laws prevented shop owners from trading in the area of a racial group to which they did not belong, blacks were allowed to operate trading enterprises in black urban areas. At the same time, black trading was restricted through the issuing of trading licences, and the business sectors in which blacks could operate (mainly general dealers' stores and transport, notably taxis) were limited.[9] Even so, a black petty capitalist class was to survive – and to expand as greater opportunities were opened up by the steady increase in the black urban population. Between 1946 and 1964 the number of black entrepreneurs increased tenfold to 12,426.[10]

Most black businesses were small, and were undertaken to provide the means of survival. Yet the most successful of them were driven by their owners' determination to succeed in the face of enormous adversity: not merely legalised racial restrictions, but difficulties in raising loans. The prospects for black enterprise were to improve steadily from the mid-1970s, as the government slowly relaxed restrictions upon black business in urban areas, and made efforts to develop a black capitalist class. Even so, black business was still limited to operating in racially restricted townships and homeland areas, and even then had to confront competition from white firms. Such entrepreneurs did not have access to the buying power of white-owned competitors, and so often came under attack from black consumers for charging inflated prices. Accordingly, black businesses had to find ways to negotiate a restricted environment; this often involved illegal activity with the attendant risk of fines, imprisonment or confiscation of goods. An alternative was to identify sympathetic whites who were willing to bend rules in the provision of finance or premises or by acting as fronts for black businesses in white areas.

Many black businesses and business associations that exist today have their origins in this period. For all its limitations, the bantustan programme promoted the development of a black proto-capitalist class which spanned the different homelands and which reached into the black urban areas. Their emergence was consolidated by the setting up of the National African Federated Chamber of Commerce (NAFCOC) in 1968 and the Black Management Forum (BMF) in 1976. The South African Black Taxi Association, forerunner of the South African National Taxi Association, was likewise founded in the mid-1980s and gave birth to the Foundation for

African Business and Consumer Services in 1988. NAFCOC went on to found the African Bank in 1975, the African Development and Construction Company in 1977 and the Black Chain Supermarkets organisation in 1978. Further projects included the launch of the Shareworld entertainment centre in Soweto in 1987 and the multi-million-rand buyout of National Sorghum Breweries in 1990. Black business leaders who were to become prominent after 1994 – such as Richard Maponya, Ndaba Ntsele, Sam Motsuenyane, Don Ncube, Gloria Serobe, Jabu Mabuza, Dawn Mokhobo and Wendy Luhabe – were all involved in black ventures or professional activities well before 1994. They formed the core of what Sipho Maseko was to describe as a 'vibrant' black entrepreneurial class which had developed during late apartheid.[11]

These businesses were sometimes assisted by government through agencies such as the Industrial Development Corporation (IDC), the Small Business Development Corporation and homeland development corporations. Foreign sponsors, notably the European Union and the US Agency for International Development, also played their part in helping black entrepreneurs.[12] Small business programmes were similarly launched by some of the major companies, such as the Rembrandt Group, Barlow Rand and Anglo American. In particular, the Anglo American Litet business development initiative (rebranded Anglo Zimele in 1989) was to become especially successful, and its example inspired the foundation of Real Africa Investments Ltd (RAIL) by Don Ncube. RAIL acquired the African Life Assurance Company from Anglo American for R200 million in 1994. Anglo Zimele was also to provide assistance to a former employee, Patrice Motsepe, who some two decades later was listed by one account as the wealthiest person in South Africa. Similarly, the insurance giant Sanlam, through its subsidiary Sankorp, initiated a wide-ranging project in the mid-1980s to facilitate black advancement and establish closer links with black leaders, 'especially those anticipated to control the direction of South Africa in the future'.[13] The project culminated in 1991 when, funded by the IDC, a group of carefully selected, politically influential blacks acquired 10 per cent of one of its subsidiary insurance companies, Metropolitan Life, the overwhelming majority of whose policy-holders were black. The deal was concluded in March 1993 and provided the financing model that would later become a template for Black Economic Empowerment (BEE) transactions.

Since the early 1980s business representatives had been meeting intermittently with the ANC in exile, but stepped up their efforts to forge a close working relationship with what was seen as the future government as the democratic transition loomed. Government had always been a major client of business, and expectations were high that a post-apartheid successor would spend heavily on development projects. Big business also backed scenario-planning exercises which urged the necessity of private enterprise if the ANC's aspirations were to be realised.[14] In so doing, the corporations laid the foundations for BEE.

Political deployment and the rise of the ANC's party-state

The ANC's election victory in 1994 provided the foundations for its subsequent domination of the political arena and the erection of a 'party-state', that is, one in which the boundaries between the party and the state become blurred.

Even though the ANC's political power was initially constrained by transitional constitutional prescriptions that it serve in coalition with the leading minority parties, its overwhelming political dominance (a large majority in parliament and control over seven out of the nine provinces) enabled it to establish control over the 'strategic sectors' of state and society, in line with the prescriptions of the 'national democratic revolution' (NDR). Given limitations imposed by the constitution and the economic dominance of private capital, as well as severe human resource constraints (for the ANC was hugely short of appropriately educated personnel), this project could only be implemented piecemeal. Nonetheless, over the first 20 years of democracy, the ANC was to massively extend party control over the state and many public institutions. In so doing, it was to transform itself, in effect, into a massive jobs agency whereby it presided over the appointment of personnel: not merely to political positions at all three levels of government, but to the huge number of posts in the public sector more generally. For this, it was to rely heavily upon the practice of 'deployment'.[15]

Initially, deployment provided for the appointment of ANC elites to high political and state office, but its practice rapidly became entrenched at lower levels of government as well. Its importance was enhanced by the limitations of an economy which, despite higher rates of growth after 1994, was unable to provide enough jobs to go around. This was especially the case for the majority black population, most of whom were unskilled and poorly educated. As a result, access to the political favour of the ANC was to become the only realistic path to material betterment for many black South Africans. For some, it was to become a route to personal enrichment.[16]

Deployment has remained shadowy because it operates behind closed doors. Susan Booysen has tracked how a de facto deployment committee established in 1994 was formalised at the ANC's conference in Mafikeng in 1997. This saw the passage of a resolution that deployment committees should be established by the party's committees at national, provincial, regional and branch executive levels. She also records that, in response to concerns about its integrity, the National Deployment Committee (NADECO) was suspended in 2001; and national deployment was then undertaken by ANC officials reporting to the party's National Executive Committee and its associated National Working Committee. Thereafter, while the new NADECO assumed responsibility for the appointment of key officials, such as the mayors of metropolitan councils and district councils, deployment committees at the lower levels continued to appoint other officials to state positions.[17]

Notionally, ANC 'cadres' were to be selected for deployment according to their qualifications and abilities together with their demonstrated political commitment. In practice, however, deployment became inextricably tangled up with intra-party factionalism as party members scrambled for positions and jobs. This tendency was to be intensified by the battle for the party leadership in the lead-up to the party's Polokwane conference in December 2007, when President Mbeki's bid to secure a third term as party leader was defeated by Jacob Zuma, who had been ejected from the deputy presidency in 2005 under a cloud of suspicion around corruption. Zuma had remained deputy president of the party, and used this as a platform to mobilise support. Following his victory at Polokwane, his supporters used the deployment committees to instigate a massive replacement of officials at the various levels of government, and followed up by securing the selection of mostly Zuma loyalists as ANC candidates at national and provincial levels for the 2009 general elections. Nonetheless, even though the Mbeki supporters were largely replaced, factionalism continued unabated, as battles for positions and resources led to widespread cronyism and corruption.

The problems were particularly acute at the local government level, where extensive popular protests against 'service delivery' failures and the unaccountability of ANC councillors aroused concern among the national leadership. This prompted NADECO to conclude that appointments to public positions should become increasingly open to qualified non-members of the ANC and all South Africans. The decision was to become embodied in a Municipal Systems Amendment Act in 2011, which aimed to prevent political parties at local level from placing loyalty above merit in their appointments. However, little had been done to implement this vision prior to the 2014 general elections, when ever higher levels of protest around the country provided the backdrop to the ANC's worst electoral performance since 1994.[18]

For all that the ANC decried factionalism, it remained an entrenched dimension of its internal dynamics, motivated in significant part by the dedication of Zuma loyalists to protecting the president from the consequences of his excesses (above all, his determination to deny responsibility for large public expenditure on his Nkandla homestead in KwaZulu-Natal).[19] With the occupation of numerous public positions effectively secured by loyalty to Zuma (albeit with provincial variation, particularly in Gauteng), official commitments to giving greater weight to merit in appointments were rendered largely valueless. Furthermore, although the ANC signalled after the 2014 election that it would devote major efforts to bringing about the better functioning of provincial governments and local councils, it faced the intractable problem that politicking was already beginning to take place around the selection of a successor to replace Zuma as state president at the next general election (probably 2019) – if not before.

The rise of factionalism has also been associated with the emergence of a 'party-state bourgeoisie'. This is defined by its high position in party and state (or both), and its resultant ability to accumulate wealth, to illegally appropriate state resources, and to dispense patronage in the form of appointments of followers to jobs or the award of state contracts to friends or family. In turn, although the party trumpets its efforts to combat corruption by prosecuting alleged offenders, its efforts are seriously undermined by their being heavily dependent upon political considerations, not least the fact that the party is currently led by a president who is seriously compromised, morally and legally.[20] In short, the party-state and deployment have facilitated an alarming extent of corruption, which has come to characterise the ANC's South Africa.

Deployment has enabled a diversion of massive public resources into private pockets, providing wealth and status for a politically influential minority. For the majority of those who were disadvantaged under apartheid, on the other hand, it has been the ANC's determined pursuit of 'equity employment' which has provided the better prospect of material betterment and upward mobility.

Equity employment

After 1994 the ANC acted quickly to transform the employment landscape. COSATU received an early reward for its alliance with the ANC by the passage of the Labour Relations Act (LRA) of 1995, the Basic Conditions of Employment Act of 1997, the Skills Development Act of 1998, and finally the Employment Equity Act of 1998. As a package, these laws massively strengthened workers by providing them with new rights. For instance, organisational rights accorded to labour made it illegal for employers not to recognise representative unions: workers now enjoyed freedom of association alongside protections against arbitrary dismissal. In addition, a Commission for Employment Equity (CEE), operating under the Department of Labour, was established in 1999 to monitor 'employment equity', the South African variant of affirmative action. These various laws applied to all employees, regardless of level, but while the first three Acts served largely to empower all workers, the Employment Equity Act was mainly aimed at bringing about fairer representation of 'historically disadvantaged individuals' (blacks, women and the disabled) in white-collar and managerial positions.

The ANC had a long-standing commitment to affirmative action, elaborated successively through the Freedom Charter (1955), its Constitutional Guidelines for a Democratic South Africa (1989), and 'Ready to Govern' (1992) and other position papers. Eventually, all this prior elaboration was to culminate in 1995 in a White Paper on the Transformation of the Public Service, which identified the goal of creating a genuinely 'representative' public administration. A year later, a White Paper on Affirmative Action in the Public Service paved the way for the passage of the Employment Equity Act.[21]

The Employment Equity Act of 1998 sought to make the South African workforce broadly representative of the demographics of the country; prohibited 'unfair discrimination' on 19 grounds (notably race, gender and disability); and compelled 'designated employers' (those with 50 or more employees or with a turnover in excess of specified financial thresholds) to draw up plans for affirmative action which would include numerical goals for equitable representation and time frames for realising them. The Act also obliged employers to reduce 'disproportionate' income differentials between categories of staff. Under its provisions, employers were required to submit reports on the composition of their workforces; and compliance with the Act became a precondition for securing government contracts.[22]

Affirmative action is usually strongly contested: South Africa has proved no exception. Generally, those who criticise employment equity argue from a zero-sum perspective, in which blacks are cast as unambiguous winners and whites and other minorities as losers.[23] From this perspective, employment equity is depicted as 'apartheid in reverse' and presented as leading to 'unfair discrimination', the appointment of poorly educated and unqualified blacks, loss of capacity of the entities involved, and the demoralisation of existing staff. Supposedly, all this adversely affects government performance or the efficiency of business, at cost to the economy. Furthermore, because the implementation of equity employment is strongly associated with 'deployment', it has been seen as contributing to the rise of a sense of racial entitlement among blacks alongside an increase in the levels of corruption, particularly in the public service.

Those who favour equity employment stress that apartheid's discriminatory legacy has to be actively addressed. Continuing de facto racial privilege for a minority is unacceptable, and blacks cannot be expected to wait for the working out of long-term measures (such as improvements in education). In any case, discrimination in the job market has severe consequences in that the abilities among disadvantaged groups are not realised. At the same time, transformation of the state has been necessary to ensure its legitimacy, for if it continued to be staffed mainly by minorities it would remain an object of distrust. Furthermore, one of the outcomes of discrimination is that disadvantaged groups receive lower incomes. Apart from being inherently unjust, this concentrates economic rewards among advantaged groups, mainly the white minority, and places constraints on the workings of the market. On the other hand, a more equal distribution of incomes tends to boost demand, and hence encourages greater opportunities for profit. In any case, if the potential of the economy is to be properly realised, it must embrace notions of fairness and equality.[24]

The debate about affirmative action will continue indefinitely. Be that as it may, my concern here is to consider the consequences of employment equity for the formation of the black middle class. It makes sense, first, to examine how employment equity has reconfigured the public sector.

Employment equity and upward mobility in the public sector
According to Vinothan Naidoo, in 1989 black Africans contributed 50 per cent of the total composition (915,545) of the combined workforce of central government, the four provinces and the 'self-governing' (the 'non-independent') bantustans, while whites accounted for 33 per cent, Coloureds

13 per cent and Indians 3.4 per cent. Black Africans (and other blacks) were largely confined to lower-level occupations, while senior occupational categories were overwhelmingly staffed by whites, who accounted for between 89 and 94 per cent of management.[25] There were another 438,599 public servants in the 'independent' bantustans, and here again there was a disproportionate number of white senior managers.[26] Unsurprisingly, the 1993 Interim Constitution declared that public administration must be rendered 'broadly representative': employment practices were to be based not just on ability, but on 'the need to redress the imbalances of the past'. In turn, the 1996 White Paper on Affirmative Action in the Public Service argued that realising a 'broadly representative public administration' was key to achieving 'legitimacy' and 'credibility' in the eyes of the majority of South Africans.

Initially, targets of 50 per cent black (African, Indian and Coloured) and 30 per cent African were set by 1999. When these targets were met, they were subsequently raised again. Indeed, by as early as 2004, the composition of the public service (at national and provincial levels) had become broadly representative of the country's demographics in racial terms, with nearly 75 per cent of its managers now being black. Women had fared less well. They had started from a low base of a mere 7.9 per cent of public service managers at the time of the transition, and thereafter gender imbalances were not reduced at the same pace as racial imbalances. Nonetheless, female representation had climbed by 2004 to around 34 per cent of senior management positions. All this did not mean that the legacies of the past had been overcome, for black representation remained higher in the more junior posts. Even so, by 2006 nearly 60 per cent of senior managers were black, and black representation in senior posts in the public service had increased far more rapidly than in the private sector.[27]

Further indication of the extent of upward mobility within the public service is provided by the report of the Commission for Employment Equity for 2013/14. Reports of their equity profiles are required annually from employers with over 150 (permanent) employees, and biannually from those with 50 employees. Over the years, the CEE's reports have come in for considerable criticism on methodological grounds, notably because they rely heavily upon submissions made by 'designated' employers themselves, and because of initially low levels of compliance by employers. Nonetheless, the CEE is confident that with increasing levels of compliance (encouraged by carrot – an online submission system – and by stick – increased fines levied

▌Table 4.1: Workforce profile of national government, 2013/14

	BM	BF	CM	CF	IM	IF	WM	WF	FM	FF
Top management	40.4	25.8	5.6	2.9	6.3	2.7	11.7	3.9	0.5	0.2
Senior management	39.0	23.8	5.4	2.6	4.4	2.9	13.4	7.7	0.5	0.3
Professionally qualified	30.1	36.6	4.2	5.7	2.3	2.8	8.5	8.3	1.0	0.5
Skilled technical	30.5	48.4	3.9	4.2	1.2	1.3	3.7	6.1	0.5	0.2

Note: BM black male, BF black female, CM Coloured male, CF Coloured female, IM Indian male, IF Indian female, WM white male, WF white female, FM foreign male, FF foreign female.

Source: Commission for Employment Equity Report, 2013–14, Tables 9, 18, 23, and 30.

on non-compliers) the accuracy of its reports will improve. Table 4.1 records how the CEE reported the workforce profiles of national and provincial levels of government for 2013/14.

Tables 4.1 and 4.2 indicate that black Africans account for two-thirds or more of top management at both national and provincial levels, 64 and 74 per cent at senior management level at national and provincial levels respectively, and over two-thirds of posts requiring professional qualifications. In comparison, blacks compose 75 per cent of the workforce as a whole. At skilled technical level, blacks are somewhat overrepresented (although the CEE data does not allow us to disaggregate these jobs into manual and non-manual). In sum, in those categories in government in which blacks do not yet predominate, it would seem that they will achieve 'representivity' relatively soon.

The transformation of the public service has been a highly complex process. Firstly, after 1994, there was the new government's need to undertake a massive restructuring of the public service. Above all, the national-level civil service needed to be reworked in accord with the new constitution. At provincial level, the four former provinces had to be carved up into the nine new provinces, and simultaneously merged with the bureaucracies of the ten former homelands. At the time, advocates of reform urged the desirability of introducing requisite qualifications for positions. Their pleas were strengthened by widespread acknowledgement of the lack of technical and managerial capacity within the former homeland services, which had also become notorious for their cultures of patronage and corruption. In the event, despite their dubious past political leanings, former black homeland

■ Table 4.2: Workforce profile of provincial governments, 2013/14

	BM	BF	CM	CF	IM	IF	WM	WF	FM	FF
Top management	43.4	28.1	6.7	2.1	4.3	1.8	7.9	5.8	0.3	0.3
Senior management	45.1	28.5	5.6	3.4	3.1	2.0	7.4	4.5	0.4	0.0
Professionally qualified	28.5	40.2	3.5	6.5	2.1	3.0	6.2	8.0	1.3	0.6
Skilled technical	27.2	56.9	1.6	3.9	0.6	1.2	1.6	5.8	0.8	0.3

Note: BM black male, BF black female, CM Coloured male, CF Coloured female, IM Indian male, IF Indian female, WM white male, WF white female, FM foreign male, FF foreign female.

Source: Commission for Employment Equity Report, 2013–14, Tables 9, 18, 23, and 30.

officials were progressively promoted as the new ANC government privileged affirmative action and demographic change.[28]

Secondly, the ANC government was distrustful of most senior public servants whom it had inherited. The overwhelming majority of these were not only white but supported the National Party.[29] Under the constitutional settlement, civil servants were guaranteed their jobs and privileges for five years. Unsurprisingly, the government rapidly introduced schemes for voluntary retirement (golden handshakes) to facilitate the early departure of numerous white senior officials, whose places were rapidly taken by black appointees. By 1999, 63 per cent of directors-general (DGs) and deputy directors-general (DDGs), the two highest grades, were black, at a time when blacks accounted for just 39 per cent of directors and chief directors (the levels below).[30] Such changes took place within a wider context of 'right-sizing': from 1996 the government sought to slash costs by reducing the overall size of the public service, which shrank between 1994 and 2001 by some 125,000 employees. Even so, there was an upward drift in the level of appointments, with the number of 'managers' increasing from around 24,000 in 1995 to over 70,000 by 2001. Overall, by 2008 the composition of the public service was 78 per cent black African, 10 per cent Coloured and nearly 3 per cent Indian – figures that are virtually identical to the racial composition of the national workforce.[31] As the National Planning Commission (NPC) was later to observe, affirmative action within the public service clearly played a major role in the growth of the black middle class.[32]

The NPC's statement is reinforced if reference is made to local government, where about another 240,000 people (60 per cent as many as those who

■ Table 4.3: Workforce profile of local government, 2013/14 (expressed as percentages)

	BM	BF	CM	CF	IM	IF	WM	WF	FM	FF
Top management	48.2	21.7	5.7	1.2	5.8	1.3	13.3	2.7	0.3	0.0
Senior management	41.7	19.4	6.5	1.9	4.7	1.4	18.3	5.7	0.3	0.1
Professional	28.7	23.2	10.2	5.3	3.6	1.6	19.4	7.6	0.3	0.1
Skilled technical	33.6	23.8	13.5	6.4	5.0	2.1	9.9	5.4	0.1	0.0

Note: BM black male, BF black female, CM Coloured male, CF Coloured female, IM Indian male, IF Indian female, WM white male, WF white female, FM foreign male, FF foreign female.

Source: Commission for Employment Equity Report, 2013–14, Tables 9, 18, 23, and 30.

work at national-government level) are employed. From the mishmash of local structures for different racial groups, the Local Government Transition Act of 1993 provided for the establishment of transitional urban, rural and metropolitan councils. Further reform in the late 1990s saw the emergence of a more consolidated structure of some 284 municipalities.

These massive changes were accompanied by a rapidly changing demographic dynamic. Thousands of white staff, many of them skilled, were retrenched or took voluntary retirement, as local governments were targeted for the employment of hitherto marginalised segments of the population. Notoriously, too, local government became a site for widespread political jostling. The large majority of councils fell to the ANC from the first democratic local-government elections in 1996. Since then, demographic 'transformation' has been at the heart of local politics, as Table 4.3 shows. The race and gender profiles reported by the CEE for local government in 2013/14 are not dissimilar to those at national level. Black Africans have recorded high levels of upward mobility in local authorities, even if they have not yet achieved 'representivity' at any of the senior levels of employment.

It is more difficult to generalise about changes in the racial and class composition of the public sector more generally. Parliament, provincial legislative assemblies and local councils have of course become predominantly black since the onset of democracy, although detailed figures are not available. Similar difficulties attend attempts to specify changes in the employment composition of the state-owned enterprises (SOEs). In fact, it is probably safe to say that the government itself has no fully accurate idea. The report of the Presidential Review Committee on State-Owned Entities, which was presented to President Zuma in 2013, indicated that while there were some

▌ Table 4.4: Workforce profile of SOEs by race and gender (expressed as percentages)

	BM	BF	CM	CF	IM	IF	WM	WF	FM	FF
Top management	33.4	16.0	4.1	3.1	9.3	2.7	24.1	5.8	0.6	0.8
Senior management	26.8	18.3	4.4	2.8	6.4	3.0	24.7	10.6	2.0	0.9
Professionally qualified	26.7	19.6	4.2	3.0	5.3	3.2	26.1	9.3	1.9	0.6
Skilled technical	34.7	28.7	5.0	3.7	2.4	2.1	15.9	6.8	0.5	0.2

Note: BM black male, BF black female, CM Coloured male, CF Coloured female, IM Indian male, IF Indian female, WM white male, WF white female, FM foreign male, FF foreign female.

Source: Commission for Employment Equity Report, 2013–14, Tables 9, 18, 23, and 30.

300 SOEs recognised by the Treasury, there were 'approximately' 715 SOEs if such bodies as municipal entities, trusts and section 21 companies were counted alongside constitutionally protected entities like the Independent Electoral Commission and the Human Rights Commission.[33]

From the moment that the ANC took power, the parastatals were identified as 'sites of transformation'. The 300-odd 'core' SOEs inherited by the ANC in 1994 employed around 300,000 people, with the 'big four' – Transnet, Eskom, Telkom and Denel – making up over 75 per cent of that number. These SOEs accounted for something like 15 per cent of GDP, and under the previous government had played a major strategic role in not only priming the economy but in promoting Afrikaner upward mobility. Unsurprisingly, they were identified by the ANC as important vehicles for driving a 'developmental state' and for promoting black empowerment. It was against this background that early enthusiasm for privatisation, espoused by Presidents Mandela and Mbeki, came up against heavy resistance within the ANC and the Alliance. Such limited privatisation as did take place was often to be linked to BEE (with the sale of state assets to black consortia).[34]

In its bid to 'transform' the SOEs, the ANC government took concerted moves, firstly, to 'deploy' appropriately loyal and black appointees to their boards; and secondly, to replace considerable numbers of white senior and technical staff at such bodies as Transnet and Eskom with black managers and professionals. Overall, some indication of black upward progress into 'middle-class' categories within SOEs is given for 2013 in Table 4.4. Again, from Table 4.4 we find that black Africans have made major inroads into the higher levels of employment in the SOEs, although at a somewhat slower pace than in the public service. Given the specialised nature of many of the parastatals, and the likelihood that they employ proportionately fewer manual workers than the different arms of government, it is reasonable to propose that equity employment targets have had to take more account of education and qualification than in the public service.

It is clear that there is considerably more differentiation in equity employment levels within the wider public sector than within the more constricted confines of the public service itself. Nonetheless, it is incontestable that, even if they do not fall directly under ministerial control (the universities, for instance, zealously guard their autonomy and have been subject to considerable criticism for alleged failures to transform),[35] public-sector organisations generally have become major sites for black upward mobility. In contrast, rates of black upward mobility within the private sector have been considerably slower.

Equity employment and black upward mobility in the private sector
Equity employment is far less advanced in the private than in the public sector. This is true despite the fact that, since the 1980s, the large corporations had made efforts to increase the recruitment of blacks into managerial positions in order to assuage domestic and international critics, offset skills shortages and increase their abilities to penetrate the black consumer market. The more farsighted were also aware of the need to prepare for political change. Even so, the private sector continued to be overwhelmingly staffed by whites, especially at senior managerial levels. Since 1994, despite large companies' increasing enthusiasm for recruiting politically influential blacks to their boards, progress towards 'representivity' has been relatively slow, although the rate of black advance has begun to increase substantially in recent years.

The detailed story of black penetration of the corporate sector remains to be told. This is partly, no doubt, because there are a large number of private employers, few of whom were under pressure until the passage of the Equity Employment Act to track black advance. In any case, even if companies did record the changing composition of their workforces, there was no single body with the authority to collate the results. Even though this situation changed with the passage of the Act and the establishment of the CEE, the commission's early reports made only rudimentary distinctions between the employment profiles of the public and private sectors. For instance, when the CEE's report for 1999/2001 recorded that black representation in the

▌Table 4.5: Workforce profile of the private sector by race and gender (expressed as percentages)

	BM	BF	CM	CF	IM	IF	WM	WF	FM	FF
Top management	8.8	3.8	3.2	1.5	6.6	1.8	58.6	11.0	4.2	0.6
Senior management	10.2	4.8	4.3	2.4	7.4	3.2	47.5	16.9	2.8	0.6
Professionally qualified	15.3	9.8	5.7	4.5	6.9	4.6	32.8	18.0	1.8	0.6
Skilled technical	32.7	16.6	6.9	6.1	4.1	3.2	16.8	11.7	1.6	0.3

Note: BM black male, BF black female, CM Coloured male, CF Coloured female, IM Indian male, IF Indian female, WM white male, WF white female, FM foreign male, FF foreign female.

Source: Commission for Employment Equity Report, 2013–14, Tables 9, 18, 23, and 30.

private sector was significantly lower than in government employment, the sole elaboration it offered was that while black Africans composed 71 per cent of managers in government, they accounted for only 9 per cent in the private sector (the figure for all blacks being 20 per cent).[36] Beyond that, the report had no further comparisons to make.

Fast-forward to the report for 2013/2014, and the picture becomes much clearer, as Table 4.5 shows. The contrast with the public sector is dramatically apparent in the 2013/14 report. Despite claims by large companies to have implemented employment equity, there appears to have been relatively little change on the ground. Except at the skilled technical level, where black representation is not dissimilar to that in the public sector, black African representation is substantially lower at all three higher levels. In contrast, white representation becomes higher as the level of employment increases, reaching nearly 70 per cent at top management level, where Indians (at 8.4 per cent) are also substantially overrepresented. The overriding question is: why? Why has black upward mobility within the private sector been so backward? Does the answer simply lie in white resistance to greater black participation in and ascent up the ranks of management? Or do the reasons for slow black penetration of the corporate sector lie more outside the realms of business, in the wider societal environment in which the private sector operates? Or does the answer lie in some combination of the two? We may speculatively propose as follows.

Lack of commitment to equity employment in private-sector circles reflects a generic critique by business of official transformational initiatives. This argues, variously, that equity employment legislation imposes major costs upon companies, which discourage investment and entrepreneurship, while the burden of monitoring and compliance also impacts negatively upon taxpayers. Furthermore, shortage of skills in some sectors makes black skills more expensive and less affordable, especially to smaller companies, which are meant to drive the attack upon unemployment. There is the additional danger that continuing race classification will increase rather than decrease racial tensions within companies, stoking resentments among minority groups. Although such criticism may be excessively ideological in nature, perhaps the most convincing critique of the government's equity employment demands is that they are demographically unrealistic.

Private employers complain consistently about the lack of a sufficiently educated pool of black talent from which to make appointments. Without any shadow of doubt, the poor performance of the public educational system over recent decades and the high drop-out rate among blacks at tertiary level suggest that there is considerable substance to employers' complaints. For instance, a characteristically robust critique of employment equity has been provided by Anthea Jeffery of the South African Institute of Race Relations. She is adamant that although the ANC may seek 75 per cent black African representation at management level, the required level of suitably qualified human material is simply not available.

> In 2013 a mere 36% of economically active Africans fell within the 34–65 age cohort from which managers can realistically be drawn. In addition, more than 1.2m Africans within this age group were unemployed. Factoring in age and employment status, the target for African representation should be put at 30%, not 75%. If the need for post-school education for many management jobs is taken into account as well, then even a 30% target is too ambitious as only 4.1% of Africans have any tertiary training.[37]

Some endorsement of Jeffery's position is provided by Standard Bank, which recorded its failure in 2012 to achieve its targeted levels of black employment at senior management level (37 versus 43 per cent), even though it had achieved its target of 62 per cent at middle-management level, and somewhat overachieved its target at junior management level (77 per cent versus 74 per cent).[38] This suggests that while blacks are steadily rising through the Bank's hierarchy, it is going to take some time – perhaps a decade or more – to achieve targets as age cohorts move upwards.

How representative the record of Standard Bank is compared with that of other major companies remains difficult to say, but note the judgement of the *Financial Mail* (which knows a thing or two about the corporate sector) that a 'quiet revolution' has taken place over recent years in business. This has involved a 'burgeoning number of black professional cadres who are assuming operational and strategic responsibility in major companies – a marked departure from the previous era, when black professionals were seemingly confined to non-executive roles and government-owned entities'.[39]

Nonetheless, even if blacks are beginning to advance at a faster rate within the corporate sector, this raises the question why and how the public sector has managed to achieve rates of black representation that are so much higher than in the private sector. The answers would seem to be several.

Firstly, it is difficult to avoid the conclusion that the commitment of the public sector to affirmative action has been far higher than in the private sector. It may well be, too, that the requirements made of candidates for appointment by government are often lower than in the private sector. This would seem to be especially the case where political factors, such as ANC deployment and factional squabbles, appear to intervene: some of the most notorious instances of this have taken place at the South African Broadcasting Corporation (SABC).[40]

Secondly, it is probable that many blacks look primarily to government or public bodies for employment. Apart from the fact that big private employers are effectively absent from large areas of the country, leaving government as the only source of local employment, there are strong cultural factors which attract blacks into the public sector. After 1994, numerous opportunities for blacks opened up in the public sector, and it is natural that they should have moved into it. Subsequently, with blacks now dominating the public sector and finding their way into the top jobs, many young blacks are likely to feel more comfortable working in such an environment, rather than taking what a number are likely to feel is the risk of facing racial obstacles in the private sector. Their fears appear to have substance, for there is considerable evidence that when blacks do move into the private sector as managers, they often feel they are having to confront 'whiteness' in one form or another: demands that they conform to 'white' patterns of behaviour or pressures to perform better than whites to prove that they were not appointed merely because they were black.[41] As one participant in a middle-class focus group put it in relation to the financial sector:

This is a white environment, it is not a black environment. And black people will not excel in this environment ... Because us as black people have always been seen as miners, rock-drill operators, teachers, policemen, soldiers and all that sort of stuff ... So ... before anybody gives us a chance and before anybody believes that you can do something, they want you to prove yourself ... The same laws do not apply to your other compatriots, those of a lighter shade.[42]

The converse also applies. White job hunters are likely to perceive the public sector as essentially black territory, where their individual prospects are limited. On the other hand, while whites within the private sector may not be explicitly or consciously racist, they may put forward 'commonsense' arguments about the difficulties of hiring blacks. As Geraldine Martin and Kevin Durrheim argue, blacks are often regarded by white employers as 'deficient in terms of skills, experience and personality'. At the same time, 'contemporary forms of racial talk are characterized by vigorous denials of racism', and 'the "good reasons" they [whites] provide justify the kinds of discrimination that are doing the work of ensuring racial exclusion'.[43] Unsurprisingly, research indicates that even where equity employment measures are in place, companies fail to address the need for promoting cultural diversity. One study conducted in more than 400 companies between 2000 and 2008 concluded that most employees perceived their firms to be largely untransformed in terms of inclusive practices.[44] This may partially account for a high turnover of 'equity employment candidates' in many private-sector companies. Apart from the much-cited practice of 'job hopping' by ambitious and able black managers, they often come up against 'institutional barriers which may be deep-seated and unconscious – such as beliefs that only 20 years' experience can qualify a person for a certain position'.[45]

The debate about equity employment clearly needs to encourage deeper analyses of corporate culture in a country that is still emerging from centuries of racial discrimination. However, the debate also needs to be related to BEE, with which it is closely associated.

Black economic empowerment

Pains have been taken in this chapter to stress the independent origins of black capitalism under apartheid, as there has been a marked tendency in recent literature for them to be brushed aside as insignificant. Such a reading of history undermines notions of African agency. As all the stories of the early black capitalists reveal, they achieved their successes against huge odds and as a result of enormous determination. If there has been a heroic age of black capitalism in South Africa, then it was almost certainly before 1990 – because its trajectory after that was to be profoundly altered by the dynamics of the political transition and, then, by ANC rule.

The discussion that follows deals with black economic empowerment (BEE) in a narrow sense, as it refers largely to the changing racial complexion of ownership and control of the private sector, rather than in a 'maximalist' sense, which seeks to assess how blacks have been empowered more generally (in terms of employment and improved access to economic opportunity). Suffice it to say that BEE from this narrow perspective was a product of two complementary forces. The first was initiatives by large-scale capital in the 1980s to forge an alliance with the ANC; the second was the ANC's determination after 1994 to transform a racialised capitalist economy.

The apartheid years had provided conditions for the steady concentration of capital. The major mining houses, which dominated the economy for years, had diversified into manufacturing; the banks and financial institutions had diversified into mining and manufacturing; and English and Afrikaner capital had steadily merged their interests with each other and with the foreign capital that had poured into the country during the post-1945 period. A further development was the extensive interpenetration of private capital and the parastatals, of which the major ones – Eskom, Transnet, Sasol and the Industrial Development Corporation (IDC) – themselves played a major role in lubricating the wheels of South Africa's 'minerals–energy complex'.

By 1981, over 70 per cent of the total assets of the top 138 companies were controlled by state corporations and eight privately owned conglomerates spanning mining, manufacturing, construction, transport, agriculture and finance. Further concentration was to come as, with the mounting political crisis of the 1980s, foreign companies divested and sold their assets locally. Unable to invest widely abroad during late apartheid, the conglomerates devoted their excess capital to buying local assets that were often distant from their core business. By 1990, just three conglomerates – Anglo American, Sanlam and Old Mutual – controlled fully 75 per cent of the total capitalisation of the Johannesburg Stock Exchange (JSE). After 1994, the opening up of the economy brought about a dramatic change in the capital market. Firstly, the conglomerates chose to 'unbundle' and sell their non-core businesses; secondly, they were desperate to spread risk by moving assets abroad. The realisation of these objectives threw them into the arms of the ANC, which they were eager to embrace after the end of the Cold War.[46]

For their part, ANC negotiators found they were seriously underprepared to run a relatively advanced capitalist economy. Furthermore, they were subject to multiple contradictory pressures. Large-scale capital was joined by Western leaders, the International Monetary Fund (IMF) and the World Bank in lobbying the ANC for market-friendly policies, promoting the necessity of attracting foreign investment if urgent developmental needs were to be addressed. On the other hand, many within the ANC itself, the SACP, COSATU and civil society called for radical economic policies if the legacy of apartheid was to be overcome. The initial outcome was the ANC's adoption of the Redistribution and Development Programme (RDP). This outlined a broadly social-democratic scenario, which received enthusiastic endorsement by the electorate in April 1994. Yet in June 1996 those in control of ANC economic policy abruptly announced the replacement of the RDP with the Growth, Employment and Redistribution programme (GEAR). This introduced the familiar neo-liberal mantras of reducing the deficit, countering inflation by cutting state expenditure, adopting a strict monetary policy, committing to a competitive exchange rate, promoting exports, privatising 'non-essential' state-owned enterprises while commercialising the others, seeking wage restraint and introducing 'regulated flexibility' into the labour market.[47]

GEAR was to set the economy along a road from which it has never fundamentally deviated, except in so far as the government has steadily increased public expenditure to pay for social grants and improvements in areas like health, education and infrastructure. The model envisages the government's role as creating an environment in which the private sector works in tandem with SOEs to provide the wherewithal for the government to fulfil its social objectives. Broadly speaking, the model worked reasonably well until the global financial crisis of 2008, delivering rates of growth which reversed the stagnation of the late-apartheid era. Since then, however, the economy has been faced by declining growth combined with increasing pressures from within the Alliance for greater government intervention to address alarming levels of unemployment and tackle a mounting crisis.

BEE was a fundamental part of the transition. Politically, the negotiation of the constitution provided for a parliamentary democracy underpinned by the protection of property rights (albeit with some qualifications).[48] Economically, the white elite which controlled the large conglomerates struck a deal with the ANC negotiators: market-friendly policies were to be combined with the incorporation of politically influential blacks into the business elite. Three broad phases of BEE were to follow.

Three phases of BEE

By the transitional years, the ANC elite was already subject to increased lobbying from black business for inclusion in a settlement, and was eager to dismantle the racial restrictions which had blocked black access to economic opportunity. For their part, the white elites recognised that if capitalism was to survive, it needed to transform its profile.

The chosen route, largely agreed in boardrooms hidden from public view, involved the striking of a series of deals whereby state institutions such as the IDC, private banks and the financial wings of the conglomerates transferred assets (subsidiaries and shares in major companies) to carefully selected blacks and appointed them to boards; such agreements were underpinned by commitments to promoting black participation in the managerial hierarchy.[49] As indicated above, the first two important deals of this nature featured the launching of RAIL and NAIL (New Africa Investments Ltd). Over the next few years empowerment deals along these lines took off, with substantial funding being provided to promote black ventures across wide swathes of the economy: in mining, telecommunications, finance, manufacturing, and the retail and wholesale sectors. The ANC itself also stepped into the fray with the foundation of Thebe Investment Corporation in 1992. Its example was soon followed by trade unions and other entities, which similarly launched their own investment companies.

This initial burst of empowerment saw blacks acquiring up to 10 per cent of the shares on the JSE between 1994 and 1997. Some shares were simply carved out of existing shareholdings and essentially given to black beneficiaries. But the predominant device was for the black acquisition of shares to be funded by borrowed money, the basic idea being that the shares thus acquired would be paid for out of dividends. This was all very well on a rising market, but it was inherently a gamble – and it was one which largely failed when the JSE was hit by the 'Asian crisis' of 1997–98. As share prices tumbled, black debts mounted, and many of these BEE deals came badly unstuck. By the end of the decade, the number of directly owned black shares on the JSE had fallen back to between 1 and 4 per cent.[50]

Most of those 'empowered' during the first phase of BEE were politically connected. As a result, the black capitalist stratum that had developed under apartheid was largely left out, in part because the ANC remained suspicious of its political past. However, during the early 1990s the established black business lobby became increasingly vigorous in the representations it made to the ANC. These were reinforced by the cries of those who had been burnt by the collapse in the market. These developments were to culminate in a resolution passed at a Black Management Forum conference in November 1997, which called for a Black Economic Empowerment Conference (BEEC) to propose measures for taking BEE forward. Subsequently, the BEEC was established in May 1998 under the auspices of the Black Business Council, an umbrella body of 11 business organisations. It was placed under the chairmanship of Cyril Ramaphosa who, sidelined from government by Thabo Mbeki, had opted to go into business, initially joining NAIL.

Although unofficial, the BEEC report enjoyed the Treasury's blessing, and, when delivered to President Mbeki, it recommended the adoption of a state-driven programme that would set guidelines, fix targets, and establish obligations for the private and public sectors over a ten-year period. Mbeki responded positively, announcing the drawing up of a 'transformation charter' that would set BEE benchmarks, time frames and procedures. The government followed up with a flurry of legislation.

The most significant law was the Mineral and Petroleum Resources Development Act of 2002, which required mines to cede ownership of their mineral rights to government, and then apply for 'new order rights' or licences in order to carry through the business of mining. Part of the qualification for acquiring such licences would be the applicant's commitment to a variety of empowerment targets (notably, 15 per cent of ownership to be placed in the hands of 'historically disadvantaged South Africans' (HDSAs) by 2007 and 26 per cent by 2012, and 40 per cent of management positions to be held by HDSAs by 2007). This was followed by agreement to a charter between government and companies involved in the manufacture and sale of liquid fuels. Although not legally binding, this committed the companies to transferring 25 per cent of the value of businesses in the sector and 25 per cent of control over these companies to HDSAs by 2010, while simultaneously reserving 9 per cent of all offshore development projects for HDSAs during the same period. A public procurement policy, which sought to link the award of government contracts to companies with specified levels of empowerment (according to the value of the contract concerned), was also introduced, together with new efforts to promote the development of small, medium and micro enterprises (SMMEs).

These initiatives forced the pace of change, as companies scrambled to set in place increased black ownership, recruitment and other targets, which were formalised in a rash of voluntary empowerment charters across the different sectors of industry. However, the progress of BEE was hampered by the slow pace of stock market recovery (black companies accounted for only 4.9 per cent of the JSE's total market capitalisation in early 2001).[51] Furthermore, adverse attention was attracted to BEE by the fact that the principal deals of the period regularly favoured a small, politically connected empowerment elite: the Department of Trade and Industry reported that 72 per cent of the total BEE deal value in 2003 involved just six BEE heavyweights.

Extensive criticism of 'elite empowerment' inaugurated a third phase of 'Broad Based' BEE, which sought to move beyond a narrow concentration on ownership. This was initiated by the Broad Based Black Economic Empowerment (BBBEE) Act of 2003, which set out to consolidate BEE through the issue of ten codes of good practice (to which industrial sector codes would have to conform). A first round of codes related to the measurement of ownership (generally, 25 per cent of equity), management and control; and a second round, introduced in December 2005, covered employment equity, skills development, preferential procurement, enterprise development, residual matters, and the measurement of qualifying small enterprises. Together, the codes would provide the basis for a 'generic scorecard' against which firms' empowerment credentials would be measured when they competed for government contracts. The various industry charters would also have to prove that they had been sufficiently consultative when drawn up, and embodied the broad objectives of BEE.

Successive revisions of the government's 'generic code' have increased the demands imposed upon companies. Notably, the amended BBBEE Act of 2014 sought to clamp down on 'fronting' (basically, presenting a company as suitably empowered when it is not so in practice), to promote compliance with BEE by all state organs and entities, and to establish a BBBEE Commission to oversee adherence to the Act. How far this succeeds in promoting the progress of BEE remains to be seen, for in practice representations by business have rendered the levels of compliance negotiable, with the government often making major concessions.[52]

The problem has not merely been resistance by large corporations, but a lack of access to capital among would-be black purchasers. According to Jenny Cargill (who has provided one of the most detailed analyses of the workings of BEE), whereas almost 30 per cent of all major deals in the pre-codes era transferred control of companies to black investors, this figure was just 10 per cent for the post-codes period up to 2008. Even so, she continues, whereas the value of disclosed transactions between 1996 and 2003 was some R90 billion, this figure escalated to around R350 billion between 2004 and 2008. However, if the 25 per cent ownership milestone was to be achieved, then between another R450 and R700 billion would need to be transferred to BEE entities.[53] By 2014, it was clear that this level of transfer of assets into black ownership had not been achieved: figures supplied by Ernst & Young indicated that with the onset of the global recession, the number and value of BEE transactions had fallen back dramatically.[54]

The outcomes of BEE are highly disputed. Definitions of BEE vary markedly across different government departments, and numerous policies and programmes work at odds with one another.[55] Further, as already noted, criticism that BEE has led principally to 'elite empowerment' and 'crony capitalism' is common.[56] Estimates of how far empowerment has extended down into the lower levels of society are rare to nonexistent, despite substantial evidence of the extensive practice of 'tenderpreneurship' – that is, the allocation at all levels of government of contracts to friends, relatives and associates of politicians and public officials.

A further difficulty is that there is little agreement about how BEE should be measured. Should it refer only to individual black shareholders in relation to ownership? Or should it include indirect black ownership (vested in trade-union investment companies or pension funds)? And how does share ownership translate into control of companies? The resulting judgements vary considerably. In 2010, for instance, a study of the top 100 companies on the JSE indicated that direct shareholding by BEE firms was 8 per cent, but the BMF responded that this figure had been arrived at by 'mathematical manipulation' and the real figure was 5 per cent.[57] Subsequently, the JSE claimed that by 'digging deeper', researchers had found that by 2012 direct shareholding by black companies and individuals had moved up to 9 per cent, and that black South Africans held a further 12 per cent of shares in the top 100 companies indirectly.[58] In contrast, President Zuma claimed in 2015 that direct black shareholding on the JSE amounted to only 3 per cent, insufficient to allow for the development of black industrialists. Subsequently, the Department of Trade and Industry indicated that it would introduce changes to official BEE calculations that would hugely downgrade the value of broad-based schemes in comparison with direct black ownership.[59]

Whatever its limitations, BEE has played an important role in developing a black corporate elite. That the black elite has grown in size, wealth and power since the early 1990s is undisputed. In 2013 New World Wealth, a global wealth consultancy, reported a 'huge spike in SA black [dollar] millionaires', whose number had grown from 4,300 to 7,800 over the previous seven years (despite a 25 per cent fall in the value of the rand to the dollar over this period).[60] (In this and most other such listings, the definition of 'black' is all-inclusive.) In the same year, Patrice Motsepe was ranked second on the South African Rich List, his total wealth amounting to some R22.6 billion. Two other black billionaires (Cyril Ramaphosa, worth R2.15 billion, and Sipho Nkosi, worth R1.6 billion) also made it into the top 25, at number 19 and 24 respectively, and seven other blacks advanced into the top 50.[61] Superficially, this might appear impressive, but one commentator complained that the rise in the number of the black super-rich was 'not nearly enough'.[62] The vast majority (40,900) of South Africa's 48,700 dollar millionaires in 2013 were still white; Motsepe's fortune (a meagre $2 billion) fell far behind that of South Africa's richest white man, Allan Gray (worth $8 billion), who did not even feature on the Rich List as he lives in Bermuda; and whereas the white millionaires were drawn from a small minority, black millionaires came from the vast majority of the population. New Wealth estimated that it will take 25 years to reach parity between black and white millionaires.

Even so, the growth in the number of black millionaires reflects a change in the composition of boardrooms. According to Trailblazers, one of the most consistent regular surveys, in 1992 there were only 15 black directorships of listed companies in South Africa; by 2012 there were 1,046 black directorships. (How many directorships were held by black Africans specifically is not given.)[63] Note, however, that individual directors will quite often occupy multiple directorships, and so the actual number of blacks sitting in boardrooms is smaller than it seems. Cyril Ramaphosa, ranked as the most influential black director by Trailblazers, sat on the boards of eight of the largest companies listed on the JSE in 2012; Mfundiso Njeke, who came second, sat on six; and third-placed Mamphela Ramphele, the most influential black female director, held four.

As influence is calculated according to the market capitalisation of the firms in which directors have a say, notionally Ramaphosa was helping direct the fortunes of firms worth R1.1 trillion. Comparative figures for Njeke were R556 billion and for Ramphele R544 billion. Yet the extent to which such influence is real is hard to gauge. Overwhelmingly, black directors hold non-executive (869 in 2012) rather than executive directorships (177 in 2012), and, on the whole, real power lies with the latter. As Trailblazers observed, non-executive directors, although bringing to boards an external awareness, are outsiders looking in, and real decision-making is undertaken by executive insiders.[64] As a result, many black directors take the money, but feel patronised.[65] Furthermore, only five of the JSE's top 40 companies were headed by black CEOs in 2009 (and three of these had either significant black or government ownership). Except for the appointment of Sizwe Nxasana as CEO of FirstRand in January 2010, little has changed since then. 'It's still an old boys' club out there, and breaking in will always be difficult,' asserted Reg Rumney, an established BEE analyst. 'The bottom line is, people don't give up power easily.'[66]

In conclusion, we can say that a black presence within the corporate elite is definitely growing, yet there are few blacks who wield independent corporate power.

Black class formation under the ANC

The ANC's transformation agenda has been the major driver of the growth of the black corporate elite and the black middle class. Undoubtedly, demographic factors have played their role, as the flow of younger white workers onto the labour market declines as the years go by. Yet deployment, equity employment and BEE have been more influential, and the ANC's political strategy has had profound consequences for South Africa's class structure. Consequently, two decades into democracy, the black middle class has come to outnumber the white middle class. But its economic foundations are precarious, and it remains heavily dependent upon the ANC's party-state.

This is dramatically illustrated with regard to the small black capitalist elite specifically. BEE was constructed around a deal bartering corporate wealth and position for political influence and connections. As such, it largely excluded the thin but impressive stratum of black capitalists who had developed businesses in the late-apartheid era. As Wendy Luhabe has put it (mixing her metaphors), 'whereas Afrikaner empowerment was about growing the cake, BEE was about cutting people into the existing pie'.[67] Herman Mashaba, founder of Black Like Me, and chairman of the Free Market Foundation, has expressed similar disillusion. Although he regards the legislative framework of BEE as satisfactory, it has been distorted by politicians themselves wanting to become its beneficiaries. 'I am no use to big business,' he declared, 'as I don't have political connections.'[68] Although Broad

Based BEE was supposed to correct the problem of elite empowerment, this has not altered the strong dependence of BEE upon the ANC.

Whether or not the early BEE pioneers were specifically 'deployed' by the ANC to the corporate sector remains a moot point. What is less in doubt is that the movement of party stalwarts into key sectors, notably mining, energy and finance, suited the party's objectives of promoting black control of the commanding heights of the economy. Three out of the BEE 'fab four' – Cyril Ramaphosa, Tokyo Sexwale, Saki Macozoma – were all ANC heavyweights before they moved into business, and all have enjoyed strong backing from financial and mining capital. The fourth, Patrice Motsepe, has eschewed a direct political role, but plays an important backroom role as a party adviser and financier; and, as an emerging philanthropist, he exemplifies the 'patriotic capitalist'. Ramaphosa, of course, has now moved back into politics as deputy president, and hence is reckoned a strong contender to succeed Zuma as president. Consequently, he has been required to formally divest himself of his business role, transferring his assets into a blind trust. Nonetheless, with massive backing from leading corporate players such as Standard Bank, Alexander Forbes and Anglo American, Ramaphosa – the former trade unionist – is widely regarded as a 'safe pair of hands', and a counterweight to the SACP and COSATU. Besides the 'fab four', numerous other ANC politicians have stakes in either BEE enterprises or established corporations. According to one database, 29 out of 60 of the 80 members of the ANC's National Executive Committee who could be tracked in 2011 held directorships (20 of them holding more than one), and 43 owned shares in companies. These figures included all members of the cabinet at the time in one way or another.[69]

Many such involvements by politicians are cultivated to secure contracts from government. It has become commonplace for ANC deployees to leave the public service or parastatals either to enter existing businesses, or to start up on their own, secure in the knowledge that their contacts in the state will bring appropriate reward in the name of empowerment. This is only one dimension of the widespread phenomenon of 'tenderpreneurship', the parlaying of political position or influence into the award of tenders to BEE companies. Although there is no accurate account of how pervasive tenderpreneurship is, media accounts indicate that it is extensive. Many of the 1,135 public officials reported by the Public Service Commission in 2009/10 as suspended for financial misconduct were accused of involvement in the wrongful allocation of tenders, yet this is probably only the tip of the iceberg.[70] In part, 'tenderpreneurship' is a product of South Africa's difficult business environment and the low rate of survival of small and medium-sized businesses, forcing black businessmen into dependence upon the state. Yet in greater part, it is an outcome of the rent-seeking, cronyism and corruption that have increasingly become central to the reproduction of the ANC's party-state bourgeoisie.

Tenderpreneurship blurs the line between the black elite and the black middle class proper, yet they share a dependence upon the ANC. The black middle class is overwhelmingly rooted in public-sector employment, which has not merely been protected, but has grown since the onset of the global recession in 2008, while private-sector employment has been declining.[71] Such growth has been accompanied by an increase in the white-collar and managerial component of public-sector employment, alongside the vigorous pursuit of employment equity. Finally, the black middle class has been sustained by the growth in public-sector unions.

Prior to 1993, unions had not been formally recognised in the public service, although a number of unions had been active in parastatals since the late 1980s and a few had begun to recruit in the health services, education and the police. In the public service itself, only staff associations had hitherto been recognised. It was in the early 1990s that the state began informal discussion with newly emerging unions and staff associations that now began to transform themselves into unions. By 1996, there were some 20-odd organisations within the public service representing 760,000 employees. By 2011, there were a total of nearly 1.2 million union members in the public service (excluding parastatals), roughly 36 per cent of total union membership in the country. Correspondingly, this growth has seen the increasing influence within COSATU of militant public-sector unions such as the South African Democratic Teachers' Union (SADTU) and the National Education, Health and Allied Workers' Union (NEHAWU). Overall, the proportion of public- to private-sector membership within COSATU increased from 7 per cent in 1991 to 39 per cent in 2012.[72]

Public-sector unions have responded to their growing constituency by lodging above-inflation wage demands.[73] By mid-2014, with the public-service wage bill now accounting for 40 per cent of recurrent expenditure, and with public-sector employment increasing while private-sector employment was falling, the government faced a major fiscal crisis. In his mid-term budget speech of that year, the new finance minister, Nhanhla Nene, warned of the need to reduce public expenditure without hurting the poor. Whether the government will have the political courage to follow through on its plans by confronting the public-sector unions, at a time when divisions within COSATU are threatening the stability of the Alliance, remains uncertain. What is certain is that tackling the fiscal crisis will have undoubted political costs.

Peter Bruce of *Business Day* posed the government's dilemma as follows: 'The African National Congress (ANC), after just 20 years, is almost where the Afrikaner Nationalists were after 40 years. They both created vibrant middle classes in their core constituencies, and like the old National Party, the ANC is about to make its middle class poorer. And middle class blacks will do the same to the ANC as the Afrikaner middle class did to the Nats – they will leave it.'[74] Such a statement suggests a political unanimity that the black middle class does not actually have. However, Bruce was correct in asking whether, having created a black middle class, the ANC would be able to retain its loyalty. Part of the answer to that conundrum might lie in whether the government is able to slake the thirst of the black middle class for better education.

5

Education and black
upward social mobility

'Through education you can change your class
into middle class.'[1]

Education is intimately related to social class. In Weberian terms, 'life chances' are heavily dependent upon education and qualifications. Elites use wealth and influence to gain access for their children to privileged schools and high-ranking universities, not only because of the status these confer, but because they generally offer a 'better' education than is available in less well-endowed segments of the educational system. Less well-off parents equally aspire to gain the best possible education for their children: some will seek advantage by dispatching their offspring to private schools, others will choose to live in districts known for the quality of their state schools, and many others, even in the poorest areas, will scrimp and save to pay fees for schooling to gain whatever advantage they can for their children. Many parents will subscribe in lofty terms to the progressive ideals of a 'liberal' education as enabling the individual child to develop his or her talents to the full. However, most parents will tend to view education in terms of market opportunity, in appreciation of how possession or non-possession of a 'good education' opens or closes doors to secure, well-paying, perhaps even prestigious jobs.[2]

Educational opportunity both reflects and shapes class systems. Even where policy-makers display the best of intentions, wealthier areas will tend to have 'better' schools, while the least well-performing schools will usually be found in the poorest areas. This is generally a matter of resources: even where state policies implement corrective measures to equalise resources, 'better' schools will boast better facilities, smaller classes and better teachers, and usually staff and parents will fight hard to maintain such advantages. Often these struggles revolve around admission policies and the capacity of schools to decide who may be admitted. Exclusion of would-be pupils may be justified on numerous grounds: the need to maintain smaller classes, pupils' demonstrated ability, the capacity to pay, and the 'ethos' of particular schools (such as denominational foundations). Struggles around admission are, in fact, very often class struggles: keeping the unwanted out, to maintain perceived advantage for those children who have been let in. Talented or fortunate individuals from less advantaged backgrounds may prove able to buck the system, and rise up through it, even gaining entry to the best universities (the 'scholarship' boy or girl being a well-known phenomenon). Generally, however, individuals' class backgrounds will determine their classroom experience, although some countries' educational systems are more open to upward social mobility than others and, likewise, individual countries' educational systems may be more open during some historical periods than others.

It is against this background that the role education plays in shaping the black middle class in contemporary South African society can be evaluated.

Education and class mobility after 1994

The inequities of the education system under apartheid – epitomised by the inferiority of Bantu Education for African students – had long been a major grievance of black South Africans. Indeed, it was an educational issue, the introduction of Afrikaans as a medium of instruction in black schools, that was the immediate cause of the Soweto uprising in 1976, which marked the beginning of the end of apartheid. 'The doors of learning shall be opened', proclaimed the ANC's Freedom Charter, and after 1994 they were. ANC policy in government sought to counteract three features of apartheid education in particular: fragmentation along racial and ethnic lines, unequal access by race, and lack of democracy. Accordingly, the National Education Policy Act of 1996 stated as its goal 'the democratic transformation of the national system of education into one which serves the needs and interests of all the people of South Africa and upholds their fundamental rights'.

Within a few years, there was a flurry of policy Acts seeking to bring about a far-reaching 'transformation' of the educational system as a whole.[3] Fifteen racially and ethnically defined education systems were combined into a single national system, which would work in cooperation with education departments in each of the nine new provinces; 'absolute priority' was to be given to introducing ten years of free and compulsory general education, which would require massive investments in training adequate numbers of teachers and improving the infrastructure of classes and equipment needed by schools; major changes in curriculum and language policy were to be introduced in order to tackle past divisions along lines of race, class and gender and to provide an education more appropriate to a developing economy; and education was to be integrated with training in order to facilitate vocational mobility.[4] Central to this drive for transformation were two notions: firstly, equal opportunity in relation to educational access and outcomes; secondly, positive discrimination in favour of those who had been racially and socially disadvantaged by apartheid. In practice, however, the realisation of these noble objectives was constrained not merely by limited resources, but also by the specifics of the democratic settlement as they affected education as well as the highly unequal nature of the inherited educational order.

The constitutional settlement might have been democratic, but it was also a compromise. ANC designs for a centralised system of governance were confronted by the demands of its opponents for a more decentralised system which would locate considerable power in the hands of lower-order governments. The result was the establishment of nine new provinces, which were to work in tandem with national government in such areas as education, with the central government setting norms and standards, which the provincial governments were then meant to implement. However, the inherited reality has intervened. The nine provincial governments possess hugely different resources and capabilities. The two wealthiest and administratively coherent provinces of Gauteng and Western Cape have proved far more able to provide for the educational aspirations of their populations than poorer provinces, such as Limpopo and the Eastern Cape, which were created more or less from scratch by bringing together bits and pieces of former white provinces and impoverished homelands. Furthermore, although the national government has attempted to direct the schooling system towards greater equality, it has encountered numerous difficulties. For instance, attempts to impose uniform learner-to-teacher ratios have met with resistance from more advantaged provinces and run up against the reluctance of teachers to be posted to rural areas. Often, too, with provincial governments having become fiefdoms of local ANC elites, the best efforts of the national education department to steer improvement have often been hampered by sheer incompetence, incapacity or resistance to central direction.

The second dimension of the settlement that was to impede the realisation of substantive equality in education was the pre-1994 transfer of de facto control of schools to parents. In anticipation of political change, the National Party government had granted ownership of the physical property of schools to locally elected school governing boards (SGBs), composed of parents, teachers and students, along with significant powers over hiring and admission. Critically, they were permitted to augment state resources by imposing school fees. For whites (especially those Afrikaners who wished to retain control over the linguistic, cultural and religious aspects of their children's education), these changes were crucial. Faced by the scary prospect of the hitherto orderly movement of blacks into 'their' schools transforming into a flood, they could take advantage of the devolution of autonomy to school boards to erect 'flood barriers' that would prevent schools, in the terminology of previous eras, from being 'swamped'.

For the ANC, the devolution of such extensive control to SGBs posed a severe problem. From an ideological perspective, it was strongly inclined to reassert state control in order to drive for greater equality and redress. On the other hand, it encountered compelling arguments in favour of the system of 'Model C' schools – fee-paying, formerly whites-only public establishments. The first set of arguments, urged strongly by the Model C schools themselves, was that they had already admitted large numbers of black children from the early 1990s, they provided a high quality of education, they were well run, and they could provide models for less advantaged schools to emulate. The second set of arguments reasoned that, given scarce financial resources, the government could not afford to fund schools for middle-class children at the same levels as previously, and alternative sources of finance would be needed if their standards were to be maintained. Correspondingly, school fees would bring private resources into the system, freeing the government to direct state expenditure towards the schools in greatest need. Thirdly, there were fears that if standards in Model Cs declined, middle-class parents would shift to private schooling, depriving the public school system of its most influential advocates, as 'business people, professionals, politicians, senior public servants and even teachers would no longer depend on public schools for the education of their children and grandchildren'.[5] Fourthly, the government may also have feared that, because the Model Cs (together with elite private schools) supplied the most highly qualified cohorts of university entrants, interruption of the flow of private funding might have a negative impact on the country's ability to produce high-level skills. Finally, there was considerable black support for democratic, local control over schools, an outcome of the 'people's education' movement, which had evolved as part of the struggle against apartheid education.

It was against this background of intense debate that the ANC made a fateful deal. On the one hand, the South African Schools Act of 1996 sought to establish a single national system of public and private schools guided by a uniform set of norms and standards while simultaneously making nine years of education compulsory for all learners. The Act provided a statutory basis for school funding in that schools were to be classified into wealth quintiles and subsidised accordingly, the aim being to abolish fees in quintiles 1–3, while those in quintiles 4 and 5 (effectively including what were now technically 'former' Model Cs) were to be fee-paying.[6] On the other hand, the Act made all schools self-governing. As Fiske and Ladd observe, 'The political trade-off involved in this move was momentous. It gave Model C schools the power to set their own policy on admissions (albeit subject to a number of limitations, including no racial discrimination), school language, the hiring of teachers, and obligatory school fees. While former black schools also gained those powers, they were much less well equipped to use them in ways to enhance school quality.'[7]

The Act indicated that all SGBs were expected to supplement state funds in order to improve the quality of the education they offered. They could do this by levying fees or raising funds by other methods, although fee levels were to be approved by meetings of parents. Once approved, fees became compulsory and all parents were obliged to pay them, unless they applied for and received exemption. Somewhat contradictorily, the Act also laid down that children could not be excluded from a school if their parents did not pay their fees, nor could they be denied admission if their parents could not afford to pay.[8]

In practice, many schools – especially those in poorer areas – found that parents were simply unable to afford fees. Even when the government sought to prevent any adverse impact of fees upon black school enrolments by providing full or partial fee waivers for poor families, numerous schools found it simply too difficult to chase up parents who notionally could afford them. Moreover, even though the law did not allow learners to be turned away on financial grounds, SGBs that were inclined to do so (most of them serving predominantly white middle-class constituencies) were to devise policies, or pursue practices (not always legal), that served to limit the admission of learners from disadvantaged backgrounds. In any case, when placed against the other costs of attendance of a 'good school' (such as uniforms, books, laptop computers and sports equipment), the imposition of substantial fees was often daunting.[9]

Overall, by 2011, 55 per cent of learners in the public system were paying no fees at all, and only 23 per cent paying annual fees of R501 or more.[10] On the other hand, parents sending their children to former Model Cs (in the two highest quintiles) were by now being required to pay what were often very substantial fees.

The new government's educational policies were designed to eliminate race-based disparities and to equalise schooling. The intentions have been admirable. The proportion of government expenditure upon education compares favourably with that of other developing and African countries.[11] Per capita expenditure upon pupils has increased substantially.[12] Determined efforts have been made to equalise expenditure, not merely across the country, but across income levels, with the quintile system (implemented in practice from 1998) providing a systematised basis for proportionally higher public funding to be channelled to poorer schools.[13] Major efforts have been made to increase school attendance, increase teacher–pupil ratios, train more teachers, improve their qualifications, upgrade school facilities, and so on. Furthermore, there has been a substantial reform of the school curriculum. Although this has encountered many difficulties, it has signalled a major move away from an authoritarian, top-down pedagogical approach to embrace new values and methods that are more appropriate to a schooling system within a democracy.[14] Overall, however, the outcomes have been hugely disappointing. Indeed, the lower reaches of the public education system are today generally accepted to be in acute 'crisis', even if the government seems reluctant to admit it and is inclined to gloss over the public schooling system's multiple deficiencies.[15]

Massive inequalities within the system remain. Despite the intention to achieve redress for poorer provinces, overall per capita expenditure upon schooling across the different provinces differs considerably, and spending upon pupils in the better-off provinces is significantly higher than in the poorer ones.[16] Above all, the quality of education delivered in many schools, especially those in black townships and poor rural areas, remains extremely poor, by international and virtually any other standards.

According to a recent review by the Stellenbosch academic Nicholas Spaull, only 25 per cent of public schools are 'mostly' functional, while the rest are failing to provide children with functional numeracy and literacy skills. Learning deficits that children acquire in primary school accumulate over time and become 'insurmountable'; educational achievement in areas such as maths and science, as measured by matriculation results, may have improved marginally in recent years, yet this comes off a dismally low base; and teachers, especially those serving poor and rural communities, lack the basic content knowledge to teach. South Africa's education system, Spaull concludes, is in 'a dire strait'.[17]

What matters here is that the inequality of educational opportunity and provision has remained systemic. After two decades of democracy, note Saleem Badat and Yusuf Sayed, South Africa has a 'two nations' educational structure which is reflected in

> a two tier system of education, resulting in a poorly resourced educational sector serving the poor and mainly black population, while the wealthy have access to private and semi-private schools that serve mainly whites and the new black elite, and attend 'research' universities. These new geographies of inequality in the schooling sector are the direct results of national policy; in the search to retain the middle class within the public school system, the state created, by design or default, a differentiated and bifurcated educational system that permits the charging of school fees and the control of schools by school governing bodies. Government policy, such as the South African Schools Act, has allowed the middle class to secure control of the historical ex-white school sector, empowering 'a new deracialised middle class' to obtain semi-private education.[18]

Similarly, Spaull observes:

> Analysis of every South African dataset of educational achievement shows that there are in effect two different public school systems in South Africa. The smaller, better performing system accommodates the wealthiest 20–25 per cent of pupils who achieve much higher scores than the larger system, which caters to the poorest 75–80

per cent. The performance in this latter, larger category can only be described as abysmal. These two education systems can be seen when splitting pupils by wealth, socio-economic status, geographic location and language.[19]

It is within this context that we may now turn to the manner in which the black middle class has engaged with this changing schooling system. We look successively at, firstly, the extent and nature of increased black access to the upper tiers of the public schooling system; secondly, the out-migration of aspirant black middle-class children from schools in historically black areas; and thirdly, the growing flight of such black children to private educational institutions.

The integration of public schools

The change in the demographic composition of the upper tiers of the public schooling system (quintiles 4 and 5) has been significant, often heartening. Nonetheless, admission to these schools is, for the overwhelming majority of learners, dependent upon the ability to pay fees. From 2011, when the distinction between no-fee and fee-paying schools was confirmed, the Department of Basic Education provided provinces with recommended financial allocations per learner.[20] By 2013, it was recommending to provincial education departments that schools in quintiles 1–3 should receive R1,010 per learner in government funding,[21] while schools in quintile 4 should receive R505 per learner, and those in quintile 5 R174. This allowed for a degree of provincial variation, with the Western Cape, for instance, increasing the learner allocations for quintile 5 schools to R252.[22]

These limited levels of state funding for the schools in the upper tiers reinforce their need to impose often substantial fees if they are to maintain their standards. In practice, keeping up standards mostly involves a determination to limit class sizes,[23] and to recruit extra teaching staff. The provincial education departments pay the basic employment costs of an agreed number of teachers, even in schools located in quintiles 4 and 5. However, the SGBs of these schools are allowed not only to top up these teachers' salaries, but also to employ other teaching staff out of their own budgets. This capacity to employ extra staff is perhaps the most important privilege these schools enjoy, and it is extensively exercised: whereas in 1997 there were just 5,943 teachers directly employed by SGBs, by 2012 the number had increased to 24,714.[24] Undoubtedly, their favourable teacher–

pupil ratios constitute one of their strongest selling points, and a major attraction to parents.

By design and effect, the levying of school fees is exclusionary (even though some wealthier schools are able to offset fees for deserving students by the award of scholarships). In addressing projected fee levels for 2013, Paul Colditz, CEO of the Federation of Governing Bodies of South African Schools, divided fee-paying public schools into three categories: those with few sports facilities and offering few extramural activities, charging between R5,000 and R12,000 per annum; those with additional subjects, more sports facilities and more extramural activities, charging up to R20,000; and the highest category, charging upwards of R20,000, but often exceeding R30,000.[25] Colditz predicted that the average cost per pupil each year in primary schools would be between R6,000 and R7,000, and between R8,000 and R12,000 in high schools. All this was too much for the national education minister, Angie Motshekga, who expressed dismay at the high levels of fees set for 2013, and accused SGBs of 'privatising public education' and rendering them 'unaffordable to parents'. Her views were echoed by Matakanye Matakanye, secretary of the National Association of School Governing Bodies (mainly representative of historically black schools), who declared high fees a 'rip-off', and bluntly accused the fee-paying schools of being 'created by the middle class and the rich to exclude the poor'.[26] A headmaster of a leading public high school admitted as much to the author, stating that because its first obligation was to children in its immediate area, and because this was largely white and middle class, the social composition of its pupils was much the same as in the past.[27]

Despite the fees imposed by former Model Cs and other schools in the top quintiles, black parents with the means or opportunity to do so have eagerly sought to gain admission for their children. Their motivation is forthright: 'For me education is everything. So I don't care if you've got clothes or not but you must have an education.' 'I always say I will pick up a child from the streets and give them education, not money. But I will give them education because to me education is opportunities.'[28] The demand for schools with reputations for strong discipline and high quality of teaching is particularly strong, and it is only those parents with no choice who send their children to poorly performing schools.[29] In 2014, for instance, it was reported that some black parents were so 'desperate' to get their children into former Model C schools that they were prepared to lie, cheat and fake documents.[30] Another report indicated that black parents are keen to send their children to 'white schools', even if in reality some of them may have become run-down.[31] Unsurprisingly, while there has been 'a flight of children out of the former black schools, there has been no movement whatsoever in the direction of black schools'.[32]

It is difficult to gauge with accuracy the rate of entry of blacks into schools in the upper quintiles. For a start, although few schools will openly admit to limiting black entry, it is clear that some juggle admissions to maintain their 'culture', 'traditions' or 'ethos', and seek to avoid reaching 'tipping points' where they will become predominantly black. Crain Soudien refers to this sort of adjustment as a 'class settlement', whereby the old white middle class seeks buy-in by the new black middle class around the notion of 'good schooling'. Referring to a study conducted at a middle-class school in Durban in the early 1990s, he notes that the school chose its first Indian and African entrants highly selectively. Although they had different racial, religious and cultural backgrounds, their socio-economic status was very much the same as that of its white pupils. Correspondingly, black parents entering their children for these schools were very much aware that they were buying into such a deal, and that effectively they were purchasing a package, essentially an educational commodity, to enable their children to succeed in the world of work.[33] Interviews conducted recently by this author in high-ranking state schools suggested that such dynamics remain very much in play today.

Reviewing integration in the public schooling system after ten years of democracy, Soudien observed that there had been very little change in the racial composition of the 75 per cent of schools formerly designated as black.[34] In contrast, there had been substantial change in the composition of the other 25 per cent. Notably, he challenged the assumption that the major changes had taken place with the migration of black children from black schools to white. While the level of entry into white schools had been considerable, the movement from former African schools to former Indian and Coloured schools had been as strong as, if not stronger than, that of blacks into former white schools.[35] Black African pupils had been migrating to former Indian and Coloured schools that were close to their homes, and convenient for purposes of travel, and many such schools had by then enrolled a majority black African student body. At the same time, because they still tended to be held in the highest regard, there was a tendency for pupils to hop from former Indian or Coloured schools to former white ones. Ultimately, Soudien identified three trends which appear to be continuing today. Firstly, there has been no movement of white, Coloured or Indian students into former black African schools, and hence racial integration is only taking place in the schools previously reserved for the racial minorities. Secondly, black African children appear to constitute a larger proportion of total school populations in former Indian and Coloured schools than in former white schools. Thirdly, black Africans were not entering Afrikaans-speaking former white schools in significant numbers.

This last-mentioned trend would seem to reflect not merely the association of Afrikaans with political domination, but strong black preference for children to be taught in English. The English language, notes Nomalanga Mkhize, a history lecturer at Rhodes University, is associated in black minds with educational excellence and 'bourgeois airs in South African society'. Among her black colleagues, parents strive to get their toddlers into preschool as early as possible in order for them to become fluent in the kind of suburban English that will place them at advantage when they start applying for limited space in good primary schools. Even young children, she laments, rapidly learn what kind of performance gains approval in 'Anglo-Saxon spaces', and try to 'act a little less black'.[36] Mkhize's observations endorse findings made by Vivien de Klerk, based on research in Grahamstown, that black parents showed a clear preference for English-language schools, even if their children stood to lose their Xhosa culture.[37]

Mkhize's observations speak to the necessity of black students having to assimilate into school cultures that may be quite different from their home backgrounds. The adaptation required of them is likely to be extraordinarily demanding. In a study of integration in former white schools, Soudien refers to the unavoidably complex ways in which race and class are rearticulated in 'spaces of privilege'. In this regard, he makes a distinction between the demands made upon, and realignment of identities by, black pupils coming from the 'previously disenfranchised elite' (in other words, basically, from middle-class homes) and those he terms the 'newly emerging elite' (coming from lower- or working-class homes).

The 'previously disenfranchised elite' parents were highly ambitious for their children and sent them to former white elite schools, which proved largely hospitable. These schools were geared to producing young people who were expected to be 'confident, worldly and familiar with the cultural capital that is dominant in Western curriculum', and had the same expectations of their black pupils as of their white. Such schools were 'powerful cultural machines'. Black pupils tended to respond positively, embracing the schools' values, making white friends, and often distancing themselves from the country's racialised past and present by working hard and proving that they were as good as white students. Sometimes this led to an unquestioning acceptance of privilege, although, equally, many came to appreciate the ambiguity of their social location, as both insiders and outsiders of the privileged school world they inhabited. Ultimately, whatever the particular modes of their adjustment, the broad alignment of black pupils' home environment with that of their elite school was to open up immense possibilities, which extended even beyond those offered by staying in South Africa, to the global environment.

Adjustments required of 'newly emerging elite' pupils attending former white schools, who were generally less privileged, tended to be more demanding. While some responded positively to the intellectual challenges posed by the schools, more often pupils were eager to fit in socially, across both racial and class boundaries, than to do well academically. This could take different forms, from excelling at sport through to 'proving themselves' by resisting bullying. Even where the schools were most racially mixed, black pupils were expected to assimilate into a white middle-class culture. In contrast to the experience of black middle-class pupils in the elite schools, this tended to elicit a more robust, counter-cultural response. Typically, it involved pupils defiantly speaking home languages rather than English, sometimes explicitly assuming African identities. Very often, they displayed a remarkable ability to switch between dialects, languages and class behaviours, a capacity especially demanded of them if they had to return home to poor black areas. Overall, they were required to engage far more creatively with racial and class issues than the black pupils attending elite schools. They displayed much more ambiguity about the world around them, as they struggled to 'articulate their identities in relation to white people and poorer black people'. Their schooling experience was charged through with 'turbulence, as they [made] their way into privilege'.[38]

Although black pupils who attend upper-tier schools encounter a variety of experiences, few doubt that they are being prepared for elite or middle-class lives. This is why so many parents go to enormous lengths to gain admission for their children to former Model C schools.

The flight from township schools

The desegregation of schooling has given rise to a highly competitive educational market in which black parents scramble to find the best particular option for their children, given their socio-economic circumstances. This market was not entirely absent under apartheid. Black parents who could afford to do so might send their children to schools outside the country (for instance, to the famous non-racial Waterford school in Swaziland) or, ironically, to the bantustans, notably in the Eastern Cape, where, despite the severe damage done by Bantu Education, a network of elite, former mission schools continued to enjoy relative prestige and function reasonably well at a time when many township schools had descended into chaos.[39] Nonetheless, for the overwhelming majority of black parents, the market in schooling was nonexistent, their children condemned to attend local schools in rural areas or townships, many of which were hugely disrupted by the youth revolts of the 1980s. All this was to change from the late 1980s, when the possibility arose that parents could gain access for their children to schools previously reserved for the racial minorities.

Vuyisile Msila has demonstrated how township parents in the post-apartheid era have increasingly exercised their choice to secure good schooling for their children. Where possibilities have arisen, by virtue of their being affordable and physically accessible, some parents have tended to opt for better schools, especially former Model Cs, outside their township neighbourhoods.[40] In contrast, most parents still send their children to township schools, but only with considerable reluctance, many citing the cost of school fees and travel outside the township as beyond their means. Even so, they differentiate *between* township schools, choosing when they can to send their children to those which are regarded as performing better than others. Often, these choices revolve around perceptions of discipline, teaching standards and their capacity to teach their children English. Such parents may not realistically aspire to their children ascending into the middle class, but they are very conscious that a better education may enable their children to obtain better-paying jobs.[41]

In practice, the movement of pupils out of townships may be less a matter of 'flight' than of hopping from one school to another. Mark Hunter, drawing on research in Durban, refers to 'circuits of schooling' in which the strategies of both parents and schools come together to drive scholar mobility and rework apartheid's social-spatial hierarchies. Schools in the public system, especially those in the upper tiers, now engage in intense competition on such matters as reputation, admissions policies, fees and success in sports to attract their chosen parent clientele. In turn, parents of all races engage in complex strategies shaped by patterns of residential segregation. In the early 1990s, the large majority of white parents accepted the inevitability of their neighbourhood 'white' schools being opened to all races. However, as socio-demographic change occurred, parents sought admission for their children in schools, often outside their immediate locality, that were deemed to stand higher in the hierarchy. Better-off parents might opt for private schooling; the places their children vacated at the more high-status public schools were filled by parents who were less well-off. Interestingly, Afrikaans-speaking parents in the Bluff in Durban (a largely white working-class to lower-middle-class area) abandoned historically Afrikaans schools in that area in favour of English-medium schools or an Afrikaans-medium school located in the Berea (a solidly white middle-class area), and so on. Rarely were they required to move house, because they were capable of financing out-of-area travel.

Related developments were identified among black parents and children. Professional and middle-class blacks moved into the central business district of Durban or the Berea, and sought to send their children to nearby prestigious, former white schools. Such better-off black parents were reported as having a class interest in retaining the 'whiteness' of such schools to reinforce their distinction. Blacks who were less well-off, but could afford to do so, moved out of Umlazi township into the Bluff, where they could access affordable family housing. They looked to send their children to what they colloquially termed 'multiracial' schools, sometimes in former Indian or Coloured areas, even though in poorer districts such schools had already become majority black African in pupil composition (although most of them still had teachers – presumably white – whose native language was English). Yet even parents who continued to live in Umlazi, often female nurses or teachers, gave high priority to sending their children to 'multiracial' schools, and bore the cost of the children's travel by train, bus or taxi. Others who could not afford to do so tried hard to access the 'best' schools for their children within the township, while rural parents (those at the bottom of the heap) might move to the townships to obtain better education. Finally, black female domestic workers in both white and black households sought to place their own children in neighbourhood 'multiracial' schools.[42]

Unfortunately, the effect of such highly competitive dynamics may be to encourage the further spiral downwards of many township schools.[43] A growing response is for black parents to opt out of the state system altogether.

Parental choice and private schooling

Historically, the private school system in South Africa catered to the English-speaking white elite. The private schools – such as Diocesan College (Bishops) in Cape Town, St Andrew's College in Grahamstown, Hilton College in Natal, St John's in Johannesburg (all for boys) and Roedean in Johannesburg (for girls) – planted strong roots, and established an associated network of preparatory schools and mutual associations, although overall they catered for only a tiny, well-off proportion of English-speakers. From some 90 in 1948, the total number of private schools soared to nearly 200 in 1990.[44] Most of them were church foundations and their prevalent ethos rested on the notion of a liberal education. Furthermore, just as the English public schools had admitted the sons of colonial (especially Indian) elites with a view to turning them into English gentlemen, some private schools in South Africa proved willing to admit individual pupils from racially diverse backgrounds with the ability to pay.

But it was only in the 1970s, in the wake of the Soweto upheavals, that the church schools, under the leadership of the Roman Catholic Southern African Bishops Conference, decided as a matter of policy to open their doors to black pupils. By 1986, although various obstacles (such as attempts to impose 'racial quotas') had been thrown up by the state, 143 out of 170 English-medium private schools were admitting blacks, albeit in small numbers.[45] Thereafter, the current towards formally non-racial or 'open' education became steadily stronger as political change loomed closer. By this time, the government had moved towards a 'grudging acceptance' of private schools as 'pressure valves' for the non-racial tendency, although under its Private Schools Act of 1986 it required them to register, the carrot being the potential receipt of a state subsidy.[46]

Even so, the move towards non-racial entry was distinctly uneven. Robust, often bitter battles were fought on school governing boards. Even when such battles were won by progressive forces, most private schools opened their doors in the expectation that black pupils would assimilate to dominant white, Western and largely capitalist values.[47] Generally, there was always concern to ensure that the 'ethos' of the schools was not jeopardised. In this they were conforming to the patterns of elite education elsewhere: of socialising students to conform to elite norms and values, educating an upper class, and preparing pupils to occupy powerful political and economic positions.[48]

Today, notwithstanding soaring fees, which range from anything between double and six times those of even the most expensive state schools,[49] the elite private schools (now referred to as 'independent' schools) are thriving. They punt themselves as offering unparalleled advantages: academic excellence (often entering pupils for overseas qualifications such as British A-levels), small classes, fine facilities, and access to the latest, up-to-date gadgetry. They also provide a startlingly wide range of sporting and cultural activities. Furthermore, many now stress their 'cultural difference and diversity': this is proudly displayed in photographic portrayals of beaming and gleaming racially mixed groups of pupils, and much is made of black 'high achievers' who gain exam distinctions at the culmination of their school careers. Indeed, most such schools present themselves as not merely 'preparing pupils for life', but for entering the 'global village', the implicit suggestion being that their schooling will equip students, once they have attended university (which most will do), to leave South Africa (a tempting prospect for many white parents).[50]

Unsurprisingly, the composition of pupil bodies at the long-established independent schools seems to have remained overwhelmingly white, notwithstanding an increasing minority presence of black students. Apart from those who have been sent by elite parents from neighbouring countries or those few who have been able to gain scholarships, it would seem that the black pupils are children of affluent parents who are either drawn from the professions or who have climbed into the corporate elite.[51]

A major reason why the highest tier of independent schools has remained predominantly white is that there has been a very substantial increase in competition from lower-priced institutions pitched at an expanding middle-class market for private education. Writing in the early 1990s, Johan Muller divided private schools into three categories, 'traditional, 'new' and 'others'.

The 'traditional' schools were those just discussed, mostly Anglocentric and with a religious (including Jewish) and denominational background. In contrast, the 'new' schools were much more varied, a number of them emerging in the wake of the Soweto uprisings, created principally to cater for black learners, and in direct reaction to apartheid. Some of the most prestigious were established to educate the 'black cream', the emergent black middle class. These were self-consciously 'progressive', belonging to the Leadership Exchange & Advancement Programme (LEAP) and New Era Schools Trust (NEST) groupings, which espoused non-racialism, multiculturalism and egalitarianism, and placed a strong emphasis upon providing comprehensive academic support for students from disadvantaged backgrounds. Some developed from a strong anti-apartheid background, attracting international donor support, while others were fostered by the charismatic church movement. Among the latter, the Accelerated Christian Education schools, launched in 1984, and associated with the Rhema Church, were the most notable. Finally, the unsatisfactorily named 'other' category was made up of a hugely diverse group of ventures; some profit-making, others not; some registered in the 1980s with 'own affairs' education departments and receiving state subsidies, others not; some 'open' to all races, some established to cater for black students only. Often termed 'street academies', they were mostly found in urban areas, where they encroached upon market niches occupied by such institutions as Damelin. Established in 1943 as a correspondence college, Damelin was quite openly a 'for profit' institution which had catered for thousands of black students, preparing them for university entry or providing them with a host of technical and other qualifications. Others, pejoratively termed 'fly-by-night' schools because of their supposed ephemerality or the alleged tendency of their unscrupulous owners to abscond with fees, provided schooling of variable quality at the lower end of the market.

Today, the private school sector has become even more diverse. Surveying it in 2003, Du Toit indicated that this sector had enjoyed very significant growth in the 1990s, with 61 per cent of all independent schools having been registered between 1990 and 2001.[52] The Centre for Development Enterprise (CDE), investigating the quality and extent of low-fee independent schools in 2009 (based upon six selected areas with high concentrations of poor people across the country), also recorded a substantial increase in private schooling. In the areas the CDE looked at, as many as 30 per cent of the schools were in the low-fee and private category, far in excess of the Department of Education's national estimate for 2008 of 4.3 per cent. Thus in Braamfontein, a district on the edge of the Johannesburg city centre and adjacent to Wits University, private schools far outnumbered public schools. Even more surprising was the more-or-less even split between public and private schools in Butterworth, an impoverished town in the former Transkei, and the significant presence of low-fee private schools in remote rural areas of Limpopo and the Eastern Cape.[53]

According to other reckonings by independent school associations, there were probably 2,500 registered independent schools (counting primary and secondary schools separately) with some 500,000 learners by 2008, constituting over 4 per cent of total learners at school level.[54] It is generally recognised that this underestimates the total: the CDE, for instance, found that almost a quarter of the schools they mapped were unregistered, and therefore illegal, although earlier in the decade Hofmeyr and Lee had suggested that the number of unregistered schools (perhaps as many as 3,000) was quite possibly far in excess of those that were registered (just under 2,000).[55] They went on to differentiate between religious schools (44 per cent of those registered in 2001), community schools (meeting demand in rural areas, inner cities and informal settlements), profit-making schools (serving all rungs of the socio-economic ladder, despite being ineligible for government subsidy), and expatriate schools (serving expatriate and diplomatic communities).[56]

The lack of clear information renders it difficult to draw firm conclusions about the class content and significance of private schooling. However, it would seem that three generalisations can be safely made. Firstly, when parents – whether black or white – opt for private schooling, they do so because they perceive private schools as offering a higher-quality education than in the public sector. Black parents want to earn a big salary, asserted a focus group participant, in order to put their children into 'even better schools, private schools'.[57] The willingness of parents to make sacrifices by working longer hours, taking second jobs or cutting down on unnecessary consumption such as eating out is a common theme: 'I don't have a pet because a pet is a luxury. I buy my clothes on sales. You will not find any designer-wear in my closet,' insisted one black parent who had sent his son to Hilton College.[58]

Private schools, most of which offer better teacher–learner ratios than public schools, are widely seen as offering better teaching, especially in English (which is of enormous importance for black pupils), and very often, too, in maths and sciences. Frequently, such perceptions are based heavily upon the 'excellence' of schools' physical resources, as well as the quality of the teaching. Yet the CDE report found strong parental sentiments that indicated that teaching staff in even low-fee private schools were regarded as more committed to their jobs than in public schools, classes were seen as being smaller, and the schools as more disciplined and better managed. Above all, there is a widespread presumption that private schools obtain better results. In the words of a black woman general practitioner, who was 'moonlighting' at two HIV/AIDS clinics to earn extra income for her son's private school fees, 'There's no discipline, no consequences, kids do whatever they want [in state schools]. In schools like Michaelhouse you see your child grow from an ordinary boy into something special.'[59]

Secondly, although the profile of private schooling continues to bear the heavy imprint of racial segmentation – whites are significantly more able to send their children to high-fee-paying schools, and low-fee schools are patronised almost entirely by blacks – race is being 'replaced by economic class as the determinant of who goes where'.[60] Although there was a drop in black enrolment at private schools when apartheid policies were initially dismantled (blacks could now easily gain access to former Model Cs), the proportion of black pupils attending private schools has grown steadily since the turn of the century. In part, suggests Francine de Clercq, this may be because many Model C schools, which have become majority black and which largely cater to black children from lower-middle-class homes, have declined badly in quality.[61] Correspondingly, the independent sector seems destined to grow, 'as private education groups are increasingly aiming at middle-income homes and offering more affordable private education'.[62] In other words, as black parents ascend the socio-economic ladder, the more likely it becomes that they will send their children to private schools.

Thirdly, the profit-making school subsector is growing substantially, and becoming increasingly competitive with the generally more expensive traditional elite schools and with the former Model Cs. In part, this is a global trend, in line with the rapid growth of the 'global middle class', but in South Africa it appears to be driven by widespread perceptions of declining quality in the public schools system. The leading private education companies in South Africa are Advtech and Curro, both of which are listed on the Johannesburg Stock Exchange. The former owns the higher-fee Crawford group of schools (established in 1993) and the less expensive Trinity Colleges. In recent years it has been 'snapping up schools and even expanding across the border', its pupil numbers increasing to 32,000 in 2015. Curro, a more recent arrival, has concentrated initially on high-fee schools (classified as its 'boutique' and 'elite' models). In the recent years, it has launched increasing numbers of low-fee schools (its 'meridian' model): these grew in number from three schools in 2009 to 41 schools (with 36,000 pupils, 24,000 of whom were black) in 2015, and it aims to have 80 schools in total by 2020. Many such schools are opened near to public schools that are deemed to be failing.[63] Both groups indicate that profits in the sector are currently modest, but exude confidence that their increasing forays into the low-fee sector (by implication, of enormous attraction to the black middle class) are more and more attractive to private investors.[64] Meanwhile, non-profit private school ventures, such as the Basa Educational Institute Trust and SPARK schools, which are establishing networks in township and lower-class areas, are also beginning to register their presence.

The growth in private schooling is not without its contradictions. While low-fee private schools are expanding apace and increasingly finding their market among the black lower-middle and working classes, there is the danger of a race to the bottom. Many tend to employ recently qualified, lower-cost, un-unionised teachers; and cost-cutting to render them more price-competitive may have a negative effect on the quality of education they offer. For the moment, however, private schooling is continuing to play an important role in the production and expansion of the black middle class.

Black social mobility through higher education

Many of the pronounced class-related tendencies depicted within the educational system at school level reappear in higher education. As with the schooling system, post-1994 higher education reflects the existence of 'two nations': the poor and mainly black population is served by a 'poorly resourced educational sector', while the wealthy have access to well-resourced, higher-tier universities which serve 'mainly whites and the black elite'.[65]

The restructuring and deracialisation of higher education

In 1994, the public higher-education sector consisted of 36 universities and technikons, which, although by this time officially open to all races, effectively served different racial constituencies. Hence the terminology of the time, which referred to 'historically white' and 'historically black' universities. Subsequently, thinking about the shape of an integrated system resulted in the release in early 2001 of a National Plan for Higher Education, which recommended that the number of institutions be reduced. A further document, 'Restructuring of the Higher Education System', released later in that year, recommended the reduction of the number of universities and technikons to 21 through processes of merger. A parallel process was already being pursued with regard to colleges of education: by 2003 almost all had been closed down or incorporated into universities and technikons, with two key distance institutions having been merged into the (distance)

University of South Africa (UNISA). Within a short period, therefore, 21 pre-existing universities had been reduced to 11; 15 technikons had become 5 technikons and 6 'comprehensive' universities (mergers of universities and technikons); 150 colleges of education became 50 merged technical colleges; and another 120 colleges of education had become only 2, with the rest either incorporated into universities or technikons or 'disestablished'. In sum, not counting a restructuring of nursing and agricultural colleges, some 306 separate institutions had become 72, and the process continued to evolve thereafter.[66]

The processes of merger were highly uneven. Although presented in terms of an all-encompassing need for 'transformation' away from discrimination (across class, gender and geographic locality as well as racial dimensions), the restructuring was based as much upon managerial notions of 'rationalisation'.[67] The outcome was that key institutions at the apex of the system, the 'historically white' institutions of Cape Town, Pretoria, Stellenbosch and the Witwatersrand, were left untouched; Rhodes was 'freed' of its East London campus, which emerged as the urban campus of Fort Hare University; Natal was merged with the University of Durban-Westville (originally established for Indians) to become the University of KwaZulu-Natal; Potchefstroom was merged with the pre-existing North West University (previously the University of Bophuthatswana); Rand Afrikaans University merged with Technikon Witwatersrand to become the University of Johannesburg; and Port Elizabeth merged with its local technikon to become Nelson Mandela Metropolitan University. The remaining institutions, historically black universities (HBUs) and technikons, now boasted new names, but in practice they continued to serve constituencies of black and poor students. The code words 'historically white' and HBUs now dissolved into distinctions between 'research' or 'traditional' universities, 'comprehensive' universities, and universities of technology. These were not hard and fast, for some universities (notably the University of the Western Cape and the University of Johannesburg) were to rise quite rapidly up the various university ranking systems. Nonetheless, although there was some attempt to pursue historical redress in terms of facilities, funding and student intake, it was the traditional universities that continued to enjoy the highest prestige based upon their markedly superior performances in terms of both research outputs and teaching.

Although there are signs that the 50 new non-racial colleges of further education have shown 'clear signs of progress towards education, training and development goals', they very definitely remain the poor relations in the higher education system.[68]

Changing access: from race to class?
Overall, there has been a marked shift in the racial composition of university student populations since the early 1990s, as can be seen in Table 5.1.

The number of black students has more than doubled since the early 1990s, while the number of whites has increased by just two-thirds. Furthermore, although whites continue to be markedly overrepresented, the proportion of blacks enrolled at university is approaching representivity. Yet beneath the headline figures there are important qualifications to be made. Firstly, as far as they have been able to do so, black students have migrated to former white universities. Numbers of black students attending universities of technology (overwhelmingly former HBUs) have increased from 107,581 to 127,982 (or by 19 per cent) during the period 2007–2012. There has been a comparable rise in the number attending comprehensive universities (from 87,006 to 105,560, or 21 per cent). However, the numbers attending 'traditional' universities have increased from 135,973 to 189,004, or 39 per cent. Of course, there are numerous factors accounting for this shift, not least the pressures upon the 'traditional' universities to achieve more representative student bodies. Nonetheless, the shift also reflects black students' perceptions of where the best quality of education lies.

Secondly, because of the socio–economic background from which large numbers of black students come, and the relatively poor schooling they have experienced, many arrive at university underprepared. Furthermore, many students struggle to pay their fees and survive financially. The result, against a wider background of disappointing outcomes among all South African university students, is that considerably lower proportions of black students graduate and higher proportions drop out than is the case with students from the racial minorities. Just 19 per cent of black students who enrolled at university in 2007 graduated at the end of their three-year degree in 2009, compared with 42 per cent of whites. (Comparable patterns appear for four-year degrees.)[69]

Thirdly, black attendance at university is directed at gaining a marketable outcome. In 2010, for instance, 32 per cent of black students who graduated did so in business, commerce and management sciences; 9.2 per cent in the health professions and clinical sciences; 8 per cent in education; 7.2 per cent in life and physical sciences; and 4 per cent in public management. To be

▌Table 5.1: Enrolment at universities and universities of technology by race, 1995–2010

	Black	Coloured	Indian	White	Total
1995	286,000	33,000	37,000	214,000	570,000
	50.2%	5.3%	6.5%	37.5%	100%
2010	595,777	58,175	54,492	178,189	886,633
	67.2%	6.6%	6.1%	20.1%	100%
2012	662,123	58,692	52,296	172,654	945,765*
	70.1%	6.2%	5.5%	18.3%	

*Total for 2012 excludes 7,608 students of unknown racial classification.
Source: SAIRR, South Africa Survey 2012, pp. 496–497; Council on Higher Education, VitalStats: Public Higher Education 2012, p. 3.

sure, 8.4 per cent graduated in social sciences, yet sadly (from this particular sociologist's perspective) the humanities and social sciences seem often to be fields which black students enter if they cannot obtain admission into other degree programmes, which are seen as 'more useful'.[70]

There are numerous other tendencies that higher-education specialists might choose to elaborate. What is important to highlight here is that the salience of race per se is beginning to fall away as 'the background class and regional character of students at urban institutions are strengthened and deracialised while rural universities remain marginalized in terms of institutional capacity, racial character and class status'.[71] This 'two nations' division seems to be reproduced in the perceived employability of students. It is more than recycling an urban myth to indicate that, while virtually all graduates eventually obtain jobs, those who have attended the traditional universities are more likely to obtain better employment, and more quickly, than their peers who have attended the former HBUs.

Despite such qualifications, acquisition of a university education hugely facilitates black entry to the job market, especially in an economy with such disastrously high levels of unemployment. Possession of a degree remains a ticket of entry to the black middle class.

The alternative: black participation in private higher education
Private post-school education bodies provide other avenues for advancement. According to one overview, they are more complementary to than competitive with the public sector, stressing career-oriented and customer-focused programmes 'with flexible non-traditional delivery' modes directed at 'working adults and other non-traditional markets, particularly those not served by the traditional higher education sector'.[72]

The private higher-education sector, which grew rapidly from the early 1990s, is increasingly being gobbled up by major international education companies, such as Advtech and Educor (owner of Damelin colleges and other 'brands') – in a local reflection of the huge expansion of 'academic capitalism' globally. They compete openly and vigorously in an education 'marketplace', which is served by both profit and not-for-profit entities. They do not receive any subsidy from government, and are overwhelmingly dependent upon fees, which are therefore very often higher than those of public institutions.

During the 1990s there was an escalation in the number of private institutions providing courses, diplomas and degrees validated by foreign and local universities. The period also saw the establishment of South African campuses by two Australian universities, Bond and Monash. The first was short-lived, but Monash South Africa, operating on a non-profit basis, continues to flourish. Having opened its campus on the fringes of Johannesburg in 1991, it has now expanded from an initial focus upon business, management, and information technology to include faculties of health and social sciences. It remains the only private university in South Africa.[73]

A moratorium was placed upon the establishment of new public–private partnerships in early 2000, partly in response to the concerns of local universities. When the moratorium was lifted in 2001, the government made it clear that public universities should take full academic responsibility for partnership programmes, and thereby effectively limited further foreign incursions into South Africa. Thereafter, the ministry introduced a set of regulations for the registration of private higher-education institutions which established criteria for eligibility, rules of compliance regarding quality and delivery, and so on.[74]

At the present time, this means that the private higher-education sector is composed of three groupings (apart from the exception of Monash). Firstly, there are a relatively small number of institutions, such as Milpark Business School and the Regent College group, which are accredited by the Department of Higher Education to offer master's and undergraduate degrees as well as a wide array of diplomas and certificates. Secondly, there are institutions in partnership with public universities, notably UNISA, which offer local teaching for diplomas or degrees in a way that distance institutions are usually unable to provide. Finally, there is a set of highly diverse programmes, which range from those providing basic business and technical training through to highly specialist courses, offered by a mix of local entrepreneurs, correspondence colleges owned by corporates, professional institutes, Bible colleges and large firms providing in-house training. All such institutions are required to register with the Department of Higher Education and comply with national quality-assurance requirements (although there are probably many unregistered institutions, especially in urban areas).

In total, by 2011 there were 113 officially registered private higher institutions, two of them offering doctoral, 12 master's and 53 undergraduate programmes, with the majority simply offering various diplomas and certificates.[75] Many of these programmes are part-time, as are quite a few of the lecturing staff, some of whom are primarily employed by public institutions. Statistics about the number of students who enrol and pass through these programmes are not easily available (although they now probably far exceed the nearly 86,000 enrolled in 2002).[76] However, student motivations have a familiar ring. Overwhelmingly, students are employment-oriented; some see private education as being 'better' than that publicly offered; and some (especially racial minority students) regard private campuses as offering higher levels of personal safety and security. Unsurprisingly, several institutions have benefited from 'white flight' from public institutions, but at the same time many provide alternatives for black students who have failed to gain university admission. Some have deliberately sited their campuses in middle-class areas, while others have targeted the black student market by locating themselves along taxi and public transport routes or in inner-city areas. Few are explicitly motivated by the goal of achieving equity and redressing past inequalities; rather, they claim to be opening up access to professional and vocational fields which may have been blocked by racial barriers, formal and informal, in the past.

Although it is difficult to assess the importance of private higher education as an avenue of upward social mobility, it is one that should not be ignored.

Education and the black middle class
Three major conclusions can be drawn from the way the changing educational system has reshaped the South African class structure, and the black middle class more specifically, over recent decades.

The most fundamental point is that deracialisation and expansion of the educational system, starting in the 1970s and hugely gaining pace since

1994, have massively improved opportunities for black upward mobility. In significant part, this has unfolded in response to the changing needs of the economy. As white upward movement into the higher ranks of society has opened up class space below, as industry has expanded, and as requirements for a more highly skilled and educated workforce have increased generally, so have the opportunities for blacks to obtain a good education. Already by the 1960s, the hapless Bantu Education model – designed to produce a docile black working class – was becoming hopelessly outdated, and the government was henceforth to widen opportunities for blacks, albeit within segregated institutions, in order to expand the ranks of a subaltern black middle class. By the 1980s, when it was confronting combined political and economic crises, the government became increasingly inclined to quietly allow increased rates of black admission into private schools, the upper tiers of the public schooling system, and the historically white universities. Subsequently, democratisation brought with it a historic transformation of the education system. Segregated educational structures have been completely swept away and, formally at least, the system has become deracialised. Both the schooling and higher education systems have been radically restructured and, above all, levels of black access to educational opportunities have been massively increased. These openings are being seized upon by black parents and students themselves, who recognise the crucial role played by education in enhancing life opportunities. A good education is explicitly perceived as necessary for staying within, or entering, the middle class.

If this is the good news, the bad news is that there is as much continuity as change. The deracialisation that has taken place has remained heavily skewed along class lines. While the top tiers of the system, public and private, previously exclusively serving whites, have been opened up to blacks, the bottom tiers – which are generally poorly resourced and often of poor quality – continue to serve overwhelmingly poor and black constituencies. No wonder that black parents do their utmost to avoid sending their children to this bottom tier, putting major effort into getting them into former Model C schools, opting for private education, or simply ensuring that they attend the 'best' public schools available to them geographically. They view education primarily in instrumental terms, as enabling children to access the job market.

Equally, the two-tiered system lends itself to the preservation of privilege. Elites, black and white, look to the private schools, top-rank public schools and the 'traditional' universities to protect their familial status and children's prospects. Far from importing middle-class energy, critique and pressure into the entirety of the public schooling system, the retention of the Model Cs has further entrenched the advantage already enjoyed by the top tiers of that system, effectively leaving the lower tiers to degenerate. Within this elite context too, there remain many instances of parents using their influence to contain deracialisation, thereby ensuring the continuation of a significant element of racial privilege. Where, in contrast, some institutions employ racial criteria in the proclaimed interest of furthering black advance at a perceived cost to whites, it provokes huge middle-class angst.[77] In sum, rather than race having simply been replaced by class within the educational sphere after 1994, race and class now play off against each other in a complicated dialectic around shared notions of 'middle-classness' and contested notions of how the apex of South African society should be reformed.

Finally, by seeking on the one hand to satisfy the needs of the changing economy, and by continuing on the other to provide for class privilege and high status, the education system reinforces the dominant values of capitalist society. Today, while the top schools and universities make much of their pursuit of personally liberating models of education, they join the lower tiers of the system in almost universally gearing their practice to the instrumental end of enabling their learners and students to enter the capitalist job-market. If this is the manifest function of the education system, then the French sociologist Pierre Bourdieu would also propose that, consciously or otherwise, it channels students towards an unquestioning acceptance of the established social system, as part of the natural order of things. In short, he would argue that its hidden purpose is to reproduce the values of the dominant class.[78]

In South Africa today, education remains intimately related to social class.

6

The black middle class at work

Relatively little attention has been paid to the work experiences of the black middle class, yet it is 'at work' that black South Africans are most likely to have had to negotiate the boundaries between race and class as they have moved up the occupational ladder. Some insight into the changing racial profile of the workforce is provided by Table 6.1. This summary table of data has obvious limitations. For instance, although 'service workers, shop and market sales workers' are regarded here as falling into the 'lower middle class', and 'manual workers' are consigned to both the 'core' and the 'marginal' working class, in practice they almost certainly overlap. Nonetheless, what Table 6.1 makes quite clear is the steady upward movement of black African, Coloured and Indian employees into occupational categories previously dominated by whites.

In chapter 1, a strong case was argued for regarding occupation, together with ownership or non-ownership of capital and possession or non-possession of wealth, as providing the foundation of the class structure of capitalist societies. It was also argued that ultimately, too, political power is largely exercised through occupations whose authority is derived from the state. In other words, it is the jobs people obtain and the roles they fulfil in the division of labour in society that largely determine their income, ranking and social status. Consequently, what follows is an examination of the work experiences of blacks as, first, state managers; second, corporate managers; third, professionals; fourth, semi-professionals; and fifth, white-collar workers.

▌ Table 6.1: Changing racial and occupational composition of the South African workforce, 1997–2014

	Black African	Coloured	Indian/Asian	White
Legislators, senior officials & managers	1997: 202,000 2014: 532,000	1997: 60,000 2014: 125,000	1997: 53,000 2014: 110,000	1997: 306,000 2014: 520,000
Professionals	1997: 76,000 2014: 451,000	1997: 64,000 2014: 75,000	1997: 41,000 2014: 60,000	1997: 294,000 2014: 236,000
Technicians & associate professionals	1997: 337,000 2014: 1,014,000	1997: 85,000 2014: 177,000	1997: 37,000 2014: 83,000	1997: 286,000 2014: 318,000
Clerks	1997: 321,000 2014: 1,031,000	1997: 108,000 2014: 231,000	1997: 66,000 2014: 84,000	1997: 279,000 2014: 305,000
Sales & services	1997: 586,000 2014: 1,866,000	1997: 109,000 2014: 193,000	1997: 43,000 2014: 77,000	1997: 165,000 2014: 143,000
Manual *	1997: 3,436,000 2014: 6,177,000	1997: 703,000 2014: 801,000	1997: † 2014: 71,000	1997: 380,000 2014: 312,000
Unspecified	1997: 143,000	1997: 25,000	1997: 11,000	1997: 76,000

* Skilled, agricultural and fishery; craft and related trades; plant and machine operators and assemblers; elementary occupations; and domestic workers.
† Sample size too small for reliable estimates.
Sources: 1997: Statistics South Africa, October Household Survey; 2014: Statistics South Africa, email communication, reported in SAIRR, South Africa Survey 2014/15, p. 236.

The state managers

As we have seen in chapter 4, the rise of the black middle class since 1994 has been the necessary accompaniment of the rise of the ANC's party-state. After coming to power, the ANC government was committed to the state's 'transformation'. To achieve this, it needed to integrate multiple apartheid-era bureaucracies into a unified structure of government; it wanted to secure control of the state by deploying party loyalists and cadres to the top ranks of the public bureaucracy; and it was determined to address past inequities by implementing affirmative action to render the public service, local government and other public institutions 'demographically representative'.

All three objectives were to be more or less achieved within the first two decades of democracy. By 2011, 74 per cent of employees in the public service were black African, 8.5 per cent were Coloured, 4.5 per cent Indian and 13 per cent white. The ranks of senior state management were similarly populated. However, the outcomes have been contradictory. According to official discourse, the goals of the 'transformation' process were to promote a public service that was professional, impartial, accountable, transparent, efficient, equitable and developmental. To its credit, the 'transforming' public service was to register numerous achievements, notably with regard to the extension of basic services and social security payments to previously disadvantaged citizens. On the other hand, the steady penetration of party influence into state structures has resulted in an extended crisis, with the public service having become 'overwhelmed by the political'. Party agendas have eroded the independence and professionalism of state institutions; equity employment has seen the recruitment of officials lacking requisite skills and experience; public servants are often prized more for their obedience than for their qualifications and competence; and corruption has flourished at senior management level and cascaded down the ranks, as (some) public officials at all levels have indulged in the looting of state coffers and 'primitive accumulation'. Efficiency has suffered accordingly. Such a 'party-state' is reluctant to render itself publicly accountable, and displays an increasing penchant for secrecy.[1]

The state managers constitute the core of the 'party-state bourgeoisie' – a term derived from several sources. Ultimately it harks back to the analysis of Frantz Fanon, who argued that, lacking the capacity to fulfil the developmental role of a 'proper' capitalist bourgeoisie, the 'native middle class' sought merely to step into the shoes of the departing colonialists, replacing them as public officials, professionals or private-sector functionaries, its sole mission being to ape their behaviour, enjoy their lifestyle and accumulate resources.[2] In the South African context, this analysis was originally applied to black politicians and officials running the bantustans and black municipalities before 1994, notably by Blade Nzimande, who described this subaltern class as a 'bureaucratic bourgeoisie', and characterised it as authoritarian and kleptocratic.[3] After 1994, class theorising within the liberation movement confronted a difficulty, for it was reluctant to probe the class characteristics of those deployed by or aligned with the ANC who would exercise state power. In theory, these were to be dedicated revolutionaries, devoted to the determined pursuit of transformation. In practice, the character of this 'new class', whose foundations Milovan Djilas would recognise as deriving from political rather than economic power, was to prove much more messy and ideologically ambiguous.

The party-state bourgeoisie was constructed around the notion of the liberation movement as a revolutionary vanguard. In the words of Geraldine Fraser-Moleketi, minister for the public service and administration under President Mbeki, the task of overcoming the apartheid legacy 'compelled a political effort after the transition to democracy to establish control over the bureaucracy and to inculcate a new value system and philosophy, in tune with the agenda of the ruling party'.[4] Although public-sector reform efforts were presented in the quasi-scientific clothing of 'new public management', the reality was that ANC ideology was at odds with professionalism and the constitutional obligations of the state machinery to remain politically independent.[5] Many of the new public servants were to serve the state with integrity. But the legitimacy of the ANC as guardian of the revolution was to cloak the predatory ambitions of many individuals, both those who had been previously feeding at the public trough in the homelands and those who had made enormous sacrifices during 'the struggle'. Furthermore, the blurring of the distinction between party and state went hand in hand with a profound blurring of public and private interests.

Borrowing from C. Wright Mills's analysis of the power elite in 1950s America, we may identify the 'political directorate' in post-1994 South Africa as operating at three levels.[6] Firstly, there is an inner circle of power surrounding the president, the deputy president and those heading the most powerful ministries – always the Presidency and Treasury, and usually the ministries, such as minerals and energy, and trade and industry, that cluster around them. Additionally, as the years have passed, the ministries responsible for security have risen in political stature, and have been steadily incorporated into decision-making at the highest levels. Finally, the inner circle is joined by other ministers who wield heavy political clout. At the second level, there is an outer circle of power, composed of ministers beyond the inner circle, along with individuals outside the ministerial sphere who enjoy major political influence or hold high position within the ANC. Together, these highest levels of power are sustained by the topmost ranks of the public service, notwithstanding the perpetual tensions which seem so common between ministers and their directors-general (the most high-ranking public servants), and between ministers and those who command the major parastatals.

The two highest levels of power are distinguished by their responsibility and capacity to make decisions that are both national in their implications and formative – that is, they shape policy, sometimes even in the teeth of opposition from within the ruling party and the Alliance. This distinguishes them from the third level of power within the party-state, which is wielded principally by premiers and their ministerial executives in the provinces, together with those who preside over local government. These have far less scope to shape policies and they are largely restricted to the sphere of implementation, and thus are judged by their success in 'delivery'. At the same time, along with the broad body of the party and the Alliance (inclusive of members of parliament, and party office-holders at national and provincial levels), this third level of power enjoys some limited capacity of constraint, by which they can on occasion nudge the power elite into changing policies or making concessions. Nonetheless, on the whole, it remains subordinate to the executive, its interest being to exercise its own power while holding external intervention from above at bay. As Doreen Atkinson has shown, provincial governments have shown far more interest in protecting their own patch than seeking to extend their powers by challenging central government.[7]

The influence of the party-state extends beyond the immediate government sphere over a broad array of public institutions and services. Generally, this influence has been less than benign. Ivor Chipkin has highlighted how the absorption into the public service of as many as 650,000 former homeland public employees, at a time of rapid implementation of affirmative action, served to compromise the efficiency of the public service from the very dawn of democracy. Apartheid-era corruption continued and improvements in service delivery failed to follow the unification and integration of previously discrete racial bureaucracies. Consequently, a deterioration of the quality of many public services was widely reported as accompanying 'the blackening of public service managers and officials'.[8]

This unfortunate outcome was often to result in highly defensive responses by public servants to perceived threats to their authority. Within the public service itself, there is an established culture of passing the buck, of scapegoating individual officials, usually but not always those lower in the party-state hierarchy. Above all, where ANC deployment has resulted in the placing of party loyalists in positions for which they are not qualified, they respond fearfully and negatively to criticism, and display a marked ambivalence about the value of skill: on the one hand, poorly qualified state managers depend upon those with high qualifications and skills to 'deliver', while, on the other hand, they tend to regard skill and competence as a threat. As a result, there is an in-built tendency to appoint other unqualified people who will not challenge their superiors, while many who are competent seek greener pastures elsewhere (usually in the private sector).[9]

These dynamics have been explored most extensively in the public hospital system. Karl von Holdt and Mike Murphy have pointed out how after 1994 public hospitals were buffeted by massive institutional changes, major financial constraints, acute shortage of human resources and wholly unmanageable workloads. Their functioning was also severely compromised by provincial officials displaying a highly autocratic attitude towards senior hospital managers, treating them as junior officials. As a result, hospital managers feared to rock the boat, innovate or display initiative because they were dependent upon those same provincial officials for the development of their careers. In turn, senior managers disempowered clinicians and nurses, in the process creating institutional paralysis and demoralisation.[10]

State managers operate within an extensive system of political patronage. Under the National Party, governments directed resources largely to Afrikaner enterprises, while the expansion of Afrikaner-dominated para-statals favoured rent-seeking by party supporters. The saving grace of this system, before it degenerated into an era of looting by white elites as democracy loomed, was that it was substantially 'developmental' in so far as it underpinned the partnership of state and capital in forging a 'minerals-energy complex'.[11] In contrast, the ANC's rule has become increasingly predatory.

Until the party was banned in 1960, the ANC's development had been deeply infused with personalistic politics.[12] Then, during its time in exile, it became not only a dispenser of employment, welfare, education and scholarships to many who had fled South Africa, but deeply entangled with criminal networks.[13] Subsequently, after 1994, its grip on state power would be severely constrained by white ownership and control of the private sector. Even so, as well as granting the ANC control over the public service, state power also put it in charge of the parastatals. These were responsible for something like 15 per cent of GDP and wielded considerable resources. Effectively, therefore, the ANC now became the country's single largest employer. In a context where the ANC's black majority constituency had historically borne the burden of systemic inequality, the ANC's 'party-state' was to develop into a huge employment agency.

Political 'deployment' has translated into an extensive network of 'big men' (and not a few women) across the state at all levels who allocate political goods to followers in return for their support. The importance of 'political connectivity' for those wanting to access employment and state resources has provoked bitter and often violent intra-party competition, compromising the functioning of state institutions. These tendencies developed under Mbeki, rising in a crescendo during his succession struggle with Zuma, when key state organs became the site of unrestrained intra-

ANC factional battles. Subsequently, the Zuma presidency has taken them to new heights. The president himself has used his office to enrich himself, his family and those around him; he has extended his direct influence over key public positions, such as the SABC and major parastatals; and he has appointed individuals close to him to run the various state security agencies. Key to all these moves was his securing control of the ANC's machinery following his victory over Mbeki. Subsequently, the ANC's determination to protect Zuma from demands for personal accountability has underpinned a wider concern to neutralise anti-corruption initiatives and to protect all those around him who benefit from the largesse of the party-state. For many within Zuma's ANC, their position in the party-state has become the platform for private accumulation.[14]

Critical to this has been the rise of 'tenderpreneurship', the allocation of public tenders by public servants and politicians that is skewed towards family and friends as well as those enjoying political connections to ANC elites. This is in part a product of the GEAR economic strategy. Initially, under the influence of international financial institutions, GEAR favoured the privatisation of state industries. But this was swiftly abandoned in the face both of opposition within the Alliance and of the ANC's growing appreciation of the extensive opportunities for patronage which its control over the parastatals would allow. Even so, the implementation of GEAR did encourage an extensive outsourcing of functions, such as refuse collection, to private operators. This was to massively extend the influence of politicians and officials over the award of tenders, which in turn have become an important de facto component of BEE. Black entrepreneurs have looked to the state for business, and the party-state has looked to operate its businesses through black entrepreneurs. It is through BEE, and its capacity to award contracts, that the state has interfaced with the corporate sector, and has sought to promote a black corporate bourgeoisie.

The corporate managers

In chapter 4 we recorded the growth of black business, against huge odds, during the latter years of apartheid, as well as the shift in the recruitment patterns of large corporations. Since 1994, ANC commitment to BEE has seen the advance of a small number of blacks into the top corporate elite. All the same, despite the large corporations today trumpeting the best of intentions, levels of black representation in corporate management have lagged significantly behind those in the public sector. This relative lack of progress results from a mix of factors. One has been a corporate reluctance to embrace equity employment, another the lack of qualified black candidates. Yet another has been a widespread preference among blacks for employment in the public sphere, which is viewed as more culturally welcoming and, for many, offering better prospects of advancement. In contrast, many blacks regard entry into the world of corporate employment as perilous and likely to prove distinctly challenging in racial terms:

> I think if you look at the fund management space, or the financial services sector – it is the one sector that is not transformed … I mean horribly not transformed. And furthermore, the bulk of the financial services sector is run by white people. OK? So obviously with that situation, it means that there is always those issues, that this is a white environment, it is not a black environment. And black people will not excel in this environment.[15]

Nonetheless, despite all the constraints, there is now a significant cohort of black managers in the corporate sphere, and increasingly they have become visible – in the media and in the workplace. So we need to ask: Who are these managers? Why have they eschewed the comfort zone of public-sector employment? What have been their experiences? How do they relate to corporate power?

Our knowledge about the black corporate middle class remains sketchy, although it is clear from biographies of successful black businesspersons that they tend to share some similar characteristics. Firstly, many are likely to come from humble, if recognisably lower-middle-class, backgrounds, with parents who were teachers, storekeepers and the like. Secondly, virtually all possess the classic qualities of individualism and readiness to overcome obstacles placed in their way. Particularly valuable insights have been provided by Wendy Luhabe, herself one of the most successful black businesswomen in South Africa, who is famous for having played key roles in the founding of Women's Investment Portfolio Holdings (Wiphold) and Alliance Capital, investment companies geared to mobilising investments from within the black community (especially from black women). In her book *Defining Moments*, published in 2002, drawing upon rich interviews with black managers who had made it to the top, she has reflected upon the experiences of black entrants into the corporate world.

Luhabe differentiates black managers' experiences by decade. Blacks began to penetrate the junior ranks of management from the early 1970s (though it was only in 1978 that legislation prohibiting blacks from working as managers in white areas was removed). While few in number, there were enough of them to 'see themselves as a class'. But they were entering a corporate world whose culture was exclusivist and dismissive of other traditions of business practice. The experiences of Reuel Khoza, who was to rise through the ranks to serve on numerous boards and eventually to chair Nedbank, were typical, recording a long struggle against racism and discrimination by white peers. Many managers like him had acquired degrees at black universities, and found that their qualifications were looked down upon. Most worked as perpetual 'trainees', 'technicians' and 'clerks', even though their jobs were clearly managerial. Most confronted the emotional challenge that they did not receive the same recognition for equal or better work performance as their white colleagues. Those who stayed the course showed a steely determination to prove their worth by outperforming their white counterparts. These early pioneers, explained Eric Mafuna (one of the founders of the Black Management Forum), displayed two major qualities. One was resilience in the face of adversity; the other was their 'hunger', their determination to overcome all the obstacles placed in their way by apartheid. Yet they were also personally conflicted, for although culturally they were closer to their companies' workers than their fellow managers, they nonetheless aspired 'to elements of the "white" managerial culture and lifestyle: to have a home larger than a matchbox, to have a car and to educate their children while they earned a decent salary'.[16]

The 1980s were 'quite different'. Trade unions were becoming a formidable force, and corporations began to appreciate that black managers could be a major asset (although tokenism was still widely practised). A significant cohort of black managers with qualifications in science, commerce, business and management emerged, some having studied overseas. Black professionals and managers became increasingly upwardly mobile. Black women began to appear in corporate ranks – a marked departure from their apartheid-era roles as 'servants, nurses, teachers and social workers'. Yet black progress was uneven. Although it was now becoming acceptable for blacks to be appointed as 'managers', many found themselves still stuck as perpetual 'trainees'. Likewise, although corporations responded to the rise of black trade unionism by appointing black managers to posts in industrial relations, too many found themselves confined to handling 'Native affairs' and barred from moving into other operational areas. Conservative racial attitudes remained strong, and black managers continued to experience extensive discrimination, if not from their immediate colleagues, then from their firms' white customers. Unsurprisingly, quite a few confronting such experiences chose to opt out, and form their own businesses. Nonetheless, towards the end of the decade, more opportunities for blacks in management opened up, notably in sales and communication. Furthermore, as political struggles intensified, more managerial opportunities developed in NGOs, and black managers became more confident in confronting 'corporate subversion of their career prospects'.

Finally, in the 1990s, 'there was a huge increase in the number of black professionals and managers'. Political change brought with it many more opportunities. BEE and equity employment now rendered the attraction, retention and promotion of black managers a political necessity. More black faces began to appear in boardrooms, as corporations sought to leverage political influence. Meanwhile, career prospects in public service management opened up and provided a highly attractive alternative to the private sector for educated blacks who wanted to contribute to the national agenda. Far more opportunities became available for black women, along with many new career avenues for black professionals in banking and finance – Luhabe singled out Standard Corporate and Merchant Bank for its role in training a large number of black managers.

A quantitative study of black managers undertaken by Johannes Mokoele during this period indicated that most felt that their employers were failing dismally to provide adequate management development programmes. Indeed, Mokoele's survey-based study gave quantitative backing to Luhabe's qualitative finding that black managers continued to experience marginalisation in the workplace, often by being excluded from the informal networks which grease the wheels of business. Although outright expressions of crude racism became less common, many subtle intimations of black inferiority remained, demanding patience and pragmatism together with a willingness to confront continuing discrimination.[17] As one black manager noted: 'I think people have got no idea how much black talent gets suppressed … It's in the form of you first don't have an education; then you have the education; then you don't have the experience; and then … (interjection: "you're incompetent!").'[18]

The experiences of black managers have improved as the democratic era has moved on. BEE and employment equity legislation has accelerated the need for such managerial appointments. Black managers are seen as vital by corporations for understanding and penetrating a growing black market. Many companies now position themselves to become 'employers of choice', and there is a marked shift towards greater workplace equality, in terms of both racial and gender imperatives. Overt discrimination at management level has now largely disappeared. Nonetheless, black managers remain hugely outnumbered by whites at senior management level. Richard Calland reports that in 2013 only 85 out of a total of 274 directors of the top 20 companies (listed by capitalisation) on the JSE were black African, and that the overwhelming majority of these occupied non-executive positions. Calland does not discount the importance of non-executive directors in providing strategic direction to a company board, yet notes that barriers to black entry into executive positions clearly remain.[19]

Another recent study indicates that black managers continue to feel that corporations are failing to provide them with appropriate responsibilities and opportunities. As a result, many engage in 'job hopping'. Far from this being a result of black managers' fixation on obtaining higher salaries (generally thought by white management to be the primary motivation for moving firms), 'job hoppers' display widespread dissatisfaction with their employing firms' corporate cultures. A sense of racial marginality remains despite the entrenchment of formal equality and firms' acceptance of the importance of 'diversity management'. Nonetheless, what stands out is that 'job hoppers' move firms because they feel that corporate employers do too little to develop their careers, offer them too little support, and display too little trust in their capacities. They therefore move jobs in order to take control of their own careers, advancing from one employer to another in order to build their repertoire of skills and competence. Alternatively, they opt to go independent, with all the risk that this entails. 'I have been on the coalface of just experiencing private sector racism,' remarked one entrepreneur who had started her own company:

> When we first started our company we could not get a job in the private sector for love or money. If the government had not been there we would just have folded in the first six months ... I mean BEE existed but it wasn't even a consideration. It was like no, no, we've got our own companies ... one of the very few jobs actually that we got in the private sector was with a motor manufacturer and it was a black man who consciously said I want to give you guys a chance because all our suppliers are white and it's a problem.[20]

The ambivalent feelings displayed by black managers – wanting to participate fully in the corporate world, yet feeling alienated from it – have been analysed by Geoffrey Modisha as resulting from their 'contradictory class location'. He argues that there is an acute disjunction between their formal position and their ability to influence decision-making. Modisha's 21 black managerial interviewees were largely situated at middle- and lower-management level, two-thirds having acquired degrees or diplomas, some of them also with a trade union background. Interestingly, although they were very clearly members of the middle class, the majority of interviewees chose not to classify themselves as such: this was linked to the fact that they were black and came from a racial majority which had been severely discriminated against historically. Most had close relatives who were unemployed or poor. Furthermore, although some exercised degrees of authority over workers, most felt that they were not entrusted with the requisite means to do their jobs properly. For them, BEE and equity employment now meant that there were many more opportunities for promotion; yet, even so, interviewees cited obstacles placed in their way by whites in higher managerial positions. There were perceptions that their skills were undervalued; that they were given fancy titles but limited authority; that they were perpetually being told that they needed more experience; and that informal white social networks demeaned them even if they did not actively block their upward mobility. It was difficult for their views to be properly heard and considered, and their participation in the making of decisions that really mattered was limited. Ultimately, although they were 'middle class', their class location was undermined by their lack of power within the workplace.[21]

Today, corporate employment policies actively embrace diversity and equality. But it would seem that many black managers continue to feel that they have to perform better than their white peers, and express feelings of alienation from what is still seen as an overwhelmingly Eurocentric world. It is understandable, therefore, that even though their immediate class location is determined by their position in the corporate hierarchy, most continue to give strong support to state-sponsored policies such as BEE. Unsurprisingly, many opt out of corporate employment to launch their own enterprises, and look to do business with the state to further their careers.

The professionals

In the 1960s, when discussing the black middle class as professionals, Leo Kuper focused upon their experiences as teachers, clergy, nurses and what he termed the 'residual professions' – lawyers, doctors, journalists, writers, social workers and civil servants. Five decades later, the black presence as professionals is far more substantial and the professions in which blacks participate are far more varied. Apart from their increased presence in public administration and management (both of which like to claim for themselves status as professions), blacks have become much more prominent as lawyers, doctors and academics; black entry into engineering and accountancy is viewed as of vital importance; blacks now predominate as teachers, nurses and social workers; and while black bishops and archbishops proliferate, the dog-collared ranks of the established churches now face hugely increased competition for black recruits to the ministry from the burgeoning charismatic churches. Despite these very considerable changes, the sociology of the professions lags behind, and it is extraordinarily difficult to offer anything approaching an overview of the advances of black professionals. In this and the following section, a preliminary effort is made to do so by way of a somewhat arbitrary distinction between 'the professions' and 'the semi-professions'.

Professions operate on a basis of trust, deriving from the possession of knowledge and expertise, which are validated by accredited qualifications guaranteed by professional associations or institutions of higher learning (or often both). Furthermore, while they recognise the need for backing by the state if they are to be enabled to regulate entry and standards, the professions simultaneously attempt to maintain their autonomy. This they regard as vital, for they are also interest groups, dedicated to maintaining their market position as purveyors of scarce resources. In turn, they buttress self-interest with a formal commitment to adherence to professional ethics and delivery of high standards of service. Indeed, an ideology of 'professionalism' is central to any understanding of the professions, even though in practice professionals may fall short of the altruism and disinterestedness they nominally espouse. In fact, professions may pursue strategies of 'social closure', practising forms of discrimination (on grounds of gender, ethnicity, race and so on) in the services they offer or the opportunities they allow.[22]

Historically, the professional bodies in South Africa were white-dominated and restricted black entry to the professions or else directed those blacks who did manage to obtain qualifications to provide services only to their own communities. Today, the official discourse stresses the urgency of black recruitment and important strides have undoubtedly been made in this respect. Yet, while the racial complexions of the major professions

▌Table 6.2: Degrees awarded to black African students in selected professional disciplines

	Number of black graduates 1991	Number of black graduates 2010	Proportion of total graduates 1991	Proportion of total graduates 2010
Architecture	8	486	2.3	3.7
Business, commerce & management	303	9,941	21.6	31.0
Engineering	36	2,165	5.7	7.5
Law	522	1,636	8.9	7.8

Source: SAIRR, South Africa Survey, 2012, pp. 504–507.

have begun to change, they all remain white-dominated. In 2011, almost two-thirds of practising attorneys were white, and black Africans just 20 per cent;[23] over 80 per cent of chartered accountants (CAs) were white, and only 7 per cent were black in 2012;[24] 86 per cent of engineers were white, and only 14 per cent were black in 2013.[25] All three professions similarly recorded marked gender imbalances: 67 per cent of lawyers, 69 per cent of CAs and a massive 97 per cent of engineers were male in those respective years. Similar patterns were recorded in academia, where 53 per cent of academics were white and 55 per cent male in 2012.[26] Yet the lament everywhere is that there is an insufficient supply of qualified black entrants to force the pace of change.[27] The fundamental problem is the slow through-put of black students in the relevant courses at university. While numbers and proportions of black African students gaining degrees in professional disciplinary fields are increasing, they are very clearly inadequate, and offer little immediate prospect of rendering the major professions demographically representative, as Table 6.2 shows.

The position is similarly acute in medicine. The demand for doctors is extraordinarily high, but the available places for students at the country's eight medical schools are very limited. The number of black African medical students registered for the MBChB degree increased from 2,675 (32 per cent of the total) in 1999 to 3,832 (45 per cent) in 2005, with the proportion of black African students graduating in medicine in those years increasing from 27 to 40 per cent.[28] This is clearly an improvement, but some medical schools still struggle to find what they consider to be suitably qualified black African entrants.

In any case, the acquisition of a first degree is only an initial step in qualifying as a professional. After that, prospective CAs have to sit a preliminary exam (which had a pass rate of only 41 per cent in 2011), followed by three years of articled apprenticeship before sitting a final exam administered by the South African Institute of Chartered Accountants (SAICA). Lawyers wanting to be attorneys must not only obtain their first degree (the LLB, reached by two routes that take a minimum of four or five years) but also serve two years as an articled clerk, and thereafter sit an attorney's exam administered by the Law Society of South Africa (LSSA). Those wanting to become advocates have first to qualify as an attorney, and then serve an additional year's apprenticeship and pass a Bar exam to become members of one of the country's eleven Bar councils. Engineers have to jump through various hoops as candidates in the different fields of engineering, usually taking a minimum of three years, before finally being recognised by the Engineering Council of South Africa (ECSA). Following successful completion of university study, medical graduates must complete a two-year internship and a further year of community service before registering with the Health Professions Council and being allowed to practise as a doctor. Prospective academics will need a minimum of a master's degree, and are increasingly expected to obtain a PhD, if they wish to obtain a lectureship at a university. In short, it not only takes ability and determination to gain entry to the professions, but requires access to considerable resources. This is very often far too much for black students, many of whom come from families that are eagerly awaiting the time when the graduate starts to earn.

Given the absolute shortages of potential recruits, different professions have put programmes in place to improve qualification rates among disadvantaged students. One of the most notable examples is the Thuthuka Bursary Fund, established by the Institute of Chartered Accountants to raise funds from the private sector, which are in turn matched by government.[29] Such initiatives have been prompted by the government's efforts to promote black advance through the negotiation of BEE charters. A chartered accountancy code, gazetted in May 2011, targeted 32.5 per cent black ownership and control, 50.1 per cent black senior management, 60 per cent black managers generally, and 70 per cent black staff within the profession by 2016. The engineers were hurried along by the BEE sector code for the construction industry, gazetted in June 2009, which set similar targets to be achieved within ten years. Such levels of targets are widely deemed to be unrealistically ambitious, although this does not seem to discourage the government, which by means of its BEE Amendment Act of 2013 indicated its intention to ratchet empowerment targets upwards across the board. Perhaps the government feels that it is only by regularly raising its demands that its message will get heard: for instance, in 2011, the CEO of Consulting Engineers South Africa lamented that, while 83 per cent of firms reported difficulties in recruiting black engineers, spending by firms on bursaries averaged between just 0.15 and 0.20 per cent of their salaries and wages bill, compared with the construction industry charter target of 0.3 per cent.[30]

Broadly, the professions register two types of concern at this sort of government intervention. The first is that political pressures will lead to declining entry standards in order to promote black representation. Such fears can easily degenerate into arguments about race. A very explicit example is provided by the furore aroused in 2010 by the terms of admission at the University of Cape Town medical school. Facing high demand for entry but with only 200 places available, the university had opted to restrict the number of places available for whites and Indians in order to offer places for black African and Coloured students. Because these gained entry with lower marks for matric than whites and Indians did, the strategy provoked major controversy, with white parents and not a few doctors crying foul.[31]

The second concern about government intervention relates to professional autonomy. It is no coincidence that it is the legal profession which, schooled in argument, has been the most prickly. As Richard Calland has demonstrated, the law profession is not only white-dominated, but also extremely hierarchical. While attorneys and advocates are interdependent, it is the latter who constitute the cream of the profession. Attorneys tend to spend relatively little time in court, and then largely in the lower ones. In contrast, it is advocates – briefed by attorneys – who appear before the major courts. Unsurprisingly, around three-quarters of advocates are white, and only some 15 per cent black African. Yet even within an already elite profession, there is an elite within this elite that wields oligarchical power by virtue of 'their consummate skills and their command of the marketplace'.[32] This oligarchy tends to regard itself as the guardian of the public interest, and is extraordinarily jealous in guarding its privileges. No wonder then that the legal services sector charter, drawn up in 2007, committed the legal profession to empowerment and equity objectives only in rather woolly terms and, unlike the charter for CAs, set no specific targets. However, the government refused to be thwarted, and, over the following years, introduced different draft bills to speed up the pace of transformation.

After major battles between the government and the legal establishment, a Legal Practice Act was passed in 2014, whose declared objectives were to provide for the transformation of the legal profession in line with constitutional imperatives. While the government claimed that its objectives were to render the legal professional more representative and accountable, its opponents complained that its real objectives were to bring the profession under political control and would undermine its independence. When eventually passed, after the government had made important concessions, it provided for the establishment of a Legal Practice Council, which would regulate both branches of the profession.[33] Formally, it was welcomed by the LSSA, yet the reality was that the association was deeply divided, with the divisions tracing racial fault-lines. Furthermore, the LSSA (which is more accessible to black lawyers) admitted that it had failed to find any consensus with the General Council of the Bar, which represents advocates. Given arguments by its opponents that important aspects of the Act are unconstitutional, in time it may well find its way to the Constitutional Court. The outcome could prove crucial in determining how far the executive may go in regulating the professions.[34]

While professional associations are traditionally disposed to resist government intervention, the continuance of white dominance breeds black reaction. Black lawyers have long been active. They complain that the conservative nature of their profession has obstructed the delivery of legal services to the poor; that lack of black advance impedes rapid transformation of the judiciary; that racist practices continue to limit black opportunity, and that the majority of attorneys and corporate clients continue to brief mainly white advocates. Complaints are also made that legal firms 'co-opt' black lawyers to boost their BEE credentials, but do not match this by providing blacks with responsibility. Worse, when cases get listed in front of a black judge, opposing parties will opt to resolve their differences through arbitration usually conducted by a retired white judge. Whatever the truth behind such allegations, it is clear that divisions along lines of race within the legal profession remain very real.[35]

The transformation process within the accountancy profession has been less turbulent. From a low base of a mere 77 qualified black accountants in 1994, the figure had crept up to just 207 (out of 19,493 CAs) by 2001. SAICA responded by setting a target of achieving 3,000 registered black CAs by 2005, and has put in place various measures to assist black trainees. However, this target was missed, and progress has been modest. Overall, only 6,929 black accountants were registered by as late as 2013. Of these,

2,484 were black African (out of 34,600 registered CAs). Black accountants welcomed the advances being made, but deplored their slow pace. Their attitudes were captured by a survey conducted by Elmarie Sadler in 2002.

At this time, there were more black CAs employed by the corporate sector than by accounting firms. This was ascribed to investment banks and large firms luring black CAs away from accounting practices with higher salaries. However, Sadler's survey suggested this was only part of the answer: 52 per cent of respondents indicated that they had left accounting firms to find better career opportunities. While accounting firms complained that their trainees were being poached, black CAs cited the conservative nature of the profession. Generally, there was greater dissatisfaction with perceived obstacles to career development than anything else. Thus, although Sadler's respondents highlighted the perceived racial bias of supervisors, their principal concerns were the limited nature of the work expected of them, the lack of black mentors, client resistance, and lack of recognition of their work. In other words, black CAs' perceptions of workplace discrimination revolved principally around the sense that their abilities were not entirely trusted and that they were not granted the same level of responsibilities as their white peers.[36] As William Ramoshaba, one of the founders of the Association for the Advancement of Black Accountants of Southern Africa, recalled about his experiences when he joined a top accounting firm in 1976: '[Coopers and Lybrand] took me not knowing what they could do with me … After six months of realizing that I was not going anywhere I went in there, where other white clerks were sitting, and I said I will see who will remove me. I started drinking from their cups and some of them tried to stop me.' His breakthrough came when he gatecrashed a white colleague's birthday party: 'That evening, when we were drinking, people started talking and opening up. The following Monday I was doing audits with them.'[37]

According to Sadler's survey, while there was widespread suspicion that their white colleagues were paid more, the more general concern was that employers were not doing enough to promote their professional development.[38] Against such a background, it is not wholly surprising that a significant number of black accountants have opted to form their own companies, confident that they will be able to secure contracts from government. The most prominent of these has been SizweNtsalubaGobodo, which has now emerged as the fifth largest accounting company in the country.[39]

The experiences of black lawyers and accountants bear a remarkable resemblance to those of black managers. Fundamentally, they are characterised by the ambivalence which flows from their location as black minorities within white-dominated work environments demanding high skills and qualifications. This is captured by the problems posed to black professionals by official policies of equity employment. Very few question the need for government intervention and affirmative action in order to transform the profiles of their professions. On the other hand, black professionals are reluctant to be stigmatised as affirmative action appointees, resenting the implication that they are less competent than their white peers. Indeed, one study of the attitudes of black academics indicated that they themselves questioned the limits of affirmative action, recognising the absolute shortages of adequately trained black candidates to fill vacant academic posts.[40]

This is not to say that empowerment efforts should not be broadened if the professions are to become 'transformed'. For instance, Xolela Mangcu – one of the most vocal critics of 'whitewash' in academia[41] – has suggested a battery of measures (such as increasing the proportion of black students studying for PhDs full-time; developing post-doctoral programmes; employing black academics as consultants to government to increase their salaries at the beginning of their careers; endowing professorships for blacks; and so on) – to accelerate matters and overcome what he sees as inertia in high quarters.[42] In response, university authorities say that they are doing much of all this already, and that the implementation of crash programmes such as Mangcu suggests would demand resources that are simply not available unless the government increases its financial subventions.[43] In any case, the wooing of leading black intellectuals working outside academia might well serve as a boost to the universities, but would arguably lead only to a recirculation of scarce supplies of qualified black talent. Yet Mangcu is undoubtedly correct in his judgement that South African universities will not operate to their potential without a critical mass of blacks within the academy. This would provide for a very different cultural experience for black academics in formerly 'white' universities, where at present 'the "black experience" is often one of feeling undermined, misunderstood and marginalised'.[44]

If this holds for the universities, then it also holds for the established professions. Debate will continue for a long time about how to balance the imperatives of transformation against the continuing requirements of quality.

The semi-professionals

If there is a justification for distinguishing between professions and 'semi-professions', it relates to their relative exclusivity and status. Both require the acquisition of specialised knowledge and skills, but the professions are more demanding. It is far harder to be accepted for training as a doctor than as a nurse, it is far more expensive and it takes a lot longer to qualify. As a result there are far fewer doctors than nurses. The rewards, too, are commensurate with professionals' relative scarcity. Once they are established, professionals are far better paid than semi-professionals, and they enjoy higher status. A widespread outcome is that whereas professionals generally promote their corporate interests through their associations, semi-professionals have increasingly sought to combine their aspirations towards professional status with trade unionism. 'Professional unions' have thus become widespread throughout the world, not least because large numbers of semi-professionals – such as teachers and nurses – are employed directly by the state. This has also been the case in South Africa, where teaching and nursing have long served as core areas of employment for the black middle class. Indeed, this justifies reference to their experiences as representative of those of other black semi-professionals (such as pharmacists and technicians).

In the early twentieth century, the earnings of black teachers and nurses, although modest, ensured that they were substantially better off than the mass of their communities. Furthermore, they were relatively few, they were awarded high status, and they bolstered this with devotion to 'professionalism'. However, from the 1970s on, a massive increase in the numbers of both teachers and nurses was matched by a simultaneous degradation of their work conditions. This prompted a turn to trade unionism, whose development was to become inextricably entangled with the politics of liberation. In 1990 the South African Democratic Teachers' Union (SADTU) was formed and rapidly established itself as the dominant teachers' union. Among nurses, the Democratic Nursing Organisation of South Africa (DENOSA) became the largest union, though it was never able to achieve the kind of unity among nurses to which it aspired. This emergence of 'professional unionism' was to prove hugely problematic, involving intense debate about whether a commitment to 'professionalism' or to trade unionism should predominate. The battle continues to this day.

The contradictions of 'professional unionism': teachers and nurses after 1994
Both SADTU and DENOSA profess a commitment to improving the

working conditions of their members and enhancing their professional development. They have combined this with a belief that their political alignment with the ANC and their affiliation to COSATU will grant them a voice in policy-making while providing them with increased leverage in industrial relations. Yet they have enjoyed only partial success. Teachers and nurses have shared in the benefits which have flowed from the progressive labour legislation passed by the ANC after it came into power. Job security and protection have been enhanced, and, on the whole, their members have benefited from the rise in income which has characterised public-sector employment. Even so, neither profession is particularly well paid, and the membership of both unions works overwhelmingly in a public sector that is widely regarded as underperforming. Morale in both professions has remained low. Although the ANC government has lavished substantially increased expenditure upon both schooling and health care, the quality of outcomes has left much to be desired. The reasons are diverse. These range from the government's policy failures through to its de facto endorsement of two-tier strategies for both education and health: its promotion of 'Model C' schools has been matched by its provision for many public servants of medical aid, which flows into private rather than public health care, leaving the latter mainly for the poor. The resulting low standards in many public schools and hospitals are often blamed upon the unions themselves. SADTU in particular has become the butt of much public criticism, perennially facing allegations that it protects incompetent, lazy and uncommitted teachers; that it is blocking educational reform and the raising of standards; and that it puts politics well above professionalism. Such critiques revolve essentially around the contradictions of 'professional unionism'.

SADTU has attempted to address these contradictions by reference to teachers' role in the struggle for liberation. The apartheid regime, it argues, created 'a race-based working "class" structure that had "class" similarities within a race prism ... The teacher as a "middle class" candidate was racially defined as belonging to either the "sub" or "middle" and/or "superior" of the "middle class". This misclassification continues to inform the "class identity" of teachers and thus their position in the nation-building order.'[45] 'Misclassified' as middle class, teachers became enforcers of white supremacist ideology, but were to challenge this role when they threw their support behind the liberation movement. Prior to 1994, the National Party government had restricted recognition to 'professional associations' as bargaining partners within the legal bargaining framework. In contrast, the ANC government rapidly extended recognition to teachers' unions. SADTU cites this as a major gain, yet at the same time argues that it posed the danger that the middle-class identity assumed by many teachers might transform it into becoming a 'pro-capital teachers' union'.[46] Consequently, a strategic decision was made to build SADTU into a 'working class and pro-poor social force' committed to the 'national democratic revolution' and to socialism. This required that it reorganise itself as a 'developmental and progressive teacher movement';[47] redefine the 'adversarial relationship' with government it had inherited; and channel 'the inherent "middle class" nature' of its members' into 'a pro-poor biased transformation trajectory'. From this perspective, SADTU now presents its membership, not as objectively middle class, but as 'educational workers'.[48] It projects the fight for their better remuneration and working conditions as therefore inextricably linked with their professional development and the struggle for free and equal quality public education.[49]

Whatever its claims, this rhetoric has merely adapted liberation movement ideology to the educational sphere. In practice, SADTU has become deeply embedded in the politics of the party-state and its leadership closely identified with the Communist Party. Its large membership has enabled it to become one of the most powerful affiliates within COSATU. Nonetheless, while committed to its alliance with the ANC, it has demonstrated its willingness to confront the government in the interests of its members. This has been expressed in terms of both policy engagements and contestations around wages and working conditions.

SADTU's major introduction to the policy sphere was provided by negotiations around the South African Schools Act from 1994 to 1996. It was to prove an unhappy experience. SADTU had called for free and compulsory education, and approached the negotiations with confidence. It was in alliance with the ANC; it had made a significant input into ANC educational policy debates; and three of its former leaders sat on parliament's education portfolio committee. However, it failed to assess the broader political situation accurately. Although the ANC was the majority party, it shared power with the National Party in a Government of National Unity, and the major concern of the Mandela administration was to secure the democratic transition. This meant making concessions to the NP, which was strongly supported by conservative educational lobbies pressing for the right of public schools to charge fees, for the retention of significant powers in the hands of parent-dominated school governing boards, and for the protection of private schools. The unions NAPTOSA and SAOU (essentially representing white middle-class interests) were major players within this grouping.[50] Although they professed political non-alignment, they engaged in vigorous lobbying. Indeed, the ANC was in no way immune to their blandishments, for its leadership anticipated the advantages of preserving Model Cs for an aspirant black middle class. Consequently, the passage of the Schools Act in the form it assumed set the stage for the entrenchment of the two-tier educational system constructed around the Model Cs. Ultimately, SADTU experienced a major defeat, and it was to draw from this the importance, firstly, of maintaining substantial autonomy, even from a ruling party with which it was in alliance; and, secondly, of ensuring that political goals were properly backed by research expertise and policy-making capacity. A sympathetic commentator regards this realisation as having given it a major shove towards genuinely 'professional' unionism.[51]

In spite of their differences SADTU and NAPTOSA (which had shifted from their prior stance of 'professionalism' to embrace a trade union orientation) were to pursue mutual interests. By running joint campaigns which united teachers from across the political spectrum, they achieved notable gains. They secured salary increases and parities which addressed historical inequities of race and gender; pensions and other benefits, such as medical aid, were brought into line with those elsewhere in the public service; and they secured major concessions on teacher retrenchments even while the state was engaging in cutbacks in spending. Subsequently, both NAPTOSA and SAOU were to join SADTU in participating in a public-sector strike around salary increases organised by COSATU in 1999.

SADTU also engaged with the government on the effects of GEAR. Within the educational sphere, the government sought to combine a move to greater equality with fiscal restraint by redistributing resources from richer to poorer schools. 'Excess' teachers would be offered the option of moving to different schools, sometimes in remote areas, or taking voluntary severance packages. Although highly critical of the spending cutbacks, SADTU endorsed the new policy, 'rather romantically anticipating that socially motivated teachers would flock to poorer schools'.[52] In practice, few did. Instead, over 15,000 teachers – many of them highly experienced – opted for the packages and headed for the school door. Although the freezing of posts now allowed some scope for increasing salaries, higher pupil–teacher ratios imposed greater burdens on the teachers that remained, and many members of SADTU were to become highly critical of the deal.

Continuing fiscal restraint throughout the early 2000s resulted in further strains with the government. SADTU regularly complained that the Mbeki government's 'neo-liberal' strategies were leading to desperate conditions in poorer communities, that teachers were having to cope with appalling conditions, pay was too low, and schooling provision was deteriorating. The response from the government was unsympathetic. Unsurprisingly, SADTU moved easily into the anti-Mbeki camp as, from 2005, Jacob Zuma launched his bid for the ANC presidency. Then, in mid-2007, after public-sector wage negotiations had broken down, SADTU was a key participant in a bitter public-sector strike which was only brought to a halt after four weeks when the government conceded above-inflation wage increases (although they fell short of union demands).[53]

The arrival of the Zuma government was to intensify SADTU's loyalty to the Tripartite Alliance. COSATU looked to wield greater influence within government, and SADTU within COSATU. Increasingly, there were suggestions that SADTU leaders were using union muscle to entrench their power in the guise of strengthening local democracy or enhancing school autonomy. In many communities they dominated SGBs, controlled appointments and seemingly made promotion dependent upon union membership. SADTU-controlled SGBs fought attempts by government to appoint school principals; and in 2014 allegations were made that in some provinces SADTU officials had been selling posts of school principals and heads of department. Officially, SADTU decried such abuses, but critics complained that it was doing all it could to block the accountability of its members, whatever their misdemeanours.[54] In particular, SADTU proved strongly resistant to all government attempts to link future pay increases to performance and productivity.[55]

During the 1980s, there had been bitter resistance by black teachers to attempts by the government to control their work through an authoritarian and often corrupt school inspectorate. Today, SADTU tends to dismiss proposals for monitoring and evaluation as 'neo-liberal' or as a revival of some hated dimensions of Bantu Education. Indeed, so powerful has SADTU become that the state seems reluctant to challenge the union. Rather than being known for its commitment to 'professional unionism', SADTU is now widely regarded as interested only in protecting an irresponsible membership. This is doubtless unfair to many of its members, yet it does suggest that the SADTU leadership is losing touch with its rank and file. There has long been a gender dimension, for SADTU's leaders are largely male within a majority female profession. Meanwhile, SADTU leaders have become divided by the factional battles which threaten to pull COSATU apart. Indeed, clashes within SADTU in 2014 led to the expulsion of its president, prompting the breakaway of disgruntled members, who threatened to form a new union. All this seems to explain why SADTU's membership appears to have peaked, while that of NAPTOSA is steadily climbing.

In contrast to SADTU's prominence in the national consciousness, DENOSA has struggled to have an impact. Unlike SADTU's impressive rate of growth (more than quadrupling its membership from around 59,000 in 1994 to around 260,000 in 2013), DENOSA's numbers have done little more than stagnate: from an initial 73,000, membership dropped to 64,000 in 2006 before climbing to 80,000 in 2012. This compares with a 40 per cent rise in the number of nurses (registered and training) to 249,000 in 2013. In short, DENOSA's level of representation in the health care sector has been declining. Furthermore, it is fragmented across levels, with around 60 per cent of its membership concentrated in the lower employment categories (students, enrolled nursing auxiliaries, and enrolled nurses) and overwhelmingly in the public sector (with only about a sixth of its numbers employed in the private sector). Simply put, DENOSA has failed to develop any substantial industrial muscle, let alone political weight.

Formally, DENOSA has remained in alliance with the ANC and as an affiliate of COSATU, but it has never sought to play an active political role. Nor indeed has it been prominent in wage negotiations. Although it has worked closely in alliance with other public–sector unions within the General Public Service Sector Bargaining Council, which was established in 1999, it has been threatened with exclusion from negotiations by a proposal that only unions with a membership of 100,000 or more should be admitted. Thus, while on occasion it has hit out at government for failing to implement new salary structures as agreed within the council, it has done little more than dispatch verbal volleys. On the other hand, it has been active in producing worthy position papers on important aspects of health care, backing these up with the launch of a DENOSA Professional Institute in 2009 to offer a variety of courses on a number of aspects of health care management.

DENOSA has failed to substantially increase its membership even though the burdens upon nurses have increased significantly. The government's early move towards greater provision of primary health care depended heavily upon nurses. Increased access and utilisation of health services as a result of the provision of free health care for women and children added to workloads, as did the interventions to tackle the crises posed by HIV and TB. Shortages of health professionals in other fields also heaped other tasks on nurses, many of them having to assume new administrative and managerial roles. Meanwhile, the supply of nurses in the public sector declined. A rationalisation of nursing colleges during the 1990s was to see a drop in student intake, resulting in an ageing nursing population (more than 45 per cent of nurses in 2013 were over 50, and fully 77 per cent of registered nurses were over 40). During 2008, around 40 per cent of professional nurses' posts were vacant, the highest levels of vacancy being in the poorest provinces, resulting in long shifts, inflexible hours and mandatory overtime. Although enrolment and training of nurses were to increase thereafter, the lack of nurses remained chronic, and the impact of improved recruitment was to be diminished by a lack of trained nursing educators, a constant drain of nurses to the private sector, and migration to other countries, such as the UK, where salaries and working conditions were substantially better. At the same time, there was an extensive movement of nurses out of the profession as a result of declining morale. The immediate issue was low salaries, but there was also widespread dissatisfaction to do with other factors such as the increasingly unsatisfactory physical state of hospitals, the poor work conditions, and threats to safety (by 2008, around 13 per cent of nurses had been infected by HIV). Other complaints included lack of respect from doctors and nurse managers, and abuse from patients and their families.[56]

Such conditions present a major challenge to the nurses' sense of professionalism. Generally, there is a widespread feeling that standards of nursing are dropping. When addressing DENOSA in 2006, President Thabo Mbeki warned of 'the erosion of the ethos that had guided nurses for such a long time'. This echoed a widespread view among older nurses that deplores the lack of commitment to be found among their younger colleagues, who for their part blame work pressures and low salaries for their lack of caring. An important study cites two younger nurses as follows. One commented: 'I don't think in this age the nurses really just care for the patient – nursing is just a job; you come to get your money at the end of the day, finish and *klaar*. I mean, nursing is not that caring profession any more.'[57] The other complained: 'It might happen that you enter nursing with caring – okay. I want to make a difference in people's lives; but we have to face the reality. In order for us to maintain ourselves we need money, and then you study for four years doing a lot of work ... then at the end of the day you get paid peanuts.'[58]

Other nurses complain that they are doing menial and dirty jobs; that they are wasting their time and their talents; and some lament the modern uniforms, complaining that they are little different from those worn by supermarket cashiers and bank tellers. In turn, the proliferation of lower nursing categories is said to have lowered the image of nursing, as the public is on the whole not aware of the different gradings, and simply regard all as 'nurses'. Generally, too, there are significant generational differences in attitudes: older nurses are deemed to be more 'caring', while younger ones are more concerned with 'getting the job done'. In turn, the declining status of nursing is said to result in a lower standard of recruits, and a resultant drop in work ethics. In addition, there is ambivalence about the recruitment of male nurses (who now constitute around 5 per cent of the total). On the one hand, many are regarded as anomalies, labelled as homosexuals, and are accused of being mainly attracted by the prospect of money or obtaining a bursary while they study, although they have no intention of staying within the profession. On the other hand, female nurses also treat them with respect, as a disproportionate number of them rise to high administrative positions, as they do indeed within DENOSA.[59]

DENOSA blames the poor working conditions and low salaries that nurses receive as lying behind the falling status of nursing, yet, given its overall minority status, it has been reluctant to initiate industrial actions. There have been various strike actions by nurses since 1994, perhaps the most famous of which involved 2,000 nurses at Baragwanath Hospital and several thousand other nurses in Soweto. But when DENOSA has engaged in strike actions, it has tended to follow in the wake of the nurses, rather than lead. Although it was to give full backing to the many nurses who participated in large-scale public-sector strikes in 2007 and 2010, it did so under a wider COSATU umbrella covering some 17 striking unions, which also involved low-level civil servants, teachers and hospital workers.

Part of DENOSA's reticence to engage in strike action reflects that of nurses themselves. Many continue to feel that participating in industrial action runs contrary to nursing ethics, and is damaging to the status of the profession. In one study, conducted among a large sample of post-basic nursing and midwifery students in the late 1990s, more than half (53 per cent) were against strike action, in contrast to just 33 per cent who regarded it as a constitutional and legal right, although even among the latter there were reservations about actually striking, mainly because of the impact on patients. While the study did not claim to represent the views of nurses across the breadth of the profession, it concluded that on balance 'the nurse of today opposes strike action'.[60] A reluctance to strike may also reflect awareness of wider opinion. A survey undertaken in the wake of the 2007 and 2010 public-sector strikes among the general public reported that, while 52 per cent of respondents supported the right of health care workers to strike, fully 70 per cent disapproved of nurses exercising that right, indicating that they should take other remedies rather than full-blown strike action to demand better wages and conditions. Worrying, too, for nurses was the survey finding that the public pays them little respect, and regards them as neither reliable nor dependable.[61]

Teaching and nursing remain core professions of the black middle class, yet their standing has declined dramatically. Previously, they were widely regarded within black communities with admiration and respect. Today, black teachers and nurses are viewed much more ambivalently. In sum, the resort to 'professional unionism' has failed to address the fundamental contradictions of their class position: how to reconcile the continual striving for middle-class status with the long-term undermining of their conditions of work.

White-collar workers

'The white collar people slipped quietly into modern society … a new cast of actors, performing the major routines of twentieth century society.' So went the opening of C. Wright Mills's classic study of white-collar workers in the United States. His notion of the white-collar worker was exceptionally broad: it ranged from corporate managers through the 'old professions' of law and medicine, and lower down the class structure, to the technicians, sales people, office workers and clerks. The white-collar people had upset the expectation that the world would be divided between entrepreneurs and wage workers. Capitalism had changed, and the rise of the modern corporation had invented a proliferation of new occupations – what Mills termed the 'new middle class'. This grouping inhabited a bleak world. It had lost all pretensions to independence (which to some extent the old middle class continued to enjoy), it was subject to 'command hierarchies', had no history and was the passive recipient of a popular culture manufactured by forces beyond its control. At the same time, there was another side to the picture. Despite all its woes, the new middle class was 'gratifyingly middle class'. Its cohorts received a salary not a wage, they or their parents had climbed out of the working class, and they had a 'yearning for the quick American climb'. In short, the new middle class was extraordinarily aspirational, even while it combined this with a deep-seated fear of being thrown out of work and thrust back into the ranks of the working class from whence it had come.[62]

These days sociologists tend to reserve the term 'white-collar workers' for the lower end of the 'new middle class', rather than for that class as a whole. It is in that sense that it is used here. Nonetheless, over half a century later, Mills's perceptive analysis speaks directly to the condition of the lower end of the lower middle class – the bank tellers, the sales people, the junior public servants and so on – in contemporary South Africa, the majority of whom are black. These are categories of workers (in the generic sense) who themselves 'slipped' into South African history from the early 1950s, becoming steadily blacker from the 1970s as employers were drawn into quietly substituting cheaper black employees in occupational zones vacated by upwardly mobile whites. Such employees regarded the stable white-collar occupations provided by both government and large private firms as offering a significant step up, and they themselves were imbued with middle-class aspirations. Today, however, white-collar work in South Africa has become more precarious.

Any definition of white-collar workers raises the problem of boundary definition between classes. What is the substantive difference between the work of a clerk in a courier's office receiving parcels for delivery by customers (non-manual work), whom this study would tend to identify as 'lower middle class', and the delivery van driver in the same firm (manual work), whom it would pigeon-hole as 'working class'?[63] Not really very much at all. Similarly, how would we categorise the supermarket check-out cashier, or the clerk behind the counter at the bank, or the petty bureaucrat dealing directly with the public? Ultimately, there is never likely to be one generally accepted answer to such questions, for there will always be different theoretical perspectives, methodologies and study purposes. Suffice it to say that this study is in sympathy with the approach of Owen Crankshaw, who, in his highly sophisticated analysis of the changing racial division of labour during the 1970s and 1980s, distinguished between professional occupations and routine 'white-collar work' by reference to the level of education and qualification that was required. Professional occupations he saw as requiring as a minimum 'post-matriculation certification'; white-collar work, merely

❚ Table 6.3: White-collar occupational categories, 2001 and 2013

	2001	% of all occupational categories	2013	% of all occupational categories
Clerks	1,202,000	9.6	1,474,000	10.7
Sales and services	1,796,000	14.4	1,970,000	14.4
All occupations	12,494,000	100	13,721,000	100

Source: SAIRR, *South Africa Survey, 2012*, pp. 504–507.

a 'Standard 8 or matric certificate'.[64] The specifics of the qualification levels he listed matter far less than the principle of distinguishing between layers of the middle class according to such levels, although we must always recognise that in real life such boundaries can be blurred by the intrusion of other factors, such as political authority. In today's South Africa, for example, major controversy has arisen with the case of Hlaudi Motsoeneng, who, with manifest backing from President Zuma, has clung to the post of chief operating officer of the SABC even though he has been exposed as not even possessing a matric certificate.

Some impression of the growth in white-collar work, as well as of its changing racial and gender composition, is given by Tables 6.3 and 6.4. These refer only to the two of the ten categories of occupation[65] distinguished in official statistics that may be identified most unambiguously as 'white collar'. Although these tables only provide an approximate guide, it would seem that 'white-collar workers' account for around a quarter of the total employed population (or some 3,440,000 employees), and that black Africans constitute around 60 per cent of that figure. As aspirant members of the middle class, they have a profound interest in maintaining their job security.

As we noted in chapter 1, Guy Standing distinguishes between two layers of what here are regarded together as 'middle class'. Firstly, there is the 'salariat', which continues to enjoy secure employment with related benefits (such as pension and paid holidays); and secondly, there are the 'proficians', a motley group which, although possessing various levels of qualifications and skills, are employed irregularly and usually on contract. The second category, it is implied, ultimately belongs to the precariat, which is defined by its fragile grasp on or its total lack of work and income security. This distinction does not apply neatly to the employment status of the lower middle class in today's South Africa. Nonetheless, it points to an

▌Table 6.4: White-collar occupational categories by race and gender (proportions), 2013

	Black	Coloured	Indian	White	Total
Clerks male	19.7	4.5	2.1	3.3	29.6
Clerks female	39.8	9.9	4.3	16.4	70.5
Sales male	43.3	4.5	2.1	3.3	26.9
Sales female	39.0	5.3	1.1	3.0	48.4

Source: SAIRR, South Africa Survey 2013, p. 253.

important characteristic of the 'white-collar' black middle class: the drive for employment security has led it into a strong embrace with the state and public-sector trade unions. There are two steps to this argument.

Private employment and the growth of insecurity

The first argument is provided by the move away in the world of work from the provision of secure employment to greater employment flexibility by means of the more extensive use of contracts, part-time and casual jobs, and outsourcing. As a result there has been an erosion of stable employment relations by precarious ones, a process often mediated by external agents such as labour brokers or subcontractors. This represents a fundamental shift away from the post-Second World War social contract between employers and employees (centred around the notion of 'decent work'), towards a dystopian, neo-liberal world of authoritarian employer domination over increasingly rightless workforces. Furthermore, it is a transformation that has swept the world, driven by forces of technology and globalisation which have allowed transnational corporations to decentralise and disaggregate production processes across the globe in order to optimise costs of production and marketing; at the same time, it has been massively assisted by the fall of Communism and the entry into the global labour market of huge supplies of 'surplus labour', which were previously inaccessible to capitalist employers.

A host of studies have indicated how these trends have increasingly transformed employment relations in South Africa. The huge corporate conglomerates have internationalised and 'unbundled', moving key operations overseas while fragmenting production processes by transferring them to subsidiaries or external contractors. In order to become globally competitive, they have increasingly mechanised while simultaneously 'rationalising' the size and rights of their labour forces (although even these major shifts have failed to stem the gradual decline of manufacturing). Even though this has been somewhat offset by the rise of financial and other services, the labour market has become characterised by a relative shrinkage of workers in 'core' jobs (enjoying permanent employment, with benefits and access to trade union rights). This has been matched by an expansion of workers in 'non-core' jobs (in precarious formal employment) and those in a 'peripheral' employment zone where people scratch a living from informal activities or are simply wholly unemployed.

Most studies explore how these global trends have impacted upon manual labour and have tended to ignore how they have affected white-collar work. The indications are that its impact has been extensive. Certainly, black employees in white-collar work who are securely employed by one of the major companies are generally highly advantaged compared with most of their peers within the private sector. Even so, the retention of stable employment relations in such major companies appears to have come at the cost of jobs. In banking, for example, blacks now largely represent the front line as bank tellers, yet automatic teller machines (ATMs) have severely reduced the overall need for bank clerks. In retail, where blacks now predominate as sales staff, giant companies routinely bypass wholesalers by buying directly from suppliers and franchising a proportion of their outlets, thereby rendering jobs increasingly insecure further down the employment chain. Even among reputable employers, there has often been some slippage in employment conditions, so that, for instance, most large companies have shifted from providing defined-benefit pension schemes (whereby the employer guarantees retirees a certain level of income) to defined-contribution schemes (whereby, although employer contributions are guaranteed, retirement income is not, as the risk of investment of pension contributions passes from the employer to the employee).[66]

Beyond the major employers, security of white-collar employment conditions tends to decrease. A well-known example is provided by the rapidly expanding call centre industry, which now employs something like 210,000 people. Operating in both the public and private sectors, call centres embody a 'new informational capitalism', which has introduced a labour process entailing 'extreme regimentation, control and surveillance of workers by management'. The work of an individual operative within a call centre requires a certain minimum proficiency in English, ability to operate a computerised call distribution system, willingness to work unsocial hours, and highly routinised work processes. It is also highly supervised: performance is closely monitored, and failure to reach targets often results in job loss. Above all, the work is experienced by many operatives as highly stressful, involving the emotional capacity to endure abuse (sometimes racial) from customers who are often irritated by long waits for their calls to be answered and what they (often rightly) interpret as corporate reluctance to address their problems.[67]

The shift away from stable employment relations has been far more pronounced in the private than the public sector. Membership in trade unions nearly doubled between the early 1990s and 2012, yet it has not kept up with the absolute increase in employment. In particular, union density (the proportion of a workforce that is unionised) has decreased in sectors like manufacturing and retail, which are dominated by large-scale corporations, where the implementation of more 'flexible' employment policies has been most pronounced. In contrast, whereas the ability of trade unions to defend worker rights in the private sector has decreased, trade union organisation within the public sector has substantially advanced.[68]

Public employment and private security
The second step in the argument about the white-collar black middle class relates to perceptions of the greater security offered by jobs within the public sector. In early 2015, the Institute for Security Studies reported that respondents to a representative survey of 2,000 young South Africans identified public-sector employment as offering an 'easy way' to make money.[69] They were not misguided, for there are solid indications that – at lower levels of employment at least – public-sector jobs pay better than ones in the private sector.[70] This reflects the growing influence of public-sector unions. Today, around 80 per cent of civil servants are unionised, their number having increased from around 1.2 million in 1994 to around 3 million today. Most of these are white-collar workers, albeit inclusive of semi-professionals. In 1994, there were just three unions within COSATU (NEHAWU, SAMWU and SADTU) whose membership was overwhelmingly located in the public sector, and they were all newcomers; by 2012, the number of public-sector unions had climbed to seven. Meanwhile, the overall proportion of white-collar workers (including semi-professionals) among COSATU's membership has increased from around 7 per cent in 1991 to 39 per cent in 2012.[71] Furthermore, as Carol Paton has observed, such trade unionists tend to have bonds on houses and own cars (or, in other words, to have middle-class rather than working-class aspirations).[72] Consequently, even though they may take industrial

action against the state, such white-collar workers are likely to see the ANC as having served their interests and remain loyal to it politically. In addition, state employment has the advantage of being perceived as largely 'unaccountable'. It is thus also identified by the politically connected as opening the door to joining the party-state bourgeoisie.

Paton's view that white-collar workers are disposed to have middle-class aspirations is backed by arguments that the trade union movement has become the protector of a 'labour aristocracy', its membership being largely composed of formally employed workers amid a sea of informally employed and unemployed workers. The standard rebuttal of this thesis is that such workers receive relatively modest wages, and generally have to share these among a large number of impoverished dependants. Even though this argument undoubtedly has some force, the 'labour aristocracy' thesis has considerable application in the way in which, since 1994, trade unions have opened up paths to upward social mobility for a minority of workers that were not previously available.

Among the most critical observers of this process has been Sakhela Buhlungu, who has examined the changing nature of union leadership within COSATU since 1994. He describes what he calls a 'profound transformation' in the federation. As COSATU has grown, it has undergone a process of advanced bureaucratisation. This has involved a progressive introduction of full-time positions for union office-bearers and (some) shop stewards: they now occupy jobs that have become increasingly professionalised and specialised, and for which they receive regular salaries backed up by benefits such as provident fund, medical aid, car and housing allowances, and study leave. In turn, such processes have led to the development of hierarchical relationships among the union leaders themselves, and a widening gap between leaders and the shop floor. Meanwhile, the institutionalisation of trade unions has massively increased the resources at unions' disposal. This has followed both from the deduction by employers of union membership fees from wages and from the launch of union investment companies. Although these companies are supposedly sealed off from direct union interference, the reality has sometimes proved very different. What follows from these diverse changes is that top union leaders have become powerful bureaucrats; they have also become increasingly distanced from the workers they represent; and the vastly greater resources over which they preside have served as a major source of temptation, with the resultant spread of corruption to the union movement. In sum, whereas trade unionists during the 1970s and 1980s were overwhelmingly drawn from the same humble circumstances as their members, the democratic era has created numerous opportunities for union leaders to improve their lifestyles. As Buhlungu narrates, it is not only that COSATU leaders enjoy competitive salaries and benefits, but that their strategic location in unions provides them with opportunities to move onward and upward outside the trade union sphere: into political position (parliament, provincial legislatures or municipalities); into the public service; and, for some, into the private sector.[73]

The opportunities for upward mobility seized by union leaders may be exceptional. Nonetheless, they illustrate how black white-collar workers aspire to become middle class.

The contradictions and fragility of the black middle class

As I argued in chapter 3, if we want to understand the location and identity of the black middle class, we need to relate it to the two major sources of power in contemporary South African society: the post-apartheid state and the large corporations that dominate the economy. This perspective has underlain the analysis of the black middle class at work in this chapter. The black middle class has been presented as highly differentiated. Different layers – or 'fractions' – of this class are offered various opportunities and face various dilemmas, and their strategies and alliances are correspondingly different. All are faced with contradictions; all have to grapple with the fragility and insecurities that characterise a new and upwardly mobile class.

This book has acknowledged that the origins of the black middle class lie in pre-1994 history, yet it has also argued that the black middle class as it exists today is very much the product of the post-apartheid state. Its arrival in government enabled the ANC to extend its hold over the machinery of state and the resources which the state deployed. Accession to state power allowed the ANC to people the public service, the parastatals and other public organisations with appointees overwhelmingly drawn from the party's historical constituency. In turn, this provided for the rise of the 'state managers', who function at every level, and in every nook and cranny, of the state. This is a category whose position has strong resonance with the notion of the 'service class'. In post-apartheid society, their role was to restructure the state, render it democratic, engage with private capital to forge a genuinely 'developmental state', and generally push the political economy in a progressive, more inclusive, more equal direction. Many were to pursue this role with integrity. Many still do. Increasingly, however, the class location of state managers has been incorporated within the party-state, in which the functions of the party and the state have been merged. The party itself has become the means to access state power and resources, and, for the emergent 'party-state bourgeoisie', state power offers the opportunity for private accumulation. The party-state bourgeoisie, after all, is a class fraction in a hurry. Its prospects for accumulation are shaped by political allegiances, which are often shadowy and indeterminate, continuously fluctuating as battles for control over positions, institutions and resources play out in frequently brutal ways. Such struggles are urgent, for hold on position and power can be extraordinarily fragile. Yesterday, you were out; today you are in; tomorrow you may be out again, so grab what you can while you can. 'Accumulate! Accumulate! That is Moses and the Prophets!'[74] No wonder, then, that faced by such uncertainty, some state managers seek to cash in their political leverage by looking to the private sector.

In the post-apartheid era, the state and capital are locked in a contradictory relationship; both are highly dependent upon each other, yet the relationship is also highly antagonistic. As the costs of apartheid mounted, large-scale capital had looked to the ANC to restore profitability and gain South African business access to the global economy. After 1994, collaborative state–business relations were sealed by large corporations seeking out individual black appointees with political clout for placement on their boards and inclusion in the restructuring deals that characterised the first wave of BEE. Yet, while equity employment and BEE were accepted as necessary costs of the transition, they were to become increasingly viewed as burdensome. The large corporations had already begun to recruit black managers since the late 1970s. They were not unaware of the wastage of black talent under apartheid, yet they were more comfortable at moving at their own pace rather than being propelled into faster rates of transformation. Black managers inevitably confronted embedded racism and, as time moved on, increasingly thrust the corporations on the defensive. Today, some have ascended to the very top of the ladder of a corporate structure which is formally colour-blind, yet many black managers continue to exude profound ambivalence about their experiences within the corporate hierarchy. Many feel held back and marginalised, their qualifications and talents not properly recognised. Hence, although they are often critical of the state's interventions in corporate affairs, they simultaneously extend support for state policies that demand 'transformation' of the corporate workplace.

Black professionals exude a similar ambivalence. Professional qualification is arduous and costly. Many black aspirants fall by the wayside. Once qualified, black professionals expect high reward – yet many confront professional structures and practices which they construe as placing them at a disadvantage. Consequently, although as a grouping they are likely to endorse the virtues of professional autonomy, they too look to state support to force the pace of 'transformation'. Some will strike out on their own to take control over their own careers; others will join black-owned practices. Whatever they do, their survival and success are likely to be highly dependent upon their securing of state contracts.

The black professionals are still few. In contrast, the black semi-professionals are far more numerous, their numbers swelled by the expansion of public services. Overwhelmingly, they are employed by the state. Historically, the status of black teachers was degraded by Bantu Education, while under apartheid black nurses were subjugated within a racially structured health system. Black teachers rebelled openly, tied their fortunes to the emerging trade union movement, and threw in their lot with the civil society movements that aided the ANC to gain power. Black nurses, more constrained by professional norms, were to follow their example, albeit belatedly and with considerable ambiguity. Correspondingly, for both semi-professions, which had long formed the core of the black middle class, democracy was potentially transformative. The trade unions which they had formed and which now represented their interests were in formal alliance with the ANC. Their new political leverage promised to restore the dignity of their callings, to grant them policy influence, and to offer them job security and improved incomes – intertwined objectives which they sought to pursue through the turn to 'professional norms', a formula designed to twin professional status with trade union representation of collective interest.

In practice, the results of professional unionism have been mixed. In policy terms, democracy has given the professional unions voice, yet the government has proved hard of hearing, and little of significance in policy terms has been granted. SADTU has sought to compensate by seeking political influence within the Tripartite Alliance and by asserting its control over local school structures to resist unwanted policy intrusions by government. Black nurses, far less organised, differ among themselves about the demands of professionalism and the virtues of occasional militant action. Both teachers and nurses gear up for contestation with the state as their employer in successive trials of strength around public-sector salaries and wages, yet both professions now face the prospect that, under the impact of global recession and government mismanagement, the state under Zuma is beginning to run out of money. For both teachers and nurses, the relative gains they have made under the ANC are now increasingly at risk.

On the lowest rung of the ladder, the white-collar black middle class is the most in peril. At the margin, it is indistinguishable from the core working class, composed of skilled and formally employed workers. Indeed, many individual households, man and wife, will have feet in both camps. White-collar workers have minimal qualifications. They need to combine these with good fortune and, in the case of state employment, often with political connections, to gain scarce employment. If their jobs are in the private sector, all but a few of the most favourably positioned are subject to the ramifications of the market, corporate strategies and the performance of the economy. Their unions are losing ground, the prospect of possible retrenchment continuously looms, and insecurity is their constant companion. In contrast, the shelter provided by public-sector unions offers their members greater security and protection, although they too are now hugely threatened by the looming financial crisis of the state.

These different layers of the black middle class are extraordinarily diverse. Some will consider that they are more divided than united. Yet they do share one thing very much in common: the aspiration to do better for themselves, and to ensure themselves and their families a better standard of living and style of life. It is to an examination of how far their hopes and aspirations have been realised that we now turn.

7

The social world of
the black middle class

The black middle class has been most regularly identified by its lifestyle. Popular focus upon its rapid appearance in a previously racially segregated society stresses its newness, its visibility, its extraordinary mobility (upwards in class terms, sideways in residential terms), its adoption of middle-class behaviours, its shifting identity and, above all, its appetite for consumption.[1] In part, this comes from self-definition, and also from the notion of 'affordability' – a widespread view among black people that black middle-classness involves not only the aspiration for better standards of living and the acquisition of consumer goods, but the economic capacity to acquire them. In addition, it comes from the popularity of the term 'black diamonds', first invented by UCT's Unilever Institute and then seized upon by the media and the marketing industry, to describe the black middle class.

The 'black diamond' perspective is often picked up in the glossy magazines, which feature high-spending, hard-living and showy black individuals and 'power couples' who have cracked the racial ceiling and who inhabit a world of extravagant lifestyles, tasteless 'bling', lavish weddings and over-the-top celebrations and partying. In this portrayal, 'black diamonds' are presented as crass and materialistic, very often living well beyond their means but desperate for higher status. Often, behind the image, is the implication that new wealth is a product of corruption and political connection, rather than of the virtues of hard work, responsibility and integrity so often associated with being middle class.

To be sure, the behaviour of individual 'black diamonds' often allows the media to present them as peculiarly unpleasant. Smuts Ngonyama, the ANC's spokesperson under President Mbeki, earned justified opprobrium for his blunt statement that 'he [had] not join[ed] the struggle to be poor' when replying to criticism of his involvement in a lucrative BEE deal.[2] Yet even he was outflanked by Kenny Kunene, then an ANC-connected businessman, who in 2010 threw a birthday party at which guests were invited to eat sushi off the bodies of semi-naked women, and thereby gifted cartoonists with the means for lampooning the excessive behaviour of the new political elite – absurdity combined with offensiveness.[3] There are, indeed, many other such instances which allow the media to present the black middle class as selfish and shallow. But this one-dimensional image is a parody, for the black middle class is too complex to be reduced to a single portrayal. To be fair, many journalistic representations of the black middle class explore its aspirations, lifestyle and struggles with empathy. Similarly, a careful reading of the Unilever 'black diamond' surveys reveals much variation in black middle-class consumption patterns. Above all, an ever-increasing array of academic research into black middle-class lifestyle poses important questions about the relationship of consumerism to capitalism, debt and citizenship.

This chapter reviews changing patterns of black middle-class social life. There is no attempt to be comprehensive. Many dimensions such as leisure activities are therefore left aside in favour of the more fundamental issues of consumption and debt, changing residential patterns, and what is termed the 'precarious positionality' of the black middle class. Before we come to that, it is necessary to stress the importance of the fact that class formation takes place over generations. While today's black middle class may be 'new', it has important roots in the households of the past.

How 'new' is the black middle class? Intergenerational patterns

Thomas Piketty has argued that capitalism in the advanced countries of the global North has been characterised by the rise of a 'patrimonial middle class'. In the early 1900s, inequalities in these societies were extreme, with the richest decile owning something like 90 per cent of societal wealth. In the wake of the 'shocks' of two world wars, the richest decile lost out to an emergent middle group, representing nearly half the population, who collectively came to own a quarter to a third of nations' wealth. Today, inequality has begun to reassert itself, so that, for instance, in the US the

▌Table 7.1: Asset ownership and debt by race, 2011

	Gross private assets (Rbn)	Total private debt (Rbn)	Net private ownership (Rbn)	Net private ownership per capita (R)
Black African	3,567	641	2,925	73,712
Coloured	680	62	618	139,655
Indian	588	119	469	360,838
White	5,558	1,191	4,367	952,511
Total	10,392	2,013	8,379	167,608

Source: Mike Schussler, cited by SAIRR, *South Africa Survey 2012*, p. 288.

richest decile owns over 70 per cent of national wealth, while the poorest 50 per cent owns just 4 per cent. This leaves a middle 40 per cent, which owns around 35 per cent. Less extreme but not dissimilar distributions of wealth are to be found in Europe.[4]

Piketty stresses the importance of inheritance to the emergence of the patrimonial middle class,[5] with a key role being played by the ownership and transfer between generations of a primary residence (housing). Interestingly, although the sources for the study of the long-run dynamics of developing countries are much harder to come by than for the rich countries, he argues that the long-term trends in a select group of countries (of which South Africa is one) have been much the same.[6]

Intuitively, while we associate membership of upper and upper-middle classes with ownership of assets, easily available estimates only allow us to break down asset ownership in South Africa by race. Using data presented by the private-sector economist Mike Schussler, Table 7.1 provides basic figures relating to total asset ownership (bonds, houses, listed shares, money market and ownership of non-residential commercial property) compared to debt. Although Schussler is coy about how he arrived at these figures, the differential of around 13:1 in respect of asset ownership between whites and black Africans seems realistic – and profound. Given that whites have been hugely advantaged historically in their access to education and employment, there is little mystery about why the large majority of them are 'middle class', and how they are enabled to pass their class on to their children (even allowing for the fact that, if Piketty is right, the top decile of whites probably owns upwards of 65 per cent of white wealth).[7] In contrast, it is commonly said, blacks lack these advantages, and, in essence, today's black middle class has had to start from scratch.

There is much to this argument. Schussler's figures clearly indicate that there is far less wealth among blacks to hand down across the generations. Most of today's black middle class are genuinely 'new' and are largely a product of post-1994 government policies and the general widening of opportunities in the country. Nonetheless, it is important to nuance this argument, for while relatively few of the black middle class may have inherited material wealth, many have inherited what the French sociologist Pierre Bourdieu has termed 'cultural capital'. The evidence for this remains fragmentary, yet it is beginning to come together.

A starting point is provided by the study of the emergence of a black middle class in Mthatha (Umtata) by Nkululeko Mabandla. Following Colin Bundy, his initial focus is upon how access to land, the combination of commercial with subsistence agriculture, the acquisition of education at mission stations, and lifestyle and consumption changes led to new forms of social stratification within African society and to the rise of new, non-traditional classes – the peasantry and the black middle class – in the Eastern Cape. Further development of these classes was, however, blocked by the Natives Land Act of 1913 and the forced removals and homeland policies of the apartheid era. The result was the 'fall' of the peasantry and the propulsion of small farmers into wage employment. Yet there were exceptions.

The more successful among the peasantry and early middle class had acquired sufficient assets to invest in land. Some of these seized upon the opportunities provided by the Umtata Water Scheme of 1906, when municipal land was auctioned to finance the building of a dam. Given a lack of white buyers, the scheme was opened to blacks, who were enabled to bid for land within a substantial area (later to be known as Ncambedlana). This laid the foundation for land accumulation by an emergent, first-generation black middle class, many of whose peasant parents had invested in the education of their children. These now occupied white-collar or professional occupations in town, and earned salaries, while continuing to farm, as their parents had done, on their new plots.

Mabandla demonstrates that alongside the wider development of a black middle class, which took place after 1950 because of growing urbanisation and the creation of the bantustans, a segment of the middle class that combined professional employment and land ownership in Ncambedlana still remained. Although commercial farming within Ncambedlana had declined by 1950, the black middle class in Mthatha continued to engage in the accumulation of land. They launched a skilful campaign of resistance to efforts by local Afrikaners to remove their rights, and successfully lobbied the government into declaring Ncambedlana 'black'. As a result, they were enabled to buy out almost all of the white-owned properties within the area, ensuring that a black middle class was firmly entrenched even before the grant of so-called self-government to Transkei in 1963. This second-generation middle class joined the first generation by also acquiring education, attending university (at Fort Hare) rather than just school or college, which provided them with access to a more diversified range of occupations, better-paid jobs and a more secure income base. Importantly, too, the middle class that developed in Ncambedlana established strong social bonds centred on homes, schools, churches, choirs and medical facilities. Their sense of community was based upon middle-class values and a strong communal identity, and was forged principally by married women, who at that time were diverted into the domestic sphere because permanent positions were barred to them.

This second generation was well placed to take advantage of the new opportunities offered by Transkei's 'independence' in 1976. Consequently, a successor generation was to become increasingly professionalised as a result of the Africanisation drive pursued by the bantustan regime. This also opened up better prospects for women, many of whom came to occupy prominent positions in both business and politics. Yet this third generation was to lack both the enthusiasm and skills of its forebears for farming. Consequently, land ownership was to become increasingly commodified, not least because rapid in-migration into the area dramatically increased the demand for housing. As a result, 'real estate entrepreneurship' became a way of life for this third generation, just as agriculture had been for the previous generations.[8]

Mabandla's work demonstrates what he terms the 'time depth' of the black middle class and suggests that, despite the ravages of the 1913 Land Act, a small yet historically significant minority of Africans retained access to land ownership in 'black spots' around the country. This provided the basis for the transfers not only of material wealth, but also of 'middle-class' aspirations and values from one generation to another. It was a middle class which was to take full advantage of the massive widening of opportunities for upward mobility across the country after 1994.

Further studies need to be made to assess the extent to which the retention of pockets of land in black hands since 1913 has provided an intergenerational basis for upward mobility.[9] Nonetheless, it will surely only qualify the more general understanding that the lack of individual property rights for blacks under apartheid severely inhibited the development of the black middle class. All the same, even if lacking material wealth, the black middle class has profited from the cultural capital generated by earlier generations.

This has recently been demonstrated by Jason Musyoka in a study of the nature of inheritance among 'new' black middle-class households.[10] On the basis of a qualitative survey of 19 appropriately middle-class households in Newcastle, KwaZulu-Natal, Musyoka made several findings. Firstly, education was regarded as the most popular inheritance from the previous generation, whether this was an actual investment or simply advice and inspiration. 'Although a long term investment, education was considered as the only sustainable option out of poverty.'[11] Secondly, households were a major source of non-educational aspiration – the determination to 'succeed in life'. Thirdly, only a minority of households had benefited from the receipt of capital assets from their parents, and most had accumulated property through their personal efforts. But the accumulation of assets was rendered problematic by the need to share incomes with poorer relatives at the same time as middle-class households were acquiring a more expensive lifestyle. All of this made investment in the future generation a difficult balancing act. Even so, participants in Musyoka's survey generally aspired to make investments (notably in property and insurance schemes).

The importance of cultural capital was further conveyed to me by one participant in a focus group, who complained that the conversation about the black middle class was usually too township- and city-related. She had grown up among people in the Eastern Cape who had never had televisions, fridges or other modern consumer goods, yet even so they regarded themselves as middle class:

> They had land; they had big houses that they built themselves; they had livestock that they had developed and grown themselves; they were financing the education of their kids through either whether it's going to be selling a cow or through whatever ... How I see middle class has got nothing to do with what you have in terms of material possessions. It's probably for me more values-oriented; it's more education-related; it's more like how you see life and how the people around you value themselves and what are their aspirations for the future and it has nothing to do with what the next person

is going to be buying from tomorrow. So from that point of view
... if you look for instance, [at] all the people [who] were highly
educated in the olden days, whether you look at Mandela or Tambo
or whatever, that started huge organisations ... [they] never had all
these material possessions that we are talking about and yet I think if
they were asked to define themselves they would define themselves
as being middle class.[12]

Again and again, what comes through is how important the access to
education of earlier generations has been in providing lift-off for the
contemporary middle class. 'My mother had a store, so holidays I will go and
work in the shop,' reported a black professional woman who, having grown
up in a rural area, eventually qualified to take graduate studies overseas. She
recalled her parents as saying: 'We will educate you up until university. That's
all. That is our inheritance to you.'[13] She was representative of a much wider
pattern. A study undertaken at UCT, internationally rated as the country's
top university, indicated that something like a third of its black graduates
came from families where at least one parent had themselves attended an
institution of higher learning.[14] Similarly, two-thirds of a class of 'high-
achieving' matriculants aspiring to enter university, the overwhelming
proportion of whom were black, indicated that one or more of their parents
had had some experience of tertiary education.[15] The undeniable message is
that a favourable family background, shaped by class, counts very heavily in
determining children's life chances.[16] But once they have got into university,
access to financial resources plays a major role in determining whether
black students are able to stay there, with 'first-generation' students from
low-income, less-educated families being the most likely to drop out.[17]
While a middle class can be created within a single generation, it is likely to
take two or more generations to become consolidated.

Consumption as freedom and display

It is unsurprising that the upsurge in black spending since 1994 has been
widely celebrated as a product and demonstration of freedom. Apartheid
symbolised black oppression, poverty and exclusion from the capacity to
buy anything but the bare necessities. Democracy symbolises the freedom
for black people to improve themselves, to catch up with whites, and even
to become rich.[18] The capacity to spend embodies social agency; wealth
represents success; and black consumerism has become associated with a

realisation of citizenship. In this context, the black middle class is seen as the major social actor in South Africa, as 'driving the economy with a love of education, homes and shopping'.[19]

The Mandela–Mbeki years of government were the 'good' years, when growth replaced late-apartheid stagnation. Real GDP grew at an average of 3 per cent between 1995 and 2003, less than had been hoped for, but nonetheless double the rate recorded between 1980 and 1994; and in 2006 GDP per head (R34,185) at last climbed above the previous high of R33,841, achieved as far back as 1981. Such growth enabled the ANC government to effect a substantial transfer of resources to the old, disabled, unemployed and the poor through an expansion of welfare payments: there was a massive leap in the number of beneficiaries of social grants from 3.4 million in 2001 to 12.4 million in 2008.[20] More money found its way into black hands, one survey reporting that by 2007, whereas spending by whites accounted for 40 per cent of disposable income, spending by black consumers now accounted for 47 per cent.[21]

Above all, it was spending by the rapidly growing black middle class that was presented as 'spurring the South African boom'. The *Financial Mail* celebrated a 'black bonanza' for driving 'the astonishing performances of companies operating in the consumer market'. In 2006 black consumers, mainly middle class, were said to have accounted for recent sales growth of between 15 and 25 per cent a year in clothing stores and 76 per cent of furniture sales; black cellphone usage had 'rocketed'; black middle-class consumers were now shopping in upmarket foodstores and acquiring sophisticated tastes for food and wine; and they were buying new and expensive, rather than second-hand, cars, accounting for the purchase of 30 per cent of imported vehicles in 2007. The black middle class was also identified as driving a residential property boom, as they increasingly aspired to home ownership and, for many, a move into formerly white suburbs. The financial sector was scrambling to insure and bank the unbanked, while advertising companies were rapidly learning to turn out adverts versed in township slang.[22] Although the term 'Buppies' (black upwardly mobile young professionals) was soon replaced by the less age-constrained 'black diamonds', young blacks with money were swiftly identified as a key segment of the market,[23] ready 'to sell their souls for the right label'. The 11-year-old Pelonomi Nkosi was quoted as saying that designer brands such as Gucci, Levi, Billabong, Nike and Puma 'made her feel more confident and noticed', while a study of 300 teenagers indicated that they spent the bulk of their savings on clothing, followed by cell phones, airtime, CDs and other technology items.[24] 'You cannot be middle class if you have no credit cards,' remarked one focus group participant.[25] The young generation was said to ignore race but worship money, which was seen as bringing power and freedom.[26]

Just as black youngsters were eager to join a globalised youth culture, the new South Africa was becoming a nation of shoppers. Shopping malls spread out rapidly across the entire country. By 2013 South Africa had more large shopping centres (malls bigger than 2,000 square metres) than Australia, yet it was not yet considered to be 'over-shopped'. By now, large retail chains (Woolworths, Debonairs, Mugg & Bean, News Café, Game, Dion, Makro, Builders Warehouse and the like) had headed for the townships. The Maponya Mall in Soweto, a venture of the black magnate Richard Maponya ('with the blessing of Nelson Mandela') in 2007, became the largest indoor mall in the country. By this time there were 13 shopping centres in the townships in Cape Town, Durban and Johannesburg, and more were following. 'Shop till you drop' was now the slogan for 'retail therapy'.[27] For black middle-class shoppers in particular, malls were becoming synonymous with 'modernity and abundance', and a way of identifying with the new society.[28] They had even become a space to celebrate a quasi-religious experience: 'The mall is where we pay our tithes and make our offerings.'[29] The 'malling' of black townships was declared a victory for capitalism, freedom and individual achievement.[30] 'These blacks', observed a journalist who spent nights covering the most fashionable watering-holes in Soweto, were 'not emerging anythings'. 'They are already here, and when the next stories of how the rich live feature, it will be their tales being told. Their obvious affluence is an emphatic and unapologetic statement that these natives, or those they know and grew up with, never struggled to be poor.'[31]

'Obvious affluence', or 'conspicuous consumption', is one of the behaviour traits most commonly ascribed to the black middle class. It is an image which has been much strengthened by the black elite's penchant for expensive cars and large mansions along with indulgence in the lavish parties and fashionable weddings that are regularly splashed over the weekend press. Yet 'conspicuous consumption' is an image which many within the middle class decry, complaining that they are dismissed as unwholesomely materialistic if not downright greedy. The reality, of course, lies between these extremes, and scholars' attention to black middle-class expenditure patterns, and what these signify, reveals a far more complicated picture.

For some of the black middle class, the deliberate flaunting of new wealth and possession of goods conforms to Thorstein Veblen's notion of 'conspicuous consumption', as an attempt by individuals to transform wealth into status. Veblen identified two ways in which an individual can display wealth. One is through leisure activities, the other through lavish expenditure upon consumption and services, the linking thread being 'the element of waste that is common to both ... In the one case it is a waste of time and effort, in the other it is a waste of goods.'[32] For Veblen, the capacity to engage in such wasteful activities was the key way in which members of the 'leisure class' were able to display their wealth and assert their status. In turn, lower strata in society would seek to emulate the consumer behaviour of those above them, so that even the poor would feel pressured into open display in order to assert their 'respectability'.

Veblen developed his theory in relation to a 'leisure class' in early twentieth-century America that sought to differentiate itself from the bourgeoisie. Massive changes have taken place in industrialised capitalist countries since then, as 'leisured' classes have tended to merge with upper segments of a considerably better-off middle class while often themselves embracing the styles and tastes of 'popular' culture. Nonetheless, his notion of 'conspicuous consumption' continues to enjoy considerable purchase as a mode of behaviour that enables individuals to demonstrate openly their rapid upward mobility.

Kunene's 'sushi party' was a prime instance of conspicuous waste, a public display that he had 'made it'. 'My birthdays were never celebrated when I was growing up, mainly because we couldn't afford it.'[33] Now he could celebrate success through excess, brushing off criticism of the party's R700,000 cost made by COSATU's Zwelinzima Vavi, by proudly announcing, 'It cost more than that.'[34] The Kunene example may be extreme, yet there are many other examples. For instance, S'bu and Shauwn Mpisane, a couple who had risen from a humble background to secure major contracts from the provincial government and eThekwini (Durban) municipality in KwaZulu-Natal, soon outspent Kunene with a R1 million Ancient Egyptian-themed wedding anniversary party (they dressed as Pharaohs) at the five-star Fairmont Hotel and Resort in Zimbali, which was attended by, among others, Jacob Zuma and his nephew Khulubuse Zuma. Indeed, by the time the couple were later subject to investigation by the authorities for fraud and corruption, they reportedly owned a fleet of 60 'exotic' cars (inclusive of a Rolls Royce and two Lamborghinis) and a string of valuable properties.[35] The new black elite, claimed Zakes Mda (whose 2009 novel *Black Diamond* explored race, class and consumerism in the new South Africa), feels 'entitled to unbridled wealth', instant gratification and conspicuous consumption.[36]

'South Africans want it all and they want it now,' observed Mda, and if they have it, it is likely that they will want to play golf on one of South Africa's 500-odd golf courses. The construction of golf courses has boomed since 1994, many now built as 'golf estates' which offer 'exclusive' lifestyles and 'secure' living. The enormous financial (and ecological) cost involved in designing, laying out and maintaining golf courses ensures that golf remains an expensive sport and that those who play it are financially well-off (clubs demand hefty joining fees along with substantial annual fees). Consequently, as Jackie Cock has demonstrated, golf has come to play a highly symbolic role. On the one hand, it signifies the social inclusion of those who play with the wealthy, and the social exclusion of the poor (who are allowed entry into the 'fortified enclaves' only to work). On the other, it provides the social space in which black elites now mix with established white elites not only to play together, but also to forge political and business alliances. It is not only the sport and the leisure that golf provides that are driving increasing black participation, but the prestige and prospects it offers. It is on the golf course, Cock notes, where 'the new power elite' is coalescing: corporations, parastatals and even the ANC itself sponsor 'golf days' at which politicians and businessmen 'network', forge relationships and make deals. Golf, observes Cock, is about 'class power' and, for the black elite and middle class, the opportunity for social display.[37]

Conspicuous consumption also constitutes an assertion of racial pride. Lloyd Mbabane, a business studies academic, has implored the black wealthy to 'Say it out loud: I'm black, I'm rich and I'm proud'. There were a host of reasons why blacks should flaunt their wealth:

If you live in the townships or rural areas, please do not hide your success from us. We see enough battered cars and cheap suits in our lives. Please wear your latest suits when you come to our functions. Don't patronise us by dressing cheaply or by rocking up in an old Datsun, Mazda or Valiant. We aspire to being successful one day, and we do not want to be condemned to a life of mediocrity.[38]

His argument echoed that of journalist Fred Khumalo. Khumalo had similarly asserted that the open display of wealth by blacks who had 'made it' would provide role models for less successful blacks to emulate:

> If we can't show off our cars in the communities that we grew up in, we are doing these communities a disservice. The presence of a beautiful car in the township, by a person who grew up in that community, struggled, went to school before the eyes of the very people of that community, should serve as an inspiration … If you can't show off in your own township, where else can you show off?[39]

Khumalo went on to elaborate the further point that blacks needed to demonstrate their wealth in the townships because whites from prosperous suburbs ('the Houghtons, the Bishopscourts, the Sandtons and the Rondebosches') had grown up with wealth, and were unlikely to be impressed by anything a black man owned:

> They have holiday homes on the French Riviera, they have yachts moored in Cape Town. Don't be fooled by the hand-me-down clothes you see them wearing, or the jalopies they drive around. They know serious money, money that smells like the mildew, so old it is. They have inheritances, family trusts et cetera. They won't pay you a second glance as you wax lyrical at a fancy bar about your investment portfolio, about the Cohibas that you've received straight from Havana.[40]

Khumalo's argument recycles that of Pierre Bourdieu, who asserted that the need to display wealth may be diminished among an upper class because of the habits and particular tastes they have acquired through their upbringing. For Bourdieu, the cultural capital enjoyed by the bourgeoisie is used to secure social status through marks of distinction, and this is more powerful, 'and provides a more general means of exclusion, than conspicuous consumption'.[41] And so, while members of the middle class seek to differentiate themselves from the working class by embracing the habits and styles of the upper class, the self-confidence of the latter may free them of the need to indulge in conspicuous consumption. Within South Africa, such distinctions inevitably involve racial dimensions. Generally, whites will feel less need to indulge in social display of their wealth and status, which they have grown up with, than blacks, who have only recently acquired it. Black ostentation can therefore be dismissed as gauche, typical of the nouveau riche. Yet, along with the narrative of the black elite and middle class as conspicuous consumers, there is, simultaneously, a more subtle message, that the more blacks become established within the middle class, the less they tend to consume conspicuously.

On the basis of an analysis of the Income and Expenditure Survey conducted by Statistics South Africa from September 2010 to August 2011, Ronelle Berger and her associates distinguished between two subgroups of the middle class (across the racial spectrum), namely the emerging and more established middle class.[42] They observed that the differential 'life chances' of subgroups within a middle class (such as access to education) were likely to have implications for economic security, stability and prospects. Despite their relative affluence, new entrants to the middle class tended to be more vulnerable to insecurity. Thus, in comparison with white households, which were more likely to have benefited from some intergenerational transfer of resources, black middle-class households were characterised by 'asset deficits', which might place them at a relative disadvantage, and have an effect on their consumption patterns (for instance, black households would be more likely to purchase assets than their white counterparts).

While established black and white middle-class groups exhibited many similar characteristics, per capita income levels of white households tended to be higher than those of black. By contrast, emerging black households were likely to enjoy substantially less entrenched prosperity (household heads being generally younger, less likely to have had tertiary education, and more likely to be single and female). Hence, while it seemed likely that a portion of the emerging group would move upwards into the established group over time, many of them were structurally disadvantaged, would remain only marginally middle class, and their potential for further upward mobility would be severely constrained.

There were other key findings. Firstly, for the middle class, the share of expenditure allocated to conspicuous consumption decreases with an increase in income per capita (suggesting that the upper classes do not experience the same need to signal their wealth as the middle classes). Secondly, Coloured and black African households spend a significantly larger share of their money on items that can visibly signal wealth (this pattern is stronger for the emerging than for the established black middle class, whose consumption patterns converge towards those of the white middle class as their asset levels increase). Thirdly, the spending patterns of black middle-class households indicate that they are 'catching up' on household asset stocks, this being most pronounced among the emerging middle class. Overall, as asset ownership rises, conspicuous consumption decreases, because the need to signal economic status declines.

It is not easy to reconcile the two narratives, of the black middle class as status-conscious conspicuous consumers on the one hand, and as an increasingly 'normal' middle class on the other. Probably both narratives are right at the same time. There is clearly a strongly felt need, especially among new members of the political elite, to demonstrate their success. Equally, as the extensive work by Peter Alexander and others on class in Soweto has shown, class identity is strongly based on the comparison of the ability to consume. People will often identify as 'middle class', because they conceive themselves to be in the 'middle' of their immediate social world, but there is a world of difference between being 'middle' in an impoverished community and being 'middle' when the reference group is more national or even global.[43] On the other hand, the consumer patterns of the black middle class exhibit marked similarities to those of the white middle class, especially as they move upwards through the class structure. In any case, as the 'black diamonds' surveys indicate, consumer habits shift through the life-cycle, with the older and more established tending to engage less in conspicuous consumption than the younger and less established. However, both these narratives have to contend with a third, the narrative of the black middle class as victims of fragility and debt.

Freedom and fragility: the black middle class, taxation and debt

For Achille Mbembe, South Africa is becoming a society of consumption in the context of acute privation for the majority of black citizens and in the absence of structures of mass production. 'Ours is a democracy with a majority of propertyless citizens in a country historically shaped by the contradiction between the rule of the people and the rule of property. Even the emerging black middle class is not entirely certain that whatever it owns today (a house, a car, a fridge) won't be taken away tomorrow. This sense of precarious ownership is a key marker of its psyche as a class in the making.'[44]

In 2011 the precariousness of the living circumstances of most South Africans was to be highlighted by the high levels of indebtedness which fuelled the tragedy of Marikana. Workers at this platinum mine were said to be in debt 'up to their necks', much of it owed to moneylenders whose hunger for repayment was only appeased by the docking of debt repayments directly from salaries and by outrageous interest rates. Journalists found instances where miners had been charged more than ten times the amount they originally borrowed. 'South Africa', concluded one commentator, was 'deep, deep into an unsustainable debt spiral'.[45]

Danger signals about the rising debt levels had already been flashing for some years. In 2007 household debt had reached a record high of 77 per cent of disposable income, up from 50 per cent in 2002. Total consumer debt was said to have reached R839 billion, an increase of 134 per cent from 2004. Repossession of property, notably cars, was 'rocketing'; the issue of summonses for debt recovery was rising; and, reportedly, up to a fifth of home owners stood in danger of losing their homes following a recent interest-rate rise.[46] Yet, despite growing awareness of the extent of debt across the wider population, it was the middle class which was depicted as the most immediately vulnerable. Some discussion involved international comparisons, noting that pressures upon middle-class living standards were increasing globally as a result of globalisation and the resort by large corporations to downsizing and slashing pay and benefits. More local commentary reported that 'debt was the biggest middle-class fear', and that 52 per cent of middle-class South Africans felt they would never be financially free.[47] It was the black middle class in particular which was said to be taking the most strain, its 'credit-spending binge' having racked up 'dangerously high levels of debt'.[48] Reality began to bite in financial circles when it was realised how little disposable income many black middle-class people had available once they paid off their monthly essentials.[49]

If the financial sector began to worry, so did the state, which saw the rise in black middle-class indebtedness as a threat to its viability. Direct taxation (levied upon individuals and businesses on a progressive basis) accounted for the major portion of the state's income (57 per cent in 2012/13), largely drawn from income tax (34 per cent of revenues) and tax paid by corporations (20 per cent), the balance coming from indirect taxes (such as VAT) paid by all regardless of income. But the tax base was remarkably small, so that in 2013 only 5.1 million individuals were required to submit income-tax returns. Even so, more and more blacks had by now been brought into the tax net, including lower-middle-class government employees such as nurses and teachers. Many of them were already financially stressed and, according to one participant in a focus group, saw themselves as the 'milking cows of capitalists'.[50] Furthermore, the relatively small number of direct taxpayers contrasted with the rising number of recipients of social grants – 15.3

million in 2013 – who accounted for 16 per cent of the budget in that year. The increasing cost of social protection, along with heavy expenditures upon such social goods as education and health, was regularly said to be imposing a heavy squeeze upon middle-class taxpayers.[51]

Financial commentators argued that the tax environment for lower and mid-level earners (the vast majority) had worsened considerably since 1994, at the same time that the cost of living, once among the cheapest globally, had become among the most expensive. Then too, as the middle class was getting squeezed, the rich were escaping paying their fair share. Indeed, tax authorities estimated that, while there were 2,600 high-net-worth individuals in the country with assets above R75 million, only 360 of them were registered to pay tax.[52] By 2015, the country was in danger of falling over a 'fiscal cliff' – yet its options were limited.[53] On the one hand, a relatively poor tax base of consumers could only be taxed so much, not only for reasons of fairness but because consumption levels needed to be primed if economic activity was to be stimulated. On the other hand, tax increases, especially if levied in unfamiliar forms (such as 'e-tolls' for motorway users in Gauteng, which united middle-class with trade union revolt in 2013), were likely to incur a heavy political cost, and the ANC became worried by the prospect of losing the allegiance of the black middle class.

The squeeze was further increased by an array of other expenditures related to middle-class life in post-1994 South Africa. The changing racial complexion of once exclusively white suburbs was simply the most visible indication that the black middle class possessed the same desire for house ownership as its white counterpart. According to a not atypical market report, the proportion of black owners who owned mid-value and higher-value homes outside township areas had grown from 13 per cent in 2003 to 19 per cent in 2013, while overall black ownership of all residential property had grown from 37 per cent to 42 per cent.[54] Yet, with home ownership had come multiple other expenses, such as municipal rates, water and electricity. Meanwhile, in the absence of adequate policing, many within the middle class felt obliged to incur private security costs, all to be added to the costs of school fees and private medical insurance (to which increasing numbers of the black middle class subscribed).[55]

The most widespread narrative addressing the indebtedness of the black middle class refers to its fragility and the danger of its dropping back into the working class or the ranks of the unemployed. In some quarters, the black middle class itself is seen as largely to blame for its 'financial irresponsibility', its propensity 'to choose bling over budget'.[56] For others, it is the fault of an irresponsible financial sector, which has moved beyond both prudence and government control.[57] Yet, as Deborah James has explained, growing indebtedness among black South Africans cannot be ascribed to just one or two factors, for it is multidimensional. As well as having roots in the political economy, it is intimately bound up with identity, status and aspirations for upward mobility. While it is dangerous to reduce her complex argument to a summary, the thrust of her account points in the following directions.

James's starting point is to tackle the 'alarmist' assumption that views debt simply as a measure of social stress and unsustainability, by observing that debt also has its positive side, in that it enables people to improve their lifestyles and reconfigure relationships between different social groups (for instance, to ensure that a new black middle class can enjoy upward mobility). Yet she also recognises that neither of these views on their own can offer a complete picture of 'the rapidly shifting terrain of relationship, ambition, dependence and ostentatious display in South Africa' – but, together, they 'can tell us something about the social terrain and those who are placed within it'.[58]

The appropriation of black land by white settlers from the end of the nineteenth century led to increasing restrictions upon the capacity of blacks to obtain credit, forcing them to resort to an array of informal borrowing arrangements (notably, from traders or store owners), although from the 1930s town-dwellers (especially) – disallowed from owning their homes – invested in furniture, which was bought on hire purchase, often from large retailers.[59] Given the low earnings and financial insecurity of many of those who borrowed, there was considerable risk involved, and numerous instances of default rooted in customers' inability to pay. Partly for these reasons, the banks – which ultimately financed hire-purchase schemes – had by the early 2000s sought to move beyond this 'credit apartheid' by 'banking the unbanked'.[60] In this they were assisted by the post-1994 liberalisation of the economy, and the greatly increased grant of credit by banks and other financial institutions was bolstered by the state's interest in promoting the black middle class.

It was soon recognised that borrowing and its unintended consequences were getting out of hand. Lenders had for many years been able to recoup their money from borrowers' bank accounts ('garnishee orders'), yet generally they preferred to seek more informal (if sometimes crooked) means of repayment. By the late 1990s, lenders had begun to toughen up, and impose stricter terms of repayment. In turn, borrowers turned to assistance from an expanding micro-loans sector (mostly run by Afrikaners retrenched from the civil service who invested their redundancy packages in lending practices) and, at the bottom end of the market, from *mashonistas*, or neighbourhood moneylenders (who came to be described as 'loan sharks'). Widespread resort to dubious practices, such as confiscating borrowers' ATM bank cards and charging high interest rates (perhaps as high as 50 per cent per month), led to official concern, and resulted ultimately in the passage of the National Credit Act of 2007. This imposed increased obligations upon creditors to ascertain borrowers' financial viability, sought to curtail unsupportable lending (notably of mortgage credit, thereby preventing the occurrence of a US-style 'subprime' crisis), encouraged debt counselling and established a system of debt review. Even so, lending and 'reckless' borrowing continued apace, with creditors continuing to resort to garnishee orders or to the appropriation of borrowers' ATM cards. For their part, some borrowers became so desperate that they resigned their jobs and cashed in their pensions to settle their debts. The story, concludes James, is one of 'continuing, even deepening, indebtedness'.[61]

Beyond the economics of neo-liberalism, James explores the aspirations and obligations of the new black middle class.[62] She notes that most members frankly acknowledge that they have benefited from the opportunities provided by the post-1994 political order, although many have simultaneously built upon foundations laid down for them by their parents, especially by their paying for their education. Yet in many cases their rapid upward mobility has not been shared by their family and friends. Inevitably, this involves many in providing financial assistance to relatives, paying what is colloquially known as a 'black tax':

> Progress for me defines all of us moving forward ... I think that that's a unique condition of the black middle class that we never really talk about, like our dependants ... So I have to figure out, okay, this goes to A, B, C, D, E before I even touch my own things. So it's also those realities where you talk about being black middle class, it's like, it's a unique set of circumstances that is really defined in a large part by our blackness.[63]

Consequently, although many display their new status by the purchase of consumer goods and head into dangerous levels of debt, others are prudent, responsive to familial obligations, and forward-looking, notably with regard to educating their children. Yet, as James notes, financial responsibility brings associated emotional and social costs. Firstly, while black middle-class women embrace the greater freedom that money buys, many find that partners or husbands are reluctant to accept changes in gender roles, and expect them to conform to conservative female roles. As a result, many such women prefer to remain single, even if this requires them to bring up their children on their own.

Secondly, many within the black middle class lament the corrosive effect of consumption and individualism upon family life. For men, in particular, the costs involved in payment of lobola, or bridewealth, can be crippling. In rural societies, the protracted transfer of wealth (usually in cattle) served to establish bonds and trust between the families involved. But, while the ideals embodied in lobola remain respected, the nature of the debt relationship involved has been transformed: money has replaced cattle, and the levels of payment required have generally gone up, especially for young women in whom money has been invested for education. As a result, payment of lobola has become increasingly unaffordable, even for those in middle-class employment, while attempts to live up to the ideal may involve men in making endless payments to their partners' relatives, some even resorting to taking out loans to cover them. Among the new middle class, there is also pressure upon prospective husbands to find the money for 'white weddings', which can be hugely expensive.[64] As a result, just as young women may find themselves torn between loyalty to parents and to their partners, the young men may well conclude that the huge costs involved in getting married, and the debts incurred by doing so, would make the arrangement unsustainable – and, in any case, would conflict with other such aspirational goals as house purchase and the acquisition of consumables. James concludes that, paradoxically, while lobola and associated payments are intended to cement long-term bonds, they seem in the contemporary world of the black middle class to have the opposite effect. In fact, they may account for the increasing prevalence of single female parents, and the decline in conventional notions of two-parent families.

James's exploration of consumption and debt confronts the widespread image of the black middle class as inherently irresponsible and extravagant.[65] Behind that narrative, she argues, lies the increasingly sophisticated profiling of black consumers by marketing companies in order to better market goods and services, and persuade them to spend more money. The stereotyping of black consumers as irresponsible also plugs into racialised critiques in which blacks are advised to live up to standards of financial prudence established for them by the white minority, even while it is widely recognised that whites can generally call upon a more established asset base and are less obligated to care for their relatives. Yet, while neo-liberalism has encouraged the freedom to spend, it has not matched this with individuals' capacity to buy. Indeed, blame for indebtedness is usually placed upon the individual consumer, rather than upon the lack of regulation of those forces that are fostering the cult of individual excess.

The black middle class and residential desegregation

The broad picture about the black middle class and the substantial reordering of space and race since 1994 has been presented by Philip Harrison and Tanya Zack, in relation to change in Johannesburg.

> The expansion of the African middle class has been one of the key drivers of spatial change in post-apartheid Johannesburg. The emergent and established African middle class has moved into previously white suburbs, although some segments of the middle class have remained in historically African townships, and especially in Soweto. In making locational choices, the African middle class is responding to the opportunity to move into high-amenity residential suburbs previously reserved for whites, but also to the desire to remain physically connected to social networks and cultural experiences in the townships.[66]

This movement of blacks into white suburbs is sometimes presented as a sign of the merging of previously racially divided segments of the middle class into one that is genuinely 'non-racial', enjoying shared lifestyles and interests – a species of the euphoric 'rainbowism' presented in so many advertisements.[67] It is a vision which is endorsed in many popular portrayals. 'It gives me great pleasure', reported a correspondent to a leading newspaper, 'to see the noisy, laughing, joyful river of white, coloured, black and Indian children talking to one another. They do not agonise over such, to them, absurd and irrelevant concepts [as "transformation"] – they just live and do what they think is "cool".'[68]

Many black people are 'flocking' to the suburbs, notes another such commentary. Some leave the townships to seek 'fame and fortune'; some are 'nagged' to move by their 'wives' [*sic*]; some are driven to do so by escalating crime. But, above all, there are the better schools, able to provide one's children with a better and brighter future. 'METRObeat visited Montclair Junior Primary School, and the visit was exciting as we saw young children experiencing the joy of discovering each other on the playing fields. In the suburbs we also find schools that are now accommodating young black students with ease. It is these schools that will see a new generation groomed into a better and unbiased rainbow nation.'[69]

Meanwhile, the townships themselves are transforming. 'A new Soweto' is arising, with fancy restaurants, upmarket drinking-holes, and even sushi bars as well as a shop specialising in wine, 'serious wine, not plonk'; there are the shopping malls of Maponya, Jabulani, Protea Gardens and Bara Mall; and, compared with the barren desert of yesteryear, there are now 'trees everywhere, fresh, planted-yesterday saplings' as if some 'revolutionary environmentalist has been let loose' and told to plant trees to his heart's content. There is even less crime:

> I join a childhood friend at Masakeng Pub ... We sit outside at a wooden table ... I look up and I see that the street is still dotted with people: a pair of lovers there, a group of teenagers laughing loudly under a streetlight there and a solitary figure walking briskly. It has just turned nine. 'Aren't people afraid of criminals?' I ask. My companion launches into a long explanation of how safe the streets are these days. These are the same streets on which marauding groups of criminals once held the community hostage.[70]

The imagery of the black middle class as driving the momentum towards a desegregated South Africa and the betterment of historically black areas is a palpably attractive one. As far as it goes, it is not untrue. However, almost inevitably, a deeper telling of the story of the new-found residential mobility of the black middle class is more complicated than any romanticised eulogies imply, for it takes place against the backcloth of the far-reaching racialised segregation of space which went before. Yet even that was not one-dimensional. 'Before, during and certainly after apartheid', writes the geographer Alan Mabin, 'South African urban change' has always been 'more complex than some simple linear process'. The changes affecting the post-apartheid cities 'are far from those of racial desegregation alone'. Indeed, new forms of segregation are arising – no longer, certainly, crudely structured around race, but rather around intensified divisions relating to income, wealth, new forms of employment and culture.[71] In East London, for instance, blacks have effectively taken over the beaches previously reserved for whites, while suburban whites increasingly 'hide away from the changing city in their coastal suburban enclaves by creating fantasies of old and new forms of coastal whiteness'.[72]

Unsurprisingly, given how apartheid sought to restrict physical movement, spatial mobility has become a metaphor for upward social mobility. In turn, this is strongly associated with the right to home ownership for people to whom this was previously denied. For Arthur, a young black man whose mother had been a teacher, who worked as a graduate trainee at a large IT company, and who already owned a number of cars, it was not until he bought his own house in Soweto that he felt he had joined the middle class: 'My house, that's how you define me because of the bond, the furniture.'[73] Yet, although he now identified himself as middle class, this was only in relation to the black people around him, and he was quite unable to compare himself with the white middle class or conceive of a national middle class with shared interests. Arthur saw post-apartheid South Africa as weighed down by a burden of past racial inequality which his like would never be able to overcome.

In many parts of South Africa apartheid involved a displacement of black urbanisation into far-flung housing settlements, well away from the white towns and cities in which their inhabitants worked. During the later apartheid years, the authorities proved less able to maintain such spatial divisions, as the black urban population mushroomed and as rural people increasingly moved to the towns. The barriers separating black from white residential areas quietly began to erode. A trickle, then a rush, of black people previously disqualified by the Group Areas Act moved into white spaces; at first, into low-cost rental accommodation in high-rise apartments in central urban areas and in older, low-density white areas, as both businesses and white inhabitants left for newer, outer suburbs. This was by no means a planned deracialisation of space. Rather, it was the outcome of multiple processes transforming the cities that gathered pace from the 1980s. In Johannesburg these included the decline of gold mining in the southern areas, deindustrialisation as manufacturing slowed, and the growth of the 'service economy', symbolised by the founding of Sandton city to the north of Johannesburg, its rapid expansion and emergence as the continent's premier financial centre.[74] At the same time, the urban change under way included the outward spread of white suburbia from the city centres: this was facilitated by highway expansion from the 1970s, the rapid growth of car ownership, and the corresponding shift of commercial activity from central business districts (CBDs) to shopping centres in the suburbs. Together, these far-reaching transformations laid the foundations for new forms of social segregation:

> CBDs in many cases (Johannesburg, East London, Germiston) began to become the shopping centres of those without private cars – in most cases black residents of townships and newly integrating inner city areas. By contrast, the suburban malls afforded more affluent (in many cases, overwhelmingly white) citizens motorized access to increasingly specialized stores. In turn, investment in suburban commercial activity deepened divides between suburb and township, with the former sharing little of the public revenues derived from new developments.[75]

With the arrival of democracy in 1994, cities and municipalities across the country had to confront the challenge of how to overcome the heritage of racial fragmentation. In general, local authorities failed to respond imaginatively to the huge transformations of urban space that were occurring. During the 1990s, they were overwhelmingly concerned with deracialising the structures of local governance, merging former white and black authorities and, in the cities, creating huge metropolitan councils. Mabin argues that the restructuring involved was 'almost revolutionary', yet the new councils elected in the local government elections of 2000 were to embrace the pursuit of growth, by making themselves attractive to business, rather than any form of 'development planning' involving the direction of investment to poorer, blacker areas.

Although a number of the new councils, such as the City of Johannesburg, were to adopt planning initiatives with long-term developmental objectives and sought to regulate suburban expansion, they generally lacked the capacity to implement them. As a result, the initiative has passed to private corporations and developers. In an age of global connection, they inevitably gravitate to wealthier, more advantaged areas, and reinforce the shift to further suburbanisation and urban sprawl. Thus, while the new authorities have sought to effect some redistribution of revenues for the improvement of basic facilities to former townships and poorer districts, they have generally failed to engage in more far-reaching geographical engineering to address past inequalities and segregation. In consequence, new 'geographies of exclusion', based upon the inheritance of racial division and the unregulated workings of property and labour markets, have been further entrenched, and the poverty of the townships continues to be hidden away. Such 'neo-apartheid' has seen a further dispersion of upper-income consumption and business opportunities to the suburbs. This has brought about greater 'enclavisation' involving 'gated communities', and a shift to class-based rather than race-based segregation, as middle-class blacks increasingly move to 'town-house' complexes and more expensive, high-walled dwellings in the formerly exclusive white areas.

The changing urban pattern has involved a dramatic reordering of space, notably in the creation of 'edge cities'. For instance, the 'northern suburbs' in Johannesburg, which were developed from the 1950s as residential areas for the white middle class, have increasingly become 'totalised suburbs', comprising large clusters of offices, shopping malls, light manufacturing parks and recreation facilities (cinemas, restaurants, and sports centres); these now function quite independently of the CBD. Sandton remains the most outstanding example, yet, to a greater or lesser extent, 'edge cities' are becoming a major feature of urban space around the entire country.[76]

Owen Crankshaw's analysis of changing residential patterns in both Johannesburg and Cape Town demonstrates that 'edge cities' in South Africa are more and more being enjoyed by the black middle class, although substantial residential desegregation 'still has a long way to go'.[77] He contrasts this with patterns in the United States, where white middle classes move out of their suburbs (often closer to CBDs) as blacks move in. The major difference, of course, is that whereas in the US whites are the large majority, in South Africa they account for only a small proportion of the population. Desegregation of former white neighbourhoods is inevitable – although it is taking place along identifiably class lines.

It is mostly blacks in the upper occupational categories who are moving into the better-off, formerly white suburbs. In Johannesburg, these are concentrated in the north, and black professionals and managers have largely abandoned the suburbs in the south of the city.[78] According to Amy Selzer and Patrick Heller, the northern suburbs close to Sandton have become the favoured home of the 'elite political class'. 'Most prominent ANC officials live in the north, and even at the lower ends of the party there is a clear status premium on living in these neighbourhoods.'[79] Even so, these areas still remain predominantly white: on the whole, black middle-class residents are, on average, younger, less qualified and earn less than their white counterparts. Correspondingly, it is black Africans (and Coloureds in Cape Town) in middle-class occupations lower down the occupational scale who account for most of those moving into less well-off, more affordable white residential areas (not only because property is cheaper, but because there tend to be higher levels of rental accommodation).[80] In Johannesburg, black semi-professionals and technicians – whom Selzer and Heller dub the 'middle middle class' – are mainly to be found in both the north and south of the city, while the black 'lower middle class', composed of white-collar workers, is to be found largely in the south. Meanwhile, the upgrading of Soweto has made the township more attractive to both the middle-middle and lower-middle classes, although even there the drift to 'enclavisation' is evident.[81] The new spatial order may be entrenching inequality, concludes Crankshaw, 'but it is certainly less racially unequal' – or, rather, it is so at the top end of the market, because the former townships remain almost exclusively inhabited by blacks.

The shift from racial to class segregation may be most pronounced in the large cities, but it is occurring around the country, shaped largely by market conditions. Unsurprisingly, black buyers are more able to purchase houses in small towns like Louis Trichardt or Nelspruit, where the average price of freehold houses in the early 2000s was around R300,000–R350,000, than in Cape Town, where the cost of 'entry-level' houses in that year started at around R750,000. Interestingly, too, house-buying in white suburbia would seem to be accompanied by a shift away from black middle-class purchasers providing homes for the extended family, with most now buying only for their immediate families.[82] Once they arrive in white areas, they need to settle in, and the evidence is that they do not always find this easy, especially in suburbs where they constitute a minority.

Richard Ballard has explored the way in which white neighbours often engage in a strategy of 'othering'. 'People', he says (by which he means people in general, not just whites), 'feel comfortable living in areas where they see their neighbours as "our kind of people" and who share "our" values'. Exclusion of 'others' therefore serves to secure 'our' space and reinforce 'our' identity. We expect our neighbours to conform. Apartheid represented an extreme form of 'othering', with blacks being allowed to enter white suburbs and live there as domestic workers only on sufferance. Although legal exclusion of blacks from suburbs is now outlawed, 'othering' continues in new ways. One is the monitoring of out-of-area black people, especially those who are poor, by private armed security patrols. More subtly, black residents are expected to behave in acceptably white middle-class ways. Questioned by Ballard about his acceptance of the idea of black neighbours, one white resident of suburbia insisted it would have nothing to do with skin colour but

> what sort of people we're looking at. I mean, if they're people who want to kill a cow on the front lawn and you know we listen to this thing in its dying moments, you feel out of kilter … If you have people that want to put 15 children in a house that's only designed to take five you know it's a problem. But it's not a colour problem per se. I mean … if we had a black bachelor next door who lived quietly and respected his neighbours as we would respect him, you know, there wouldn't be the slightest problem. But it's a cultural thing you see … There are cultural differences between the races.[83]

Such an argument implies that racial newcomers to a white area should adopt the culture of established residents. Ballard is careful to stress that this conditional acceptance of blacks is characteristic only of 'some whites'. For the latter, as he explains elsewhere, the slaughter of animals in suburban backyards by blacks for cultural events is symptomatic of the encroachment of barbarism upon civilisation, and a metaphor for the threat to their own lives posed by black majority rule. Other whites, he observes, adopt a more reflective attitude, point out the publicly concealed barbarism of industrialised meat production, and, rather than viewing the suburban slaughter of animals as unacceptably cruel, adopt a relativism which recognises the cultural value of African ceremony.[84] Even so, while blacks moving into middle-class residential areas may over time refashion suburban values in conformity with their own cultures, for some this is not always easy. For these new arrivals in white suburbs, they can be uncomfortable places in which to live.

A widespread complaint about the white suburbs is that they lack the sense of community which exists in townships. High walls and other household fortifications, let alone 'racial othering', inhibit interaction with those who live close by. This often comes as a shock for black families moving from crowded townships, and can prove emotionally stressful. One study found significant levels of depression among black wives who had relocated to suburbs: most missed relatives and generally felt lonely. Of these women 35 per cent regretted they had moved and 55 per cent admitted to wanting more friends.[85] 'People miss the community spirit and warmth that thrives in the townships but is lacking in the suburbs,' remarked one researcher who had undertaken a survey of attitudes towards residential location among 2,500 adults.[86] 'White people here just leave you alone,' commented an Indian homeowner. 'Everyone minds their own business here.'[87] Unsurprisingly, there is a desire among some black residents in white areas to return 'home'.

One estate agent, Buti Mofokeng of Kuntas Properties, observed in 2006 that black families were moving back into Soweto from the southern suburbs. He ascribed this to the fact that the upgrading of Soweto was rendering its own middle-class suburbs more attractive.[88] But the suggestion made by one property industry spokesperson that 'townships are becoming suburbs with all the conveniences' and that 'in the next decade there will no longer be a clear distinction between suburbs and townships'[89] is very much an exaggeration. The gap between the elite suburbs in white areas and the black suburbs in the townships is destined to remain huge. Although former white suburbs will become more racially mixed, suburbs in townships will remain almost entirely black. The de facto racial segregation of residential areas is sure to continue as a fact of South African life for the foreseeable future.

The precarious positionality of the black middle class

During the 2014 general election, the ANC proclaimed that 'it had a good story to tell'. For the black middle class this was almost certainly so, even if the outcomes of the democratic transition have been far more ambiguous for black South Africans at lower ends of the social scale. For all its limitations, the story of the black middle class since 1994 has been one of greater opportunity, higher incomes, improved standards of living, and greater dignity. This is not something for critics to sniff at, for all that levels of unemployment and poverty remain appallingly high. Nonetheless, it is necessary to pose the uncomfortable question whether the good fortune of the black middle class will continue.

If the Mandela–Mbeki years were those of relative prosperity, today that era seems to be coming to an end. Growth in South Africa has slowed to a crawl as a result of the global slump and daunting domestic factors: the structural limitations of the economy, ANC mismanagement, expensive but poorly performing parastatals, parlous relations between government and business, extensive corruption and so on. In essence, the state is beginning to run out of money: tax revenues seem to be reaching their limits while expenditure upon social services continues to rise. Some predict that South Africa is on a path of debt growth that cannot be sustained for much longer, and any resultant financial crisis will inevitably have far-reaching political consequences.[90] Will the ANC have the capacity to self-reform, and cut back on the extensive corruption and cronyism of political elites? Will indebtedness lead to neo-liberal cutbacks on social security spending? Will demands for more financial rigour lead to retrenchments in the public service and a drive for a slimmed-down state? This is no place to debate such questions, but just posing them reminds us of the essential fragility of the black middle class. If, as suggested above, it takes more than a single generation to consolidate a middle class, will less favourable economic conditions plunge many of the black middle class back into the lower ranks of society from where they have come?

This question requires us to pay attention to how black middle-class people cope with the sense of fragility that pervades the lives of so many of them. The black middle class is not naïve. Overwhelmingly they see themselves as having benefited from a very rapid process of social change. Along with this goes a sense that the pace or even the fact of social change can be reversed, and that the black middle class may be in peril. This point was made very explicitly by one of the participants (overwhelmingly drawn from lower-middle-class occupations) in a focus group I met in East London:

What I can say now is what we are seeing in the country – let me come up with a new term – because of the inflation there is a de-growth and de-development of the middle class, like going down because of the inflation. If you look at someone who is earning R10,000 – it could be a take-home or a gross – and then if you look at how things are going up. This year [2013] we had – is it four times, five times petrol increase? Something like that. It's not only petrol. School fees, clothes, food and everything. And look at the 6.6 per cent which teachers, police and whatever they get – it's even less than the increase. So this is which we call the middle class is going down. That's why I'm saying de-development and de-growth. It's going down and as a result in Africa – I mean like it or not, 20 years is enough for a liberation organisation. That's where you start to see the change. So if you go to the history in liberation movements in Africa that [is] because [for] the ruling parties 20 years' time is enough and they start to go down.[91]

This view is expressive of a widespread sense that the black middle class is 'struggling'. Such a sense of precariousness may perhaps help us to understand the apparent growth of corruption: while greed as a factor should never be discounted when we are trying to disentangle the motivations that lie behind theft from the public purse, we should not underestimate the impact upon individuals of a pervasive feeling of economic insecurity, and a resultant willingness to take shortcuts to wealth, with all the attendant risks it may entail.

Another widespread response to precariousness which has attracted considerable attention is the turn to religion. South Africa is a deeply religious country: something like three-quarters of the population claim adherence to Christianity, another 10 per cent is made up of Muslims, Hindus, Jews and those belonging to other faiths, and only up to 15 per cent claim to have no religion. Furthermore, regular attendance at religious services is high. Within this context, it is important to make particular reference to the rapid growth of the Pentecostal and other charismatic Christian churches and what is said to be their particular appeal to the black middle class.

In terms of number of adherents, the charismatic churches remain outnumbered by the Dutch Reformed, Catholic and mainline Protestant churches, and very heavily by the African independent churches (these are also strongly associated with Pentecostalism, but constitute an earlier generation of breakaways from the colonial mainline denominations).[92] Nonetheless, they are the fastest-growing group of churches in South Africa today. As Pentecostalists, they embrace the experience of being 'born again' or acceptance of the Holy Spirit; they emphasise 'the Kingdom of God in the present, not the future'; they are 'concerned with the immediacy of what God is saying to them'; and their followers tend to be concentrated 'in the emerging and aspirant middle classes'.[93]

In Africa, the phenomenal growth of Pentecostalism since the 1980s and 1990s has been associated with vigorous American missionary activity and by the precipitous decline of African economies and the consequent withdrawal of the state from the provision of education, health and other services, a role increasingly assumed by NGOs and the churches.[94] In South Africa, although new charismatic churches emerged from the 1960s, their growth has been most marked since the early 1990s, and they have drawn adherents, white and black, away from the established churches.[95] Broadly, they are associated with the espousal of socially conservative values (notably in the sphere of sexual behaviour and orientation), hard work, and individual responsibility and morality; many lay claim to spiritual healing; and many proclaim a 'prosperity' message suggesting that religious commitment will bring earthly material reward, although some now temper that message with a commitment to poverty alleviation as much as they vaunt the merits of entrepreneurship. Furthermore, they tend to be 'non-political' in the sense that they eschew political activity in favour of worship and personal salvation, and they accept rather than challenge secular authority.

There seem to be three major assertions made about the appeal of the charismatic churches to the black middle classes. The first is that they provide a sense of social connection to communities; the second, that they provide a feeling of self-worth while endorsing a socially conservative world-view which overlaps strongly with African social attitudes; and third, that while at one level they withdraw from politics, at another they legitimise the political order and the high levels of inequality over which it presides.

These assertions can be broadly endorsed here. But there are reasons for caution in doing so. One is that the charismatic churches are enormously diverse, so it is important to distinguish between the 'mega-churches', of which perhaps the best known is the Rhema Church of Pastor Ray McCauley, and numerous 'community-based' churches found in inner cities, local neighbourhoods and townships, largely serving poor communities (predominantly in black African or Coloured but also in poorer white areas).[96] Another is that while there is much assertion about the character of such churches, it is difficult to distinguish reliably between the religious beliefs and practices of the black middle class and those of other black congregants at large. Even so, it remains possible to point to the ways in which the charismatic churches seem to shore up the black middle class.

In qualification of the last point, it would seem that the township Pentecostal churches share important features of liturgy and practice with the African independent churches, notably the emphasis upon faith healing, and its close connection to combating a range of demons and evil spirits whose identities are deeply rooted in traditional African myths and beliefs. While at one level this may resonate in township settings, it has also been associated with deeply conservative attitudes: for instance, widespread condemnation of homosexuality and lesbianism as ungodly deviation, and the belief that HIV/AIDS is a punishment for sin. Nonetheless, although an emphasis upon deliverance from evil spirits is probably stronger in those churches serving poorer communities, the language of 'spiritual warfare' against the devil is also common among charismatic churches that have originated from within white communities.[97]

In suburban areas, charismatic churches have proved particularly attractive to sections of the new, suburban black middle class:

> Separated socially from those they left behind, living behind the security fences of suburbia, they are drawn to the spiritual and emotional community offered by churches like Rhema Ministries. Highly organized, these churches cater to a range of language and age groups (children, teens, young adults, singles and families), offering emotionally-charged worship and the possibility to network between new and old elites on the common basis of faith. Combining fairly literalist theology and high-tech communication (television broadcasting, internet, and so on) with services that mingle old-fashioned revivalism with the atmosphere often of a rock concert, Rhema has also encouraged members to give of their time to socially worthy causes – from soup kitchens to health clinics. Like the African Independent Churches, Rhema largely does not engage with the state, following the (selective) biblical injunction of obedience to the state while exhorting its members to live out its socially conservative commitment to 'biblical values'.[98]

Such churches foster a sense of community and social belonging, not least in the suburbs, where many congregations are both multiracial and multiclass. In short, there is a sense that the charismatic churches enable people 'to come to terms with the unpredictability of South African social life: as a citizen (or customer) engaging with the state, the existential uncertainty generated by crime, or by sickness, for young people who are unlikely to find a job in the formal economy and for those who are unemployed'.[99] Many congregants, observes a study by the Centre for Development and Enterprise (one of the few relating to Pentecostals based upon survey work), are drawn from communities in which social problems (like teenage pregnancy, marital breakdown, alcohol and drug abuse) are rampant, and there is a perception of a 'state of siege'. Accordingly, the restrictive morality of the Pentecostal churches serves as a bulwark against 'surrounding moral chaos, protecting at least a portion of the communities from the debilitating effects of moral decay'.[100]

More positively, the teachings of the charismatic churches provide a sense of direction and personal fulfilment. Broadly, this is in conformity with Max Weber's famous thesis that the Protestant ethic gave spiritual sanction to the rational pursuit of economic gain. The prosperity gospel follows the biblical injunction that one should give in order to receive. This translates into moral pressures upon congregants to give generously to the church. Although, as Deborah James notes,[101] there is always the risk that the pastor will run away with the money, generally it would seem that such contributions, if not used to fund immediate church needs, are directed towards worthwhile projects of benefit to the poor: the emphasis on self-help and giving is 'twinned with the need to aid the less well-off'. Furthermore, tithing is linked to the deferral of gratification, and a strong stress on personal morality promoting habits of saving, capital accumulation and economic advancement.[102] While it may be difficult to judge the impact of such exhortations upon individuals, the CDE reported that 20 per cent of Pentecostals in the suburbs and 23 per cent in the townships claimed improvements in their financial or occupational circumstances as a result of their faith and practice. Although these figures are low, the CDE argued that they should not be discounted in a society combining a competitive market economy with entrenched high levels of poverty and unemployment.[103] On the other hand, Deborah James observes that emphases on controlled consumption and rational financial calculation are paradoxically accompanied by the belief in many churches that such behaviour brings material abundance: by implication, conspicuous consumption can prove evidence of God's favour.

The extent to which the charismatic churches provide solace and inspiration to the black middle classes clearly needs much more careful investigation. Nonetheless, it is important to stress the congruence between the values that these churches proclaim and the aspirations of the black middle class (even if young professional women within their congregations struggle with the patriarchal values they tend to espouse).

James cites black middle-class respondents who indicated how they had broken free of their working-class parents' alignment with mainstream or African independent churches, to join new charismatic churches whose gospels were more in line with their rapid upward mobility. Reflecting upon the problem that such church members set themselves by the need to square their success with the failure of those they left behind them, she relates the observations of one such woman, a young university lecturer, herself a member of the His People Church. While recalling the manner in which the Rhema Church had opened up its doors at a time when apartheid was dissolving, she observed:

> Being in a context where the message corresponds to the broader situation, this offers an explanation to people. But it also gives people an explanation for gross inequality. If you're able to earn R100,000 per month and others have nothing, you feel there is destiny and purpose. And so you don't have to struggle to reconcile this with the existence of inequality. You'd feel guilty if you used it all yourself, but here you are giving some of your money away. It is the church that uses it. The middle classes are removed from their own societies – or the societies to which they formerly belonged – and are not aware of the extent of poverty and marginalization out there, or the scale of injustice. Certainly, few of my students know about this, so one can assume that the people at the church are similar.[104]

James also observes that there is something of a contradiction between the entrepreneurial, individualistic values preached by the churches and the fact that so many of their black congregants have been beneficiaries of government policies geared to producing a black middle class. Indeed, she also reports that, while some pastors she interviewed were highly critical of the manner in which policies such as BEE had benefited only a few and were scornful of those who had used political position for personal benefit, they simultaneously spoke with admiration of businessmen who had come into riches quickly.

Even so, for all the criticism which pastors might direct at politicians, they proclaim a separation of the worlds of faith and politics: the emphasis upon personal transformation does not translate into a call for more far-reaching social and economic transformation. This is a distinction that has been aided by the transition from apartheid. The Pentecostal tradition in South Africa was founded upon African reaction to white domination of the mainline churches: the Pentecostal churches were among the first to desegregate their congregations. But their socially conservative orientation was to place them in opposition to the socially liberal foundations of South Africa's democratic constitution. This would provoke the entry of the African Christian Democratic Party into the political arena in order to promote Christian values. Yet the party's failure to make any significant electoral impact can only have strengthened the existing predisposition of the charismatic churches to concentrate on their more worldly engagements with the alleviation of poverty and its associated social ills rather than engaging in more searching political critique. On the other hand, this does not seem to mean that individual Pentecostals are less interested in politics than other Christians, nor that they have 'secluded themselves from the everyday culture of complaint about conditions and delivery'.[105] By virtue of their beliefs, they may be less disposed to political activism, but it would not seem to make them wholly immune from political protest. It is accordingly to the politics of the black middle class that we now turn.

8

The politics of the black middle class

Reflections about the middle class in South Africa repeat classic debates in social science. One of the most famous proponents of the middle class was Aristotle, who associated its dominance with the good society. In modern times, his views were foundational for Seymour Martin Lipset's hugely influential thesis that increases in the wealth and education of the lower classes were supportive of democracy in that they were likely to reduce their commitment to extreme ideologies.[1] While Lipset's argument paved the way for extensive work on the relationships between democracy and development, an alternative tradition challenged any assumption of an inherent predisposition of the middle class to democracy. Hence, Barrington Moore argued in his famous comparative study of modern revolutions that while the emergence of a bourgeoisie was a *necessary* condition for democracy, it was by no means *sufficient*.[2] Subsequently, his work has provided the inspiration for major studies of democratisation in the global South. Rueschemeyer and his associates (among others) have contended that the political role played by middle classes is shaped by particular interests and historical situations, often dictated by the availability of class alliances, whether with elites, working classes or peasantries.[3]

Relating these debates about the middle class and democracy to contemporary South Africa is not straightforward, simply because the issue has not previously been discussed systematically. What we have, instead of anything constituting a 'debate', are three broad propositions. The first, emanating from both historical and liberation movement literature, is the familiar argument that the development of the black middle class was stunted by the state under segregation and apartheid, and that in consequence it threw in its lot with the working class under the leadership of the ANC in the struggle for democracy. What follows, in consequence, is a second position: that, in essence, the black middle class is tied to the apron strings of the ANC. In other words, the contemporary growth, security and prospects of the black middle class are a product of historical attachment to the ANC, as well as of post-1994 ANC policies such as affirmative action and BEE. Thirdly, in an echo of Lipset, there follows a further proposition that the steady growth of the black middle class is generally 'a good thing' and will contribute to the consolidation of democracy and greater political diversity. From this perspective, it has been regularly argued that the black middle class is a particular target of the Democratic Alliance (DA), the major party of opposition, as well as various other parties created by black leadership to challenge the ANC, including the United Democratic Movement (UDM, 1997); the Congress of the People (COPE, 2009); Agang SA (2013); and the Economic Freedom Fighters (EFF, 2013).

In what follows, the three propositions are elaborated, and their overlaps and differences discussed.

Proposition 1: the black middle class was a force for democracy before the year 1994

The argument that the black middle class was overwhelmingly a progressive force in the struggle for liberation and democracy is writ large in the literature, and there is no intention here of contesting it. In reaction to military defeat by colonising forces, a small but politically conscious black middle class played the key role in forming the ANC in 1912 to protest against wide-ranging, highly oppressive impositions of imperial and settler colonial authority. Thereafter, although there is much debate about the relative political weight of different classes within the organisation, it is widely recognised that the smallness of the black middle class, its limited access to property, and its lack of opportunities for upward social mobility because of various racial restrictions imposed by white regimes, thrust it into alliance with a burgeoning urbanised working class, thereby transforming the ANC into a mass movement during the turbulent 1950s.

There is no denying the leadership offered by an emergent middle-class intelligentsia. Originally, diverse professionals, ministers of religion and writers such as Pixley Seme, J.T. Jabavu and Sol Plaatje played a critical role in articulating black grievances and subsequently founding the ANC. In later years, their baton was taken up by what would now be termed intellectual activists, such as the lawyers Nelson Mandela and Oliver Tambo, who radicalised the party's leadership, extended its roots into the working class, and transformed it into a mass movement capable of posing a major challenge to the apartheid regime. Thereafter, the ANC did maintain something of a tradition of internal debate. But, for many individuals, their commitment to liberation came at a cost. Pressure, formal and informal, upon intellectuals to follow the 'party line' led, in the words of one sceptical black intellectual, to their 'moral philosophy' being 'forever closed'. Their political discourse became 'ritualised' and propagandistic, and any pretence they might have had to intellectual independence was replaced by a slavish devotion to liberation movement ideology.[4] Unsurprisingly, when serious theoretical and political differences between black intellectuals did occur, between nationalists and communists, between leaderships and dissidents, and between the ANC–SACP and minority political traditions, they too often assumed the form of 'social combat' rather than 'a culture of careful discourse requiring premises to be defended by logic and reasoning'.[5]

It was only after the replacement of the conservative 'old guard' by the Youth League radicals in 1949 that the ANC launched out onto the road to becoming a mass movement, and that the nationalist cross-class alliance seriously took shape. Yet black middle-class support for the liberation project was never unanimous nor unambiguous. A first theme in this regard is that, especially after the clampdown on the liberation movements in the early 1960s, many if not most middle-class blacks were, if not actually accepting of defeat, then acquiescent in their racial subordination – a situation that was to be subject to a major generational challenge from the rise of Black Consciousness and the Soweto revolt among young students. Yet another theme is that several middle-class elements, in their ambition for improvement or advantage, served on various official structures, such as municipal advisory bodies, thereby accepting if not actually endorsing their subordinate racial status. This acceptance of subordination was to be writ large by the participation of middle-class elements in the bantustan or homeland project. Certainly, in retrospect, we may agree that much of this involvement was pragmatic rather than ideological for all but a particular coterie of leaders committed to ethnic nationalism. Even so, although middle-class involvement in homeland governance was heavily subject to chiefly authority, the bantustan project – as a conservative bulwark against the forces of liberation – could not have succeeded as much as it did without this participation. In short, middle-class involvement in official structures under apartheid always demonstrated a marked political ambiguity towards the liberation project as envisaged by the ANC.

None of these qualifications refutes the major narrative of the black middle class under apartheid as a leading component of the liberation movement. Nonetheless, they most certainly complicate it. A significant aspect of South African history is the way white governments sought to capitalise on the 'respectability' of the black middle class, recognising it as a basis for the forging of conservative alliances against radical elements and protest from below. This was to gather momentum from the mid-1970s onwards. The major increase in the provision of education to black children, in the access of black students to 'white' universities and technikons, the growing pace of black upward advance into occupational spheres previously dominated by whites, and the relaxation of restrictions upon African business, all played their part in what John Kane-Berman has described as a 'silent revolution'.[6] This shift was cautiously backed by large-scale capital, which saw the extension of property rights, training and professional employment opportunities to increased numbers of blacks as strengthening the stake of a subaltern middle class in the capitalist system. Eventually, of course, as the liberation movement gained traction, large-scale capital (alongside progressive elements within the white community) was to play a major role in forging a democratic transition, which accepted the fundamentals of the market economy. Such an outcome registered a defeat for the more radical wing of the ANC. While this turn of events was often wrapped up in the pretence that the democratic phase of the 'national democratic revolution' (NDR) heralded a transition to socialism,[7] in reality it provided the foundations for a middle-class democracy under the leadership of a party-state bourgeoisie.

Proposition 2: as the product of the ANC, the black middle class is also its proponent

Despite its more rapid development in the latter years of apartheid, the size of the black middle class at the dawn of democracy was still remarkably modest. In many ways the black middle class as we know it today is the creation of the ANC in government. This it has done by using its 'capture of state power' to implement policies which, whether by intention or simply outcome, facilitate black upward mobility.

Firstly, in line with the notion of the 'national democratic revolution', the ANC has 'deployed' its chosen personnel to key positions in state and society. In theory, the ANC selects individuals for positions not merely according to their dedication to revolutionary duties but also according to their qualifications and abilities. In practice, the outcomes of deployment have become increasingly problematic – for, at all levels of the state, a marked tendency to prioritise loyalty to the party (or, often, factions within it) over merit has come to predominate; and this has facilitated the rise of patron–client relations constructed around political control over the allocation of state resources. In short, deployment has emerged as a major instrument for individuals to manipulate opportunities provided by the public sector, to accumulate wealth and ascend the class structure.

The second instrument of class formation has been affirmative action. The outcome has been most dramatic in the public sector: today, even the upper reaches of the public service are largely black. In pursuing affirmative action, the ANC has massively widened access for its own political constituency to state employment on terms and levels of remuneration that appear relatively generous compared with those offered in the private sector.[8] For instance, a survey by Naledi, COSATU's research arm, reported in 2006 that the average salaries of the federation's members who worked in the public sector were very substantially higher than those paid to members in the private sector.[9] Furthermore, public-sector employment appears to have offered greater security of employment compared with the private sector, where employment levels are subject to the vicissitudes of the market. Unsurprisingly, the ANC reaps the political rewards. As one professional remarked to Amuzweni Ngoma:

I am ANC to the core … I have seen how my life has changed for the better thanks to the ANC. Some of the policies of the ANC … I am not saying that they are perfect. They've got their shortcomings, similar to every other political organization out there. However, be that as it may, I still accept that for me the ANC is the best thing ever happen to me. Reason is, I didn't have to apply to any minister to gain access to my university of choice, the policies of the ANC are of such a nature that they promote the employment of black people … Be it on merit or not merit doesn't matter to me. The fact of the matter is that due to the policies of the ANC our people can earn a salary.[10]

Meanwhile, of course, the private sector is subject to wide-ranging state pressures, legal and otherwise, to implement 'employment equity'.

Thirdly, the ANC has massively increased educational opportunities for blacks at both secondary and tertiary levels. Two key processes run contiguously. One is an impressive expansion in the absolute number of places for blacks at both state secondary schools and institutions of higher education. The second is that access to these establishments has been significantly widened by the deracialisation of education. Educational opportunity and resources under apartheid were severely skewed by race, massively favouring whites. Now, in formal terms this is no longer so, and the most notable feature of the transformation has been the increased black entry to educational institutions previously reserved wholly or overwhelmingly for whites. The new opportunities greatly increase the chances of educational success, for overall standards and facilities in former black institutions at all levels remain much inferior. This is in part because the educational advantages enjoyed by what were once racially privileged institutions are buttressed by the right to levy and set fees, effectively restricting entry to those who can afford them. The class implications and advantages of attending such schools and universities are so evident that black parents display enormous determination to meet the costs involved and even, where necessary, to buck the lottery of the public school system by sending their children to the steadily expanding private educational sector. In sum, especially given the overall disappointing results of the public school system in former 'black' areas, schools and higher education institutions that have been able to capitalise upon a legacy of racial privilege have emerged as key sites for the production and reproduction of class advantage.

Finally, the most explicit strategy of class formation pursued by the ANC has been the pursuit of black economic empowerment (BEE). If the impact of affirmative action was to be most advanced within the public sector, the objective of BEE – as it was formally established during the years of the Mbeki presidency – was to challenge the domination by whites of South Africa's corporate structure and promote the development of a black capitalist class, thereby bridging the post-1994 separation of (black) political and (white) economic power. Suffice it to say that the results have been mixed and, in many ways, disappointing for the government (not to mention often embarrassing). Share ownership of the majority of large and medium-sized firms still remains overwhelmingly white. Nonetheless, the parastatals – sites of Afrikaner power in years past – have become largely blackened, and have provided an important launch pad for ambitious individuals to transfer into the private sector. Concurrently, the lily-white racial hue of the topmost corporate ranks has been leavened by the politically leveraged development of a small but enormously rich black elite, alongside an increase in the proportion of black managers, as companies have come under pressure to render BEE more 'broadly based'. In short, even if BEE has, in the view of many, facilitated the rise of 'crony capitalism', it has also played a major role in class formation, and this redounds to the ANC's benefit. 'I'm voting for the ANC,' remarked a black engineering consultant before the 2014 election:

> I am a beneficiary of ANC policy. This is a view one can hold whether you work in corporate South Africa or as an entrepreneur – I am a beneficiary, directly. And even considering where we come from, I don't think, even with my combination of skills and call it the luck I have, the white Nationalist government would have plucked me from wherever I am and encouraged me to actually participate, and to create an enabling environment for me to participate in the mainstream economy.[11]

Another black corporate manager admitted after the election that, although he did not see much to choose from between the ANC and DA, 'I voted for business. It was more business related, I was like "between the two parties, really?" It boils down to race in this country. One party (the DA) is still going to see me as black. Another party (ANC) is going to say "let's support you in policy". It's not really implemented that way, but somehow the thought is there.'[12]

The argument that follows, broadly put, is that the black elite and middle class now in positions of power, privilege and profit are not likely to bite the hand of the party-state that feeds them. The more dependent they are upon the ruling party for their welfare, the more they are likely to support it. This view finds endorsement in the work of Collette Schulz-Herzenberg, who in her detailed analysis of voter attitudes between 1994 and 2009 found that the proportion of ANC 'partisans' among black owner/employer and professional/supervisory occupational categories had increased as blacks moved upwards: 'core support for the ANC has begun to emerge from the material beneficiaries of a post-apartheid order, shown in the increases in levels and strength of party support among the black middle classes'.[13]

From this it would seem to follow that the different segments of the 'party-state bourgeoisie' remain close to the ANC as the party of liberation, the party from whose strategies they have benefited. As many of them are 'deployees' of the ruling party, the upper level of 'state managers' – not just those around the president and provincial premiers but the general corps of senior civil servants (10,600 in 2010) and senior executives in parastatals – can be assumed to be broadly united by their loyalty to the ANC (even if they are disunited by their belonging to different factions of the party). Much the same can be said of what elsewhere has been termed a 'civil petty bourgeoisie', comprising members of parliament and provincial legislatures, middle management within the public sector (21,000 of them in national and provincial governments in 2010), the much larger mass of lower-level public employees in non-manual occupations, as well as black professionals and semi-professionals (notably teachers and nurses). Certainly, it is now widely known that membership of the ANC is regarded by many aspirants as a necessary step to gaining entry to the public service.[14] Even within the private sector, many black professionals, such as independently employed accountants and lawyers, incline strongly towards the ANC, not merely because they receive commissions from state bodies but because they may need political backing to confront perceived racism within their professional bodies. During the 2014 election, the ANC regarded such people as its natural allies and sought to organise them into a Progressive Professionals Forum.[15]

Overall, this is clearly an extremely heterogeneous category. Nonetheless, as with 'state managers', it is likely that the majority of professionals are loyal to the ANC, having benefited variously from equity employment and deployment. This does not mean that their support for the ANC is uncritical. 'Party politics ... can be quite unbecoming, can be quite nasty,' remarked one professional. Even so, the ANC was the one party that was pursuing policies she wanted to see implemented, although she also admitted that it had 'screwed up'. 'It's the best option we have at the moment ... They are the best option.'[16] 'For the moment', indicated another, who felt that the 'ANC is under siege' from the media, 'I will support the ANC.' With the breakaway from the ANC of splinter movements like COPE and the EFF, there was a danger of fragmentation of the black vote: 'The net effect [would be] the same as that desired by the National Party when they promoted tribalism, its division and conquer. So I will stay in the ANC, until I emigrate' [*Laughter*].[17]

The political orientations of the 'corporate black bourgeoisie', composed of those who have significant shareholdings in major companies or who are employed at executive or managerial level in the large corporations dominating the private sector, may be more difficult to decipher. Overall, despite official lamentations that the private sector lags behind in its enthusiasm for 'transformation', this segment has grown significantly since 1994, with blacks now constituting nearly half the number of professionals.[18] While the black senior executives and corporate managers may regard themselves as relatively autonomous of the ANC, the steady growth of this segment is a product of the democratic era. For a start, significant numbers of them will have previously served within government or the parastatals, and will have maintained connections with bureaucracies relevant to the companies for which they now work. This in turn reflects the interest of large corporations in accessing 'political connectivity' as well as their need to transform their demographic profile in conformity with official demands. Granted, there are some black businesspersons who are highly critical of the manner in which the state relates to the corporate sector. If so, they largely keep their criticisms to themselves. Odd exceptions, like Herman Mashaba – who announced he was joining the DA after the 2014 election – are likely to have steered clear of or been bypassed by state patronage.[19]

There is, finally, a black business and trading bourgeoisie, combining a mix of owners and managers of medium and small businesses. The diversity of this grouping is indicated by the fact that, at its lower levels, black operators merge into the lower regions of the informal sector of the economy. Their activities often take place outside the tax net and sometimes (according to popular legend) are spiced up by involvement in protectionism and criminality (the taxi industry being a particular example). Historically, this grouping was heavily constrained by apartheid limitations imposed upon black activity in business and, even today, given lack of capital, skills and training, it continues at a major disadvantage relative to white-owned small businesses. Unsurprisingly, therefore, since 1994 black business has become increasingly vocal and active in lobbying the ANC to promote its interests, notably under the Zuma government. Indeed, in mid-2015 it claimed a considerable victory when the Department of Trade and Industry gave notice of intention to amend BEE scorecards by downgrading the value of broad-based and employee share-ownership schemes in favour of a major upgrading of the value of individual share ownership, a move designed to promote 'active' over 'passive' black investment. The motivation behind this was said to be the need to speed up the creation of black industrialists, but it was met with criticisms that it would take BEE back to the earlier phase of elite enrichment. More particularly, the projected change in policy was greeted with cries of anguish from large corporates, which in recent years had rendered their empowerment deals increasingly 'broad-based' in conformity with existing official policy, and now faced having their BEE status hugely downgraded. With the threat of a corporate revolt, trade and industry minister Rob Davies caved in, publicly regretting his 'mistake' and promising that firms' existing BEE ratings would not be affected. Although they were thwarted in the short term, the incident highlighted how heavily black business continues to depend upon its relations with the party-state, notably in relying upon concessions and contracts from government at all three levels, and from public-sector entities more generally.[20]

The fact that the class structure of South Africa has massively changed during the democratic era has been warmly welcomed by ANC-aligned intellectuals. Many of them continue to celebrate this success and to denigrate the political opposition as hostile to progressive change and as politically reactionary. Ideologically turgid analyses of the progress of and obstacles to the 'national democratic revolution' continue to characterise many ANC discussion documents, COSATU statements and SACP publications, along with strident defences of ANC policy and strong attacks upon the government's opponents in the popular media. Yet, amid vociferous backing for the ANC from many black commentators, there are some even from the ANC's own ranks who recognise that welcome progress has come at a considerable cost. 'We used to discuss *Capital* the whole night and solve problems on the spot,' remarked one comrade to Leslie Dikeni. 'Nowadays, comrades have changed, they do not even want to hear about Marxism and Leninism. Everyone is working for companies and drives BMWs. These days it's everyone for himself. I have also changed. What can I do?'[21]

The hollowing out or dissolution of liberation movement ideology under the corrosive pressures of possessive individualism may be the least of the ANC's problems. The more pressing issue is the political ambiguity of the processes of black elite and middle-class formation. This has been explored in a particularly insightful analysis by Joel Netshitenzhe, who was close to Thabo Mbeki during his presidency. Netshitenzhe's starting point is that the advance of the black middle sector is something of which the ANC should be justly proud. 'Such progress – and the fact that the Black middle strata have been the most visible beneficiaries of the project of social transformation – should of course be celebrated.' Nonetheless, this welcome social advance has been accompanied by the 'sins of incumbency'.

As a consequence of white domination and colonialism, black bene-ficiaries of ANC rule aspire to standards of living that are associated with whites and that are 'artificially high compared to today's global middle class'. In pursuit of non-racial equality, the black middle and upper classes seek to achieve the standard of living of the metropolis, 'and many aspire to do so in one swoop'. The 'burgeoning black middle and upper strata' do not possess the historical assets of their white counterparts, and they have large nuclear and extended families to support. As a result, many are extraordinarily financially insecure, and 'resort to short-termism in the conduct of business and material self-advancement'. Unsurprisingly, many strive to obtain the resources they need 'by hook or by crook'. They lobby for positions in the civil service, view party position as the route to wealth, misuse state or trade union resources, and exploit political contacts to acquire tenders. The outcome is that, unlike the middle strata in 'mature' class societies, they are not guided so much by pride in their professions or in shaping positive value systems in society as by 'survival and climbing up the steep social ladder'.

The cost for the party is incalculable. Intra-party patronage and corruption take root; 'a toxic leadership begets toxic members'; and a nationalism of convenient victimhood arises to hide incompetence and greed. 'Because you were oppressed, you can mess up, steal and plunder, and shout racism when challenged.' Overall, the sins of incumbency pose major existential questions for the ANC, SACP and Tripartite Alliance. Have they not become so embedded in the 'mainstream of political patronage that they are in fact testing the limits of self-liquidation'? Will the class dynamics associated with the sins of incumbency allow for organisational reform? Can the ANC continue to enjoy popular legitimacy and exercise authority when it is living in a glasshouse? Netshitenzhe gave no answer to his own highly charged questions, but his doubts about whether the ANC is capable of moral and political regeneration were laid plain for all to see.[22]

Yet things do change. It may be that, if and when the state begins to run out of money, the ANC government will have little option but to implement far-reaching economic reforms in the interests of political survival. Such reforms, which might take place under a more business-aligned administration (particularly, perhaps, if Cyril Ramaphosa succeeds to the presidency), could involve the privatisation of poorly performing parastatals and the implementation of stricter budgetary control.[23] In particular, a financially stretched ANC government might feel compelled to squeeze the public sector, either by clamping down on salary increases or even resorting to retrenchments. In so doing, it would risk alienating the self-same black middle class that its own policies have created.

In any case, even while the prospect of middle-class employment becoming more precarious in the public sector represents a looming threat to the ANC, it is already facing the reality of greater black dissidence as the black middle class consolidates itself and becomes more diverse.

Proposition 3: the greater diversity of the black middle class is contributing to the consolidation of democracy

It is not without reason that the ANC is becoming increasingly nervous about the reliability of black middle-class support. It is in relation to the immediacy of party politics that potential black middle-class disengagement from the ANC is most widely discussed, but ultimately this is determined by wider factors of social and political change. Let us take each in turn.

The black middle class and party politics

Prior to the May 2014 general elections, it was widely suggested that the political alignment of the black middle class to the ANC was under stress, and that opposition parties were targeting it as an attractive constituency. Chief among these was the DA, which, having gobbled up remnants from the former National Party since 1994,[24] has been eager to rebut attacks that stereotype it as little more than a front for white interests. In recent years, it has vigorously promoted its non-racial credentials in a manner that, though designed to appeal to black voters more widely, seems particularly geared to wooing the black middle class. Under Helen Zille's leadership, the DA proclaimed its support for 'broad-based' BEE to address the legacy of racial inequality, while indicating that it was highly critical of the manner in which the ANC has implemented it.[25] Unsurprisingly, this created considerable controversy within DA ranks: its right wing complained that any embrace of policies involving recognition of racial categories constituted an abandonment of the party's liberal heritage. Zille's response was that social engineering of racial redress to counter the apartheid legacy was fully compatible with the party's mission.[26] For some observers, this debate implied that, for all its efforts to bridge the racial divide, the DA was unlikely to expand its support among black voters significantly.[27] This also seemed to be the view of Mamphela Ramphele, who – deeply critical of the ANC's performance in power – had initially chosen to launch her own party, Agang SA, in the lead-up to the 2014 election, rather than throwing in her lot with the DA, with which she had little ideological difference. In some quarters this was thought to be a shrewd move, and Agang was hailed as an attractive rival for disaffected members of the black middle class.[28] But it was not long before Agang more or less self-destructed as a result of its leader's spectacularly inept politicking. Having responded positively (and unilaterally) to an invitation that she become the DA's 'presidential candidate' for the election, Ramphele withdrew from the arrangement almost immediately afterwards when she found she had left her party followers behind her.

The view that the black middle class has become more politically diverse is backed by the findings of a survey conducted by Lawrence Schlemmer in 2003. These acknowledged that 'the race-based transformation policies of the ANC [had] created an exceptionally strong bond between it and the African core middle class'.[29] Nonetheless, they also indicated that the black middle class expressed numerous misgivings about the ANC's performance in power, with some respondents indicating support for other parties. Schlemmer concluded that their political attitudes were pragmatic, and exhibited 'anything other than a consistent, solidly based, and … durable preference'. Even so, because of the social distance between the black middle class and their white counterparts, 'the area of least convergence between the African and white middle classes [was] that of party politics'. This was linked to a widespread belief among members of the black middle class that white wealth was the product of a racist past and that, consequently, the position and privileges of the white middle class were illegitimate.[30]

Schlemmer's findings are now dated, but their thrust finds support in later work. Robert Mattes, interpreting AfroBarometer survey data in 2015, reports widening intra-black class differences in respect of electoral participation.[31] Individuals within the black middle class were less likely than other black survey respondents to have voted in the 2009 election, to have identified with any political party, and to have identified with the ANC specifically (this being most marked among the young). The black middle class also proved less likely than others to have contacted elected or government officials, or to have taken part in community action or protest.

Similar findings were reported by David Everatt after conducting focus group discussions among black middle-class participants. These indicated that black voters with relatively high incomes were looking for a party that would defend their middle-class status. They recognised that the ANC had played a major enabling role in their lives. Nonetheless, they complained about high levels of corruption, broken promises, and failures of service delivery, while simultaneously worrying about how the growing militancy of the poor might impinge upon their security. However, while guarded approval was extended to the DA for demanding accountability from the ANC, few would consider voting for it nationally, and, if they did so, it would be primarily to register discontent. There was resentment at being regarded as 'voting fodder' by the ANC, and a growing willingness, as one participant put it, to 'jump ship'. But, without any serious political choice apart from the DA on offer, the major alternative was simply that of abstaining from the polls.[32]

Mattes concludes that there is little to support the argument that the ANC has created a party-state bourgeoisie. 'South Africa's emerging black middle class are no less *loyal* … to the new, democratic South Africa. While they are less likely [than the poor] to *voice* their dissent, at least in terms of active protest action, they also show some limited signs of *exiting* from the electoral process and the larger democratic process between elections.'[33] However, this finding is problematic, as AfroBarometer data do not distinguish between the occupational backgrounds of survey respondents. Note, further, that both Mattes and Everatt refer only to what is termed here the 'core' (or upper) black middle class, and make no reference to the more extensive lower black middle class, whose politics may be different, being influenced by high levels of trade union membership. In contrast, I would argue that while the ANC certainly has good reason to be worried about the potential for greater loss of black middle-class support, this is most likely to occur among those elements of the class who are increasingly distant from the party-state: those working in the private sector, the media or civil society.[34]

It is interesting to relate this discussion to the course and outcome of the 2014 general election. During the campaign there was substantial indication that the ANC was worried by the threat presented by the DA and Agang to its support among the black middle class. Concerned that many traditional supporters were embarrassed by the image of President Jacob Zuma, party leaders in Gauteng appealed to former President Thabo Mbeki to re-enter active politics and campaign among black middle-class voters.[35] Although Gwede Mantashe, secretary-general of the ANC, expressed the national leadership's displeasure at the affront this represented to Zuma, it was widely accepted within the party that black middle-class 'grumblings' over governmental inefficiency and corruption were widespread, and that this was especially the case in Gauteng, where many among the black middle class identified with Mbeki.[36]

This should not surprise us. When, after Mbeki's ejection from the state presidency in September 2008, various of his supporters formed the Congress of the People (COPE), it was commonly predicted that the new party would attract the black middle class. This persuaded the ANC to deploy huge resources to counteract the threat. Even so, COPE still took some 7 per cent of the national vote (a not unworthy achievement for a newly launched party). Subsequently, COPE fell victim to perpetual leadership squabbles, and failed to pack any significant electoral punch in May 2014, gaining less than 1 per cent of the national vote. But its performance in 2009 underlined the threat which dissent within ANC ranks represents to the party's hegemony, especially if this were to be channelled into a wider coalition pact. Although the majority of the electorate are poor and black, the ANC's electoral hegemony since 1994 has been founded upon its claim to constitute a home for all races and classes. Accordingly, the drift of black middle-class support to parties of opposition would represent a major symbolic defeat, of far wider import than the mere loss of votes.

With Agang virtually imploding before the election, the major threat to the ANC's black middle-class vote remained the DA. After its disastrous and short-lived nomination of Agang's Mamphela Ramphele as its presidential candidate, the DA recovered to mount a vigorous campaign to attract black voters. Carefully choreographed rallies with party leaders flanked by enthusiastic black supporters, all clad in the party's bright blue T-shirts boasting the party logo, were matched by loud insistence that the DA's predecessors had played a major role in the liberation struggle. Interestingly, too, the DA in its campaigning contrasted the liabilities of the Zuma era with the more favourable records of the Mandela and Mbeki presidencies. It also came up with a remarkably effective black leader in the form of Mmusi Maimane as its front in Gauteng, where he ran an Obama-like revivalist campaign.[37] Nonetheless, while the DA was to improve its overall proportion of the vote (up nearly 8 per cent from 2009 to a total of just over 22 per cent in the national election), its performance among black voters in 2014 remains difficult to assess.

The DA claims that it secured some 760,000 black votes out of its total of 4,089,215. It improved its showing in the provincial contests in each and every province. Its worst performance was in KwaZulu-Natal, where its proportion of the vote increased from 9 to nearly 13 per cent; its best performance, relatively speaking, was in Northern Cape, where it leapt from 12.5 to 24 per cent. Above all, it could be pleased with the leap in its proportion of the vote in Gauteng, from 22 per cent in 2009 to nearly 31 per cent in 2014; here the DA made some significant inroads into more prosperous areas within Soweto such as Diepkloof. In turn, there were across-the-board increases in the DA's shares of the vote in the metropolitan areas, from 19 per cent in Buffalo City (East London) to 60 per cent in Cape Town. It was particularly gratified by gaining 40 per cent of the vote in Nelson Mandela Bay (Port Elizabeth), a result which signalled that the ANC stood in danger of losing control of the city council in the 2016 local elections.

The DA's performance in the metros suggests that it gained increased support from black voters whose personal or familial circumstances had improved materially and otherwise since 1994. It also benefited from the collapse of COPE, and it may even have gained grudging support from some who would have voted for Agang had it not run its campaign so spectacularly badly. All the same, the focus groups conducted for this study indicated that black professionals continued to remain shy of backing the DA. For all their growing alienation from the ANC, deep cynicism about incumbent politicians and wish for greater accountability from the government, they were wary of cutting their links with the ANC tradition. Some suggested, therefore, that they might vote for a black-led party like the UDM, which had emerged out of the ANC. In so doing, they would be registering a protest, while simultaneously signalling their willingness to return to the fold if the ANC's performance improved. Yet few gave an indication that they were ready to transfer support to the DA.

For many, the issue simply boiled down to one of race. Interestingly, there was substantial recognition that the DA might well prove capable of offering better service delivery than the ANC. Indeed, one entrepreneur indicated wryly that a DA (or, what he termed, a 'white') government might address the needs of the masses and prove better at quelling discontent than the ANC, because it would live in fear of the black majority.[38] Generally, however, there remained a strong feeling that the DA was ultimately a vehicle of white minority interests, and that in the Western Cape particularly it was perpetuating racial inequality. 'I would vote for the DA if they were

212

much cleaner on their transformation stance,' asserted one professional. 'Unfortunately they are not.'[39]

The subsequent election of Mmusi Maimane to the leadership of the DA suggests a concerted pitch by the party for the black vote, and promises a significant challenge to the ANC in the local government elections in 2016. Maimane himself constitutes a considerable attraction to a younger, 'born-free' generation of blacks. Born in Dobsonville, Soweto, to an ANC-supporting family, the product of a Model C school, and in possession of three university degrees (UNISA, Wits and Wales), he has enjoyed a meteoric rise within the DA, to which at the time of his victory in the leadership election he had belonged for only four years. Young and energetic, married to a white woman with whom he has two young children, he is also a pastor of the Liberty Church's Discovery branch in Cosmo City (a new multiclass black suburb on the edge of Johannesburg). Although evangelical rather than conventionally charismatic, the Liberty Church's teachings are deeply conservative and its ministers spend much time preaching the evils of adultery, pornography and homosexuality. While Maimane himself has been explicit about the supremacy of the constitution over his personal beliefs, his support for a referendum on the death penalty and his personal opposition to same-sex marriage during his leadership campaign indicate the likelihood of clashes ahead with the DA's classic liberalism and an appeal to black social conservatism.[40] Certainly, there is much in him which may appeal to significant elements within the black middle class whose loyalty to the ANC is wavering.

For its part, the DA exudes enormous confidence that Maimane mania is having a marked effect on its fortunes. On the basis of the party's latest tracking polls, the DA's Paul Boughey asserted in mid-2015 that Maimane's leadership constituted a 'tipping point' for the DA among black voters favourably inclined to the party. His election 'fully legitimated' their choice, and had 'escalated' the potential swing of black votes to the party. 'We have never polled this high ... Mmusi has truly given us momentum.' Three thousand people had turned up to hear him speak at the University of Cape Town, far exceeding the size of the venue, and the DA was 'seeing this kind of response everywhere'. At the same time, Boughey recognised that Maimane faced the challenge of ensuring not only that black middle-class voters abandoned the ANC, but that they did not shift to the EFF.[41]

The only other significant alternative on offer for black voters in 2014 (except for the declining Inkatha Freedom Party in KwaZulu-Natal and the usual smattering of small parties) was the Economic Freedom Fighters (EFF), which was established by the former Youth League leader Julius Malema after his expulsion from the ANC in 2012. Centring its support on striking mineworkers on the platinum belt in North West and in Malema's home province of Limpopo, the EFF put forward a militantly radical-nationalist programme designed to appeal, especially, to youthful unemployed blacks, the marginalised and the impoverished. Once the election campaign began in earnest, it cast its net much wider, appealing also to professionals frustrated by their inability to rise in the workplace. Nevertheless, while it swiftly acquired the support of certain student elements (some of them migrants from the Youth League), and while it gained the backing of a handful of high-profile professionals and black businesspersons who had fallen out with the ANC and who remained distrustful of the DA, its support seems to have been overwhelmingly rooted among its original target group.[42] Even so, Malema's populism may serve as a serious counter to the more measured appeal of Maimane, and could well mop up lower-middle-class support attracted by a radical-nationalist programme (with a strong element as well of Africanism blurring with anti-whiteism).

More detailed analysis is required to confirm these ruminations about how the black middle class voted in the 2014 elections, and what their longer-term implications may be. It is important to stress that the question of whether the black middle class will abandon the ANC is logically quite separate from that of whether greater diversity will contribute to the consolidation of democracy. Far too often these questions are confused, the implication being that only when black middle-class voters cut their links to the ANC will they mature as democrats. While this may be a defensible proposition, it is only that, based as it is upon the conventional view that for a genuinely competitive party system to emerge there needs to be an erosion of ANC dominance and the genuine prospect of regular alternations in power. It will take far more than the defection of the black middle class from the ANC to promote a more democratic polity, not least because democracy requires much more than just competition between parties.

On the march? The political diversity of the black middle class
In so far as the new black middle class is consolidating, it is simultaneously becoming more confident. This suggests it is developing a greater capacity for reflection and for cutting its umbilical cord to the ANC. In the wake of the 2014 election, four factors seem particularly pertinent.

Firstly, while the most powerful segments of the black elite and middle class remain strongly aligned to the ANC's party-state, the black middle class as a whole is becoming more heterogeneous. However much they come out of an ANC background, many younger black middle-class voters are becoming increasingly critical of the performance of the ruling party. They may or may not choose to gravitate to the DA under Maimane's leadership, even if it does seem likely that black middle-class resistance to the DA's blandishments will weaken. But beyond the immediate realm of party politics, what is more important is the noise made by a growing legion of black middle-class commentators who contribute energetically to the public discourse about anything and everything as editors, journalists, anchormen, commentators, letter writers, and bloggers through the established and social media.

Just a few years ago, William Gumede and Leslie Dikeni lamented 'the retreat of the intellectuals'. After 1994, their narrative went, many intellectuals previously engaged in oppositional activity joined the new government; many who had led progressive NGOs and trade unions joined the civil service; and the universities began to decline as sites of intellectual engagement.[43] This led to a massive silencing of contrary opinions. Beyond such factors, a more fundamental concern was that the legacy and practice of the ANC as a liberation movement had smothered black intellectuals and dissuaded them from engaging in criticism. Critics of the party were labelled as 'unpatriotic' and 'unAfrican', or vilified as dupes of imperial powers or former colonialists. Any criticism of ANC policies was dismissed as disloyal. Uncritical deference to the leader (at the time, Thabo Mbeki) undermined any consideration of alternative ideas, and the ANC's continued commitment to the 'national democratic revolution' became 'a substitute for thinking about solutions to the problems of our politics'. In contrast, the question that really mattered was 'how to come to terms with the market, in new and innovative ways, and how to bring about a quality democracy'.[44]

Although there was substance to Gumede and Dikeni's argument, it was nonetheless overdrawn. There has never been a uniformity of black opinion. Today, certainly, there is a cacophony of black voices, ranging in their stridency across the political and economic spectrum. There are incessant critiques of the moral degeneration of the ANC. Black celebrations of the market vie with demands for socialism and the developmental state. ANC policy positions get torn apart. Black women decry the patriarchy they see as still dominant within the ruling party. Such criticisms made by black

215

commentators hurt the ANC far more than if they were made by the DA or other opposition parties, and offer more punch precisely because of where they have come from. In a notorious attack upon such critics, Jacob Zuma once dismissed them as 'clever blacks'.[45] Reaction among black intellectuals to his epithet ranged from hilarity to scorn, and black cleverness has continued unabated.

One recent development of significance is the increasing urgency of critique by 'born-frees'. Much of this discourse revolves around the issue of black identity. In 2015 this took the form of the 'Rhodes must fall' campaign at the University of Cape Town, which rapidly spread to Rhodes University in Grahamstown, and more generally extended to attacks upon 'institutional racism' at the historically white universities.[46] As Max du Preez sagely commented, these campus campaigns reflected a much wider middle-class rage among black professionals, managers and white-collar workers about felt white racism in the workplace and in society at large. As such, they earned the ANC's approbation and support. However, the risk for the ANC was that the manifest insecurities and frustrations of the 'born-free' black middle-class generation might easily translate into anger about the party's own responsibility for the lack of 'transformation'.

The increasing depth of critical black discourse feeds into a second consideration about the construction of a democratic culture. As an ethos of 'professionalism' (centred on a set of ethical values and practices) takes hold among the black middle class, inclusive of the public sector, individuals are more likely to claim independence from the ANC.[47] Although surveys indicate that the black middle class does not as yet display high levels of involvement in independent civil society, it is inevitable that this will grow. Blacks are making their way forward in key occupations such as accounting and law, and playing a more prominent role in their professional associations. Consequently, just as poor communities across the country are choosing to make their voices heard by means of 'service delivery' protests, so it is likely that members of the black middle class will find common cause with their white counterparts in registering protests about discontents – whether about schooling, transport, municipal service, environmental issues or whatever. In short, even if black middle-class voters choose to stop short of voting against the ANC, we can be assured of their growing demands for accountability – hopefully from the private sector as much as from government.

Thirdly, it is often suggested that there is greater prospect of a fundamental challenge to the ANC from a split within the Tripartite Alliance than from a migration of black voters to the DA. Until fairly recently, commentators have tended to assume that such a split would take the form of the SACP and COSATU peeling off to the left, leaving the ANC behind. This, in turn, would supposedly lead to a significant rearrangement of the party system. According to this scenario, divergence between 'nationalist' and 'socialist' tendencies within the ANC would open up the way for a coalition between 'nationalist' elements of the ANC and pro-market opposition parties, and for 'socialists' to move into a new party of labour. If this were to happen, the further suggestion has been that the large body of the black middle class would stay with the 'nationalist' wing of the ANC, or coalesce with it under whatever label it might choose to operate.[48]

The problem with this scenario is that the looming collapse of the Tripartite Alliance will not occur along these lines. Zuma's ascendancy within the ANC has been associated with the rise of intra-party factionalism, which has far less to do with ideology than access to or distance from the powers and privileges of the party-state. Indeed, 'nationalism' versus 'socialism' does not really enter the equation at all, despite desperate efforts by the SACP leadership, locked into the party-state under Zuma, to portray his government as politically progressive and intent on pursuing the 'national democratic revolution'. Indeed, if anything, a looming struggle within the ANC about who is to succeed Zuma as president is likely to be almost entirely devoid of programmatic appeal. On the surface of things, as deputy president, Cyril Ramaphosa would seem in line to inherit former President Mbeki's support base within the ANC, and might promise something of a rapprochement between the ruling party and large-scale capital, a stronger drive to attract international investment, and the promotion of more efficient government. But Ramaphosa's succession to the presidency is far from guaranteed. Indeed, there is likely to be a strong backlash from the Zuma faction, significantly based upon the ethnic mobilisation of support within KwaZulu-Natal, the ANC's largest and most weighty province.[49] Furthermore, the Zuma faction is likely to draw support from the majority of those within the ANC machinery who have profited significantly from the post-Mbeki party-state.

Any ideological battle will take place within a much diminished COSATU, and to the ANC's left. The expulsion of the National Union of Metalworkers of South Africa (NUMSA) from COSATU, combined with the departure from the federation of Zwelinzima Vavi, its popular former general secretary, points to the likely formation of something of a socialist party to compete with the ANC. From a labour perspective, such a party will base itself on support from the largely private-sector unions, which fall in behind NUMSA, while the major public-sector unions will remain aligned to COSATU and completely dominate it. From a more narrowly party-political perspective, a new socialist party will seek to appeal not only to the black working class and working poor, but also to disaffected elements of the lower middle class.[50]

In view of their dependence upon state employment, their receipt of (on average) better pay and their enjoyment of more secure conditions of work, white-collar members of public-sector unions are more likely to stay within the ANC fold, at least for the moment. In contrast, lower-middle-class white-collar workers in the private sector, who on average receive lower pay and have to endure more precarious employment conditions than their counterparts in the public sector, would seem more disposed to desert the ANC and gravitate to political alternatives. Nonetheless, we should be wary of mechanically assuming that they will necessarily back a militant party of labour rather than opting for political withdrawal, or even backing the DA, whose pro-market policies are touted as reviving the economy.

Finally, more worrying for the ANC is what the future holds for it if – as seems increasingly likely – it has to confront a major financial crisis, forcing it to cut back drastically on the largesse of the party-state and impose retrenchments on the public service. In that case, the ANC may bleed multiclass support to the sort of popular coalition which congregated behind the Movement for Democratic Change in Zimbabwe, which – but for de facto military intervention – all but displaced the Mugabe regime in the election of 2008. Indeed, the fate of Zimbabwe's black middle class offers a salutary story. Having had to overcome a background of massive discrimination under colonialism,[51] it prospered during the first decade and more of independence. It invested very heavily in education, sending children to former white schools and university. It grew comfortable in the civil service, law, medicine, finance and business. It moved into the plush white suburbs, enjoyed all their amenities and reaped the fruits of a consumer society. Then the economy collapsed. While the political elite gained access to foreign currency and continued to enjoy the high life, the middle class sank like a stone. Many fled the country to earn a living and support families left behind. Interestingly, those who clung to their jobs continued to value education. Today, they still scrape and save to pay school fees, hoping beyond hope that a better future awaits their children. Today, their middle-class style of life is about little more than survival.[52]

South Africa remains far from having to face a similar scenario, but warning lights are already flashing. A financial meltdown will bring major fractures within the ANC party-state in its wake, and the party will strain the loyalty of many within the black middle class. The political direction or directions in which the black middle class chooses to go will prove an important factor in shaping the country's future trajectory.

The black middle class and democracy: progression or reaction?

The fundamental issue posed by this chapter is whether an emerging black middle class will be a force for democracy against authoritarianism. Much commentary in South Africa rather uncomplicatedly assumes that a growing black middle class will prove to be politically progressive. In contrast, I argue here that reality is likely to be far more ambiguous, if not downright messy. Let us refer back to the three propositions which have shaped this chapter, to place this argument in a wider context.

Firstly, there is agreement with the broad thrust of proposition 1 that the black middle class was historically a politically progressive force. Simultaneously, the argument here warned against any heroic narrative about its role in the struggle for democracy. Certainly, the leadership of the ANC (and other political movements) was heavily drawn from the middle class, and middle-class elements played prominent roles in articulating the demands for racial and political equality. Nonetheless, the role of the black middle class was historically quite uneven: at different times, in different situations, in different locations it was variously (and sometimes simultaneously) liberal, conservative, nationalist and radical. It might even be argued that the only consistent thing about the black middle class was its political inconsistency.

Proposition 2 suggested that the different layers of the black middle class are likely to maintain their broad political alignment with the ANC, though to varying degrees depending on their connection with the party-state. Despite numerous factional struggles within the party and across the state, despite a myriad of discontents, a middle class which has benefited immensely under ANC rule is unlikely to abandon a party which uses state power to dispense political goods in its favour. The perquisites of the party-state bourgeoisie are real, and the gulf between the employed and increasingly precarious working class and impoverished underclass is too great for even a fragile middle class to abandon its sponsor, even if this demands toleration of illiberalism. As in most other African countries which participated in the 'third wave of democracy',[53] the black middle class may back a drift towards 'competitive authoritarianism', a hybrid form of governance in which democratic forms belie a reality of authoritarian rule.[54]

Despite this rather gloomy argument, there must also be agreement with the thrust of proposition 3, that the growth of the black middle class will add to political diversity and a more vigorous civil society, and hence strengthen democratic trends. In line with classic theories which associate rising levels of education, urbanisation, wealth and equality with democratisation, we may trust that the emergent black middle class will increasingly demand greater accountability from society's rulers and, indeed, may even join popular revolt if its material and political rights are seriously threatened. Moreover, at all times there are likely to be courageous individuals from the black middle class, as from other groups in society, willing to take on injustice and tyranny. Yet overall I am left to wonder if – despite our hopes lying with proposition 3 – we should not grant greater weight to proposition 2. In this regard, food for thought is provided by briefly considering the political stance of the rapidly emerging middle class in China – a country for which the ANC and SACP currently display much admiration.

The piecemeal market reforms of the Communist Party of China (CCP) which opened up the Chinese economy have been accompanied by the rapid growth of a middle class (estimated at between 150 and 180 million people at the present time). This has boosted hopes that, despite major setbacks (such as the brutal suppression of protesters in Tiananmen Square in 1989), the expansion of the middle class will lead to demands for greater openness, transparency, freedom of expression and, ultimately, the right to choose their leaders: liberalisation followed by democracy. This would be bad news for the CCP, which has already sought to obscure an increasing incidence of political protest, notably in urban areas. Analysis indicates that much of this activity is driven by workers and peasants. Nonetheless, there is also a significant rise in middle-class willingness to confront state authority, and to empower individuals as citizens, even if this usually takes a supposedly apolitical form. While Chinese middle-class protests may provide a precursor for future politically motivated protests, for now the majority of them reportedly display a nimby ('not in my backyard') character, involving opposition to local 'nuisances' such as housing, corruption, policing and quality-of-life issues. Most of these protests are therefore 'reactive, conservative, and localized'.[55] The emergent middle class in China may not be politically quiescent, but it seems to fear a drift to democracy that 'would empower the unwashed masses of workers and farmers, who would fall victim to the slippery and silver tongues of demagogues and populists who would incite them to use their power in numbers to expropriate the wealth and property of their "betters"'.[56]

Should we expect significantly different in South Africa, where class tensions are rapidly rising? And should we expect a rearrangement of political parties more clearly across class lines, a breach in the ANC's multiclass alliance, and a concerted shift to more intensified class struggle? There are no easy answers to such pressing questions. In conclusion, some guide may be given by a brief consideration of how South Africa's black middle class relates to the wider narrative about 'the rise and rise' of middle classes in contemporary Africa.

9

Afterword:
South Africa's black middle class
in an African context

There is need, in conclusion, to relate the foregoing discussion about the black middle class in South Africa to the much wider discussions presently taking place about middle classes in the global South and the African continent more specifically. Whereas it is commonly said that the middle class in the global North is shrinking under the impact of neo-liberalism,[1] recent years have seen 'the meteoric rise of the new middle class' in the global South.[2] Africa, meanwhile, has been said to possess 'the fastest-growing middle class in the world',[3] an assertion that is an integral part of the narrative of 'Africa rising'. This discourse, notably as it is carried on by global institutions, is explicitly celebratory. On the one hand, the new middle classes are said to be the 'drivers of development'. In particular they are distinguished by their growing capacity for consumption, thereby providing a significant stimulus for economic growth. On the other hand, they are simultaneously portrayed as the 'drivers of democracy', challenging authoritarian rule by elites. Thus in Africa, the middle class has been proclaimed a 'politically conscious class', with 'enlightened voters' who are increasingly demanding accountability from politicians, and voting according to issues rather than traditional or ethnic allegiances.[4]

There is much in this discourse which finds strong echoes in popular discussions about the 'rise' of the black middle class in South Africa. In this book, an attempt has been made not so much to contradict such an analysis as to complicate it. The black middle class may be mostly 'new', yet it has deep roots in the pre-democratic eras. It is distinguished by its penchant for consumption, yet this is as much prompted by its struggle to escape from poverty and to 'catch up' with the white middle class as it is by the status-driven desire to display. While it is becoming more prominent as a critic of the inefficiencies and failures of the party-state, the sharpness of its critique is simultaneously blunted by its heavy dependence upon the state as its employer and as the fount of its resources. In short, the ambiguities of the black middle class make it immensely difficult to portray, and serve as a guarantee that debate about its social and political characteristics is set to continue for years to come. Hence this chapter is titled an 'afterword' rather than a 'conclusion'. Quite simply, there is far too much about the black middle class that is difficult to pin down, to finish this book with judgements that are 'conclusive'. However, what will be useful to end with are some pointers about how the study of the black middle class may be taken forward, by engaging in some broader comparisons.

The strange career of the African middle class

It is only relatively recently that concerted attention has begun to be paid to the African 'middle class'. This is not to say that there has not previously been interest in the social groups that are today described as 'middle class'. It is rather to say that they have been categorised and regarded differently, with different characteristics ascribed to them. Further, where they were labelled 'middle class', the term tended to be used descriptively rather than theoretically.

During early colonialism, the proto-middle class in Africa was regarded ambivalently. 'Middle-class' Africans were in the 'middle' because they inserted themselves between the colonialists and the huge majority of colonial subjects. On the one hand, they were ridiculed, as mimicking whites; on the other, they were feared as representing a challenge to white status and authority. During the later colonial period, and after political independence, such 'middle-class' Africans were described as 'modernising elites'. Subsequently, as disillusion with post-colonial political and economic trajectories set in during the 1970s and 1980s, they became 'bourgeoisies', and were depicted as corrupt, authoritarian, exploitative and anti-developmental. It was only from the early 1990s, after structural adjustment had slimmed African states, and neo-liberalism had been twinned with a return to multiparty democracy, that African bourgeoisies were found to have either dissolved into or spawned a 'progressive middle class'.

224

This outline of the strange career of the African middle class is, of course, a caricature. Social analysis has been more complicated and nuanced than this implies. Nonetheless, as with all caricature, it can help to illustrate how the South African black middle class fits into this wider picture.

The broad trajectory of the African elite through the bourgeoisie to the African middle class has been valuably sketched out by both Carola Lentz[5] and Danielle Resnick.[6] Both note that work on social stratification and class in Africa has deep roots. The concept of class, says Resnick, was 'widely discussed in Africanist literature' from the 1950s and 1960s. However, there were few overall analyses of class structure in Africa. Indeed, there was much debate about whether 'class analysis' as such was appropriate to Africa, where societies were still seen as rooted in 'tradition', and classes, as they were conceived of in relation to 'advanced societies', were only vaguely discernible.

Lentz notes how, within this context, studies of the 'middle class' tended to be merged with studies of 'elites' (or 'the analysis of the "upper end" of the social scale'),[7] despite the very different meanings attached to elites and social classes in the classical literature. Social groups, such as the highly educated and professionals, who elsewhere in the world would be discussed as middle classes, were usually categorised as elites, 'a category that gained prominence in the 1960s and 1970s'.[8] After the Second World War, colonial officers, anthropologists, political scientists and others had wanted to know where the future leaders of African states would come from, what their qualifications would be, and what visions they would bring to the task. Lentz accords pivotal importance to Peter Lloyd's edited volume of *The New Elites of Tropical Africa*, published in 1966, which presented case studies of a wide selection of African states.[9] Lloyd's very definition of elites, she argues, expressed the widespread hope that Western-educated Africans would play the role of modernising agents in newly independent nations. They would be bearers of new norms and values, they would mediate between modernity and tradition, and, as indicated by their moving into occupations according them high incomes, they would adopt Western styles of life. They were 'elites' rather than a 'class' because African societies were largely vertically organised, with high rates of social mobility facilitated by education, but they were bound together from top to bottom through kinship networks and cultural homogeneity. At the same time, they were divided horizontally by persisting ethnic loyalties across occupations and wealth. To be sure, Lloyd went beyond any dichotomous division of African societies into elites and masses. Notably, he drew a distinction between 'traditional' and 'modern' elites. Furthermore, he acknowledged a scale of elites, recognising both Westernised national elites and more localised sub-elites, such as traders and teachers. Even so, he steered explicitly clear of class analysis. If elites were an 'upper class', where were the 'lower classes'? Peasants were ethnically, not class-oriented, and African working classes were tiny and, in many countries, scarcely visible. 'Elite' was clearly the most suitable term, with its counterpart being the 'masses'.[10]

Lloyd's work set the tone for numerous studies of the era that discussed, variously, the origins of elites and the role of education in elite formation; educated elites' marriage strategies; the development and composition of subnational elites; and relations between national and local elites. The term 'middle class' was bandied about with considerable regularity, yet was often used interchangeably with that of 'elite', without reference to the different social and political implications which the terminologies implied.[11] The result was a 'conceptual quagmire'[12] in which the term elite was used overwhelmingly descriptively, without any explicit discussion of the relationship between elite and class concepts. Even so, as Lentz goes on to note, Lloyd himself seemed to hint that African elites might develop into classes. If they were to become hereditary, if they were to monopolise access to education, if they were to lose touch with their rural origins, and if their privilege was to provoke the hostility of the masses, then they would lose their right to be regarded as agents of modernity.[13] In retrospect, his cautious comments seemed to foreshadow the transformation of African 'elites' into 'bourgeoisies'.

As Lentz observes, the hopes placed in African politicians and public ser-vants as modernisers 'soon gave way to trenchant critiques of the parasitism of African bureaucracies'.[14] Accusations of mismanagement and corruption now came to be levelled at groups rather than individuals. 'Elite' became replaced by 'class', as structuralist analyses came to the fore, much of it rooted (often fairly loosely, it might be said) in Marxist and neo-Marxist theory. The result, declares Resnick amusingly, was 'a plethora of bourgeoisies'.[15] Initially, there was Frantz Fanon's 'national bourgeoisie', which tellingly he described as a privileged middle class that had sought to defeat colonial rule only to usurp its place of dominance over the working class.[16] Subsequently, it was joined by Issa Shivji's 'bureaucratic bourgeoisie' in Tanzania, which essentially referred to those who manned the political and administra-tive apparatus;[17] Irving Markovitz's 'organizational bourgeoisie', which referred to the same actors plus traditional leaders;[18] and Richard Sklar's 'managerial bourgeoisie', which, given the right circumstances, might be able to transform itself into a genuinely 'entrepreneurial bourgeoisie'.[19] The problem was that the circumstances and social structures were rarely right. In many countries, the consolidation of bourgeoisies occurred as a result of nationalisation and indigenisation initiatives. The former transferred numerous foreign enterprises, particularly in oil, mining, banking and insurance, into local hands, as the state assumed the major role in industrialisation and development. The latter transferred assets, property ownership and employment from foreigners to locals. As a result, national citizens gained positions in civil services and parastatals which required skills many of them did not have. Others acquired businesses, which they lacked the business know-how and capital to run. As a result, multinational corporations were enabled to skirt regulations by using middlemen, and the state responded by providing concessions and contracts. The result was what dependency theorists labelled 'comprador bourgeoisies', which, in essence, operated in alliance with and as agents of foreign capital. Amid all this conceptual morass, an energetic debate on African capitalism engaged in battle about whether African capitalists were entirely dependent upon foreign capital or whether they had autonomous origins and possessed genuine degrees of economic independence.[20]

What was distinctive about such Marxist- or neo-Marxist-inspired analyses was that, generally, the state – rather than the ownership of capital – was seen as the critical locus of class formation. This followed from the structure of African political economies. African bourgeoisies clustered around the state because capital in African hands was scarce and African business sectors were overwhelmingly foreign-owned, foreign-manned and externally oriented. At independence, therefore, African 'elites' inherited the 'political kingdom', and had little option but to regard the state as the motor of development and accumulation. If they were to branch off into private ventures on their own behalf, they generally did so with the tolerance of the state, to which they were in all likelihood linked through patronage networks and on which they remained dependent for access to capital and contracts. In contrast, African capitalists who were genuinely autonomous of the state tended to be regarded with suspicion if not outright hostility by politicians, who feared the emergence of potentially rival social forces.

Despite these marked differences in social formation from advanced capitalist societies, Africanist scholarship appropriated the terminology and baggage of Marxist and neo-Marxist analysis because of the past alignment of colonialism with capitalism, and the continuing domination of African economies by external capitalist markets and multinational corporations. Inevitably, there was marked ambivalence about 'nationalist' bourgeoisies. On the one hand, they were the product and inheritors of the nationalist struggles against colonialism, and there was reluctance in many quarters (not least among the nationalist bourgeoisies themselves) to define them as exploitative. On the other hand, for many scholars, following Fanon, they were depicted as having betrayed the national revolution by engaging in outrageous strategies of material accumulation, enjoying a lifestyle based upon wealth and privilege, and exercising political domination over the poorer majority in society. It followed that if bourgeoisies were consolidating, they were engaging in class struggle. Correspondingly, class analysis now extended to a focus on the development of African working classes, and the transition of migrants and peasantries into proletariats.

As Lentz notes, non-Marxist scholars, particularly political scientists, continued to use the term 'elites' to describe mainly the politicians and bureaucrats of the new African states. For Jean-François Bayart, for instance, the identification of a political elite was quite separate from the broader question of social stratification, for which class analysis was more appropriate. At the same time, he asserted that African societies did not really have classes, and preferred to focus upon the relations between 'old' and 'new' ruling groups, and the extent to which they coalesced into a 'dominant bloc'.[21] Other scholars pursued the path of functionalist analysis by considering the social background of institutional elites (such as parliamentarians), some linking this to notions of the 'circulation of elites', political leadership, and democratic change and stability. Within such analyses, ideas of 'neo-patrimonialism' became prominent, highlighting 'the vertical integration [of elites] with the broader population through patron–client relations, usually along ethnic lines'.[22] Stripped of their optimism, these notions clearly followed in the wake of Lloyd and all those who in an earlier era had placed such faith in African elites.

If elite analysis began to enjoy something of a renaissance from the early 1990s, this was a result of more than just a shift in academic fashion. It was rather more the result of changing political, social and economic circumstances on the ground. At the same time that African bourgeoisies were developing around the state, the state was coming under attack. The oil crises of the early 1970s, resultant depression in the US and much of

Europe, and a calamitous fall in commodity prices plunged many African states into crisis. Accordingly, they fell into the clutches of the IMF and other international financial institutions. Just as the turn to neo-liberalism in the West saw an attack upon many social programmes, so it heralded the arrival of structural adjustment throughout much of Africa, as indebted states were required to make huge cuts in their expenditures on health, education and social services and sell off their nationalised industries into private (often multinational) hands. By the 1990s, state bourgeoisies were having the ground cut from beneath their feet. The end of the Cold War and the collapse of the Soviet Union discredited African socialism and Afro-Marxism. 'Bloated' states were being shrunk and civil services reduced in size. Neo-liberal prescriptions delegitimised notions of the 'developmental state' and hailed 'entrepreneurship' as the motor of development.

State bourgeoisies adapted by entering into partnership with multi-national capitalism, though this was often presented in nationalist discourses as 'indigenisation' and 'empowerment'. Such initiatives remained heavily dependent upon the extraction of commodities and the sale of cash crops, boosted by the commodity boom of the 1990s and early 2000s. Yet there was also significant structural change. On the one hand, African working classes – always small – were further weakened by the decline of formal employment, and the necessity for the majority of the people to rely upon participation in the informal sector for survival. On the other hand, African countries were to experience, albeit very unevenly, employment growth in high value-added service sectors, such as finance, business, real estate, transport and communication, construction, hotels, catering and tourism. These were to provide the basis for the emergence, growth and, above all, celebration of the African middle class.

By the dawn of the new century the restructuring of the global economy facilitated by neo-liberalism had seen a significant shift of power and wealth to the global South. Global institutions now increasingly identified a rapid advance in the human development status of almost all countries in the South, as a result of the industrialisation of 'emerging economies' such as Brazil, China and India. The world was becoming a richer place, and the lot of the global poor was steadily improving. An important outcome was the rapid growth of middle classes. According to the United Nations Development Programme (UNDP), for instance: 'Between 1990 and 2010, the South's share of the global middle class population expanded from 26% to 58%. By 2030, more than 80% of the world's middle class is projected to be residing in the South and to account for 70% of total consumption expenditure.'[23]

This prognosis assumed that two-thirds of this global middle class were in Asia and the Pacific, and a tenth in Central and South America. Only 2 per cent were in sub-Saharan Africa, where the share of manufacturing in terms of contribution to African GDP had declined significantly between 2000 (12.8 per cent) and 2008 (10.5 per cent). Even so, the decline failed to put a damper upon what *Deloitte on Africa* had referred to rapturously as 'the rise and rise of the African middle class'.[24] According to this source, the middle class in Africa as a percentage of the population had grown steadily from 26 per cent in 1980 to 34.3 per cent in 2013. The huge drawback was that the dramatic growth in Africa's overall population was undercutting any dramatic reduction in poverty. Nonetheless, the growth of the middle class provided a major 'opportunity for profit that [was] underpinned by volume'. This middle class was urban-based, highly educated, future- and children-oriented, and hugely aspirational. Furthermore, they were highly attuned to changing technology, were culturally self-confident, and were politically assertive. In other words, the African middle class was robustly 'modern'.

Amid the excitement about the African middle class, there was recognition of a hierarchy of classes. Deloitte divided the middle class into an upper middle class, spending between US$10 and $20 a day, a lower middle class spending between $4 and $10 a day, and a 'floating class' spending between $2 and $4 a day – this figure was only slightly above the world poverty line of $2 a day. These levels of expenditure were recognised as modest, yet nonetheless they provided what *The Economist* had identified as 'a real chance to follow in the footsteps of Asia'.[25]

It was against this background that academic interest in the middle classes in the global South experienced a renaissance during the 2000s. Middle classes were believed to 'boost growth, promote desirable social dynamics, and safeguard democracy. In short, they are modernisers who embody a positive vision of social mobility and meritocratic social order.'[26] As far as Africa was concerned, the transition from 'elites' to 'middle classes' was widely regarded as coming to fruition, if not yet complete, and there were numerous 'new frontiers' to be crossed.[27]

Since the decline of such analysis in recent years, it is now increasingly recognised that 'class has the potential to once again be a topic of major importance for Africanist scholarship'.[28] This does pose particular problems about the African middle class, a few of which I broach here.

Problems in the study of the African middle class

Although the middle class in Africa has begun to attract major interest in recent years, the conceptual limitations that have characterised the study of the upper echelons of African societies have continued unabated. Perhaps this is because the objectives of policy-makers attached to global institutions and governments are different from those of scholars; perhaps it is because scholars themselves come from different disciplines and from different intellectual traditions. Overall, it seems highly unlikely that any great degree of consensus will be achieved. The origins, size and character of the African middle class will continue to be subjects of vociferous debate. Such is the nature of social science. Nonetheless, this does not prevent the identification of key problem areas in the discussion of the middle classes, which we shall relate in passing to the study of the black middle class in South Africa.

The need for middle-class history

Given that in many ways the African middle class is a recent discovery, it is not surprising that there are major gaps in its history. Because scholars concentrated on elites, bourgeoisies, petty bourgeoisies, working classes, migrants and peasantries, the 'middle class' as such received short shrift. It was deemed either to be relatively insignificant or simply subordinated to these other class categories. This was in part because many scholars, notably in earlier eras, felt that Africa lacked proper social classes and that African society was 'backward', slow to join the trajectory of advanced societies or, quite simply, was cut off from the mainstream of historical development elsewhere. Whatever the case, it is difficult to disagree with Lentz when she says that 'with regard to Africa ... in-depth studies of the emerging middle class(es) are still scarce, and scholars are barely beginning to catch up with global research trends'.[29] Given the lack of systematic attention to the study of social stratification in Africa, it is not surprising that on the whole scholars have failed to engage in recent debates on class theory that are taking place elsewhere. The result has been that the history of the African middle class has been fragmented, regarded as only a subordinate dimension of grander narratives such as the nature and techniques of colonial domination, the rise of nationalism, African underdevelopment, and the pathologies of post-colonial rule.

Lentz's argument chimes in with the observation made earlier about the lack of a specific history of the white middle class in South Africa.

Even so, comparing the South African literature with that on Africa as a whole, Lentz singles out studies of the middle class in South Africa as having a 'long tradition'.[30] As far as the white middle class is concerned, she is clearly wrong. With regard to the black middle class, she is correct if the studies by such authors as Kuper, Wilson and Mafeje, Brandel-Syrier and Dreyer during the apartheid years are contrasted with the dearth of similar studies in the overwhelming majority of other African countries. Yet, while these books offer enormously valuable insights into the social character of the black middle class during earlier eras, they were necessarily inhibited in what they were enabled to say, notably about middle-class involvement in politics. Kuper, to be fair, dwells at some length upon the political engagements and potential of the black middle class, yet he could do so because his research was undertaken before the clampdown on the liberation movements. The authors who followed in his train were much more severely inhibited by the oppressive political conditions characterising later years under apartheid. It was only towards the end of the apartheid era, as the National Party's reform strategies began to be implemented, that the politics of the black middle class came to be specifically addressed, and then only by a handful of short studies in which, on the whole, it was portrayed unsympathetically as a largely 'collaborative' petty bourgeoisie.

This book has been written from the conviction that although the black middle class is distinctively 'new', there is a need to understand its history if we are to correctly assess its social character and potential as a political actor. Whether it has succeeded in justifying this belief is not for this author to say. However, what may be ventured with relative confidence is that there is considerable value in attempting to pull the rapidly growing volume of disparate studies of diverse aspects of the middle classes together, and provide overviews.

Significant work on middle classes in different African countries is now beginning to appear. Overwhelmingly, beyond definitional issues, it seems to concentrate upon the new visibility of the middle class, as demonstrated by changing patterns of consumption and lifestyle, and how this is related to potential for economic growth. This same trend has been noted with regard to the black middle class in South Africa.

The study of consumption and lifestyle is obviously enormously important. It is also integral to how African middle classes identify themselves and relate to the rest of their societies. Yet it also imports a significant bias into how the African middle class is understood, and leaves important lacunae in our understanding (notwithstanding valuable isolated contributions). One is how the massive expansion of secondary and tertiary education, much of it offered by private providers, has played a major role in the growth of Africa's middle classes. Another is the study of the African middle class at work. How do changing patterns of employment reshape the middle class, what costs and opportunities do they imply, and what roles do middle-class Africans play within diverse employment venues – from government offices through the corporate corridors of large multinationals to the work environments provided by the professions and small business? Another gap is how changing work patterns affect socio-geographic spatial relations and the spread of suburbia. Of such subjects, and indeed many others, we know relatively little, and our understanding of African middle classes is poorer for it.

This book has been facilitated by the relative wealth of discrete studies of different dimensions of black middle-class life in South Africa that have appeared in recent years. What has been achieved here, for all its limitations, may be less easily achieved for other African countries. Even so, the plea for more holistic and integrated studies of African middle classes remains. Yet it is recognised that this will demand far greater clarity about how African middle classes should be defined.

The issue of definition

Economists and global institutions have been at the fore in defining the middle class in Africa and the global South in recent years. Overwhelmingly, they have identified the middle class according to income or consumption. As Dieter Neubert has noted, there are two different approaches.[31] One identifies middle classes relative to their specific countries and societies. For instance, Nancy Birdsall and her colleagues

> use a relative income measure to look at the households that are, literally, in the middle of the income distribution in each country, i.e. in each country, households with per capita income in the range of 75 and 125 percent of the median household per capita income. We do not pretend that this measure captures any fixed notion of the 'middle class'. What it does capture – literally – is the middle strata in income terms in each country.[32]

The other approach, widely adopted by global institutions, defines the middle class by reference to socio-economic data such as poverty levels, and income and expenditure levels and patterns, either globally or continentally. The resulting definitions vary widely. The UNDP uses as a measure an income or expenditure of between US$10 and $100 a day, which, as Henning Melber points out, is such a generous definition that it embraces a wide range of 'middle classes in the plural, right down to the precariat in industrialised countries'.[33] In contrast, Abhijit Banerjee and Esther Duflo, who define the middle class as earning between $2 and $10 per day, are much more stringent.[34] Yet the World Bank economist Martin Ravallion plumps for between $2 and $13 a day;[35] and the $2 threshold for entering the middle class is similarly applied by the African Development Bank, although it ups the ante for exiting the middle class at the top end of the spectrum to $20 a day.[36]

So it goes on. Who is right and who is wrong? Clearly there is no answer. As we noted in chapter 3, different definitions suit different objectives. Policy-makers interested in poverty alleviation and marketing companies interested in selling their products to consumers have very different purposes. Simply put, you pay your money and you make your choice. However, as Melber has observed, this range of definitions is so flexible that it can be used 'to cover almost everything "in between", thereby signifying little or nothing'. It is a far cry from class analysis and 'is devoid of almost any analytical substance'.[37] Such definitions are therefore of limited use to sociologists. While they may underlie analyses of changing middle-class consumer patterns, they tell us little else about such considerations as status, prestige, occupation, and political orientations and influence.

Despite the limitations of relying on socio-economic data for definitional purposes, economistic approaches have highlighted the array of income groupings that may constitute a middle class. As Neubert observes, thresholds between income strata within the middle class (upper, middle-middle and lower) tend to be chosen arbitrarily, yet at least they are recognised. In this, it has to be said, they have gone beyond the traditional approach of most sociological and anthropological research, which, as the early focus upon elites implies, has tended to restrict itself to notions of the 'better-off' as constituting the middle class. It is no coincidence that Lentz's wide-ranging review of the elite and middle-class literature in African studies restricts itself to what she terms 'the upper middle class'.[38] Yet if there is an upper middle class, there should obviously be a lower one as well. Quite clearly, any analytical approach employed for understanding the African middle class must attempt to take this on board. Consequently, in this book an attempt has been made to probe the social locations of an array of social strata (from corporate managers down to white-collar workers) that are usually conceived of as constituting a middle class.

The Marxist and neo-Marxist approaches that transformed African elites into varieties of bourgeoisie allowed for this to some degree. There was embedded in many such analyses a distinction between a 'real' bourgeoisie, or a bourgeoisie proper which owned and deployed capitalist property and resources, and a 'petty bourgeoisie', which did not – yet which nonetheless enjoyed class privileges over the popular mass. Amilcar Cabral, for instance, was explicit. At independence in Guinea there was

> no economically viable bourgeoisie because imperialism prevented it being created. What there [was, was] a stratum of people in the service of imperialism who have learned how to manipulate the apparatus of the state – the African petty-bourgeoisie: this is the only stratum capable of controlling or even utilising the instruments which the colonial state used against the people. So we come to the conclusion that in colonial conditions it is the petty bourgeoisie which is the inheritor of class power.[39]

In the South African historical literature of the 'revisionist' period of the 1970s and 1980s, there was similar reference to the emergence of African petty bourgeoisies (as traders, petty capitalists and administrators) in the interstices of the white-dominated economy. Subsequently, it was never really resolved by Marxist analyses whether the acquisition of state power allowed 'bureaucratic' or 'organisational' bourgeoisies to become 'real' bourgeoisies, while, on the other hand, the characterisation of those who occupied positions above the working class tended to be largely ignored. Thus, although in later literature distinctions were to be drawn between 'old' and 'new' segments of the middle class, reflecting the changing nature of the occupational structure, these were horizontal rather than vertical distinctions. In contrast, there was considerable debate about whether the relatively high wages earned by skilled manual workers, backed by union power, placed them so far above the position of unskilled workers and the peasantry that they qualified as 'privileged'. Generally, the answer given was 'no', maintaining the fundamental divide between workers and managers (and hence the integrity of the working class). In turn, this meant that little attention was paid to the class character of new categories of employees (junior office staff and other white-collar workers) who were emerging in significant numbers within the state itself and within neo-liberalising economic structures. Studies, such as that of bank workers in India offered by Fernandez (see chapter 1), have few equivalents within the literature on Africa.

The approach taken by this book has attempted to move beyond the limitations of the existing literature by drawing upon diverse theoretical traditions. At its heart is the neo-Weberian assertion that class structures are constituted of a hierarchy of occupations which are differentiated by skill and income. Critically, this allows for the identification of a hierarchy of classes, with different 'life chances', descending from a power elite or bourgeoisie at the top down through upper- and lower-middle classes and reaching 'core' and marginal working classes at the lowest levels of society. In turn, following the neo-Marxist tradition, it asserts the critical importance of the nature and levels of power and authority which these different classes wield or are subject to, and which in turn derive from two principal sources of power and authority within post-apartheid society (and, it may be said, the more general post-colony): the state and the market (principally, multinational and large corporations). It is not claimed that this framework resolves all issues. It has difficulties in dealing with the problem of the ownership of capital (whether as shares, investments, property or whatever). Nor does it deal satisfactorily with the issue of how class location translates into distinctive political and social attitudes (to address which, for instance, Neubert refers us to Bourdieu's concepts of habitus and milieus). Hopefully, it offers some pointers to how the class analysis of the modern African state might be pushed forward. Yet this, in turn, raises the potential difficulty of South Africa's 'exceptionalism'.

The black middle class and South African 'exceptionalism'
The black middle class in South Africa has followed as strange a career as its counterparts in the rest of sub-Saharan Africa. As the overview in chapter 2 relates, historians have been very free with their terminology, variously distinguishing between the modernising mission-school elites and the traditional chiefly elites, proto-middle classes and emergent petty bourgeoisies. The Congress Alliance has generally been conceived of as a class alliance of middle-class elements, workers and peasants (or an alliance between elites and masses) as much as a political alliance between racially

subordinated blocs of Africans, Indians and Coloureds. Later liberation literature referred to the frustrations of African petty capitalists, while those Africans wielding authority and accessing material reward by participating in homeland and official urban structures were denounced as a collaborative bourgeoisie. Blade Nzimande, steeped in the dominant Marxist tradition of the 1970s and 1980s, identified the emergence of a 'new African middle class', yet proceeded to chop it up into state, corporate, civil and trading 'petty bourgeoisies'. In contrast, the post-Soweto period saw urgent efforts by the government and capitalist-allied organisations such as the Urban Foundation to expand the African middle class to serve as a moderating influence in an era of radical turmoil. Today, the 'petty bourgeoisie' has withdrawn to the wings, and the 'black middle class' occupies centre stage.

Despite this confusion of terminology, it is nonetheless possible to identify the broad transition, from elites to bourgeoisies to middle class, which has characterised the wider African literature. Even so, although we need to be very wary of claims of South African exceptionalism, one can argue that the post-1994 African middle class in South Africa is 'exceptional' in terms of its having today become 'black'.

As noted in the Introduction, there are significant controversies around the appropriation of this label in this way. The historical literature has generally referred to the 'African middle class', and from the 1970s Black Consciousness theorised the overall community of Africans, Coloureds and Indians as 'black'. Yet, today the term 'black middle class', referring to Africans as distinct from Coloureds and Indians, has come to predominate – despite the formal use of 'black' in a more inclusive manner in legislation under the rubric of BEE. This is more than a ploy by the marketing industry and the promotion of 'black diamonds'. It is rather a matter of identity.

Michael West has offered one of the few extensive histories of an African middle class outside South Africa. It seems no coincidence that he is writing about 'colonial Zimbabwe', a country subject like South Africa to settler colonialism, in which the emergence of an African middle class faced particular challenges. In his enormously rich account, he explores how, initially, the colonists assumed 'the power to name', only to be met by the counter-claim by Africans to 'the right to name' as a matter of identity: 'For the colonialists, the question was: What shall we call them? The Africans, in a quest for self-identity, which involved nothing less than a subversion of the colonial will, responded with a question of their own: What shall we call ourselves?'[40]

237

Initially, the colonists and the British used the term 'Kaffir'. This only acquired its derogatory connotations towards the end of the nineteenth century as the colonial project intensified. Thereafter, from the early twentieth century, it was replaced in officialdom by the term 'native' as a more respectable alternative until the 1960s. Central to this naming process was the depersonalisation of the colonised and the denial of individuality. The native had no name: he or she was given a generic European name, such as Tom or Jim, and African males were referred to as 'boys' and women as 'girls'.

Understandably, Africans objected. Despite its dubious etymological beginnings, writes West, 'native' as a term of self-designation was initially accepted by Africans, partly perhaps 'as a result of their own internalisation of the devaluation of Africanness inherent in the colonial project – yet it certainly undermined the use of "Kaffir"'.[41] It therefore appeared in the titles of most of the political and other associations formed by Africans in Southern Rhodesia up to the mid-1930s. Thereafter, elite Africans began objecting to the designation, and demanded that the authorities refer to them as African (alongside requests that in correspondence officialdom should dignify recipients with the honorific 'Mr' or 'Mrs'). Yet, meanwhile, an alternative self-designation, 'Bantu', also gained currency among the African elite (as in the Rhodesian Bantu Voters' Association), the word having been used quite widely in various parts of southern Africa by scholars, colonialists and Africans alike in this period. Yet 'Bantu' in turn fell by the wayside. 'The Bantu, it was now claimed, were really Africans who had been robbed of their true cultural and historical designation', and the word signified both insult and historical dispossession. In turn, the more white settlers resisted this latest twist in terminology (for were they not also 'African'?), the more 'African' acquired agency as the preferred mode of identity. Its widespread adoption was integral to the rise of African self-consciousness, alongside the adoption of cultural and ideological practices imported from South Africa such as the singing of 'Nkosi Sikelel' iAfrika' (God Bless Africa) as the anthem of emerging African nationalism.

A similar terminological trajectory could be tracked in South Africa (although the renaming of the South African Native National Congress as the ANC as early as 1923 indicates that the process of African self-assertion in reaction to white settler domination was always ahead of what was happening in Southern Rhodesia). During the apartheid era, of course, the National Party imposed the term 'Bantu' upon Africans as a way of differentiating them linguistically and politically into discrete ethnicities and nations, only for this designation to be repudiated with scorn[42] by the overwhelming majority of Africans. Subsequently, during the heyday of popular resistance to the apartheid regime, the unity of the oppressed was expressed by the merging (however uneven) of African identity into the more socially inclusive moniker 'black'. It is only since 1994, perhaps indeed later, that there has been a growing assertion of 'African' identity as 'black' – while in contrast, there are signals of a reassertion of separate Coloured and Indian identities (alongside a growing awareness at least in scholarly circles of the persistent salience of 'whiteness'). This argument should not, perhaps, be pushed too far. It needs validation by a more careful analysis of how linguistic terminology is linked to social and political identity than can be provided here. However, what can be argued with a greater degree of certainty is that today the 'African' middle class self-identifies as 'black'. This is in line with the greater racial assertiveness associated with the contrast between Mandela's emphasis upon 'reconciliation' and Mbeki's emphasis upon 'Africanism', and the continued division of post-apartheid South Africa into two nations (white/rich versus black/poor). In turn, electoral studies indicate the growing extent to which its former white, Coloured and Indian supporters are deserting the ANC, which is becoming increasingly 'black'. It is arguable that as the post-apartheid project unravels, racial tensions are beginning to rise.

Identification as 'black' was very evident during the meetings of focus groups conducted for this book. Indeed, in her MA thesis also based upon these, Amuzweni Ngoma asserts that black professionals are more race conscious than they are class conscious.[43] Similarly, Leslie Bank, in his fascinating account of changing racial attitudes in East London, argues that in reaction to a vociferous white racism in the city, 'the black middle class is strongly anti-white and would often rather throttle local initiative than allow it to fall into "white hands"'.[44] Official statistics now increasingly substitute the word 'black' for 'African'.

Herein lies the distinctiveness of the 'black' middle class. It sees itself as 'black' in reaction to the historical political and economic oppression by whites, and in resentment at what it perceives as continuing white dominance of the economy. In the demand for 'transformation', many of the niceties of whether Coloureds and Indians are also 'black' regularly get pushed aside. In this regard, developing race consciousness does not so much trump as express the class consciousness and interests of the black middle class. Elsewhere in Africa, with the exception of Namibia and Zimbabwe, which were similarly subject to settler colonialism, it would make no sense for the African middle class to identify as 'black'. In South Africa, it does.

A research agenda for the study of the African middle class

This book opened with Alec Brown's plea to the middle classes of 1930s Europe to join the proletariat in the struggle against Fascism. However, my introduction promised only the much more modest intention of furthering the greater understanding of post-apartheid society through an exploration of the 'rise of the black middle class', linking this to the greater attention being given to the rapid expansion of the middle class across Africa and the global South more generally. Yet the political message that Brown conveyed should remind us that the question of the middle class is one of major importance. The discourse of the global institutions may be unduly celebratory, yet it is correct in linking the expansion of the middle classes to questions around democracy and development. This requires that in future work greater attention should be given to elaborating African class systems, the way the middle classes are located within them, and, in turn, the manner in which they are integrated into global structures.

Hitherto, debate about the middle classes in Africa has been more reactive than proactive. An enormous amount of ink has been spilled in engaging with the varying definitions of the middle class put forward by the global institutions and allied economists, and correctly so. There has been concerted attention to exploring changing lifestyle patterns associated with the expansion of incomes at the middle level of the spectrum, and how rampant consumerism is a product and reflection of neo-liberal capitalist development. All these and related discussions are important and necessary. Even so, they have arguably come at the cost of attention to larger issues to which the global institutions point – yet which they leave largely hanging in the air. Accordingly, I now pose a series of questions about the African middle classes that need to be addressed.

Can it be assumed that a larger, better-off and more educated African middle class will have the capacity to undertake a formative, perhaps leading, role in the long-term sustainable development which will bring about the general improvement of people's lives in African countries? What is meant by such a capacity? Does it require a middle class to develop into a genuine capitalist bourgeoisie? If so, is there any genuine prospect of that, given the continuing dependence of African 'development' on inflows of foreign investment? To what extent is that happening already, even if principally centred on extraction and import–export activities?

In any case, can it be assumed that the expansion of the middle class will continue? Or will it contract if and when investment dries up in response to downturns in the global economy? What types of middle class are being produced by present patterns of investment in Africa (still heavily minerals-led, though accompanied by an expanding financial and services sector)? Will they be pioneering and innovative, enabling African development to leap forward in an age when technology is progressing by leaps and bounds? Will the middle classes save for productive investment, or will they simply opt for unproductive consumption? Will they place personal enrichment above 'development'? Can 'development' in Africa simply be consumption-led? What are the implications for the middle class if consumption-led development is fuelled by unsustainable levels of personal and national debt?

Even supposing that African middle classes are sustainable and continue to grow, can it be assumed that they will challenge authoritarian political patterns laid down by their forebears, the post-independence elites? Is the expanding African middle class sufficiently independent of the state to demand accountability from those who run it? If development is leading to highly unequal distribution of incomes, why should the better-off, upper-middle class side with the lower-middle class, workers and the unemployed, and in what circumstances, rather than allying with Africa's oppressive elites? What are the class structures and formations being promoted by present patterns of development, and will they lead to class coherence or conflict between differently privileged segments of the middle class? Is the middle class sufficiently homogeneous to construct and sustain a progressive political project, or will it fragment along ethnic or other lines?

Furthermore, research needs to be pursued across national lines. In South Africa, we often ask whether today's black middle class can emulate the development role played for Afrikanerdom by the Afrikaner middle class from the 1920s. What similar historically based questions need to be asked in other African countries? How do class formations and emergent middle classes differ across different African countries? Is the black middle class in semi-industrialised South Africa more advanced – or less so – than middle classes in other major countries in Africa such as Angola and Nigeria? How should we compare middle classes in such widely variant African countries as Nigeria, Chad, Sudan, Rwanda, Kenya and Zimbabwe? To what extent is a process of transnational formation of an African middle class taking place, and what would be the implications of such a process for the continent as well as for individual African countries?

Similar questions need to be posed across continents. Despite their rapid recent growth, middle classes in Africa are much smaller than in most other 'emergent' regions. Furthermore, although sharing a common experience of colonial conquest and subordination, countries in Latin America and Asia have evolved widely varying class formations and structures. So how should we compare the developmental and democratic potential of middle classes in Africa with those in countries such as China, India and Brazil? Does the South African middle class have more in common with, say, its counterpart in Brazil than it does with its equivalent in Nigeria? If it does, so what?

Numerous other such uncomfortable questions come crowding in. Nonetheless, they are the sorts of issues − beyond the present obsessions of so much middle-class research with issues of lifestyle, consumption and identity − which should be guiding the developing research agenda around the middle classes in Africa. They will demand that we go back to the classical debates about the nature and historical role of the middle class outlined at the beginning of this book, and determine how these should be carried over into discussion about development (or the lack of it) in Africa. There will be no easy answers, and much blood will be spilt in debating those that are given. Yet they will serve to remind us that, for all its exceptionality, the development of the black middle class in South Africa is taking place against a much wider global canvas.

Notes

Introduction

1 Alec Brown, *The Fate of the Middle Classes*. London, Victor Gollancz, 1936, pp. 238–239.

2 Leo Kuper, *An African Bourgeoisie: Race, Class and Politics in South Africa*. New Haven, Yale University Press, 1965.

3 Alan Cobley, *Class and Consciousness: The Black Petty Bourgeoisie in South Africa, 1924 to 1950*. Westport, Greenwood Press, 1990.

4 Monica Wilson and Archie Mafeje, *Langa: A Study of Social Groups in an African Township*. Cape Town, Oxford University Press, 1963; Thomas Nyquist, *African Middle Class Elite*, Institute of Social and Economic Research, Rhodes University, Occasional Paper No. 28, 1983; Nkululeko Mabandla, '*Lahla Ngubo*: The Continuities and Discontinuities of a South African Black Middle Class', MA dissertation, University of Cape Town, 2012.

5 Notably André Odendaal, *The Founders: The Origins of the ANC and the Struggle for Democracy in South Africa*. Auckland Park, Jacana Media, 2012.

6 Honourable exceptions include Peter Alexander, Claire Ceruti, Keke Motseke, Mosa Phadi and Kim Wale, *Class in Soweto*. Scottsville, University of KwaZulu-Natal Press, 2013; and Deborah James, *Money from Nothing: Indebtedness and Aspiration in South Africa*. Johannesburg, Wits University Press, 2014. The literature on the black middle class before 1994 is examined in chapter 2.

7 See chapter 2 for more detailed discussion.

8 For a review of the changing terminology used to label historically subordinated 'racial' groups and the reasons why individuals among such groups appropriate labels (such as 'black') to identify themselves, readers should refer to chapter 9. Suffice it to say that I use the term 'black middle class' because I judge it to be the preferred self-designation of the collective I am writing about.

9 *The Economist*, 13 May 2000.

10 I return to this theme in chapter 9.

Chapter 1: The 'middle class': problems and controversies
1 Karl Marx, *Capital: A Critique of Political Economy*. Vol. 3, *The Process of Capitalist Production as a Whole*. London, Lawrence and Wishart, 1974 [1884], p. 885.
2 Tom Bottomore (ed.), *Interpretations of Marx*. Oxford, Blackwell, 1988, p. 19.
3 Tom Bottomore, *Classes in Modern Society*. London, HarperCollins Academic, 1991, pp. 10–11.
4 Eduard Bernstein, *Evolutionary Socialism*. New York, Schocken, 1961 [1899].
5 Francis Klingender, *The Condition of Clerical Labour in Britain*. London, Martin Lawrence, 1935.
6 Renner's work was introduced to the English-speaking world by Ralf Dahrendorf, *Class and Class Conflict in an Industrial Society*. London, Routledge and Kegan Paul, 1959.
7 David Lockwood, *The Black-Coated Worker* (2nd edition, with postscript). Oxford, Clarendon Press, 1989 [1958]. See also Michael Crozier, *The World of the Office Worker*. Chicago, University of Chicago Press, 1971.
8 Harry Braverman, *Labour and Monopoly Capital*. New York, Monthly Review Press, 1974.
9 Nicos Poulantzas, *Classes in Contemporary Capitalism*. London, New Left Books, 1974.
10 Erik Olin Wright, 'Class Boundaries and Contradictory Class Locations', in Anthony Giddens and Held David (eds.), *Classes, Power and Conflict: Classical and Contemporary Debates*. Berkeley, University of California Press, 1982, pp. 112–129.
11 James Burnham, *The Managerial Revolution*. New York, John Day, 1941.
12 Nicholas Abercrombie and John Urry, *Capital, Labour and the Middle Classes*. London, Allen and Unwin, 1983, p. 153.
13 Bottomore, *Classes in Modern Society*, pp. 45–47.
14 Frank Parkin, *Class Inequality and Political Order*. St Albans, Paladin, 1972, p. 26.
15 Anthony Giddens, *Capitalism and Modern Social Theory: An Analysis of the Writings of Marx, Durkheim and Weber*. Cambridge, Cambridge University Press, 1971, p. 188.
16 On Weber's relation to Marx and Marxism, see ibid., pp. 190–195.
17 Thomas Piketty, *Capital in the Twentieth Century*. Cambridge, The Belknap Press of Harvard University Press, 2014, p. 251.
18 Piketty's recent work demonstrates the continuing major role played by inheritance and income from ownership of capital in underpinning growing inequality.
19 As was explored notably by Antonio Gramsci, who theorised how the bourgeois class under capitalist society tended to exercise 'hegemony' over – that is, ideologically dominate – other classes in society.
20 For an early contribution to what became known as the 'embourgeoisement' thesis, see John Goldthorpe and David Lockwood, 'Affluence and the British Class Structure', *Sociological Review*, 11, 2, 1963, pp. 133–163.
21 Werner Sombart, *Why Is There No Socialism in the United States?* London, Macmillan, 1976 [1906].
22 C. Wright Mills, *White Collar: The American Middle Classes*. Oxford, Oxford University Press, 1951, pp. 351–354.
23 Wright, 'Class Boundaries and Contradictory Class Locations', pp. 112–129, citation from p. 121.
24 Ibid., p. 121.
25 Ibid., pp. 124–127.
26 For a valuable discussion, see Dahrendorf, *Class and Class Conflict*, pp. 77–84.
27 Milovan Djilas, *The New Class: An Analysis of the Communist System*. London, Thames and Hudson, 1957, p. 35.

28 Dahrendorf, *Class and Class Conflict*, p. 83.

29 Ibid., p. 66.

30 Ibid., p. 68.

31 The growth of inequality in recent decades is at the centre of the analysis presented by Piketty.

32 Guy Standing, *The Precariat: The New Dangerous Class*. London, Bloomsbury Academic, 2011, pp. 7–8.

33 Ibid., p. 8.

34 Leela Fernandes, *India's New Middle Class: Democratic Politics in an Era of Economic Reform*. New Delhi, Oxford University Press, 2006, p. 106.

35 Ibid., p. 108.

36 Barrington Moore, *The Social Origins of Dictatorship and Democracy: Lord and Peasant in the Making of the Modern World*. Harmondsworth, Peregrine Books, 1969, p. 418.

37 Dietrich Rueschemeyer, Evelyne Stephens and John Stephens, *Capitalist Development and Democracy*. Cambridge, Polity Press, 1992, p. 272.

38 Seymour Martin Lipset, 'Some Social Requisites of Democracy', *American Political Science Review*, 53, 1959, pp. 69–105.

39 Gabriel Almond and Sidney Verba, *The Civic Culture: Political Attitudes and Democracy in Five Nations*. Princeton, Princeton University Press, 1963.

40 Samuel Huntington, *The Third Wave: Democratization in the Late Twentieth Century*. Norman, University of Oklahoma Press, 1991.

41 Francis Fukuyama, 'The Future of History: Can Liberal Democracy Survive the Decline of the Middle Class?', *Foreign Affairs*, January/February 2012.

42 Joshua Kurlantzick, 'One Step Forward, Two Steps Back', 2013, www.foreignpolicy. com/articles/2013/03/04/one_step_forward_two_steps_back?page=full&wp_login-redirect=0.

43 Standing, *The Precariat*, pp. 132–154.

44 E.P. Thompson, *The Making of the English Working Class*. Harmondsworth, Penguin, 1968, pp. 9–11.

Chapter 2: The black middle class in South Africa, 1910-1994

1 The CPSA dissolved in the face of the Suppression of Communism Act of 1950, only to re-form underground as the South African Communist Party (SACP).

2 For the tortuous debates within the CPSA around the Native Republic, see Sheridan Johns, *Raising the Red Flag: The International Socialist League and the Communist Party of South Africa, 1914–1932*. Bellville, Mayibuye Books, UWC, 1995.

3 Paul Maylam, *A History of the African People of South Africa: From the Early Iron Age to the 1970s*. Cape Town, David Philip, 1986, p. 223.

4 For instance, Harold Wolpe, 'The Changing Class Structure of South Africa: The African Petty-Bourgeoisie', in Paul Zaremfka (ed.), *Research in Political Economy*. Greenwich, JAI Press, 1977, pp. 143–174; and Owen Crankshaw, 'Theories of Class and the African "Middle Class" in South Africa, 1969–1983', *Africa Perspective*, 1, 1, 1986, pp. 3–33.

5 Note that the subservice of clergy of the Reformed Churches during and after the period of Dutch rule in the Cape to settler interests led them to refusing baptism to slaves and indigenous peoples, thereby denying them access to civil rights, reinforcing their racial subordination and blocking any possibility of upward social mobility (except on an occasional individual basis, such as black female slaves marrying white slave

owners). See Robert C.-H. Shell, *Children of Bondage: A Social History of the Slave Society at the Cape of Good Hope, 1652–1838*. Johannesburg, Wits University Press, 1997.

6 Alan Cobley, *Class and Consciousness: The Black Petty Bourgeoisie in South Africa, 1924 to 1950*. Westport, Greenwood Press, 1990, p. 59.

7 Ibid., p. 60. See also Colin Bundy, *The Rise and Fall of the South African Peasantry*. London, Heinemann, 1970, ch. 2, who emphasises (p. 38) how the creation of a 'respectable' class of 'civilised' Africans out of 'savage' society was linked to 'a whole constellation of beneficial results': not merely the defeat of 'heathenism, polygamy and barbarism', but the consumption of manufactured goods and an increase in commerce.

8 Cobley, *Class and Consciousness*, p. 61.

9 Meghan Healy-Clancy, *A World of Their Own: A History of South African Women's Education*. Pietermaritzburg, University of KwaZulu-Natal Press, 2013.

10 According to Hilda Kuper, who provided a chapter on nursing in Leo Kuper, *An African Bourgeoisie*. New Haven, Yale University Press, 1965, there were some 3,446 qualified African teachers by 1910. Virtually all these would have been trained to teach only at the primary level.

11 Fort Hare was a product of the Inter-State Native College Scheme, supported by the Cape government and promoted by J.T. Jabavu among enthusiastic African supporters in all four colonies. See André Odendaal, *The Founders: The Origins of the ANC and the Struggle for Democracy in South Africa*. Auckland Park, Jacana Media, 2012, pp. 326–341.

12 Cobley, *Class and Consciousness*, pp. 61–63.

13 Cherryl Walker, *Women and Resistance in South Africa*. Cape Town, David Philip, 1991, p. 19.

14 Anne Digby, 'Black Doctors and Discrimination under South Africa's Apartheid Regime', *Medical History*, 57, 2, 2013, pp. 269–290.

15 Phillip Tobias, 'Apartheid and Medical Education: The Training of Black Doctors in South Africa', *Journal of the National Medical Association*, 72, 4, 1960, pp. 395–410.

16 Table CXLVII, Report of the Fagan Commission, U.G. 28, 1948; and Occupational Census, 1936, in U.G. 11/12, 1942, cited by Pallo Jordan, 'The African Petty Bourgeoisie: A Force for Change or for the Status Quo', 1984, Paper Prepared for the Weekend Seminar of the Economics Unit of the ANC; www.disa.ukzn.ac.za/webpages/DC/.../cnf198400000.026.021.000pdf.

17 There were 8,204 African teachers and 2,429 clergymen in 1936; and 14,002 teachers and 2,697 clergymen in 1946.

18 Cobley, *Class and Consciousness*, pp. 64–66.

19 Nkululeko Mabandla, '*Lahla Ngubo*: The Continuities and Discontinuities of a South African Black Middle Class', MA dissertation, University of Cape Town, 2012 (available online at https://openaccess.leidenuniv.nl/handle/1887/20897). Mabandla builds upon the study by Sean Redding, 'Peasants and the Creation of an African Middle Class in Umtata', *International Journal of African Historical Studies*, 26, 3, 1993, pp. 513–539.

20 Cobley, *Class and Consciousness*, p. 68.

21 Ibid., p. 69.

22 Ibid., pp. 78–81.

23 One example of institutionalised discrimination was provided by the Anglican Church, which was more liberal than certain Nonconformist churches, and certainly more so than either the Catholic Church or the Dutch Reformed Churches. In 1934, it had more African adherents than white, but all its bishops were white (and usually from England). Meanwhile, the stipends of African priests were a third or less of those of

white priests. White priests were in charge of 'black work', but no black priests were in charge of 'white work'. See Alan Paton, *Apartheid and the Archbishop: The Life and Times of Geoffrey Clayton*. Cape Town, David Philip, 1973, p. 46. I am indebted to the late Bishop David Russell for this reference.

24 See, notably, in this regard, the influential study by Shula Marks, *The Ambiguities of Dependence in South Africa: Class, Nationalism and the State in Twentieth Century Natal*. Johannesburg, Ravan Press, 1986.

25 See notably Odendaal, *The Founders*.

26 Peter Limb, *The ANC's Early Years: Nation, Class and Place in South Africa before 1940*. Pretoria, University of South Africa Press, 2010, p. 117.

27 Mary Benson, *South Africa: The Struggle for a Birthright*. London, Penguin, 1966, p. 24.

28 P. Walshe, *The Rise of African Nationalism in South Africa: The African National Congress, 1912–1952*. London, Hurst, 1970, p. 34.

29 Benson, *South Africa*, p. 25.

30 Ibid., p. 24.

31 Saul Dubow, *The African National Congress*. Johannesburg, Jonathan Ball, 2000, p. 4.

32 Limb, *The ANC's Early Years*, pp. 122–123.

33 Ibid., p. 27.

34 Ibid., pp. 483–493.

35 The Congress Alliance initially linked the ANC to the (South African) Indian National Congress, the Coloured People's Congress and the Congress of Democrats (for whites) before being joined by the South African Congress of Trade Unions (SACTU) after its formation in 1955.

36 Edward Feit, *African Opposition in South Africa: The Failure of Passive Resistance*. Stanford, Stanford University Press, 1967.

37 For instance, Robert Fine with Dennis Davis, *Beyond Apartheid: Labour and Liberation in South Africa*. London, Pluto Press, 1990, pp. 266–275; and Robert Lambert, 'Political Unionism and Working Class Hegemony: Perspectives on the South African Congress of Trade Unions, 1955–1965', *Labour, Capital and Society*, 18, 2, 1985, pp. 244–277.

38 For 1945, *State of South Africa: Economic, Financial and Statistical Year-Book for the Republic of South Africa, 1967*. Johannesburg, Da Gama Publications, p. 107; for 1970, South African Institute of Race Relations (SAIRR), *A Survey of Race Relations in South Africa, 1971*. Johannesburg, SAIRR, 1972, p. 257.

39 There were a total of 5,407 African students enrolled in South African universities in 1971 (albeit 2,804 by correspondence at UNISA). See SAIRR, *Survey 1971*, p. 289.

40 Jordan, 'The African Petty Bourgeoisie', citing Table 4, ch. 31, in the *South African Year-Book* for 1975. For the feminisation of the teaching profession, see Shirley Mahlase, *The Careers of Women Teachers under Apartheid*. Harare, SAPES Books, 1997, pp. 56–59.

41 Kuper, *An African Bourgeoisie*.

42 Ibid., p. ix.

43 Ibid., pp. 1–8.

44 Ibid., p. 8.

45 Monica Wilson and Archie Mafeje, *Langa: A Study of Social Groups in an African Township*. Cape Town, Oxford University Press, 1963, p. 7.

46 Ibid., p. 15.

47 Ibid., p. 147.

48 Mia Brandel-Syrier, *Reeftown Elite: A Study of Social Mobility in a Modern African Community on the Reef*. London, Routledge and Kegan Paul, 1971, pp. 8–20.

49 Thomas Nyquist, *African Middle Class Elite*, Occasional Paper No. 28, Institute of Social and Economic Research, Rhodes University, 1983, p. 21.

50 Actually, there were five tiers, with the profession of 'Doctor' standing alone as 'very high', and 'latrine worker' similarly on its own as 'very low'.

51 Nyquist, *African Middle Class Elite*, pp. 260–261.

52 But see Lynette Dreyer, *The Modern African Elite of South Africa*. Basingstoke, Macmillan, 1987.

53 Dan O'Meara, *Forty Lost Years: The Apartheid State and the Politics of the National Party, 1948–1994.* Johannesburg, Ravan Press, 1996, pp. 272–274.

54 Owen Crankshaw, *Race, Class and the Changing Division of Labour under Apartheid*. Oxford, Taylor and Francis, 2002.

55 Hermann Giliomee, *The Last Afrikaner Leaders: A Supreme Test of Power.* Cape Town, Tafelberg, 2012, p. 146.

56 SAIRR, *Survey 1971*, pp. 257 and 289; SAIRR, *Race Relations Survey 1989/90.* pp. 824, 862 and 872.

57 Dreyer, *Modern African Elite*, Table 2.1, p. 16, cites a total of 2,860 Africans in managerial and administrative occupations.

58 Roger Southall, 'The Beneficiaries of Transkeian "Independence"', *Journal of Modern African Studies*, 15, 1, 1976, pp. 1–26; Roger Southall, *South Africa's Transkei: The Political Economy of an 'Independent' Bantustan.* London, Heinemann Educational, 1983. An interesting follow-up, by a dissident daughter of Transkeian President Kaiser Matanzima, argued more strongly that 'there is no evidence that teachers favour collaboration with the Nationalist Government'. See Xoliswa Jozana, 'The Transkeian Middle Class: Its Political Implications', *Africa Perspective*, 1, 7 & 8, 1989, pp. 94–104, citation from p. 96.

59 Sam Nolutshungu, *Changing South Africa: Political Considerations*. Manchester, Manchester University Press, 1982.

60 Jeff Peires, 'The Implosion of Transkei and Ciskei', *African Affairs*, 91, 1992, pp. 365–387. For a similar analysis, see Peter Delius, 'Chieftainship, Civil Society and the Political Transition in South Africa', *Critical Sociology*, 22, 1996.

61 O'Meara, *Forty Lost Years*, pp. 272–274.

62 Stuart Jones and Andre Miller, *The South African Economy, 1910–90*. New York, St Martin's Press, 1992, p. 321.

63 Charles Kekana, 'The Effect of Influx Control on the African Middle Class', MA thesis, University of the Witwatersrand, 1990.

64 Joe Slovo, 'South Africa: No Middle Road', in Basil Davidson, Joe Slovo and Anthony Wilkinson (eds.), *South Africa: The New Politics of Revolution*. Harmondsworth, Penguin, 1976, pp. 103–210. Also Harold Wolpe, *Race, Class and the Apartheid State*. London, James Currey, 1988.

65 Jordan, 'The African Petty Bourgeoisie', p. 32.

66 Bonginkosi Nzimande, 'Managers and the New Middle Class', *Transformation*, 1, 1986, pp. 39–62.

67 Ibid., p. 56.

68 For a more extended treatment, see Bonginkosi Nzimande, 'Class, National Oppression and the African Petty Bourgeoisie: The Case of the African Traders', in Robin Cohen, Yvonne Muthien and Abebe Zegeye (eds.), *Repression and Resistance: Insider Accounts of Apartheid*. London, Hans Zell, 1990, pp. 165–210.

69 Philip Eidelberg, 'Guerrilla Warfare and the Decline of Urban Apartheid: The Shaping of a New African Middle Class and the Transformation of the African National Congress

(1975–1985)', *Comparative Studies of South Asia, Africa and the Middle East*, 19, 1, 1999, pp. 51–65.

70 Ibid., p. 51.

71 Ibid., p. 54.

72 Ibid., p. 62.

73 Roger Southall, 'The ANC: Party Vanguard of the Black Middle Class?', in Arianna Lissoni, Jon Soske, Natasha Erlank, Noor Nieftagodien and Omar Badsha (eds.), *One Hundred Years of the ANC: Debating Liberation Histories Today*. Johannesburg, Wits University Press, 2012, pp. 325–346.

Chapter 3: The black middle class in post-apartheid South Africa

1 But note the recent publication of statistical data on the middle class by the South African Institute of Race Relations, *FastFacts*, 7/2015, July 2015, Issue 287.

2 There is, however, a decent literature on Indian merchant capital and entrepreneurship, and numerous passing references to a subaltern Indian bourgeoisie. For an important treatment, see Vishnu Padayachee and Gillian Hart, 'Indian Business in South Africa after Apartheid: Old and New Trajectories', *Comparative Studies in History and Society*, 42, 4, 2000, pp. 683–712. Even so, the profiling of an 'Indian middle class' would need the scholar to cut deeply into the historical undergrowth. This would be even more the case for any analysis of a 'Coloured' middle class.

3 HSRC, *Opinion Survey – Electronic Data*. Pretoria, HSRC, 2000.

4 Carlos Garcia Rivero, Pierre du Toit and Hennie Kotze, 'Tracking the Development of the Middle Class in Democratic South Africa', *Politeia*, 22, 3, 2003, pp. 6–29.

5 Jan Cronje, '"Meteoric" Growth of Black Middle Class', 2013, *IOL News*, www.iol. co.za/new/south-africa/western-cape/meteoric-growth-of-black-middle-class-1.1514101#VCJ8_5SSy8A. Unfortunately, my access to the Unilever Institute's 2013 report, '4 Million and Rising', has been blocked by lack of available research funds to pay the commercial price required.

6 Eric Udjo, 'The Demographics of the Emerging Black Middle Class in South Africa', Bureau of Market Research, College of Economic and Management Sciences, University of South Africa, Research Report No. 375, 2008.

7 Hopefully, the analysts whose work I am citing will excuse its summary form, and its skipping over the often highly technical methodologies they employ.

8 Deloitte on Africa, 'The Rise and Rise of the African Middle Class', 2013; www.deloitte. com/assets/Dcom-South Africa/ local%20 Assets/Documents, rise_and_rise.pdf.

9 The ADB recognises this is too low for inclusion in the middle class in the developed world, but deems it appropriate in the world's poorest continent, where average income is much lower than in the West.

10 V. Mahajan, *Africa Rising: How 900 Million African Consumers Offer More Than You Think*. New Jersey, Pearson Education, 2009.

11 Hilde Ibsen, 'Black Diamond: The Jewel in the South African Developmental State', forthcoming.

12 S. Burton and P. Hawthorne, 'South Africa: The New Black Middle Class', *Time*, 29 February 1988.

13 See, notably, L.M. Ungerer, 'Activities, Lifestyles and Status Products of the Newly-Emerging Middle Class in Gauteng', Bureau of Market Research, UNISA, Research Report, 1999; and J.H. Martins, 'Income and Expenditure by Product and Type of Outlet

of Middle and Upper Class Black Households in Gauteng, 1999', Bureau of Market Research, UNISA, Research Report No. 275, 2000.

14 Paul Haupt, 'The SAARF Universal Living Standards Measure (SU-LSM): 12 Years of Continuous Development', www.saarf.co.za/LSM/lsm-article.asp. Note, however, that Haupt's reference to a 'wealth' measurement refers largely to possession or non-possession of consumer goods, and not ownership of houses and financial assets – the principal measures of 'capital' in contemporary South Africa.

15 These include the following: hot running water; fridge/freezer; microwave oven; flush toilet in house or on plot; VCR in household; vacuum cleaner/floor polisher; washing machine; computer; electric stove; TV; tumble dryer; Telkom telephone; hi-fi or music centre; built-in kitchen sink; home security service; deep freeze; water in home or on stand; M-Net or DStv (private TV channels); dishwasher; metropolitan dweller; sewing machine; DVD player; house/cluster/town house; motor vehicle(s); no domestic worker; no cell phone in household; 1 cell phone in household; none or only one radio; and living in an urban area.

16 C.J. van Aardt, 'Forecast of the Adult Population by Living Standards Measure (LSM) for the Period 2005 to 2015', Bureau of Market Research, UNISA, Research Report 348, 2006.

17 Haupt, 'The SAARF Universal Living Standards Measure'.

18 University of Cape Town Unilever Institute of Strategic Marketing, 'Black Diamonds: Unearthing South Africa's New Black Middle Class', 2005, CD PowerPoint Presentation (African Studies Library, University of Cape Town).

19 UCT, 'Booming Black Middle Class Weighs In with a Whopping R 400 Billion Annual Consumer Spend', University of Cape Town, *Monday Paper*, 13–26 May 2013.

20 Cronje, '"Meteoric" Growth of Black Middle Class'.

21 For instance, Sharda Naidoo, 'Black Power: Exploding Number of Affluent Africans Set to Propel Economic Growth', *Sunday Times*, 20 May 2007.

22 Cronje, '"Meteoric" Growth of Black Middle Class'.

23 Claire Bisseker, 'Breaking Class', *Financial Mail*, December 2004. See also Edward Stoddard, 'Black Middle Class Is "Great for Stability" and Vindicates Mbeki's Policies', *Business Report*, 11 July 2006.

24 Cited in Ibsen, 'Black Diamond'.

25 Where else, for instance, other than a Black Diamonds survey, would you have 'sex' listed as a hobby of the black middle class?

26 Justin Visagie, 'The Development of the Middle Class in Post-Apartheid South Africa', Paper Presented at the Microeconometric Analysis of South African Data Conference 2011, Salt Rock Hotel, October 2011; and Justin Visagie and Dorrit Posel, 'A Reconsideration of What and Who Is Middle Class in South Africa', *Development Southern Africa*, 30, 2, 2013, pp. 149–167. See also Ronelle Burger, Cindy Lee Steenekamp, Servaas van der Berg and Asmus Zoch, 'The Middle Class in Contemporary South Africa: Comparing Rival Approaches', Stellenbosch Economic Working Papers, 11/14, Bureau for Economic Research, University of Stellenbosch, 2014. Using the same data base (mainly the National Income Dynamics Study, a national household panel study undertaken by entities at the University of Cape Town), they similarly demonstrate significantly different outcomes regarding the size of the middle class according to whether it is defined by occupation and skill, vulnerability (defined by a panel of experts), income and, lastly, self-identification.

27 They recognise a sociological tradition of class analysis centred around occupation, but

fault this for being based upon the work status of individuals, thereby failing to classify (for instance) the unemployed or those outside the labour force.

28 'Including not only labour market income, but also government grant income; other government income; investment income; remittance income; and agricultural income' (Visagie and Posel, 'Reconsideration', p. 4).

29 Thus, they explain:
- 'The middle tercile' definition defines the middle third of households, according to per capita household income distribution, as constituting the middle class.
- The second definition identifies the middle class in terms of its falling between 75 per cent and 125 per cent of median income in the per capita income distribution (the 75–125% median definition).
- The third definition adopts an income range of between 50 and 150% of median income, (the 50–150% median definition).

Correspondingly,
- The middle tercile definition has the widest income boundary for the middle class, with 4.56 million households falling within this income threshold.
- The 50–150% income definition selects a total of 4.25 million middle-class households, of which 1.52 million fall below the poverty line.
- The 75–125% median definition identifies the smallest range for the middle class, placing only 1.96 million households into the middle class.

30 The 'mean' is the 'average'. All numbers are added together and then divided by the number of numbers. The 'median' is the 'middle' value in a list of numbers. So to find the median, numbers are placed in value order, with the middle number constituting the median. Example: find the median of {13, 23, 11, 16, 15, 10, 26}. The middle number is 15, so the median is 15. (If there are two middle numbers, you average them.)

31 Lawrence Schlemmer, 'Lost in Transformation? South Africa's Emerging African Middle Class', Centre for Development Enterprise, *CDE Focus*, 8, 2005.

32 Visagie and Posel, 'Reconsideration', p. 165.

33 Visagie, 'Development of the Middle Class', p. 8, Table 2.

34 Visagie and Posel, 'Reconsideration', p. 159.

35 Ibid., p. 166.

36 Ibid., p. 166.

37 Garcia Rivero, Du Toit and Kotze, 'Tracking the Development of the Middle Class', p. 19.

38 Ibid., p. 23.

39 Jeremy Seekings and Nicoli Nattrass, *Class, Race and Inequality in South Africa*. Scottsville, University of KwaZulu-Natal Press, 2006, p. 26.

40 Owen Crankshaw, *Race, Class, and the Changing Division of Labour under Apartheid*. London, Routledge, 1997.

41 Seekings and Nattrass, *Class, Race and Inequality in South Africa*. My condensation of their approach as depicted in Figure 3.1 is drawn from chapters 7 and 9.

42 PSLSD (Project for Statistics on Living Standards and Development), *South Africans Rich and Poor: Borderline Household Statistics*. Cape Town, South African Labour and Development Research Unit, University of Cape Town, 1994.

43 Seekings and Nattrass, *Class, Race and Inequality*, p. 254.

44 An interesting critique of Seekings and Nattrass's triangular conception of the class structure is offered by Ben Scully, 'Development in the Age of Wagelessness: Labor, Livelihoods, and the Decline of Work in South Africa', PhD thesis, Johns Hopkins

University, 2013. Scully opts for a diamond-shaped model divided across a top band (composed of 10–20% of households), a 'middle majority' band (67–77% of households), and an 'isolated underclass' (13% of households). His major argument is that for the large majority of the 'middle majority', 'sharing and cooperation across various labor market positions are essential to both short and long time livelihood' (so, for instance, employed workers may rely upon unemployed family members for child care, or for dependence upon access to rural housing to provide stability during a future retirement' (p. 156)). Such interdependence, he argues, shapes workers' *ways of life,* through which workers' material interests extend beyond their own immediate labour market position. However, while Scully's argument is clearly important, I am not sure that it is helpful for identifying a 'middle class', as Scully's 'middle majority' would seem to throw the middle class and the better-off segments of the working class into one broad category.

45 Seekings and Nattrass, *Class, Race and Inequality,* pp. 308–314.
46 Roger Southall, 'Political Change and the Black Middle Class in Democratic South Africa', *Canadian Journal of African Studies,* 38, 3, 2004, pp. 521–542; reprinted in Alan Jeeves and Greg Cuthbertson (eds.), *Fragile Freedom: South African Democracy 1994–2004.* Pretoria, University of South Africa Press, 2008, pp. 31–49.
47 Blade Nzimande, 'Class, National Oppression and the African Petty Bourgeoisie: The Case of African Traders', in Robin Cohen, Yvonne Muthien and Abebe Zegeye (eds.), *Repression and Resistance: Insider Accounts of Apartheid.* London, Hans Zell, 1990, pp. 165–210.
48 Southall, 'Political Change', p. 540.
49 Roger Southall, *Liberation Movements in Power: Party and State in Southern Africa.* Scottsville, University of KwaZulu-Natal Press, 2013.
50 Roger Southall, 'The Power Elite in Democratic South Africa: Race and Class in a Fractured Society', in John Daniel, Prishani Naidoo, Devan Pillay and Roger Southall (eds.), *New South African Review 3: The Second Phase – Tragedy or Farce.* Johannesburg, Wits University Press, 2013, pp. 17–38.
51 Thomas Piketty, *Capital in the Twentieth Century.* Cambridge, The Belknap Press of Harvard University Press, 2013, p. 326, observes that the limitations of historical sources make it much harder to study the long-run dynamics of wealth distribution in developing countries than in the rich countries. Thus, although he notes that tax data are available for South Africa from 1913, which are useful for calculating income inequalities, there is no equivalent source available for the examination of inequalities of wealth.

Chapter 4: Black class formation under the ANC

1 I have explored the dynamics of the transition and the NDR in Roger Southall, *Liberation Movements in Power: Party and State in Southern Africa.* Woodbridge. James Currey; Scottsville, University of KwaZulu-Natal Press, 2013.
2 Sampie Terreblanche, *A History of Inequality in South Africa 1652–2002.* Pietermaritzburg, University of Natal Press, 2002, pp. 73–84.
3 Ibid., p. 76.
4 Owen Crankshaw, 'Changes in the Racial Division of Labour during the Apartheid Era', *Journal of Southern African Studies,* 22, 4, 1996, pp. 633–656.
5 Ibid., pp. 643–645.
6 Ibid., pp. 645–649.

7 Ibid., pp. 649–642.

8 This section draws on valuable interviews conducted by the author and Don Lindsay with Dr Sam Motsuenyane, former president of the National African Federated Chamber of Commerce, 5 December 2012; Mr Julian Ogilvie-Thompson, former director of Anglo American, 6 December 2012; Ms Wendy Luhabe, prominent businessperson and founder of the Women's Investment Portfolio Holdings, 10 December 2012; Professor Peet Strydom, formerly adviser to Sankorp, 31 January 2013; and Mr Herman Mashaba of Lephatsi Investments and chairman of the Free Market Foundation, 11 February 2013.

9 Sipho Maseko, 'Black Bourgeoisie in South Africa: From Pavement Entrepreneurs to Stock Exchange Capitalists', Seminar, Centre for African Studies, University of Cape Town, 19 May 1999.

10 SAIRR, *A Survey of Race Relations in South Africa, 1975*. Johannesburg, SAIRR, 1976, pp. 228–229.

11 Maseko, 'Black Bourgeoisie'. See also Wendy Luhabe, *Defining Moments: Experiences of Black Executives in South Africa's Workplace*. Pietermaritzburg, University of KwaZulu-Natal Press, 2002; and Sam Motsuenyane, *A Testament of Hope: The Autobiography of Dr Sam Motsuenyane*. Johannesburg, KMM Review Publishing, 2012, for insider accounts of this period.

12 Maseko, 'Black Bourgeoisie'.

13 Grietjie Verhoef, '"The Invisible Hand": The Roots of Black Economic Empowerment, Sankorp and Societal Change in South Africa, 1995–2000', *Journal of Contemporary History*, 28, 1, 2003, pp. 27–47.

14 Patrick Bond, *Elite Transition: From Apartheid to Neo-Liberalism in South Africa*. Pietermaritzburg, University of Natal Press, 2000, ch. 3, 'Social Contract Scenarios'.

15 Southall, *Liberation Movements*, ch. 6.

16 Ibid., ch. 9.

17 Susan Booysen, *The African National Congress and the Regeneration of Political Power*. Johannesburg, Wits University Press, 2011, pp. 373–378.

18 Collette Schulz-Herzenberg, 'The 2014 National and Provincial Results', in Collette Schulz-Herzenberg and Roger Southall (eds.), *Election 2014 South Africa: The Campaign, Results and Future Prospects*. Auckland Park, Jacana Media, 2014, pp. 188–227.

19 This was a long-running saga involving the ANC's use of its majority in parliament to protect the president in defiance of a demand, issued in a report of the public protector, Thuli Madonsela, that he assume financial responsibility for unjustified or illegal expenditure at Nkandla, which had redounded to his personal advantage.

20 Zuma's ascent to the presidency saw the apparent use of political pressure upon the then acting national director of public prosecutions to drop some 783 charges relating to corruption, fraud and racketeering in connection with the ANC's 1998 Arms Deal. Zuma was thereafter to face a long-running legal campaign by the opposition Democratic Alliance to have the charges reinstated. Zuma's presidency was also associated with the rise of 'Zuma Inc', whereby an interlocking group of Zuma family, friends and associates appears to have secured massive financial advantage through their close connection to the party and the state. See Southall, *Liberation Movements*, pp. 293–326.

21 I am indebted to Don Lindsay for the tracing of this lineage.

22 SAIRR, *South Africa Survey 1999/2000*. Johannesburg, SAIRR, 2000, p. 250.

23 Affirmative action is often presented as deliberately discriminatory against Afrikaners in particular. See for example Dan Roodt, *The Scourge of the ANC*. Dainfern, Praag, 2004, which includes an essay entitled 'Afrikaner Survival under Black Rule'.

24 Those wishing to track the debate on affirmative action are well advised to follow the letters columns in the media. More formally, they may refer to Blade Nzimande and Mpumelelo Sikhosana (eds.), *Affirmative Action and Transformation*. Durban, Indicator Press, 1996; and Omano Edigheji, 'Affirmative Action and State Capacity in a Democratic South Africa', *Policy: Issues and Actors*, 20, 4, Johannesburg, Centre for Policy Studies, 2007.

25 Vino Naidoo, 'Assessing Racial Redress in the Public Service', in Kristina Bentley and Adam Habib (eds.), *Racial Redress and Citizenship in South Africa*. Cape Town, HSRC Press, 2008, pp. 99–128.

26 Louis Picard, *The State of the State: Institutional Transformation, Capacity and Political Change in South Africa*. Johannesburg, Wits University Press, 2005, p. 301.

27 Naidoo, 'Assessing Racial Redress'.

28 Ivor Chipkin and Sarah Meny-Gibert, 'Why the Past Matters: Studying Public Administration in South Africa', *Journal of Public Administration*, 47, 1, 2012, pp. 102–112.

29 Picard, *The State of the State*, p. 302.

30 Geraldine Fraser-Moleketi, 'Public Service Reform in South Africa: An Overview of Selected Case Studies from 1994–2004', MAdmin thesis, University of Pretoria, 2006, p. 99.

31 C. Milne, 'Affirmative Action in South Africa: From Targets to Empowerment', *Journal of Public Administration*, 44, 4.1, 2009, pp. 969–990.

32 National Planning Commission, Diagnostic Report 2011, https://pmg.org.za.

33 The Presidency, Republic of South Africa, Presidential Review Committee on State-Owned Entities, Vol. 1, Executive Summary of the Final Report, 2013.

34 Roger Southall, 'The ANC, Black Economic Empowerment and State-Owned Enterprises: A Recycling of History?', in Sakhela Buhlungu, John Daniel, Roger Southall and Jessica Lutchman (eds.), *State of the Nation: South Africa 2007*. Cape Town, HSRC Press, 2007, pp. 201–225.

35 See, for instance, Kesh Govinder, Nombuso Zondo and Malegapuru Makgoba, 'A New Look at Demographic Transformation for Universities in South Africa', *South African Journal of Science*, 109, 11/12, 2013, pp. 1–11.

36 *Commission for Employment Equity Report, 1999–2001*, pp. 41–42, www.labour.gov.za.

37 Anthea Jeffrey, 'Employment Equity Bill: Taking an Unnecessary Big Stick to Business', *Daily Maverick*, 18 October 2014.

38 Standard Bank, '2012 Black Economic Empowerment Report', 2012, p. 6. Note, however, that the Standard Bank uses the term 'black' in an all-inclusive sense.

39 *The Little Black Book 2009/10*. Johannesburg, Financial Mail, 2010, p. 7.

40 Gavin Davis, 'The Zumafication of the SABC', *Sunday Times*, 19 October 2014. Davis explores the political dynamics, protective of President Zuma, which lay behind the appointment of Hlaudi Motsoeneng as chief operating officer of the SABC, despite the fact that he has been proven not to have passed his matric.

41 Geoffrey Modisha, 'A Contradictory Class Location? The African Corporate Middle Class and the Burden of Race in South Africa', *Transformation*, 65, 2008, pp. 120–145.

42 Participant in Konrad Adenauer Foundation Cape Town Middle Class Focus Group, 11 September 2013.

43 Geraldine Martin and Kevin Durrheim, 'Racial Recruitment in Post-Apartheid South Africa: Dilemmas of Private Recruitment Agencies', *Psychology in Society*, 33, 2006, pp. 1–15.

44 Christo Nel, *Transformation without Sacrifice*. Cape Town, Village of Leaders Products,

cited by South African Board for People Practices (SABPP), 'SABPP Position Paper on Employment Equity and Transformation', 2013, p. 16.

45 Ibid., p. 22.

46 Southall, *Liberation Movements*, pp. 88–91.

47 Ibid., pp. 91–92.

48 Under the 1993 Constitution, section 25, property might only be expropriated in the public interest, with payment of compensation that is 'just and equitable'.

49 One of the criticisms levelled at white business was that it was handpicking black elite partners, but part of its problem was that white corporate leaders knew few blacks, and hence tended to deal with the few they knew.

50 Much of my discussion of the three phases of BEE is drawn from Southall, *Liberation Movements*, pp. 220–226.

51 William Gumede, *Thabo Mbeki and the Battle for the Soul of the ANC.* Cape Town, Zebra Press, 2005, p. 222.

52 Roger Tangri and Roger Southall, 'The Politics of Black Economic Empowerment in South Africa', *Journal of Southern African Studies*, 34, 3, 2008, pp. 699–716.

53 Jenny Cargill, *Trick or Treat: Rethinking Black Economic Empowerment.* Auckland Park, Jacana Media, 2010, p. 59.

54 Ernst & Young's figures differ considerably from those provided by Cargill (just R166 billion worth of BEE deals between 1996 and 2003, and R319 billion between 2004 and 2008), yet indicate a sharp drop in the number (from 125 and 58) and value (from R96 billion to R36.5 billion) of deals by 2009. SAIRR, *South Africa Survey 2010/2011.* Johannesburg, SAIRR, 2012, p. 351.

55 Don Lindsay, 'BEE Reform: The Case for an Institutional Perspective', in John Daniel, Prishani Naidoo, Devan Pillay and Roger Southall (eds.), *New South African Review: New Paths, Old Compromises?* Johannesburg, Wits University Press, 2011, pp. 236–255.

56 For instance, Gumede, *Thabo Mbeki*, pp. 215–233; Moeletsi Mbeki, *Architects of Poverty: Why African Capitalism Needs Changing.* Johannesburg, Picador Africa, 2009. For a valuable discussion see also Ben Turok, *From the Freedom Charter to Polokwane: The Evolution of ANC Economic Policy.* Cape Town, New Agenda, 2008, pp. 168–175.

57 'JSE's BEE Study Is Misleading, Says BMF', *Mail & Guardian Online*, 14 September 2010; www.mg.co.za/article/2010-09-14-jses-bee-study-is-misleading-says-bmf.

58 Media Club South Africa, 'JSE Black Ownership on the Increase', 12 December 2012, www.southafrica.info/businesstrends/empowerment/jse-121212.htm#. VDPDrWeSy8A.

59 Loni Prinsloo, Thekiso Lefifi and Brendan Peacock, 'Big Salute for New BEE Rules', *Sunday Times*, 10 May 2015.

60 Theresa Taylor, 'Huge Spike in SA Black Millionaires', *Business Report*, 15 Nov. 2013.

61 *Who Owns Whom 2014.* Johannesburg, Who Owns Whom, 2014, pp. 57–60.

62 Taylor, 'Huge Spike in SA Black Millionaires'.

63 Trailblazers 2012 Report, www.empowerdex.co.za/Portals/5/.../Trailblazers%20 report%202012.pdf.

64 Ibid.

65 Georgina Murray, 'Black Empowerment in South Africa: "Patriotic Capitalism" or a Corporate Black Wash?', *Critical Sociology*, 26, 3, 2000, pp. 183–204.

66 Malose Monama, 'Black CEOs Thin on the Ground', *Fin24*, 21 June 2009, www.fin24. com/Business/Black-CEOs-thin-on-the-ground-20090621.

67 Wendy Luhabe, interview with Don Lindsay and Roger Southall, 10 December 2012.

68 Herman Mashaba, interview with Don Lindsay and Roger Southall, 11 February 2013.
69 Richard Calland, *The Zuma Years: South Africa's Changing Face of Power.* Cape Town, Zebra Press, 2013, p. 341, citing 'Who Owns What', a database compiled by the Institute for Security Studies.
70 Parliamentary Monitoring Group, 'State of the Public Service Report 2011: Public Service Commission Briefing', www.pmg.org.za/report/20111123-state-of-the-public-service-report -2011.
71 According to Statistics South Africa, private-sector growth declined from 6.3 to 6.1 million between 2008 and 2012, while public-sector employment grew from 2.1 to 2.4 million. See Felicity Duncan, 'Employment Trends: A Hard Look at the Numbers', 2013, www.moneyweb.co.za/moneyweb-south-africa/employment-trends-a-hard-look-at-the-numbers.
72 Ian Macun, 'The State of Organised Labour: Still Living Like There's No Tomorrow', in Devan Pillay, Gilbert Khadiagala, Prishani Naidoo and Roger Southall (eds.), *New South African Review 4: A Fragile Democracy, Twenty Years On.* Johannesburg, Wits University Press, 2014, pp. 39–55.
73 *Business Day,* 24 October 2014.
74 Peter Bruce, 'Zuma: The One Button Nene Can't Press', *Business Day,* 24 October 2014.

Chapter 5: Education and black upward social mobility

1 Participant, Konrad Adenauer Foundation Middle Class Focus Group, East London, 15 July 2013.
2 On 'parentocracy' in schooling in Western societies, see Maria Alice Nogueira, 'A Revisited Theme: Middle Classes and the School', in Michael Apple, Stephen Ball and Luis Gandin (eds.), *The Routledge International Handbook of the Sociology of Education.* London, Routledge, 2010.
3 Badat and Sayed observe that 'Between 1994 and 2013, there were about seven white papers, three green papers, twenty-six bills (of which seventeen were amending bills), thirty-five acts, eleven regulations, fifty-two government notices, and twenty-six calls that encompassed basic to higher education'. See Saleem Badat and Yusuf Sayed, 'Post-1994 South African Education: The Challenge of Social Justice', in Robert Rotberg (ed.), 'Strengthening Governance in South Africa: Building on Mandela's Legacy', *Annals of the American Academy of Political Social Science,* 652, 2014, pp. 127–148 (citation from p. 131).
4 Edward Fiske and Helen Ladd, *Education Reform in Post-Apartheid South Africa.* Cape Town, HSRC Press, 2004, pp. 62–65.
5 John Pampallis, 'School Fees', *Issues in Education Policy No. 3,* Centre for Education Policy Development, Braamfontein, 2008, p. 10.
6 Raj Mestry and Raymond Ndhlovu, 'The Implications of the National Norms and Standards for School Funding Policy on Equity in South African Public Schools', *South African Journal of Education,* 34, 3, 2014, pp. 1–11.
7 Fiske and Ladd, *Education Reform,* p. 69.
8 Pampallis, 'School Fees', p. 11.
9 Fiske and Ladd, *Education Reform,* pp. 69–86.
10 SAIRR, *South African Survey 2012.* Johannesburg, SAIRR, 2013, p. 438.
11 World Bank, 'Government Expenditure on Education, Total', 2015, www.data.worldbank.org/indicator/SE.XPD.ROR.GB.ZS; chapter 3, Education, www.

treasury.gov.za/publications/igfr/2015/prov/03%20Chapter%203%20-%20 Education.pdf.

12 From a national average (based on rand value in 2000) of R3,250 in 2000 to R4,439 in 2007. SAIRR, *Survey 2012*, p. 418.

13 See the Department of Education, *Norms and Standards for School Funding*, 1998.

14 For overviews of the introduction and results of Outcomes Based Education, see Fiske and Ladd, *Education Reform*, pp.173–200; and Yusuf Sayed and Anil Kanjee, 'An Overview of Education Policy Change in Post-Apartheid South Africa', in Yusuf Sayed, Anil Kanjee and Nkomo Mokubung (eds.), *The Search for Education Quality in Post-Apartheid South Africa: Interventions to Improve Learning and Teaching*. Cape Town, HSRC Press, 2013, pp. 5–38.

15 Nicholas Spaull, 'Education in South Africa: Still Separate and Unequal', 2014, http:// nicspaull.com/2014/01/12/educations-in-sa-still-separate-and-unequal-extended-version-of-city-press-article.

16 The proportion of provincial budgets spent on education ranged from a high of 10.9% in Gauteng to a low of 5.0% in Limpopo during the period 2010–2013/14. See chapter 3, Education, www.treasury.gov.za/publications/igfr/2015/prov/03%20Chapter% 203%20-%20Education.pdf.

17 Nicholas Spaull, *South Africa's Education Crisis: The Quality of Education in South Africa 1994–2011*. Centre for Development Enterprise, Johannesburg, 2013, p. 58.

18 Badat and Sayed, 'Post-1994 South African Education', p. 134.

19 Spaull, *South Africa's Education Crisis*, p. 6.

20 Note that although schools in quintiles 1–3 were no longer allowed to charge fees for children in Grades 1–9 (catering for the years of compulsory school attendance), learners in Grades 10–12 have to pay fees, even if they live in the poorest areas. See Lee-Ann Collingridge, 'Schools Quintile System to Change?', 2014, www.corruptionwatch. org.za/content/schools-quintile-system-to-change.

21 Research had previously indicated that the quintile system was not working effectively, and that the schools most disadvantaged were those assigned to the middle rather than the lower quintiles. Amita Chudgar and Anil Kanjee, 'School Money: Funding Flaws', *HSRC Review*, 7, 4, 2009, pp. 8–19.

22 Media Release, Minister of Education Donald Grant, Western Cape, 'Background to the National Quintile System', 14 October 2013, www.wced.pgwc.gov.za/comms/ press/2013/74_14oct.html.

23 Note a judgment of the Constitutional Court in 2013 which instructed the principal of a primary school in Rivonia to admit a learner in excess of the limit in its admission policy, on the grounds that the school did not have an absolute right to lay down the maximum capacity of a public school, given that unequal education perpetuates historical inequalities. The implication was that an appropriate balance was required between provincial education departments and SGBs in relation to admissions policies.

24 SAIRR, *Survey 2012*, p. 456. Note, however, it is not clear whether, prior to 2011, some of these teachers might have been employed in SGBs running schools in quintiles 1–3, although it may be presumed that the large majority would always have been employed by SGBs in quintiles 4 and 5.

25 At least one school, Rondebosch Boys' High School, located at the apex of the public school system, also invited parents to pay a tax-deductible 'voluntary development levy'.

26 'Public School Fees "Shocking"', *City Press*, 27 October 2012.

27 In the school concerned, figures for 2005 recorded 69% of students were white, 22% Coloured, 4% African, and 4% Indian (figures supplied by headmaster to author). Although the interview was conducted in 2013, these seemed to be the latest figures available.

28 Konrad Adenauer Foundation Middle Class Focus Group, Gauteng, 12 July 2013.

29 Shireen Motala, 'Equity, Quality and Access in South African Education: A Work Still Very Much in Progress', in John Daniel, Prishani Naidoo, Devan Pillay and Roger Southall (eds.), *New South African Review: The Second Phase – Tragedy or Farce?* Johannesburg, Wits University Press, 2013, pp. 221–338.

30 Sipho Masondo, 'Desperate to Get Their Children into Former Model C Schools', *City Press*, 13 April 2014.

31 Zwelani Ncube, 'Plight of the Privileged "White Schools"', *Daily Dispatch*, 9 November 2013, presumably referring to some of such schools in the Eastern Cape.

32 Crain Soudien, '"Constituting the Class": An Analysis of the Process of "Integration" in South African Schools', in Linda Chisholm (ed.), *Changing Class: Education and Social Change in Post-Apartheid South Africa*. Cape Town, HSRC Press, 2004, pp. 89–114 (citation from p. 89).

33 Ibid., pp. 109–110.

34 Ibid., p. 97.

35 In an earlier study, Soudien cites how in Gauteng in 2002, 'only 5% of former Indian schools, 45% of former Coloured schools, and 34% of former White schools were deemed to have low levels of integration'. See Crain Soudien, 'The Reconstitution of Privilege: Integration in Former White Schools in South Africa', *Journal of Social Issues*, 66, 2, 2010, pp. 353–366 (citation from p. 353).

36 Nomlanga Mkhize, 'Quest for English Robs Our Schools of Language', *Business Day*, 21 October 2014.

37 Vivien de Klerk, 'Language Issues in Our Schools: Whose Voice Counts? Part 1: The Parents Speak', *Perspectives in Education*, 20, 1, 2002, pp. 1–14.

38 Soudien, 'The Reconstitution of Privilege'.

39 On this, see chapter 4, 'Old Mission Schools, 1963–1980', in Timothy Gibbs, *Mandela's Kinsmen: Nationalist Elites and Apartheid's First Bantustan*. Auckland Park, Jacana Media, 2014, pp. 70–90.

40 Vuyisile Msila, 'The Education Exodus: The Flight from Township Schools', *African Review of Education*, 2, 2, 2005, pp. 173–188.

41 Vuyisile Msila, 'School Choice and Intra-Township Migration: Black Parents Scrambling for Quality Education in South Africa', *Journal of Education*, 46, 2009, pp. 81–98.

42 Mark Hunter, 'The Remaking of Social-Spatial Hierarchies: Educational Choice and a South African City', Paper for RC21 Conference on 'Resourceful Cities', Berlin, 29–31 August 2013; and 'Circuits of Schooling and the Production of Space: The Family, Education, and Symbolic Struggles after Apartheid', Seminar Paper, WISER, 2014.

43 Jonny Steinberg, 'Competition Is Detrimental to Township Schools', *Business Day*, 14 November 2014.

44 Jane Hofmeyr and Simon Lee, 'The New Face of Private Schooling', in Chisholm, *Changing Class*, pp. 143–173.

45 Johan Muller, 'Schools without the State: A Study of Private and Alternative Schooling in Johannesburg', Education Policy Unit Research Report, University of the Witwatersrand, 1990, p. 4.

46 Hofmeyr and Lee, 'The New Face of Private Schooling', p. 152.

47 Pam Christie, *Open Schools: Racially Mixed Catholic Schools in South Africa 1976–1986*. Johannesburg, Ravan Press, 1990.

48 Agnes van Zanten, 'The Sociology of Elite Education', in Apple, Ball and Gandin, *Routledge International Handbook*, pp. 329–337.

49 Kentse Radebe, 'The Costly Choice between Public and Private Schooling', 2013, www.moneyweb.co.za/moneyweb-south-africa/the-costly-choice-between-public-and-private-school.

50 The content of this last paragraph is drawn from school 'advertorials' which regularly appear in the press.

51 Admittedly, these generalisations are largely impressionistic.

52 J. du Toit, *Independent Schooling: Assessing Its Size and Shape*. Pretoria, Research Programme on Human Resources Development, HSRC, 2003.

53 CDE, *Hidden Assets: South Africa's Low Fee Private Schools*. Johannesburg, CDE, 2013.

54 Jane Hofmeyr and Lindsay McCay, 'Private Education for the Poor: More, Different and Better', 2010, https://hsf.org.za/resource-centre/focus/focus-56-february-2010-on-learning-and-teaching/private-education-for-the-poor-more-different-and-better.

55 Hofmeyr and Lee, 'The New Face of Private Schooling', p. 153.

56 They also included a category of 'spontaneous' schools, which come and go in poorer areas, but were unable to say much about them except to record their impression that the number of such 'fly-by-night' schools was increasing, although the CDE was later to dispute this.

57 Konrad Adenauer Foundation Middle Class Focus Group, Cape Town, 11 September 2013.

58 Prega Govender, 'The Great Migration: Parents Working Longer Hours and Making Huge Sacrifices to Move Their Children to Private Schools', *Sunday Times*, 30 November 2011.

59 Ibid.

60 Du Toit, *Independent Schooling*.

61 Private communication with the author.

62 SAIRR, *Survey 2012*, p. 446.

63 I am indebted to Francine de Clercq of Educational Leadership and Policy Studies at Wits University for this observation.

64 Tina Weavind, 'Investors Go Gaga for Private Schools', *Sunday Times*, 11 January 2015.

65 Badat and Sayed, 'Post-1994 South African Education', p. 134.

66 Jonathan Jansen, 'Changes and Continuities in South Africa's Higher Education System, 1994–2004', in Chisholm, *Changing Class*, pp. 293–314.

67 This was an extraordinarily complex process, ranging across systems of governance through to the 'transformation' of academic staff profiles, but it goes well beyond the scope of this chapter.

68 Simon McGrath, 'The State of the South African Further Education and Training College Sector', in Simon McGrath, Azeem Badroodien, André Kraak and Lorna Unwin (eds.), *Shifting Understandings of Skills in South Africa*. Cape Town, HSRC Press, 2004, pp. 158–174.

69 Figures drawn from Council on Higher Education, *VitalStats: Public Higher Education 2012*. Pretoria, CHE, 2015, pp. 33, 35 and 63.

70 SAIRR, *Survey 2012*, p. 504. See also A. de Lannoy, 'The Stuff That Dreams Are Made Of: Narratives on Educational Decision-Making among Young Adults in Cape Town', *Journal of Education*, 51, 2011, pp. 53–72.

71 Jansen, 'Changes and Continuities', p. 301.
72 Glenda Kruss, *Chasing Credentials and Mobility: Private Higher Education in South Africa*. Cape Town, HSRC Press, 2004, p. 2.
73 Note, however, that Curro Holdings is planning to build a private university for 10,000 students by the early 2020s: '"And I'm Not Talking a Mickey Mouse University" Claims Curro Founder Chris van der Merwe', *Sunday Times*, 8 February 2015.
74 Council on Higher Education, 'The State of Private Higher Education in South Africa', *Higher Education Monitor*, 1, 2003, pp. 1–17; Mahlubi Mabizela, 'Recounting the State of Private Higher Education in South Africa', in N.V. Varghese, *Growth and Expansion of Private Higher Education in Africa*. Paris, International Institute for Education Planning, 2006, pp. 131–163.
75 SAIRR, *Survey 2012*, p. 512.
76 Mabizela, 'Recounting the State', p. 147.
77 I reference here the huge controversy aroused by the University of Cape Town's policy of maintaining 'race' as a proxy for historical disadvantage. See, notably, Max Price, 'In Defence of Race-Based Policy', *Mail & Guardian*, 6 January 2012, www.mg.co.za/article/2012-01-06-in-defence-of-racebased-policy/; and Osiame Molefe, 'UCT's Admissions Policy Unearths Black Middle-Class Angst', *Daily Maverick*, 26 February 2013, www.dailymaverick.co.za/article/2012-03-14-ucts-admissions-policy-unearths. The policy was to be changed from 2014, when race would become just one of several factors to be considered in assessing an applicant's historical disadvantage.
78 For instance, Pierre Bourdieu, 'Cultural Reproduction and Social Reproduction', in J. Karabel and A.H. Halsey (eds.), *Power and Ideology in Education*. Oxford, Oxford University Press, 1977.

Chapter 6: The black middle class at work

1 Peter Franks, 'The Crisis of the South African Public Service', *Journal of the Helen Suzman Foundation*, 7, 2014, pp. 48–56.
2 Frantz Fanon, *The Wretched of the Earth*. Harmondsworth, Penguin, 1974, pp. 119–124.
3 Blade Nzimande, 'Class, National Oppression and the African Petty Bourgeoisie: The Case of the African Traders', in Robin Cohen, Yvonne Muthien and Abebe Zegeye (eds.), *Repression and Resistance: Insider Accounts of Apartheid*. London, Hans Zell, 1990, pp. 165–210.
4 G. Fraser-Moleketi, 'Public Service Reform in South Africa: An Overview of Selected Case Studies from 1994–2004', MAdmin thesis, University of Pretoria, 2006, p. 23.
5 Ivor Chipkin, 'Histories and Cultures of the Public Service in South Africa', 2011. www.pari.org.za/wp-content/uploads/2011/08.
6 Roger Southall, 'The Power Elite in Democratic South Africa: Race and Class in a Fractured Society', in John Daniel, Prishani Naidoo, Devan Pillay and Roger Southall (eds.), *New South African Review 3: The Second Phase – Tragedy or Farce?* Johannesburg, Wits University Press, 2013, pp. 17–38.
7 Doreen Atkinson, 'Provinces as Bulwarks: Centrifugal Forces within the ANC', *Transformation*, 87, 1, 2015, pp. 32–54.
8 Chipkin, 'Histories and Cultures of the Public Service', p. 4.
9 Peliwe Mnguni, 'Deploying Culture as a Defence against Incompetence: The Unconscious Dynamics of Public Service Work', *South African Journal of Industrial Psychology*, 38, 2, 2012.

10 Karl von Holdt and Mike Murphy, 'Public Hospitals in South Africa: Stressed Institutions, Disempowered Management', in Sakhela Buhlungu, John Daniel, Roger Southall and Jessica Lutchman (eds.), *State of the Nation: South Africa 2007*. Cape Town, HSRC Press, 2007, pp. 312–341.

11 Ben Fine and Zavareh Rustomjee, *The Political Economy of South Africa: From Minerals Energy Complex to Industrialisation*. London, Hurst, 1996; Jonathan Hyslop, 'Political Corruption: Before and after Apartheid', *Journal of Southern African Studies*, 31, 4, 2005, pp. 773–789.

12 Tom Lodge, 'Neo-Patrimonial Politics in the ANC', *African Affairs*, 113, 450, 2014, pp. 1–23.

13 Stephen Ellis, *External Mission: The ANC in Exile*. Johannesburg, Jonathan Ball, 2012.

14 Estimates of the cost of corruption vary. The amount of R30 billion per annum or more is regularly bandied about, and on one occasion Sipho Pityana, president of the Council for the Advancement of the South African Constitution, reckoned it to be as much as 20% of GDP (*The Times*, 16 May 2011).

15 Cited in Amuzweni Ngoma, 'Professional and Political Identity Repertoires of South Africa's Black Middle Class'. MA Research Report. Department of Sociology, University of the Witwatersrand, 2015, p. 85.

16 Wendy Luhabe, *Defining Moments: Experiences of Black Executives in South Africa's Workplace*. Pietermaritzburg, University of Natal Press, 2002, p. 66. The following paragraphs draw from this valuable source.

17 Johannes Mokoele, 'Perspectives of Black South African Managers Regarding Advancement into Senior Corporate Management Positions', PhD dissertation, Virginia Polytechnic Institute and State University, 1997.

18 Black Middle Class Focus Group, Konrad Adenauer Foundation, 12 July 2013.

19 Richard Calland, *The Zuma Years: South Africa's Changing Face of Power*. Cape Town, Zebra Press, 2013, pp. 337–338.

20 Black Middle Class Focus Group, Konrad Adenauer Foundation, Johannesburg, 12 July 2013.

21 Geoffrey Modisha, 'A Contradictory Class Location? An Exploration of the Position and Roles of the African Corporate Middle Class in South African Workplaces and Communities', MA Research Report, School of Social Sciences, University of the Witwatersrand, 2007.

22 Keith Macdonald, *The Sociology of the Professions*. London, Sage, 1995, pp. 29–35.

23 Calland, *The Zuma Years*, p. 369. Coloured attorneys, at just 1.3%, were severely underrepresented, but Indian lawyers were significantly overrepresented.

24 Ibid., p. 358. Coloured CAs formed just 2.8% and Indian CAs 9.6%.

25 Abram Molelemane and Nicholas Owsley, 'There Are Signs of Change in the Engineering Sector', *Creamer Media's Engineering News*, 10 May 2013. The use of the term 'black' in this instance was inclusive of Coloureds and Indians.

26 Higher Education South Africa (HESA), 'South African Higher Education in the 20th Year of Democracy: Context, Achievement and Key Challenges', HESA Presentation to the Portfolio Committee on Higher Education and Training, 5 March 2014.

27 For instance, Allyson Lawless, *Numbers and Needs: Addressing Imbalances in the Civil Engineering Profession*. Halfway House, South African Institution of Civil Engineering, 2015.

28 Human Sciences Research Council, Development Policy Research Unit, and Sociology of Work Unit Research Consortium, 'The Shortage of Medical Doctors in

South Africa', Research Commissioned by the Department of Labour, 2008, Tables 20 and 23.

29 Calland, *The Zuma Years*, pp. 258–359.

30 Luphert Chilwane, 'More Engineers than Before', *New Age*, 3 October 2011.

31 Prega Govender, 'UCT Urged to Scrap Race Criteria', *Sunday Times*, 15 August 2010. In 2010, UCT medical school was making 200 offers, 80 for whites and Indians, 80 for African and Coloured students. UCT vice-chancellor Max Price argued that although race was only a proxy for disadvantage, black students coming from township schools and obtaining 65–70% in matric would probably have obtained 90% if they had gone to a 'good' school. The debate about the use of 'race' by UCT as a proxy for historical disadvantage was to result in a change of policy in 2014. From 2016, 75% of student intake at first year would be based upon marks alone, only 25% on 'marks weighted upward by an index of disadvantage'. This was justified on the grounds that increased numbers of black applicants, most of whom now came from 'good schools', were able to compete with white students on more or less equal terms.

32 Calland, *The Zuma Years*, p. 382. Calland, himself a lawyer by training, provides an excellent overview of the complexities of the legal profession for the layman.

33 The government had earlier backed down on its intention to fuse the two branches of the profession, although the opponents of the eventual Act claimed that their being brought under the same regulatory authority was a back-door way of achieving this objective. The opponents of the Act also claimed that the proposed composition of the initially 'transitional' legal practice council would effectively enable the minister of justice to secure a majority in favour of government-sponsored transformation objectives.

34 Wyndham Hartley, 'Legal Practice Bill Forced Through Despite Opposition', *Business Day*, 13 November 2013. For a useful summary of the provisions of the Bill, see SAIRR, *Survey 2012*, pp. 756–759.

35 Dinga Nkhwashu, 'Here's Why Black Lawyers Struggle', *Politicsweb*, 31 July 2013; www. politicsweb.co.za/politicsweb/view/politicsweb/en/page7169?oid+395444&sn=Det ails&pid=71616. However, a black entrepreneur relating how she overcame delay in receiving payment for a job for government observed, 'We had to bring our white lawyers in and it worked … this boy looks fifteen, and said, we're going to get this money!' Black Middle Class Focus Group, Konrad Adenauer Foundation, Johannesburg, 12 July 2013.

36 Elmarie Sadler, 'A Profile and the Work Environment of Black Chartered Accountants in South Africa', *Meditari Accountancy Research*, 10, 2002, pp. 159–185.

37 Phakamisa Ndzamela, 'Black Accountants Body Celebrates 30 Years, but Challenges Remain', *Business Day*, 11 September 2015.

38 Sadler, 'Profile and the Work Environment'.

39 Phakamisa Ndzamela, 'What a Black Accounting Firm Tells Us about Transformation', *Rand Daily Mail*, 16 February 2015, http://www.rdm.co.za/business/2014/10/28/ what-a-black-accounting-firm-tells-us-about-transformation.

40 Keith Durrheim with Merridy Boetigger, Zaynab Essack, Silvia Maarschalk and Chita Ranchod, 'The Colour of Success: A Qualitative Study of Affirmative Action Attitudes of Black South African Academics', *Transformation*, 64, 2007, pp. 112–139.

41 Xolela Mangcu, 'Academic Whitewash', *City Press*, 6 January 2015. Mangcu has hung his more general criticisms around what he deems to be the dismal rate of transformation at the University of Cape Town, where he is a professor in sociology.

42 Xolela Mangcu, '10 Steps to Develop Black Professors', *City Press*, 20 July 2014; and 'SA's Black Academics Are Getting Raw Deal', *Business Day*, 3 November 2014.

43 Max Price, 'Staff Transformation at UCT', University of Cape Town/Newsroom & Publications/ Daily News, 14 July 2014.

44 Lieketso Mohoto, 'Black Rage in Privileged Universities', *Mail & Guardian*, 16–22 January 2015.

45 SADTU, 'The South African Democratic Teachers Union's 2030 Vision', 2010, www. sadtu.org.za/docs/disc/2010/2030vision.pdf, p. 2.

46 Ibid., p. 3.

47 Ibid., p. 5.

48 Ibid., p. 7.

49 Ibid., p. 7.

50 NAPTOSA, the National Professional Teachers' Organisation of South Africa; SAOU, the Suid-Afrikaanse Onderwysersunie.

51 Logan Govender, 'Teacher Unions, Policy Struggles and Educational Change, 1994 to 2004', in Linda Chisholm (ed.), *Changing Class: Education and Social Change in Post-Apartheid South Africa*. Cape Town, HSRC Press, 2004, pp. 267–291.

52 Clive Glaser, 'Champions of the Poor or "Militant Fighters for a Better Pay Cheque"? Teacher Unionism in Mexico and South Africa, 1979–2013', NRF Research Chair Seminar, University of the Witwatersrand, 20 August 2014 (unpaginated).

53 Ibid.

54 Gareth van Onselen, 'How SADTU and the SACE Have Damaged Accountability in SA Education', 2012, www.inside-politics.org/2012/06/25/how-sadtu-and-the-sace-have-damaged-accountability-in-sa.

55 Glaser, 'Champions of the Poor'.

56 Mignonne Breier, Angelique Wildschut and Thando Mgqolozana, *Nursing in a New Era: The Profession and Education of Nursing in South Africa*. Cape Town, HSRC Press, 2009, esp. ch. 7; Elizabeth Mokoka, Martha Oosthuizen and Valerie Ehlers, 'Retaining Professional Nurses in South Africa: Nurse Managers' Perspectives', *Journal of Interdisciplinary Health Sciences*, 15, 1, 2010; Lilian Dudley, 'Nurses Strike Action Highlights Human Resources Crisis within Public Health System', Health Systems Trust, 2007, www.hst.org.za.

57 Breier, Wildschut and Mgqolozana, *Nursing in a New Era*, p. 113.

58 Ibid., pp. 100, 113.

59 At the time they were writing, Breier and associates. (ibid., p. 100) reported that although DENOSA was led by a female secretary-general, Thembeka Gwagwa, one of her two deputies and six out of nine provincial secretaries were male, along with eleven out of the twelve full-time DENOSA shop stewards.

60 Marie Muller, 'Strike Action by Nurses in South Africa: A Value Clarification', *Curationis*, November 2001.

61 Ames Dhai, Harriet Etheredge, Merryll Vorster and Yosuf Veriava, 'The Public's Attitude towards Strike Action by Healthcare Workers and Health Services in South Africa', *South African Journal of Bioethics and Law*, 4, 2, 2011, www.sajbl.org.za/index.php/sajbl/article/view/163/159.

62 C. Wright Mills, *White Collar: The American Middle Classes*. London, Oxford University Press, 1951, pp. ix–xx.

63 We might add that life would become even more complicated for class categorisation if clerk and driver were married to each other.

64 Owen Crankshaw, 'Changes in the Racial Division of Labour during the Apartheid Era', *Journal of Southern African Studies*, 22, 4, 1996, pp. 633–656, citation from p. 642.

65 Manager, professional, technician, clerk, sales and service, skilled agriculture, craft and related trade, plant and machine operator, elementary and domestic worker.

66 For banking, see for example a Standard Bank report which offers details of the extensive benefits the bank provides to staff, these including what it claims are above-average salaries, pension, medical aid and wellness programmes ('Human Capital: The Competencies, Capabilities and Experience of Our People and Their Motivation to Innovate', http://sustainability.standardbank.com/wp-content/uploads/2014/04/Human-capital.pdf). For retail, see Bridget Kenny, 'The "Market Hegemonic" Workplace Order in Food Retailing', in Edward Webster and Karl von Holdt (eds.), *Beyond the Apartheid Workplace: Studies in Transition*. Scottsville, University of KwaZulu-Natal Press, 2005, pp. 217–242.

67 Rahmat Omar, 'New Work Order or More of the Same? Call Centres in South Africa', in Webster and Von Holdt, *Beyond the Apartheid Workplace*, pp. 267–288.

68 Ian Macun, 'The State of Organised Labour: Still Living Like There's No Tomorrow', in Devan Pillay, Gilbert Khadiagala, Prishani Naidoo, and Roger Southall (eds.), *New South African Review 4: A Fragile Democracy – Twenty Years On*. Johannesburg, Wits University Press, 2014, pp. 39–55. Macun notes that between 1990 and 2012 union density in manufacturing slumped from 70% to 31%; in finance from 35% to 21%; and declined from just 18% to 16.6% in wholesale and retail. See Table 2, p. 44.

69 'Public Service Jobs Yield "Easy Money"', *Business Day*, 16 March 2015.

70 According to Carol Paton, 'With the median wage in the economy at about R36,000 a year for those in formal employment, teachers at an entry-level wage of R148,000 and police and correctional service officers with starting salaries of R123,000 and R95,000 respectively, public servants are in a very different class from industrial workers.' *Business Day*, 10 July 2014.

71 COSATU, *The 11th COSATU Secretariat Report 2012*, p. 6, www.cosatu.org.za/eventslist.php?eid=31.

72 Paton, *Business Day*, 10 July 2014.

73 Sakhela Buhlungu, *A Paradox of Victory: Cosatu and the Democratic Transformation in South Africa*. Scottsville, UKZN Press, 2010, pp. 117–121.

74 Marx's sloganising of the values of the capitalist bourgeoisie is just as applicable to the party-state bourgeoisie.

Chapter 7: The social world of the black middle class

1 Élodie Escusa, 'A Class Defined by "Consumption": The Grocery Shopping Practices of the Lower-Middle Classes in Johannesburg, South Africa', Institut Français des Relations Internationales, Sub-Saharan Africa Programme, 2013.

2 *Business Day*, 16 December 2004.

3 M. Seabi, 'Tycoon's Super Sweet R700,000 Bash', *City Press*, 1 December 2010.

4 Thomas Piketty, *Capital in the Twenty-First Century*. Cambridge, The Belknap Press of Harvard University Press, 2014, pp. 260–262, 346–347, 373, 339–343 and 411–414.

5 Ibid., p. 290.

6 Ibid., pp. 326–330.

7 In this regard, Bank has observed increasing white poverty in East London, where, according to the 2011 census, some 40% of whites are struggling economically, as many

of them have lost jobs after the closure of factories. See Leslie Bank, 'The Pain and Shame of Growing White Poverty', *Daily Dispatch*, 12 April 2013.

8 Summarised from Nkululeko Mabandla, 'Rethinking Bundy: Land and the Black Middle Class – Accumulation beyond the Peasantry', *Development Southern Africa*, 32, 1, 2015, pp. 76–89.

9 See, for instance, Colin Murray, *Black Mountain: Land, Class and Power in the Eastern Orange Free State, 1880s to 1980s*. Edinburgh, Edinburgh University Press, 1992.

10 Musyoka adopted a triangulated definition of 'middle class' according to one of three indicators: household location (access to flush toilets, electricity for lighting, electricity or gas for cooking, and a phone); occupation; and household income (following Visagie) of R10,000 or more per month (a level of income which he argued provides households with distribution capabilities). See J.M. Musyoka, 'Perspectives on Emerging Wealth Distribution in South Africa's Previously Disadvantaged Households: A Systems Thinking Approach', PhD thesis, University of KwaZulu-Natal, 2015, pp. 91–96.

11 Ibid., p. 141.

12 Konrad Adenauer Foundation Black Middle Class Focus Group, 12 July 2013.

13 Ibid.

14 Interview, UCT registrar, March 2013.

15 The author distributed a questionnaire to this class of over 500 students at Wits in January 2013. Scarcely a scientific survey, yet nonetheless indicative.

16 Asmus Zoch, 'Life Chances and Class: Estimating Inequality of Opportunity for Children and Adolescents in South Africa', *Development Southern Africa*, 32, 1, 2014, pp. 57–75.

17 International Education Association of South Africa, 'In Leaps and Bounds: Growing Higher Education in South Africa', www.iseasa.studysa.org/..SA/in%20leapsand%20 bounds%Grow.

18 Deborah Posel, 'Races to Consume: Revisiting South Africa's History of Race, Consumption and the Struggle for Freedom', *Ethnic and Racial Studies*, 23, 2, 2010, pp. 157–175.

19 Lisa Steyn, 'The Black Belt Economy Kicks In', *Mail & Guardian*, 3–9 May 2013.

20 SAIRR, *South Africa Survey 2008/09*. Johannesburg, SAIRR, pp. 95–96, 526.

21 Jocelyn Newmarch, 'Black Share of Income Now Highest', *Mail & Guardian*, 26 October – 1 November 2007.

22 Fikilie-Ntsikelelo Moya, 'The Emerged Blackoisie', *Mail & Guardian*, 23 December – 5 January 2006; 'Black Bonanza', *Financial Mail*, 12 November 2004; Keith Platt, 'SA Middle Class Ravenous for Organic Foods', *Sunday Times*, 11 February 2007; Roy Cokayne, 'Black Men Keep Vehicle Sales Hopping, Says Finance House', *Business Report*, 5 November 2007; Arnold van Huyssteen, 'Black Buyers Help Drive Residential Boom', *This Day*, 17 March 2004; Rebecca Harrison, 'Advertising Turns to the Townships', *Mercury*, 22 September 2005.

23 Hilde Ibsen, 'Black Diamond: The Jewel in the ANC State Machinery', forthcoming.

24 Subashni Naidoo, 'SA Kids Would Gladly Sell Their Souls for the Right Label', *Sunday Times*, 3 February 2008.

25 Konrad Adenauer Foundation Middle Class Focus Group, East London, 15 July 2013.

26 Megan Power, 'New Generation Ignores Race but Worships Money', *Sunday Times*, 19 June 2005.

27 'Grants Boost Mall Growth', *Financial Mail*, 22–27 March; Tamlyn Stewart, 'Shop Till You Drop in Gauteng', *Sunday Times*, 14 September 2008.

28 Sophie Chevalier, 'Food, Malls and the Politics of Consumption: South Africa's New Middle Class', *Development Southern Africa*, 32, 1, 2015, pp. 118–129, citation from p. 124.

29 R. Caroll, 'South Africa's Middle Class: Young, Black and Driving a BMW', The Guardian (London), April, cited by Hilde Ibsen, cited by Ibsen, 'Black Diamond', p. 15.

30 Mlungisi Zondi, 'Capitalism Wins a Major Victory in Soweto', *The Weekender*, 1–2 September 2007.

31 Moya, 'The Emerged Blackoisie'.

32 Thorstein Veblen, *The Theory of the Leisure Class*, as cited by Andrew Trigg, 'Veblen, Bourdieu, and Conspicuous Consumption', *Journal of Economic Issues*, 35, 1, 2001, pp. 99–15, citation from p. 101.

33 Seabi, 'Tycoon's Super Sweet R700,000 Bash'.

34 *Sunday Times*, 29 October 2010.

35 *Sunday Times*, 10 February 2013.

36 Zakes Mda, 'A New Black Elite Consumed by Greed: A Half Revolution', *International Herald Tribune*, 28 April 2004.

37 Jacklyn Cock, 'Caddies and "Cronies": Golf and Changing Patterns of Exclusion and Inclusion in Post-Apartheid South Africa', *South African Review of Sociology*, 39, 2, 2008, pp. 183–200.

38 Loyiso Mbabane, 'Say It Loud: I'm Black, I'm Rich and I'm Proud', *Sunday Times*, 8 April 2007.

39 Fred Khumalo, 'We Shouldn't Be Ashamed to Show Off Our Wealth in the Townships', *Sunday Times*, 4 March 2007.

40 Ibid.

41 Trigg, 'Veblen', p. 105.

42 Ronelle Burger, Megan Louw, Brigitte Barbara Isabel de Oliveira Pegado and Servaas van der Berg, 'Understanding Consumption Patterns of the Established and Emerging South African Black Middle Class', *Development Southern Africa*, 32, 1, 2015, pp. 41–56. The middle class was set at a level of R53,271 per capita per annum in 2010/11, constituting the most affluent 15% of the population.

43 See notably Mosa Phadi and Claire Ceruti, 'Models, Labels and Affordability', in Peter Alexander, Claire Ceruti, Keke Motseke, Mosa Phadi and Kim Wale (eds.), *Class in Soweto*. Scottsville, University of KwaZulu-Natal Press, 2013, pp. 142–163.

44 Achille Mbembe, 'Consumed by Our Lust for Lost Segregation', *Mail & Guardian*, 28 March – 4 April 2013.

45 Rebecca Davis, 'Marikana: The Debt-Hole That Fuelled the Fire', *Daily Maverick*, 12 October 2012.

46 Wiseman Khuzwayo, 'Repossessions Escalate as Debt Rockets', *Business Report*, 13 January 2008.

47 Mamello Masote, 'Debt Is Biggest Middle Class Fear', *Sunday Times*, 3 February 2013.

48 Sharda Naidoo, 'Now for the Big Squeeze', *Sunday Times* (*Business Times*), 3 February 2006.

49 Business Opinion, 'We All Carry the Burden of the Middle Class', *Sunday Times* (*Business Times*), 9 July 2006; also Simpiwe Piliso, 'Black Diamonds Aren't Really Making It', *Sunday Times*, 7 October 2007.

50 Konrad Adenauer Foundation Black Middle Class Focus Group, East London, 15 July 2013.

51 RSA, *2012 Tax Statistics*. Joint Publication between National Treasury and the South

African Revenue Service, 2012; Peter Curle, 'Middle-Class Tax Squeeze', *Financial Mail,* 14 October 2013, www.financialmail.co.za/opinion/2013/09/05middle-class-tax-squeeze.

52 Lynley Donnelly, 'Who Owns What by Race', 9 December 2011, www.mg.co.za/article/2011-12-09-who-owns-what-by-race.

53 Jannie Rossouw, Fanie Joubert and Adele Breytenbach, 'South Africa's Fiscal Cliff: A Reflection on the Appropriation of Government Resources', *Tydskrif vir Geesteswetenskappe,* 54, 1, 2014, pp. 144–162.

54 Lightstone Newsletter, 'Growth in Luxury Black Property Ownership Soars', 2013, www.lightstone.co.za/Portal.../Property_Newsletter_March-2013 pdf.

55 By 2011, some 77% of public-sector workers were covered by private medical aids, by which time black African membership (3,533,000) had come to outnumber white (3,070,000), although medical aid was widely deemed to be becoming increasingly unaffordable, as its cost-inflation had well exceeded the consumer price index since the early 1990s (SAIRR, *Survey 2012,* pp. 527–528).

56 Sharda Naidoo, 'Black Diamonds Likely to Choose Bling over Budget', *Sunday Times,* 28 January 2007.

57 Patrick Bond, 'Debt, Uneven Development and Capitalist Crisis in South Africa: From Marikana Microfinance Mashonisas to Moody's Macroeconomic Monitoring', Background Paper 2/3 for the Rosa Luxemburg Stiftung Workshop, 30 November – 2 December 2012, Berlin.

58 Deborah James, *Money from Nothing: Indebtedness and Aspiration in South Africa.* Johannesburg, Wits University Press, 2014, p. 36.

59 A theme reiterated by Leslie Bank in regard to the black middle class in East London from the 1960s, when women in particular wanted to 'fill the empty rooms of their new houses with a repertoire of modern furnishings and appliances which would be indicative of their status within the new urban spatial environment'. See Leslie Bank, *Home Spaces, Street Styles: Contesting Power and Identity in a South African City.* Johannesburg, Wits University Press, 2011, p. 83.

60 James, *Money from Nothing,* pp. 92–94. According to one source, the number of bank account owners increased from 9 million in 1994 to 20 million in 2008. See Solidarity Research Institute, *Transformation in the Banking Sector: Ownership of Bank Accounts, Credit Cards, ATM Cards, Debit Cards and Mzansi Accounts in South Africa, 1994–2009.* Pretoria, SRI, 2010.

61 Deborah James, 'Deeper into a Hole? Borrowing and Lending in South Africa', *Current Anthropology,* 55, S9, 2014, pp. 17–29.

62 James, *Money for Nothing,* ch. 1, 'Indebtedness, Consumption and Marriage: The New Middle Classes', pp. 35–59.

63 Konrad Adenauer Foundation Focus Group, Johannesburg, 12 July 2013.

64 She cites the case of a young woman for whom the cost of lobola was estimated at around R50,000, with a 'white wedding' likely to cost a further R250,000.

65 Not least because she devotes considerable attention to the role of such institutions as stokvels, funeral societies and churches in mobilising black savings.

66 Philip Harrison and Tanya Zack, 'The Wrong Side of the Mining Belt? Spatial Transformations and Identities in Johannesburg's Southern Suburbs', in Philip Harrison, Graeme Gotz, Alison Todes and Chris Wray (eds.), *Changing Space, Changing City: Johannesburg after Apartheid.* Johannesburg, Wits University Press, 2014, pp. 269–292, citation from p. 286.

67 Sarah Britten, 'One Nation, One Beer: The Mythology of the New South Africa in Advertising', PhD thesis, University of the Witwatersrand, 2006.

68 Robert Stone, 'Kids Cool at School', letter, *Business Day*, 21 July 2015.

69 Themba Nyathikazi, 'The Great Trek from Townships to City Suburb', METRObeat, 15 March 2000, pp. 8–9.

70 Bafana Khumalo, 'The Dust Settles and a New Soweto Arises', *Sunday Times*, 30 September 2007.

71 Alan Mabin, 'Suburbanisation, Segregation, and Government of Territorial Transformations', *Transformation*, 57, 2005, pp. 41–63, citations from pp. 45 and 44. I draw heavily upon this valuable source in the paragraphs below.

72 Leslie Bank, 'Frontiers of Freedom: Race, Landscape and Nationalism in the Coastal Cultures of South Africa', *Anthropology Southern Africa*, 3, 4, 2015.

73 Detlev Krige, '"Growing Up" and "Moving Up": Metaphors That Legitimize Upward Social Mobility in Soweto', *Development Southern Africa*, 32, 1, 2015, pp. 104–117, citation from p. 110.

74 Keith Beavon and Pauline Larsen, 'Sandton Central, 1969–2013: From Open Veld to New CBD?', in Harrison, Gotz, Todes and Wray, *Changing Space, Changing City*, pp. 370–394.

75 Mabin, 'Suburbanisation', pp. 51–52.

76 Owen Crankshaw, 'Race, Space and the Post-Fordist Spatial Order of Johannesburg', *Urban Studies*, 45, 8, 2008, pp. 1692–1711.

77 Ibid., p. 1707.

78 Owen Crankshaw, 'Deindustrialization, Professionalization and Racial Inequality in Cape Town', *Urban Affairs Review*, 48, 6, 2012, pp. 836–862.

79 Amy Kracker Selzer and Patrick Heller, 'The Spatial Dynamics of Middle Class Formation in Post-Apartheid South Africa: Enclavization and Fragmentation in Johannesburg', *Political Power and Social Theory*, 21, 2010, pp. 147–184.

80 Crankshaw, 'Race, Space' and 'Deindustrialization'.

81 Selzer and Heller, 'Spatial Dynamics', pp. 173–176.

82 Mike Bester, 'Black Buyers Boost Property Market', *Mail & Guardian*, 31 October – 6 November 2003.

83 Richard Ballard, 'When in Rome: Claiming the Right to Define Neighbourhood Character in South Africa's Suburbs', *Transformation*, 57, 2005, pp. 64–87, citation from p. 79.

84 Richard Ballard, '"Slaughter in the Suburbs": Livestock Slaughter and Race in Post-Apartheid Cities', *Ethnic and Racial Studies*, 33, 6, 2010, pp. 1069–1087.

85 Shirley Thandiwe Matjeke, 'Some Consequences of Relocation into a White Community for Wives in Black Middle Class Families', MA thesis, University of the Witwatersrand, 1995.

86 'Middle Classes Choose Township Lifestyles', *Mercury*, 25 July 2005.

87 Makhosazana Xaba, 'Neighbours', in Liz McGregor and Sarah Nuttall (eds.), *At Risk: Writings on and over the Edge of South Africa*. Johannesburg, Jonathan Ball, 2007, pp. 90–103, citation from p. 91.

88 Roy Cokayne, 'Former Residents Home In on Soweto', *Business Report*, 19 February 2006.

89 'Middle Classes Choose Township Lifestyles'.

90 Roger Southall, 'The Coming Crisis of Zuma's ANC: The Party State Confronts the Fiscal Cliff', *Review of African Political Economy*, 42, 147, 2016.

91 Konrad Adenauer Foundation East London Black Middle Class Focus Group, 15 July 2013.

92 Precise numbers of adherents are difficult to come by. However, Anthony Egan, in a valuable overview of the Christian denominations, cites the Reformed Churches as accounting for 9.0% of congregants, Roman Catholic 8.9%, Mainline Protestant 22.0%, Pentecostal/Charismatic 7.3%, Other Churches 12.0% and African Initiated Churches as 40.8%. These figures are for 2001, and are thus outdated, but informed analysis is agreed that the charismatic Pentecostals remain the fastest-growing bloc within the Christian community. See Anthony Egan, 'Kingdom Deferred? The Churches in South Africa, 1994–2006', in Sakhela Buhlungu, John Daniel, Roger Southall and Jessica Lutchman (eds.), *State of the Nation: South Africa 2007*. Cape Town, HSRC Press, 2007, pp. 448–469, Table 18.1, p. 451.

93 Citations from Centre for Development and Enterprise (CDE), *Dormant Capital: Pentecostalism in South Africa and Its Potential Social and Economic Role*. Johannesburg, CDE, 2008.

94 Paul Gifford, 'Some Recent Developments in African Christianity', *African Affairs*, 93, 373, 1994, pp. 513–534.

95 Ivor Chipkin and Annie Leatt, 'Religion and Revival in Post-Apartheid South Africa', Helen Suzman Foundation, 2013. These authors indicate how, apart from drawing the black middle class, the charismatic churches are attracting young middle-class Afrikaners away from the Reformed Churches, enabling them to retain socially conservative attitudes while dissociating themselves from apartheid.

96 For this distinction, see CDE, *Dormant Capital*, p. 15.

97 Egan, 'Kingdom Deferred?', p. 459.

98 Ibid., p. 459.

99 Chipkin and Leatt, 'Religion and Revival', p. 44.

100 CDE, *Dormant Capital*, pp. 25–26, 40.

101 Erik Bahre, 'Liberation and Redistribution: Social Grants, Commercial Insurance, and Religious Riches in South Africa', *Comparative Studies in Society and History*, 53, 2, 2011, pp. 371–392.

102 CDE, *Dormant Capital*, p. 21.

103 Ibid., p. 45.

104 James, *Money from Nothing*, p. 213.

105 CDE, *Dormant Capital*, p. 70.

Chapter 8: The politics of the black middle class

1 Seymour Martin Lipset, 'Some Social Requisites of Democracy: Economic Development and Political Legitimacy', *American Political Science Review*, 53, 1, 1959, pp. 69–105; and *Political Man*. London, Heinemann, 1959.

2 Barrington Moore, *The Social Origins of Dictatorship and Democracy: Lord and Peasant in the Making of the Modern World*. Harmondsworth, Penguin, 1966, citation from p. 418.

3 Dietrich Rueschemeyer, Evelyne Stephens and John Stephens, *Capitalist Development and Democracy*. Chicago, Chicago University Press, 1992.

4 Themba Sono, *Dilemmas of African Intellectuals in South Africa: Political and Cultural Constraints*. Pretoria, University of South Africa Press, 1994, p. 33.

5 Ibid., pp. 32–34.

6 John Kane-Berman, *South Africa's Silent Revolution*. Johannesburg, SAIRR, 1991.

7 For how black middle-class elements shifted interpretation of the NDR within the ANC in a conservative direction, see Gillian Hart, 'Changing Concepts of Articulation: Political Stakes in South Africa Today', *Review of African Political Economy*, 111, 2007, pp. 85–101.

8 For instance, Prega Govender, '"Overpaid" Army of Civil Servants Sucking SA Dry: Billions for Salaries – and They Want Even More', *Sunday Times*, 3 May 2015.

9 In the Naledi survey, the average salary for public-sector health workers belonging to NEHAWU was R5,000, for police it was R8,500, for teachers R7,600, and the wage for municipal workers about R4,500. In contrast, in the private sector, the average wage for mineworkers was R4,000, while on average metalworkers earned R3,300 and clothing and textile workers a paltry R870. See Tumi Makgetla, 'COSATU Joins the Nouveau Riche', *Mail & Guardian*, 6–17 October 2006.

10 Amuzweni Ngoma, 'Professional and Political Identity Repertoires of South Africa's Black Middle Class', MA Research Report, Department of Sociology, University of the Witwatersrand, 2015.

11 Amuzweni Ngoma, 'Black Professionals and the ANC in the 2014 Election', *Konrad Adenauer Stiftung International Reports*, 10, 2014, pp. 55–73, citation from p. 62.

12 Konrad Adenauer Foundation Middle Class Focus Group, Cape Town, 11 September 2013.

13 Collette Schulz-Herzenberg, 'Towards a Silent Revolution? South African Voters during the First Years of Democracy 1994–2006', PhD thesis, University of Cape Town, 2009, p. 142.

14 See the special issue of *Transformation* (87, 2015) devoted to the functioning of the ANC at subnational level.

15 Karl Gernetzky, 'Manyi Organized ANC Loyalty of Professionals', *Business Day*, 2 April 2013.

16 Konrad Adenauer Foundation Middle Class Focus Group, 11 September 2013.

17 Ngoma, 'Professional and Political Identity Repertoires'.

18 SAIRR, *Survey 2010/11*, p. 246; SAIRR, *South Africa Survey 2014/15*. Johannesburg, SAIRR, p. 244.

19 Greg Nicholson, 'Black Like Who? Mashaba on Race, Business and the DA', *Daily Maverick*, 29 May 2014. Mashaba had previously been serving as chair of the Free Market Foundation, his particular mission being to argue that trade union protection of the employed amounted to a 'class war on workers'.

20 Carol Paton, 'State Makes Rapid BEE Policy Reversal', *Business Day*, 11 May 2015. Large-scale capital, already heavily locked into broad-based deals, and those with whom they had concluded them, such as the ANC's own Batho-Batho Trust (20% owned by an employee scheme), Chancellor House (100% owned by an ANC trust) and various trade union investment companies, secured a rapid reversal of an initial proposal to amend BEE ratings without taking into account existing broad-based deals. In its rapid backpedalling on the policy, the DTI now indicated that the upgrading of individual black share ownership would apply only to future deals. At the time of writing, the final outcome of the proposed amendment remains uncertain, although it would seem to indicate that individual black ownership will in future count for more in BEE ratings.

21 Leslie Dikeni, 'Our Intellectual Dilemma: The Pseudo-Intellectuals', in William Gumede and Leslie Dikeni (eds.), *The Poverty of Ideas; South African Democracy and the Retreat of the Intellectuals*. Auckland Park, Jacana Media, 2009, pp. 35–56, citation from p. 38.

22 Joel Netshitenzhe, 'Competing Identities of a National Liberation Movement and the Challenges of Incumbency', 2012, www.polity.org.za/article/competing-identies-of-a-national-liberation-movement-and-the-challenges-of incumbency-2012-06-20.

23 Roger Southall, 'The Coming Crisis of Zuma's ANC: The Party-State Confronts the Fiscal Cliff', *Review of African Political Economy*, 42, 147, 2016.

24 Or, rather, those elements of the NP which did not get gobbled up by the ANC. The latter absorbed most sitting NNP MPs, including their leader, Marthinus van Schalkwyk.

25 '"Know Your DA" Campaign: We Are Committed to BEE', *Mail & Guardian*, 9 September 2013.

26 For a discussion relating this debate to conceptions of 'negative' and 'positive' liberalism, see Randolph Vigne and Merle Lipton, 'Racial Redress Is Not Inimical to Liberalism, but Part of It', *Business Day*, 5 February 2014.

27 Eusebius McKaiser, 'My Head May Say DA, but Tell That to My Heart', *Sunday Times*, 2 February 2014.

28 Songezo Zibi, 'Can Agang Change the Game?', *Financial Mail*, 21 June 2013.

29 Lawrence Schlemmer, 'Lost in Transformation? South Africa's Emerging African Middle Class', *CDE Focus*, 8, August 2005.

30 Ibid., p. 11.

31 Robert Mattes, 'South Africa's Emerging Black Middle Class', *Journal of International Development*, 27, 5, 2015, pp. 665–692.

32 David Everatt, 'Class, Race and Politics in South Africa Today' (mimeo), July 2012, p. 37.

33 Mattes, 'South Africa's Emerging Black Middle Class'.

34 Roger Southall, 'Political Change and the Black Middle Class in Democratic South Africa', *Canadian Journal of African Studies*, 38, 3, 2004, pp. 521–542.

35 Bonga Mthembu, 'Black Middle Class Can't Support Zuma-led ANC', *The Times*, 3 October 2013; Ranjeni Munusamy, 'Jacob's Ladder: The Middle Class Conundrum', *Daily Maverick*, 11 November 2013.

36 Natasha Marrian, 'ANC Defends Zuma's Appeal to Middle Class Vote', *BDlive*, 1 October 2013, www.bdlive.co.za/national/politics/2013/10/01anc-defends-zumas-appeal-to-middle-class-vote; Marianne Merten, 'Election Crucial for ANC', *Daily News*, 1 November 2013.

37 Zweletu Jolobe, '"Ayisafani"? The Democratic Alliance Election Campaign', in Collette Schulz-Herzenberg and Roger Southall, *Election 2014 South Africa*. Auckland Park, Jacana Media, 2014, pp. 57–71.

38 Ngoma, 'Black Professionals', p. 66.

39 Ibid.

40 Gareth van Onselen, 'The Right Reverend Aloysias Maimane', *Business Day Live*, 2015, www.bdlive.co.za/opinion/columnists/2015/05/04/the-right-reverend-aloysias-maimane. The Constitutional Court has ruled that the death penalty is incompatible, and same-sex marriage is compatible, with the Constitution.

41 Gareth van Onselen and Jan-Jan Joubert, 'Maimane Magic Lifts DA's Hopes for Black Votes', *Sunday Times*, 30 August 2015.

42 Jason Robinson, '"Birth of a Giant?" Julius Malema and the Economic Freedom Fighters', in Schulz-Herzenberg and Southall, *Election 2014 South Africa*, pp. 72–88.

43 William Gumede and Leslie Dikeni, 'Introduction', in Gumede and Dikeni, *The Poverty of Ideas*, pp. 1–10.

44 William Gumede, 'Building a Democratic Political Culture', in ibid., pp. 11–34.

45 'Zuma Scolds "Clever" Blacks', *News24*, 3 November 2012, www.news24.com/ Archives/City-Press/Zuma-scolds-clever-blacks-20150429.

46 The campaign earned its name from students' demand that a statue of Cecil Rhodes on UCT's main steps be removed.

47 Amuzweni Ngoma, 'Loosening Ties? Black Professionals and the ANC in the 2014 Election', in Schulz-Herzenberg and Southall, *Election 2014 South Africa*, pp. 155–168.

48 See, for example, Patrick Laurence, 'Afro-Communists v Afro-Nationalists in the ANC', *Moneyweb*, 27 November 2009.

49 At time of writing, this is taking the form of a campaign within the ANC for a woman president. As this revolves around backing for Nkosazana Dlamini-Zuma, President Zuma's ex-wife (who it is presumed would head off continuing pressure for his prosecution for corruption around the 1998 Arms Deal), its feminist credentials are somewhat suspect.

50 Vishwas Satgar and Roger Southall, *COSATU in Crisis: The Fragmentation of an African Trade Union Federation*. Johannesburg, KMM Publishers, 2015.

51 Michael West, *The Rise of an African Middle Class: Colonial Zimbabwe 1898–1965*. Bloomington, Indiana University Press, 2002.

52 Petina Gappah, 'A Roller Coaster for Zimbabwe's Middle Class', 2010, www. theafricareport.com/Elections/a-roller-coaster-for-zimbabwes-middle-class.html.

53 Samuel Huntington, *The Third Wave: Democratization in the Late Twentieth Century*. Norman, University of Oklahoma Press, 1992. In this highly influential book, Huntington explores the global trend towards democracy which took place in more than 60 countries in Europe, Latin America, Asia and Africa in the immediate decades after Portugal's 'carnation revolution' in 1974.

54 Steven Levitsky and Lucan Way, *Competitive Authoritarianism: Hybrid Regimes after the Cold War*. New York, Cambridge University Press, 2010.

55 Andrew Wederman, 'Not in My Backyard! Middle Class Protest in China', Paper Presented to Conference on 'Middle Class Phenomenon in Emerging Markets: Multi-Disciplinary and Multi-Country Perspectives', Georgia State University, 26–28 September 2012, p. 6.

56 Ibid., p. 3.

Chapter 9: Afterword

1 Saskia Sassen, *Expulsions: Brutality and Complexity in the Global Economy*. Cambridge, Harvard University Press, 2014.

2 Max Bolt, Deborah James, Sarah Nuttall and George St Clair, 'The New Middle Class in the Global South', Circular relating to 'The New Middle Class in the Global South: A Two-Day Workshop', 21–22 September 2015, WISER, Wits University.

3 UHY International, 'The World's Fastest-Growing Middle Class', 2013, www.uhy. com/the-worlds-fastest-growing-middle-class.

4 P. Fletcher, 'Africa's Emerging Middle Class Drives Growth and Democracy', 2013, www. Reuters.com/article/2013/05/10/us-africa-investment-idUSBRE9490DV20130510.

5 Carola Lentz, 'Elites or Middle Classes? Lessons from Transnational Research for the Study of Social Stratification in Africa', Working Papers of the Department of Anthropology and African Studies of the Johannes Gutenberg University, Mainz, 2015, p. 161; http://www.ifeas.uni-mainz.de/Dateien/AP_161.pdf.

6 Danielle Resnick, 'The Political Economy of Africa's Emergent Middle Class: Retrospect and Prospect', *Journal of International Development*, 27, 2015, pp. 573–587 (citation from p. 575).

7 Lentz, 'Elites', p. 2.

8 Ibid., p. 9.

9 Peter Lloyd, *The New Elites of Tropical Africa*. London, Oxford University Press, 1966.

10 Lentz, 'Elites', pp. 9–13.

11 Lentz provides (ibid., p. 2) the valuable example of Christine Oppong's book on Ghanaian civil servants which was published as *Marriage Among a Matrilineal Elite* in 1974, and republished as *Middle Class African Marriage* in 1983, in which 'elite' continued to be used in the text and no explanation was given for the change in title.

12 Ibid., p. 2.

13 Ibid., p. 11.

14 Ibid., p. 13.

15 Resnick, 'The Political Economy', p. 575.

16 Frantz Fanon, *The Wretched of the Earth*. Harmondsworth, Penguin, 1968.

17 Issa Shivji, *Class Struggles in Tanzania*. London, Heinemann, 1976.

18 Irving Markowitz, *Power and Class in Africa: An Introduction to Change and Conflict in African Politics*. Englewood Cliffs, Prentice Hall, 1977.

19 Richard Sklar, *Corporate Power in an African State: The Political Impact of Multinational Mining Companies in Zambia*. Berkeley, University of California Press, 1975.

20 See, notably, Colin Leys, *Underdevelopment in Kenya*, London, Heinemann, 1975.

21 Jean Francois Bayart, *The State in Africa: The Politics of the Belly*. London, Longman, 1993.

22 Lentz, 'Elites', p. 13.

23 United Nations Development Programme, *The Rise of the South: Human Progress in a Diverse World. Human Development Report 2013*. New York, United Nations Development Programme, 2013, p. 14, cited in Henning Melber, 'Africa and the Middle Class(es)', *Africa Spectrum*, 3, 2013, pp. 111–120.

24 Deloitte on Africa, 'The Rise and Rise of the African Middle Class', 2013; www.deloitte.com/assets/Dcom-SouthAfrica/local%20Assets/Documents,rise-and-rise.

25 Ibid.

26 Lentz, 'Elites', p. 14.

27 Resnick, 'The Political Economy', p. 284.

28 Ibid., p. 284.

29 Lentz, 'Elites', p. 2.

30 Ibid.

31 Dieter Neubert, 'What Is "Middle Class"? In Search of an Appropriate Concept', 2014; meta-journal.net/article/view/1330.

32 Nancy Birdsall, Carol Graham and Stefano Pettinato, 'Stuck in the Tunnel: Is Globalization Muddling the Middle Class?', Center on Social and Economic Dynamics, Working Paper No. 14, August 2000.

33 Melber, 'Africa and the Middle Class(es)', p. 115.

34 Abhijit Banerjee and Esther Duflo, 'What Is Middle Class about the Middle Classes around the World?', *Journal of Economic Perspectives*, 22, 2008, pp. 3–28.

35 Martin Ravallion, 'The Developing World's Bulging (but Vulnerable) Middle Class', *World Development*, 38, 2010, pp. 445–454.

36 African Development Bank, 'The Middle of the Pyramid: Dynamics of the Middle Class in Africa', *Market Brief*, April 2011, p. 20.

37 Melber, 'Africa and the Middle Class(es)', p. 115.

38 Lentz, 'Elites', p. 3.

39 Cited in William Worger, Nancy Clark and Edward Alpers, *Africa and the West: From Colonialism to Independence, 1975 to the Present*. Oxford, Oxford University Press, 2010, p. 180.

40 Michael West, *The Rise of an African Middle Class: Colonial Zimbabwe 1898–1965*. Bloomington, Indiana University Press, 2002, p. 25.

41 Ibid., p. 29.

42 And not a little humour. There was an African newspaper columnist, I regret I never knew his proper name, who claimed the first name 'Stan' and delighted in writing as 'Bantu Stan'.

43 Amuzweni Ngoma, 'Political Identity Repertoires of South Africa's Professional Black Middle Class', MA thesis, University of the Witwatersrand, 2015.

44 Leslie Bank, 'Frontiers of Freedom: Race, Landscape and Nationalism in the Coastal Cultures of South Africa', *Anthropology Southern Africa*, 3, 4, 2015.

Select bibliography

Abercrombie, Nicholas and John Urry, *Capital, Labour and the Middle Classes*. London, Allen and Unwin, 1983

Alexander, Peter, Claire Ceruti, Keke Motseke, Mosa Phadi and Kim Wale, *Class in Soweto*. Scottsville, University of KwaZulu-Natal Press, 2013

Almond, Gabriel and Sidney Verba, *The Civic Culture: Political Attitudes and Democracy in Five Nations*. Princeton, Princeton University Press, 1963

Atkinson, Doreen, 'Provinces as Bulwarks: Centrifugal Forces within the ANC', *Transformation*, 87, 1, 2015

Badat, Saleem and Yusuf Sayed, 'Post-1994 South African Education: The Challenge of Social Justice', in Robert Rotberg (ed.), 'Strengthening Governance in South Africa: Building on Mandela's Legacy', *Annals of the American Academy of Political Social Science*, 652, 2014

Bahre, Erik, 'Liberation and Redistribution: Social Grants, Commercial Insurance, and Religious Riches in South Africa', *Comparative Studies in Society and History*, 53, 2, 2011

Ballard, Richard, 'When in Rome: Claiming the Right to Define Neighbourhood Character in South Africa's Suburbs', *Transformation*, 57, 2005

Ballard, Richard, '"Slaughter in the Suburbs": Livestock Slaughter and Race in Post-Apartheid Cities', *Ethnic and Racial Studies*, 33, 6, 2010

Banerjee, Abhijit and Esther Duflo, 'What Is Middle Class about the Middle Classes around the World?', *Journal of Economic Perspectives*, 22, 2008

Bank, Leslie, *Home Spaces, Street Styles: Contesting Power and Identity in a South African City*. Johannesburg, Wits University Press, 2011

Bank, Leslie, 'Frontiers of Freedom: Race, Landscape and Nationalism in the Coastal Cultures of South Africa', *Anthropology Southern Africa*, 3, 4, 2015

Bayart, Jean Francois, *The State in Africa: The Politics of the Belly*. London, Longman, 1993

Beavon, Keith and Pauline Larsen, 'Sandton Central, 1969–2013: From Open Veld to New CBD?', in Philip Harrison, Graeme Gotz, Alison Todes and Chris Wray (eds.), *Changing Space, Changing City: Johannesburg after Apartheid*. Johannesburg, Wits University Press, 2014

Benson, Mary, *South Africa: The Struggle for a Birthright*. London, Penguin, 1966

Bernstein, Eduard, *Evolutionary Socialism*. New York, Shocken, 1961 [1899]

Birdsall, Nancy, Carol Graham and Stefano Pettinato, 'Stuck in the Tunnel: Is Globalization Muddling the Middle Class?', Center on Social and Economic Dynamics, Working Paper No. 14, August 2000

Bond, Patrick, *Elite Transition: From Apartheid to Neo-Liberalism in South Africa*. Pietermaritzburg, University of Natal Press, 2000

Booysen, Susan, *The African National Congress and the Regeneration of Political Power*. Johannesburg, Wits University Press, 2011

Bottomore, Tom (ed.), *Interpretations of Marx*. Oxford, Blackwell, 1988

Bottomore, Tom, *Classes in Modern Society*. London, HarperCollins Academic, 1991

Bourdieu, Pierre, 'Cultural Reproduction and Social Reproduction', in J. Karabel and A.H. Halsey (eds.), *Power and Ideology in Education*. Oxford, Oxford University Press, 1977

Brandel-Syrier, Mia, *Reeftown Elite: A Study of Social Mobility in a Modern African Community on the Reef*. London, Routledge and Kegan Paul, 1971

Braverman, Harry, *Labour and Monopoly Capital*. New York, Monthly Review Press, 1974

Breier, Mignonne, Angelique Wildschut and Thando Mgqolozana, *Nursing in a New Era: The Profession and Education of Nursing in South Africa*. Cape Town, HSRC Press, 2009

Britten, Sarah, 'One Nation, One Beer: The Mythology of the New South Africa in Advertising', PhD thesis, University of the Witwatersrand, 2006

Brown, Alec, *The Fate of the Middle Classes*. London, Victor Gollancz, 1936

Buhlungu, Sakhela, *A Paradox of Victory: Cosatu and the Democratic Transformation in South Africa*. Scottsville, UKZN Press, 2010

Bundy, Colin, *The Rise and Fall of the South African Peasantry*. London, Heinemann, 1970

Burger, Ronelle, Cindy Lee Steenekamp, Servaas van der Berg and Asmus Zoch, 'The Middle Class in Contemporary South Africa: Comparing Rival Approaches', Stellenbosch Economic Working Papers, 11/14, Bureau for Economic Research, University of Stellenbosch, 2014

Burger, Ronelle, Megan Louw, Brigitte Barbara Isabel de Oliveira Pegado and Servaas van der Berg, 'Understanding Consumption Patterns of the Established and Emerging South African Black Middle Class', *Development Southern Africa*, 32, 1, 2015

Burnham, James, *The Managerial Revolution*. New York, John Day, 1941

Calland, Richard, *The Zuma Years: South Africa's Changing Face of Power*. Cape Town, Zebra Press, 2013

Cargill, Jenny, *Trick or Treat: Rethinking Black Economic Empowerment*. Auckland Park. Jacana Media, 2010

Centre for Development and Enterprise, *Dormant Capital: Pentecostalism in South Africa and Its Potential Social and Economic Role*. Johannesburg, CDE, 2008

Centre for Development and Enterprise, *Hidden Assets: South Africa's Low Fee Private Schools*. Johannesburg, CDE, 2013

Chipkin, Ivor and Annie Leatt, 'Religion and Revival in Post-Apartheid South Africa', Helen Suzman Foundation, 2013

Chipkin, Ivor and Sarah Meny-Gibert, 'Why the Past Matters: Studying Public Administration in South Africa', *Journal of Public Administration*, 47, 1, 2012

Christie, Pam, *Open Schools: Racially Mixed Catholic Schools in South Africa 1976–1986*. Johannesburg, Ravan Press, 1990

Chudgar, Amita and Anil Kanjee, 'School Money: Funding Flaws', *HSRC Review*, 7, 4, 2009

Cobley, Alan, *Class and Consciousness: The Black Petty Bourgeoisie in South Africa, 1924 to 1950*. Westport, Greenwood Press, 1990

Cock, Jacklyn, 'Caddies and "Cronies": Golf and Changing Patterns of Exclusion and Inclusion in Post-Apartheid South Africa', *South African Review of Sociology*, 39, 2, 2008

Commission for Employment Equity Report, 1999–2001, www.labour.gov.za

Commission for Employment Equity Report, 2013–2014, www.labour.gov.za

Council on Higher Education, 'The State of Private Higher Education in South Africa', *Higher Education Monitor*, 1, 2003

Council on Higher Education, *VitalStats: Public Higher Education 2012*. Pretoria, CHE, 2015

Crankshaw, Owen, 'Theories of Class and the African "Middle Class" in South Africa, 1969–1983', *Africa Perspective*, 1, 1, 1986

Crankshaw, Owen, 'Changes in the Racial Division of Labour during the Apartheid Era', *Journal of Southern African Studies*, 22, 4, 1996

Crankshaw, Owen, *Race, Class and the Changing Division of Labour under Apartheid*. Oxford, Taylor and Francis, 2002

Crankshaw, Owen, 'Race, Space and the Post-Fordist Spatial Order of Johannesburg', *Urban Studies*, 45, 8, 2008

Crankshaw, Owen, 'Deindustrialization, Professionalization and Racial Inequality in Cape Town', *Urban Affairs Review*, 48, 6, 2012

Crozier, Michael, *The World of the Office Worker*. Chicago, University of Chicago Press, 1971

Dahrendorf, Ralf, *Class and Class Conflict in an Industrial Society*. London, Routledge and Kegan Paul, 1959

De Klerk, Vivien, 'Language Issues in Our Schools: Whose Voice Counts? Part 1: The Parents Speak', *Perspectives in Education*, 20, 1, 2002

De Lannoy, A., 'The Stuff That Dreams Are Made Of: Narratives on Educational Decision-Making among Young Adults in Cape Town', *Journal of Education*, 51, 2011

Delius, Peter, 'Chieftainship, Civil Society and the Political Transition in South Africa', *Critical Sociology*, 22, 1996

Dhai, Ames, Harriet Etheredge, Merryll Vorster and Yosuf Veriava, 'The Public's Attitude towards Strike Action by Healthcare Workers and Health Services in South Africa', *South African Journal of Bioethics and Law*, 4, 2, 2011

Digby, Anne, 'Black Doctors and Discrimination under South Africa's Apartheid Regime', *Medical History*, 57, 2, 2013

Dikeni, Leslie, 'Our Intellectual Dilemma: The Pseudo-Intellectuals', in William Gumede and Leslie Dikeni (eds.), *The Poverty of Ideas: South African Democracy and the Retreat of the Intellectuals*. Auckland Park, Jacana Media, 2009

Djilas, Milovan, *The New Class: An Analysis of the Communist System*. London, Thames and Hudson, 1957

Dreyer, Lynette, *The Modern African Elite of South Africa*. Basingstoke, Macmillan, 1987

Dubow, Saul, *The African National Congress*. Johannesburg, Jonathan Ball, 2000

Du Toit, J., *Independent Schooling: Assessing Its Size and Shape*. Pretoria, Research Programme on Human Resources Development, HSRC, 2003

Durrheim, Keith with Merridy Boetigger, Zaynab Essack, Silvia Maarschalk and Chita Ranchod, 'The Colour of Success: A Qualitative Study of Affirmative Action Attitudes of Black South African Academics', *Transformation*, 64, 2007

Edigheji, Omano, 'Affirmative Action and State Capacity in a Democratic South Africa', *Policy: Issues and Actors*, Johannesburg, Centre for Policy Studies, 20, 4, 2007

Egan, Anthony, 'Kingdom Deferred? The Churches in South Africa, 1994–2006', in Sakhela Buhlungu, John Daniel, Roger Southall and Jessica Lutchman (eds.), *State of the Nation: South Africa 2007*. Cape Town, HSRC Press, 2007

Eidelberg, Philip, 'Guerrilla Warfare and the Decline of Urban Apartheid: The Shaping of a New African Middle Class and the Transformation of the African National Congress (1975–1985)', *Comparative Studies of South Asia, Africa and the Middle East*, 19, 1, 1999

Ellis, Stephen, *External Mission: The ANC in Exile*. Johannesburg and Cape Town, Jonathan Ball, 2012

Fanon, Frantz, *The Wretched of the Earth*. Harmondsworth, Penguin, 1968

Feit, Edward, *African Opposition in South Africa: The Failure of Passive Resistance*. Stanford, Stanford University Press, 1967

Fernandes, Leela, *India's New Middle Class: Democratic Politics in an Era of Economic Reform*. New Delhi, Oxford University Press, 2006

Fine, Ben and Zavareh Rustomjee, *The Political Economy of South Africa: From Minerals Energy Complex to Industrialisation*. London, Hurst, 1996

Fine, Robert with Dennis Davis, *Beyond Apartheid: Labour and Liberation in South Africa*. London, Pluto Press, 1990

Fiske, Edward and Helen Ladd, *Education Reform in Post-Apartheid South Africa*. Cape Town, HSRC Press, 2004.

Franks, Peter, 'The Crisis of the South African Public Service', *Journal of the Helen Suzman Foundation*, 7, 2014

Fraser-Moleketi, Geraldine, 'Public Service Reform in South Africa: An Overview of Selected Case Studies from 1994–2004', MAdmin thesis, University of Pretoria, 2006

Fukuyama, Francis, 'The Future of History: Can Liberal Democracy Survive the Decline of the Middle Class?', *Foreign Affairs*, January/February 2012

Garcia Rivero, Carlos, Pierre du Toit and Hennie Kotze, 'Tracking the Development of the Middle Class in Democratic South Africa', *Politeia*, 22, 3, 2003

Gibbs, Timothy, *Mandela's Kinsmen: Nationalist Elites and Apartheid's First Bantustan*. Woodbridge, James Currey; Auckland Park, Jacana Media, 2014

Giddens, Anthony, *Capitalism and Modern Social Theory: An Analysis of the Writings of Marx, Durkheim and Weber*. Cambridge, Cambridge University Press, 1971

Gifford, Paul, 'Some Recent Developments in African Christianity', *African Affairs*, 93, 373, 1994

Giliomee, Hermann, *The Last Afrikaner Leaders: A Supreme Test of Power*. Cape Town, Tafelberg, 2012

Goldthorpe, John and David Lockwood, 'Affluence and the British Class Structure', *Sociological Review*, 11, 2, 1963

Govender, Logan, 'Teacher Unions, Policy Struggles and Educational Change, 1994 to 2004', in Linda Chisholm (ed.), *Changing Class: Education and Social Change in Post-Apartheid South Africa*. Cape Town, HSRC Press, 2004

Govinder, Kesh, Nombuso Zondo and Malegapuru Makgoba, 'A New Look at Demographic Transformation for Universities in South Africa', *South African Journal of Science*, 109, 11/12, 2013

Gumede, William, *Thabo Mbeki and the Battle for the Soul of the ANC*. Cape Town, Zebra Press, 2005

Harrison, Philip and Tanya Zack, 'The Wrong Side of the Mining Belt? Spatial Transformations and Identities in Johannesburg's Southern Suburbs', in Philip Harrison, Graeme Gotz, Alison Todes and Chris Wray (eds.), *Changing Space, Changing City: Johannesburg after Apartheid*. Johannesburg, Wits University Press, 2014

Hart, Gillian, 'Changing Concepts of Articulation: Political Stakes in South Africa Today', *Review of African Political Economy*, 111, 2007

Healy-Clancy, Meghan, *A World of Their Own: A History of South African Women's Education*. Pietermaritzburg, University of KwaZulu-Natal Press, 2013

Huntington, Samuel, *The Third Wave: Democratization in the Late Twentieth Century*. Norman, University of Oklahoma Press, 1991

Hyslop, Jonathan, 'Political Corruption: Before and after Apartheid', *Journal of Southern African Studies*, 31, 4, 2005

James, Deborah, 'Deeper into a Hole? Borrowing and Lending in South Africa', *Current Anthropology*, 55, S9, 2014

James, Deborah, *Money from Nothing: Indebtedness and Aspiration in South Africa*. Johannesburg, Wits University Press, 2014

Jansen, Jonathan, 'Changes and Continuities in South Africa's Higher Education System, 1994–2004', in Linda Chisholm (ed.), *Changing Class*. Cape Town, HSRC Press, 2004

Johns, Sheridan, *Raising the Red Flag: The International Socialist League and the Communist Party of South Africa, 1914–1932*. Bellville, Mayibuye Books, UWC, 1995

Jolobe, Zweletu, '"Ayisafani"? The Democratic Alliance Election Campaign', in Collette Schulz-Herzenberg and Roger Southall (eds.), *Election 2014 South Africa: The Campaign, Results and Future Prospects*. Auckland Park, Jacana Media, 2014

Jones, Stuart and Andre Miller, *The South African Economy, 1910–90*. New York, St Martin's Press, 1992

Jozana, Xoliswa, 'The Transkeian Middle Class: Its Political Implications', *Africa Perspective*, 1, 7 & 8, 1989

Kane-Berman, John, *South Africa's Silent Revolution*. Johannesburg, SAIRR, 1991

Kekana, Charles, 'The Effect of Influx Control on the African Middle Class', MA thesis, University of the Witwatersrand, 1990

Kenny, Bridget, 'The "Market Hegemonic" Workplace Order in Food Retailing', in Edward Webster and Karl von Holdt (eds.), *Beyond the Apartheid Workplace: Studies in Transition*. Scottsville. University of KwaZulu-Natal Press, 2005

Klingender, Francis, *The Condition of Clerical Labour in Britain*. London, Martin Lawrence, 1935

Krige, Detley, '"Growing Up" and "Moving Up": Metaphors That Legitimize Upward Social Mobility in Soweto', *Development Southern Africa*, 32, 1, 2015

Kruss, Glenda, *Chasing Credentials and Mobility: Private Higher Education in South Africa*. Cape Town, HSRC Press, 2004

Kuper, Leo, *An African Bourgeoisie: Race, Class and Politics in South Africa*. New Haven, Yale University Press, 1965

Lambert, Robert, 'Political Unionism and Working Class Hegemony: Perspectives on the South African Congress of Trade Unions, 1955–1965', *Labour, Capital and Society*, 18, 2, 1985

Levitsky, Steven and Lucan Way, *Competitive Authoritarianism: Hybrid Regimes after the Cold War*. New York, Cambridge University Press, 2010

Limb, Peter, *The ANC's Early Years: Nation, Class and Place in South Africa before 1940*.
Pretoria, University of South Africa Press, 2010

Lindsay, Don, 'BEE Reform: The Case for an Institutional Perspective', in John Daniel,
Prishani Naidoo, Devan Pillay and Roger Southall (eds.), *New South African Review:
New Paths, Old Compromises?* Johannesburg, Wits University Press, 2011

Lipset, S.M., *Political Man*. London, Heinemann, 1959

Lipset, Seymour Martin, 'Some Social Requisites of Democracy: Economic Development
and Political Legitimacy', *American Political Science Review*, 53, 1, 1959

Lloyd, Peter, *The New Elites of Tropical Africa*. London, Oxford University Press, 1966

Lockwood, David, *The Black-Coated Worker* (2nd edition). Oxford, Clarendon Press, 1989

Lodge, Tom, 'Neo-Patrimonial Politics in the ANC', *African Affairs*, 113, 450, 2014

Luhabe, Wendy, *Defining Moments: Experiences of Black Executives in South Africa's Workplace*.
Pietermaritzburg, University of KwaZulu-Natal Press, 2002

Mabandla, Nkululeko, '*Lahla Ngubo*: The Continuities and Discontinuities of a South
African Black Middle Class', MA dissertation, University of Cape Town, 2012

Mabandla, Nkululeko, 'Rethinking Bundy: Land and the Black Middle Class –
Accumulation beyond the Peasantry', *Development Southern Africa*, 32, 1, 2015

Mabin, Alan, 'Suburbanisation, Segregation, and Government of Territorial
Transformations', *Transformation*, 57, 2005

Mabizela, Mahlubi, 'Recounting the State of Private Higher Education in South Africa',
in N.V. Varghese, *Growth and Expansion of Private Higher Education in Africa*. Paris,
International Institute for Education Planning, 2006

Macdonald, Keith, *The Sociology of the Professions*. London, Sage, 1995

Macun, Ian, 'The State of Organised Labour: Still Living Like There's No Tomorrow',
in Devan Pillay, Gilbert Khadiagala, Prishani Naidoo and Roger Southall (eds.),
New South African Review 4: A Fragile Democracy, Twenty Years On. Johannesburg, Wits
University Press, 2014

Mahajan, V., *Africa Rising: How 900 Million African Consumers Offer More Than You Think*.
New Jersey, Pearson Education, 2009

Mahlase, Shirley, *The Careers of Women Teachers under Apartheid*. Harare, SAPES Books, 1997

Markowitz, Irving, *Power and Class in Africa: An Introduction to Change and Conflict in African
Politics*. Englewood Cliffs, Prentice Hall, 1977

Marks, Shula, *The Ambiguities of Dependence in South Africa: Class, Nationalism and the State
in Twentieth Century Natal*. Johannesburg, Ravan Press, 1986

Martin, Geraldine and Kevin Durrheim, 'Racial Recruitment in Post-Apartheid South
Africa: Dilemmas of Private Recruitment Agencies', *Psychology in Society*, 33, 2006

Martins, J.H., 'Income and Expenditure by Produce and Type of Outlet of Middle and
Upper Class Black Households in Gauteng, 1999', Bureau of Market Research,
UNISA, Research Report No. 275, 2000

Marx, Karl, *Capital: A Critique of Political Economy*. Vol. 3, *The Process of Capitalist Production
as a Whole*. London, Lawrence and Wishart, 1974 [1884]

Matjeke, Shirley Thandiwe, 'Some Consequences of Relocation into a White Community
for Wives in Black Middle Class Families', MA thesis, University of the Witwatersrand,
1995

Mattes, Robert, 'South Africa's Emerging Black Middle Class', *Journal of International
Development*, 27, 5, 2015

Maylam, Paul, *A History of the African People of South Africa: From the Early Iron Age to the
1970s*. Cape Town, David Philip, 1986

Mbeki, Moeletsi, *Architects of Poverty: Why African Capitalism Needs Changing*. Johannesburg, Picador Africa, 2009

McGrath, Simon, 'The State of the South African Further Education and Training College Sector', in Simon McGrath, Azeem Badroodien, André Kraak and Lorna Unwin (eds.), *Shifting Understandings of Skills in South Africa*. Cape Town, HSRC Press, 2004

Mestry, Raj and Raymond Ndhlovu, 'The Implications of the National Norms and Standards for School Funding Policy on Equity in South African Public Schools', *South African Journal of Education*, 34, 3, 2014

Mills, C. Wright, *White Collar: The American Middle Classes*. London, Oxford University Press, 1951

Milne, C., 'Affirmative Action in South Africa: From Targets to Empowerment', *Journal of Public Administration*, 44, 4.1, 2009

Mnguni, Peliwe, 'Deploying Culture as a Defence against Incompetence: The Unconscious Dynamics of Public Service Work', *South African Journal of Industrial Psychology*, 38, 2, 2012

Modisha, Geoffrey, 'A Contradictory Class Location? An Exploration of the Position and Roles of the African Corporate Middle Class in South African Workplaces and Communities', MA Research Report, School of Social Sciences, University of the Witwatersrand, 2007

Modisha, Geoffrey, 'A Contradictory Class Location? The African Corporate Middle Class and the Burden of Race in South Africa', *Transformation*, 65, 2008

Mokoele, Johannes, 'Perspective of Black South African Managers Regarding Advancement into Senior Corporate Management Positions', PhD dissertation, Virginia Polytechnic Institute and State University, 1997

Mokoka, Elizabeth, Martha Oosthuizen and Valerie Ehlers, 'Retaining Professional Nurses in South Africa: Nurse Managers' Perspectives', *Journal of Interdisciplinary Health Sciences*, 15, 1, 2010

Moore, Barrington, *The Social Origins of Dictatorship and Democracy: Lord and Peasant in the Making of the Modern World*. Harmondsworth, Peregrine Books, 1969

Motala, Shireen, 'Equity, Quality and Access in South African Education: A Work Still Very Much in Progress', in John Daniel, Prishani Naidoo, Devan Pillay and Roger Southall (eds.), *New South African Review: The Second Phase – Tragedy or Farce?* Johannesburg, Wits University Press, 2013

Motsuenyane, Sam, *A Testament of Hope: The Autobiography of Dr Sam Motsuenyane*. Johannesburg, KMM Review Publishing, 2012

Msila, Vuyisile, 'The Education Exodus: The Flight from Township Schools', *African Review of Education*, 2, 2, 2005

Msila, Vuyisile, 'School Choice and Intra-Township Migration: Black Parents Scrambling for Quality Education in South Africa', *Journal of Education*, 46, 2009

Muller, Johan, 'Schools without the State: A Study of Private and Alternative Schooling in Johannesburg', Education Policy Unit Research Report, University of the Witwatersrand, 1990

Muller, Marie, 'Strike Action by Nurses in South Africa: A Value Clarification', *Curationis*, November 2001

Murray, Colin, *Black Mountain: Land, Class and Power in the Eastern Orange Free State, 1880s to 1980s*. Edinburgh, Edinburgh University Press, 1992

Murray, Georgina, 'Black Empowerment in South Africa: "Patriotic Capitalism" or a Corporate Black Wash?', *Critical Sociology*, 26, 3, 2000

Musyoka, J.M., 'Perspectives on Emerging Wealth Distribution in South Africa's Previously Disadvantaged Households: A Systems Thinking Approach', PhD thesis, University of KwaZulu-Natal, 2015

Naidoo, Vino, 'Assessing Racial Redress in the Public Service', in Kristina Bentley and Adam Habib (eds.), *Racial Redress and Citizenship in South Africa*. Cape Town, HSRC Press, 2008

Nel, Christo, *Transformation without Sacrifice*. Cape Town, Village of Leaders, 2010

Ngoma, Amuzweni, 'Black Professionals and the ANC in the 2014 Election', *Konrad Adenauer Stiftung International Reports*, 10, 2014

Ngoma, Amuzweni, 'Loosening Ties? Black Professionals and the ANC in the 2014 Election', in Collette Schulz-Herzenberg and Roger Southall (eds.), *Election 2014 South Africa: The Campaign, Results and Future Prospects*. Auckland Park, Jacana, 2014

Ngoma, Amuzweni, 'Political Identity Repertoires of South Africa's Professional Black Middle Class', MA thesis, University of the Witwatersrand, 2015

Nogueira, Maria Alice, 'A Revisited Theme: Middle Classes and the School', in Michael Apple, Stephen Ball and Luis Gandin (eds.), *The Routledge International Handbook of the Sociology of Education*. London, Routledge, 2010

Nolutshungu, Sam, *Changing South Africa: Political Considerations*. Manchester, Manchester University Press, 1982

Nyquist, Thomas, *African Middle Class Elite*, Occasional Paper No. 28, Institute of Social and Economic Research, Rhodes University, 1983

Nzimande, Bonginkosi, 'Managers and the New Middle Class', *Transformation*, 1, 1986

Nzimande, Blade, and Mpumelelo Sikhosana (eds.), *Affirmative Action and Transformation*. Durban, Indicator Press, 1996

Nzimande, Bonginkosi, 'Class, National Oppression and the African Petty Bourgeoisie: The Case of the African Traders', in Robin Cohen, Yvonne Muthien and Abebe Zegeye (eds.), *Repression and Resistance: Insider Accounts of Apartheid*. London, Hans Zell, 1990

Odendaal, André, *The Founders: The Origins of the ANC and the Struggle for Democracy in South Africa*. Auckland Park, Jacana Media, 2012

Omar, Rahmat, 'New Work Order or More of the Same? Call Centres in South Africa', in Edward Webster and Karl von Holdt (eds.), *Beyond the Apartheid Workplace: Studies in Transition*. Scottsville, University of KwaZulu-Natal Press, 2005

O'Meara, Dan, *Forty Lost Years: The Apartheid State and the Politics of the National Party, 1948–1994*. Johannesburg, Ravan Press, 1996

Padayachee, Vishnu and Gillian Hart, 'Indian Business in South Africa after Apartheid: Old and New Trajectories', *Comparative Studies in History and Society*, 42, 4, 2000

Pampallis, John, 'School Fees', *Issues in Education Policy No. 3*, Centre for Education Policy Development, Braamfontein, 2008

Parkin, Frank, *Class Inequality and Political Order*. St Albans, Paladin, 1972

Paton, Alan, *Apartheid and the Archbishop: The Life and Times of Geoffrey Clayton*. Cape Town, David Philip, 1973

Peires, Jeff, 'The Implosion of Transkei and Ciskei', *African Affairs*, 91, 1992

Phadi, Mosa and Claire Ceruti, 'Models, Labels and Affordability', in Peter Alexander, Claire Ceruti, Keke Motseke, Mosa Phadi and Kim Wale (eds.), *Class in Soweto*. Scottsville, University of KwaZulu-Natal Press, 2013

Picard, Louis, *The State of the State: Institutional Transformation, Capacity and Political Change in South Africa*. Johannesburg, Wits University Press, 2005

Piketty, Thomas, *Capital in the Twentieth Century*. Cambridge, The Belknap Press of Harvard University Press, 2014

Posel, Deborah, 'Races to Consume: Revisiting South Africa's History of Race, Consumption and the Struggle for Freedom', *Ethnic and Racial Studies*, 23, 2, 2010

Poulantzas, Nicos, *Classes in Contemporary Capitalism*. London, New Left Books, 1974

PSLSD (Project for Statistics on Living Standards and Development), *South Africans Rich and Poor: Borderline Household Statistics*. Cape Town, South African Labour and Development Research Unit, University of Cape Town, 1994

Ravallion, Martin, 'The Developing World's Bulging (but Vulnerable) Middle Class', *World Development*, 38, 2010

Redding, Sean, 'Peasants and the Creation of an African Middle Class in Umtata', *International Journal of African Historical Studies*, 26, 3, 1993

Resnick, Danielle, 'The Political Economy of Africa's Emergent Middle Class: Retrospect and Prospect', *Journal of International Development*, 27, 2015

Robinson, Jason, '"Birth of a Giant?" Julius Malema and the Economic Freedom Fighters', in Collette Schulz-Herzenberg and Roger Southall (eds.), *Election 2014 South Africa: The Campaign, Results and Future Prospects*. Auckland Park, Jacana Media, 2014

Rossouw, Jannie, Fanie Joubert and Adele Breytenbach, 'South Africa's Fiscal Cliff: A Reflection on the Appropriation of Government Resources', *Tydskrif vir Geesteswetenskappe*, 54, 1, 2014

Rueschemeyer, Dietrich, Evelyne Stephens and John Stephens, *Capitalist Development and Democracy*. Cambridge, Polity Press, 1992

Sadler, Elmarie, 'A Profile and the Work Environment of Black Chartered Accountants in South Africa', *Meditari Accountancy Research*, 10, 2002

Sassen, Saskia, *Expulsions: Brutality and Complexity in the Global Economy*. Cambridge, Harvard University Press, 2014

Satgar, Vishwas and Roger Southall, *COSATU in Crisis: The Fragmentation of an African Trade Union Federation*. Johannesburg, KMM Publishers, 2015

Sayed, Yusuf and Anil Kanjee, 'An Overview of Education Policy Change in Post-Apartheid South Africa', in Yusuf Sayed, Anil Kanjee and Nkomo Mokubung (eds.), *The Search for Education Quality in Post-Apartheid South Africa: Interventions to Improve Learning and Teaching*. Cape Town, HSRC Press, 2013

Schlemmer, Lawrence, 'Lost in Transformation? South Africa's Emerging African Middle Class', *CDE Focus*, 8, 2005

Schulz-Herzenberg, Collette, 'Towards a Silent Revolution? South African Voters during the First Years of Democracy 1994–2006', PhD thesis, University of Cape Town, 2009

Schulz-Herzenberg, Collette, 'The 2014 National and Provincial Results', in Collette Schulz-Herzenberg and Roger Southall (eds.), *Election 2014 South Africa: The Campaign, Results and Future Prospects*. Auckland Park, Jacana Media, 2014

Scully, Ben, 'Development in the Age of Wagelessness: Labor, Livelihoods, and the Decline of Work in South Africa', PhD thesis, Johns Hopkins University, 2013

Seekings, Jeremy and Nicoli Nattrass, *Class, Race and Inequality in South Africa*. Scottsville, University of KwaZulu-Natal Press, 2006

Selzer, Amy Kracker and Patrick Heller, 'The Spatial Dynamics of Middle Class Formation in Post-Apartheid South Africa: Enclavization and Fragmentation in Johannesburg', *Political Power and Social Theory*, 21, 2010

Shell, Robert C.-H., *Children of Bondage: A Social History of the Slave Society at the Cape of Good Hope, 1652–1838*. Johannesburg, Wits University Press, 1997

Shivji, Issa, *Class Struggles in Tanzania*. London, Heinemann, 1976

Sklar, Richard, *Corporate Power in an African State: The Political Impact of Multinational Mining Companies in Zambia*. Berkeley, University of California Press, 1975

Slovo, Joe, 'South Africa: No Middle Road', in Basil Davidson, Joe Slovo and Anthony Wilkinson (eds.), *South Africa: The New Politics of Revolution*. Harmondsworth, Penguin, 1976

Sombart, Werner, *Why Is There No Socialism in the United States?* London, Macmillan, 1976

Sono, Themba, *Dilemmas of African Intellectuals in South Africa: Political and Cultural Constraints*. Pretoria, University of South Africa Press, 1994

Soudien, Crain, '"Constituting the Class": An Analysis of the Process of "Integration" in South African Schools', in Linda Chisholm (ed.), *Changing Class: Education and Social Change in Post-Apartheid South Africa*. Cape Town, HSRC Press, 2004

Soudien, Crain, 'The Reconstitution of Privilege: Integration in Former White Schools in South Africa', *Journal of Social Issues*, 66, 2, 2010

South African Institute of Race Relations, *A Survey of Race Relations, 1971*. Johannesburg, SAIRR, 1972

South African Institute of Race Relations, *A Survey of Race Relations, 1975*. Johannesburg, SAIRR, 1976

South African Institute of Race Relations, *Race Relations Survey, 1989/90*. Johannesburg, SAIRR, 1990

South African Institute of Race Relations, *South Africa Survey 1999/2000*. Johannesburg, SAIRR, 2000

South African Institute of Race Relations, *South Africa Survey 2008/09*. Johannesburg, SAIRR, 2009

South African Institute of Race Relations, *South Africa Survey 2010/11*. Johannesburg, SAIRR, 2012

South African Institute of Race Relations, *South Africa Survey 2012*. Johannesburg, SAIRR, 2013

South African Institute of Race Relations, *South Africa Survey 2013*. Johannesburg, SAIRR, 2014

South African Institute of Race Relations, *South Africa Survey 2014/15*. Johannesburg, SAIRR, 2015

Southall, Roger, 'The Beneficiaries of Transkeian "Independence"', *Journal of Modern African Studies*, 15, 1, 1976

Southall, Roger, *South Africa's Transkei: The Political Economy of an 'Independent' Bantustan*. London, Heinemann Educational, 1983

Southall, Roger, 'The ANC, Black Economic Empowerment and State-Owned Enterprises: A Recycling of History?', in Sakhela Buhlungu, John Daniel, Roger Southall and Jessica Lutchman (eds.), *State of the Nation: South Africa 2007*. Cape Town, HSRC Press, 2007

Southall, Roger, 'Political Change and the Black Middle Class in Democratic South Africa', *Canadian Journal of African Studies*, 38, 3, 2004, reprinted in Alan Jeeves and Greg Cuthbertson (eds.), *Fragile Freedom: South African Democracy 1994–2004*. Pretoria, University of South Africa Press, 2008

Southall, Roger, 'The ANC: Party Vanguard of the Black Middle Class?', in Arianna Lissoni, Jon Soske, Natasha Erlank, Noor Nieftagodien and Omar Badsha (eds.), *One Hundred Years of the ANC: Debating Liberation Histories Today*. Johannesburg, Wits University Press, 2012

Southall, Roger, 'The Power Elite in Democratic South Africa: Race and Class in a Fractured Society', in John Daniel, Prishani Naidoo, Devan Pillay and Roger Southall (eds.), *New South African Review 3: The Second Phase – Tragedy or Farce?* Johannesburg, Wits University Press, 2013

Southall, Roger, *Liberation Movements in Power: Party and State in Southern Africa.* Woodbridge, James Currey; Scottsville, University of KwaZulu-Natal Press, 2013

Southall, Roger, 'The Coming Crisis of Zuma's ANC: The Party-State Confronts the Fiscal Cliff', *Review of African Political Economy*, forthcoming, 2016

Spaull, Nicholas, *South Africa's Education Crisis: The Quality of Education in South Africa 1994–2011.* Centre for Development Enterprise, Johannesburg, 2013

Standing, Guy, *The Precariat: The New Dangerous Class.* London, Bloomsbury, 2011

Statistics South Africa, *October Household Survey, 1997.* Pretoria, SSA, 1997

Tangri, Roger and Roger Southall, 'The Politics of Black Economic Empowerment in South Africa', *Journal of Southern African Studies*, 34, 3, 2008

Terreblanche, Sampie, *A History of Inequality in South Africa 1652–2002.* Pietermaritzburg, University of Natal Press, 2002

Thompson, E.P., *The Making of the English Working Class.* Harmondsworth, Penguin, 1968

Tobias, Phillip, 'Apartheid and Medical Education: The Training of Black Doctors in South Africa', *Journal of the National Medical Association*, 72, 4, 1960

Turok, Ben, *From the Freedom Charter to Polokwane: The Evolution of ANC Economic Policy.* Cape Town, New Agenda, 2008

UCT, 'Booming Black Middle Class Weighs In with a Whopping R400 Billion Annual Consumer Spend', University of Cape Town, *Monday Paper*, 13–26 May 2013

Udjo, Eric, 'The Demographics of the Emerging Black Middle Class in South Africa', Bureau of Market Research, College of Economic and Management Sciences, University of South Africa, Research Report No. 375, 2008

Ungerer, L.M., 'Activities, Lifestyles and Status Products of the Newly-Emerging Middle Class in Gauteng', Bureau of Market Research, UNISA, Research Report, 1999

Van Aardt, C.J., 'Forecast of the Adult Population by Living Standards Measure (LSM) for the Period 2005 to 2015', Bureau of Market Research, UNISA, Research Report 348, 2006

Van Zanten, Agnes, 'The Sociology of Elite Education', in Michael Apple, Stephen Ball and Luis Gandin (eds.), *The Routledge International Handbook of the Sociology of Education.* London, Routledge, 2010

Veblen, Thorstein, *The Theory of the Leisure Class*, as cited by Andrew Trigg, 'Veblen, Bourdieu, and Conspicuous Consumption', *Journal of Economic Issues*, 35, 1, 2001

Verhoef, Grietjie, '"The Invisible Hand": The Roots of Black Economic Empowerment, Sankorp and Societal Change in South Africa, 1995–2000', *Journal of Contemporary History*, 28, 1, 2003

Visagie, Justin and Dorrit Posel, 'A Reconsideration of What and Who Is Middle Class in South Africa', *Development Southern Africa*, 30, 2, 2013

Von Holdt, Karl and Mike Murphy, 'Public Hospitals in South Africa: Stressed Institutions, Disempowered Management', in Sakhela Buhlungu, John Daniel, Roger Southall and Jessica Lutchman (eds.), *State of the Nation: South Africa 2007.* Cape Town, HSRC Press, 2007

Walker, Cherryl, *Women and Resistance in South Africa.* Cape Town, David Philip, 1991

Walshe, Peter, *The Rise of African Nationalism in South Africa: The African National Congress, 1912–1952.* London, Hurst, 1970

West, Michael, *The Rise of an African Middle Class: Colonial Zimbabwe 1898–1965*. Bloomington, Indiana University Press, 2002

Who Owns Whom 2014. Johannesburg, Who Owns Whom, 2014

Wilson, Monica and Archie Mafeje, *Langa: A Study of Social Groups in an African Township*. Cape Town, Oxford University Press

Wolpe, Harold, 'The Changing Class Structure of South Africa: The African Petty-Bourgeoisie', in Paul Zaremfka (ed.), *Research in Political Economy*. Greenwich, JAI Press, 1977

Wolpe, Harold, *Race, Class and the Apartheid State*. London, James Currey, 1988

Worger, William, Nancy Clark and Edward Alpers, *Africa and the West: From Colonialism to Independence, 1975 to the Present*. Oxford, Oxford University Press, 2010

Wright, Eric Olin, 'Class Boundaries and Contradictory Class Locations', in Anthony Giddens and Held David (eds.), *Classes, Power and Conflict: Classical and Contemporary Debates*. Berkeley, University of California Press, 1982

Xaba, Makhosazana, 'Neighbours', in Liz McGregor and Sarah Nuttall (eds.), *At Risk: Writings on and over the Edge of South Africa*. Johannesburg, Jonathan Ball, 2007

Zoch, Asmus, 'Life Chances and Class: Estimating Inequality of Opportunity for Children and Adolescents in South Africa', *Development Southern Africa*, 32, 1, 2014

Index

JC JAMES CURREY

Recent James Currey titles on South and Southern Africa

The Road to Soweto:
Resistance and the Uprising of 16 June 1976
JULIAN BROWN

South Africa. The Present as History:
From Mrs Ples to Mandela and Marikana
JOHN S. SAUL AND PATRICK BOND

Liberation Movements in Power:
Party and State in Southern Africa
ROGER SOUTHALL

Mandela's Kinsmen:
Nationalist Elites and Apartheid's First Bantustan
TIMOTHY GIBBS

Women, Migration and the Cashew Economy
in Southern Mozambique
JEANNE MARIE PENVENNE

Writing Revolt: An Engagement with
African Nationalism, 1957-67
TERENCE RANGER

Colonialism and Violence in Zimbabwe:
A History of Suffering
HEIKE I. SCHMIDT